QUINTILIAN

I

LCL 124

THE INSTITUTIO ORATORIA OF
QUINTILIAN

WITH AN ENGLISH TRANSLATION BY
H. E. BUTLER

IN FOUR VOLUMES
I

HARVARD UNIVERSITY PRESS
CAMBRIDGE, MASSACHUSETTS
LONDON, ENGLAND

First published 1920
Reprinted 1933, 1953, 1958, 1963, 1969, 1980, 1989

ISBN 0-674-99138-9

Printed in Great Britain by St. Edmundsbury Press Ltd,
Bury St. Edmunds, Suffolk, on wood-free paper.
Bound by Hunter & Foulis Ltd, Edinburgh, Scotland.

TABLE OF CONTENTS

Preface.—Ch. 1: Elementary Education.—Ch. 2:
The merits of public and private education compared.—Ch. 3: General reflections on the capacity
and treatment of pupils.—Ch. 4: Grammar.—
Ch. 5: Correctness; barbarisms; pronunciation:
the aspirate; accents; solecisms; words, foreign,
compound, metaphorical, new, etc.—Ch. 6: Language; analogy; etymology; old words; authority; usage.—Ch. 7: Orthography; difference
between spelling and pronunciation.—Ch. 8: Reading; authors to be read; methods of teaching;
value of history.—Ch. 9: Composition.—Ch. 10:
Other studies necessary to rhetoric; music, geometry, astronomy.—Ch. 11: Instruction to be
derived from the stage; delivery; gesture; reci-
tation; gymnastic.—Ch. 12: Boys capable of studying a number of subjects at once.

Ch. 1: Rhetoric not begun early enough; relations
between *rhetor* and *grammaticus.*—Ch. 2: Choice
of a teacher; mutual duties of teacher and pupil.
—Ch. 3: Necessity of avoiding inferior teachers.—
Ch. 4: Elementary rhetorical exercises; narratives;
proof and refutation; panegyric and denunciation;
commonplaces; theses; reasons; preparations for
pleadings; praise and blame of particular laws; fictitious declamations.—Ch. 5: Assistance to be given
to pupils.—Ch. 6: Declamation.—Ch. 7: Ortho-

TABLE OF CONTENTS

INTRODUCTION

Life of Quintilian

Marcus Fabius Quintilianus was, like Seneca, of Spanish origin, being born about 35 A.D. at Calagurris. His father was a rhetorician of some note who practised with success at Rome. It is not surprising therefore to find that the young Quintilian was sent to Rome for his education. Among his teachers were the famous *grammaticus* Remmius Palaemon, and the no less distinguished rhetorician Domitius Afer. On completing his education he seems to have returned to his native land to teach rhetoric there, for we next hear of him as being brought to Rome in 68 A.D. by Galba, then governor of Hispania Tarraconensis. At Rome he met with great success as a teacher and was the first rhetorician to set up a genuine public school and to receive a salary from the State. He continued to teach for twenty years and had among his pupils the younger Pliny and the two sons of Domitilla, the sister of Domitian. He was also a successful pleader in the courts as we gather from more than one passage in his works. Late in life he married and had two sons. But both wife and children predeceased him.

INTRODUCTION

He died full of honour, the possessor of wide lands and consular rank. The date of his death is unknown, but it was before 100 A.D. He left behind him a treatise "On the causes of the decadence of Roman oratory" (*De causis corruptae eloquentiae*), the present work, and a speech in defence of a certain Naevius Arpinianus, who was accused of murdering his wife. These are the only works known to have been actually published by him, though others of his speeches had been taken down in shorthand and circulated against his will, while an excess of zeal on the part of his pupils resulted in the unauthorised publication of two series of lecture notes. The present work alone survives. The declamations which have come down to us under his name are spurious. Of his character the *Institutio Oratoria* gives us the pleasantest impression. Humane, kindly and of a deeply affectionate nature, gifted with a robust common sense and sound literary judgment, he may well have been the ideal schoolmaster. The fulsome references to Domitian are the only blemishes which mar this otherwise pleasing impression. And even here we must remember his great debt to the Flavian house and the genuine difficulty for a man in his position of avoiding the official style in speaking of the emperor.

As a stylist, though he is often difficult owing to compression and the epigrammatic turn which he gives his phrases, he is never affected or extravagant. He is still under the influence of the sound traditions

INTRODUCTION

of the Ciceronian age, and his Latin is silver-gilt rather than silver. His *Institutio Oratoria*, despite the fact that much of it is highly technical, has still much that is of interest to-day, even for those who care little for the history of rhetoric. Notably in the first book his precepts as regards education have lasting value : they may not be strikingly original, but they are sound, humane and admirably put. In the more technical portions of his work he is unequal; the reader feels that he cares but little about the minute pedantries of rhetorical technique, and that he lacks method in his presentation of the varying views held by his predecessors. But once he is free of such minor details and touches on themes of real practical interest, he is a changed man. He is at times really eloquent, and always vigorous and sound, while throughout the whole work he keeps the same high ideal unswervingly before him.

BIBLIOGRAPHY

EDITIONS

Ed. princeps, Campano, Rome, 1470.
Gronov, Leyden, 1665.
Gibson, Oxford, 1693.
Obrecht, Strassburg, 1698.
Burmann, Leyden, 1720.
Capperonnier, Paris, 1725.
Gesner, Göttingen, 1738.
Spalding, Leipzig, 1798–1816, with supplementary volume of notes by Zumpt, 1829, and another by Bonnell, 1834.

TEXTS

Zumpt, Leipzig, 1831.
Bonnell, Teubner texts, 1854.
Halm, Leipzig, 1868.
Meister, Leipzig, 1886–7.
Radermacher, Teubner texts, 1907 (Bks. 1–6). Second edition by V. Buchheit, 2 vols., 1959.
D. M. Gaunt, *M. Fabii Quintiliani Institutio Oratoria.* Selections with commentary and summaries of the intervening material. London, W. Heinemann. 1952.

EDITIONS OF SINGLE BOOKS

Bk. 1, Fierville, Paris, 1890; F. Colson, Cambridge, 1924.
Bk. 10, Peterson, Oxford, 1891.
Bk. 10 and 12, Frieze, New York; Bk. 12, R. G. Austin, Oxford, 1948.

Of the above the commentary of Spalding and the texts of Halm, Meister and Radermacher are by far the most important. Peterson's edition of Bk. 10 contains an admirable introduction dealing with the life of Quintilian, his gifts as a critic, his style and language and the MSS.

BIBLIOGRAPHY

In connection with the history of rhetorical theory and practice at Rome, the following works are of special importance:—

Cicero, de Oratore (Ed. Wilkins, Oxford, 1892).
Cicero, Orator (Ed. Sandys, Cambridge, 1889).
Cicero, Brutus (Ed. Kellogg, Boston, 1889).
Tacitus, Dialogus de claris oratoribus (Ed. Peterson, Oxford, 1893).

For the history of Latin rhetoric and education the following works may be consulted:—

Norden, *Die Antike Kunstprosa*, Leipzig, 1898.
Volkmann, *Die Rhetorik der Griechen und Römer*, Leipzig, 1885.
Marquardt, *Das Privatleben der Römer*, pp. 80-126, ed. 2, Leipzig, 1886.
Wilkins, *Roman Education*, Cambridge, 1905.

ENGLISH TRANSLATIONS OF QUINTILIAN

Guthrie, London, 1805.
Watson, in Bohn's series, reprinted 1903.

THE MANUSCRIPTS

The MSS. of the *Institutio Oratoria* fall into three groups:—

(1) The Codex Ambrosianus (E 153), an eleventh-century MS. now at Milan. Chs. IX. iv. 135 to XII. xi. 22 are missing.

(2) The Codex Bernensis (351) of the 10th century.
The Codex Bambergensis (M. 4, 14) of the 10th century.
The Codex Nostradamensis (Paris, Lat. 18527) of the 10th (?) century.
This group has the following *lacunae*: I. to i. 7; V. xiv. 12 to VIII. iii. 64; VIII. vi. 17 to 67; IX. iii. 2 to x. i. 107; XI. i. 71 to ii. 23; XII. x. 43 to *end*. The gaps are to be supplied from the Codex Bambergensis, in which they have been filled in by a later hand from a MS. resembling the Ambrosianus.

(3) A number of late MSS of the 15th century of the usual type.

BIBLIOGRAPHY

Occasional assistance may be obtained from the *Ars Rhetorica* of Julius Victor (Halm, *Rhet. Lat. minores*, II. pp. 373 *sqq.*), which is based on Quintilian and often transcribes whole passages: the Rhetorical treatise attributed to Cassiodorus (Halm, *op. cit.* p. 501) is also sometimes useful.

The text in this volume is that of Halm, with a few slight alterations in reading, and a considerable number in punctuation. The first family is indicated by A in critical notes, the second by B. Where particular MSS. are mentioned they are indicated by their name

BIBLIOGRAPHICAL ADDENDUM (1980)

Critical edition: ed. M. Winterbottom (*OCT*), 2 vols, Oxford 1970.

Editions with commentary: Book I, by F. H. Colson, Cambridge 1924

Book III, by Joachim Adamietz, Munich 1966

Book XII, by R. G. Austin, Oxford 1954[2].

Studies: Jean Cousin, *Études sur Quintilien*, Paris 1936.

G. M. A. Grube, *The Greek and Roman Critics*, London 1965

George Kennedy, *Quintilian*, New York 1969

M. Winterbottom, *Problems in Quintilian* (BICS Suppl. 25), London 1970

Lexicon: E. Bonnell, Leipzig 1834 (repr. 1963: vol. 6 of G. L. Spalding's edition).

Survey: Jean Cousin, 'Quintilien 1935–1959,' *Lustrum* 7 (1963) 289–331

SIGLA

A = Codex Ambrosianus I, 11th century.

B = Agreement of Codex Bernensis, Bambergensis and Nostradamensis, 10th century.

G = Codex Bambergensis in those passages where gaps have been supplied by a later 11th-century hand.

QUINTILIAN

BOOK I

M. FABIUS QUINTILIANUS TRYPHONI SUO SALUTEM

Efflagitasti cotidiano convicio, ut libros, quos ad Marcellum meum de Institutione oratoria scripseram iam emittere inciperem. Nam ipse eos nondum opinabar satis maturuisse, quibus componendis, ut scis, paulo plus quam biennium tot alioqui negotiis districtus impendi; quod tempus non tam stilo quam inquisitioni instituti operis prope infiniti et legendis

2 auctoribus, qui sunt innumerabiles, datum est. Usus deinde Horatii consilio, qui in arte poëtica suadet, ne praecipitetur editio *nonumque prematur in annum,* dabam iis otium, ut, refrigerato inventionis amore, diligentius repetitos tanquam lector perpenderem.

3 Sed si tanto opere efflagitantur quam tu adfirmas, permittamus vela ventis et oram solventibus bene precemur. Multum autem in tua quoque fide ac diligentia positum est, ut in manus hominum quam emendatissimi veniant.

MARCUS FABIUS QUINTILIANUS TO HIS FRIEND TRYPHO, GREETING

You have daily importuned me with the request that I should at length take steps to publish the book on the Education of an Orator which I dedicated to my friend Marcellus. For my own view was that it was not yet ripe for publication. As you know I have spent little more than two years on its composition, during which time moreover I have been distracted by a multitude of other affairs. These two years have been devoted not so much to actual writing as to the research demanded by a task to which practically no limits can be set and to the reading of innumerable authors. Further, following the pre- 2 cept of Horace who in his Art of Poetry deprecates hasty publication and urges the would-be author

> " To withhold
> His work till nine long years have passed away,"

I proposed to give them time, in order that the ardour of creation might cool and that I might revise them with all the consideration of a dispassionate reader. But if there is such a demand for 3 their publication as you assert, why then let us spread our canvas to the gale and offer up a fervent prayer to heaven as we put out to sea. But remember I rely on your loyal care to see that they reach the public in as correct a form as possible.

M. FABII QUINTILIANI
INSTITUTIONIS ORATORIAE

LIBER I

Prooemium

Post impetratam studiis meis quietem, quae per
viginti annos erudiendis iuvenibus impenderam, cum
a me quidam familiariter postularent, ut aliquid de
ratione dicendi componerem, diu sum equidem reluc-
tatus, quod auctores utriusque linguae clarissimos non
ignorabam multa, quae ad hoc opus pertinerent,
2 diligentissime scripta posteris reliquisse. Sed qua
ego ex causa faciliorem mihi veniam meae depre-
cationis arbitrabar fore, hac accendebantur illi magis,
quod inter diversas opiniones priorum et quasdam
etiam inter se contrarias difficilis esset electio; ut
mihi si non inveniendi nova at certe iudicandi de
veteribus iniungere laborem non iniuste viderentur.
3 Quamvis autem non tam me vinceret praestandi,

THE INSTITUTIO ORATORIA
OF QUINTILIAN

BOOK I

Preface

Having at length, after twenty years devoted to
the training of the young, obtained leisure for study,
I was asked by certain of my friends to write
something on the art of speaking. For a long time I
resisted their entreaties, since I was well aware that
some of the most distinguished Greek and Roman
writers had bequeathed to posterity a number of
works dealing with this subject, to the composition
of which they had devoted the utmost care. This 2
seemed to me to be an admirable excuse for my refusal, but served merely to increase their enthusiasm.
They urged that previous writers on the subject had
expressed different and at times contradictory
opinions, between which it was very difficult to
choose. They thought therefore that they were
justified in imposing on me the task, if not of
discovering original views, at least of passing definite
judgment on those expressed by my predecessors.
I was moved to comply not so much because I 3
felt confidence that I was equal to the task, as

5

quod exigebatur, fiducia quam negandi verecundia,
latius se tamen aperiente materia plus quam impone-
batur oneris sponte suscepi, simul ut pleniore obse-
quio demererer amantissimos mei, simul ne vulgarem
viam ingressus alienis demum vestigiis insisterem.
4 Nam ceteri fere, qui artem orandi litteris tradiderunt,
ita sunt exorsi, quasi perfectis omni alio genere
doctrinae summam in eloquentia manum imponer-
ent, sive contemnentes tanquam parva, quae prius
discimus, studia, sive non ad suum pertinere officium
opinati, quando divisae professionum vices essent,
seu, quod proximum vero, nullam ingenii sperantes
gratiam circa res etiamsi necessarias procul tamen ab
ostentatione positas; ut operum fastigia spectantur,
5 latent fundamenta. Ego, cum existimem nihil arti
oratoriae alienum, sine quo fieri non posse oratorem
fatendum est, nec ad ullius rei summam nisi praece-
dentibus initiis perveniri, ad minora illa, sed quae si
negligas, non sit maioribus locus, demittere me non
recusabo; nec aliter, quam si mihi tradatur educan-
dus orator, studia eius formare ab infantia incipiam.

6

because I had a certain compunction about refusing. The subject proved more extensive than I had first imagined ; but finally I volunteered to shoulder a task which was on a far larger scale than that which I was originally asked to undertake. I wished on the one hand to oblige my very good friends beyond their requests, and on the other to avoid the beaten track and the necessity of treading where others had gone before. For almost all others who have 4 written on the art of oratory have started with the assumption that their readers were perfect in all other branches of education and that their own task was merely to put the finishing touches to their rhetorical training ; this is due to the fact that they either despised the preliminary stages of education or thought that they were not their concern, since the duties of the different branches of education are distinct one from another, or else, and this is nearer the truth, because they had no hope of making a remunerative display of their talent in dealing with subjects, which, although necessary, are far from being showy : just as in architecture it is the superstructure and not the foundations which attracts the eye. I on the other hand hold that the 5 art of oratory includes all that is essential for the training of an orator, and that it is impossible to reach the summit in any subject unless we have first passed through all the elementary stages. I shall not therefore refuse to stoop to the consideration of those minor details, neglect of which may result in there being no opportunity for more important things, and propose to mould the studies of my orator from infancy, on the assumption that his whole education has been entrusted to my charge. This work I dedicate 6

6 Quod opus, Marcelle Victori, tibi dicamus; quem,
cum amicissimum nobis tum eximio litterarum amore
flagrantem, non propter haec modo (quamquam sint
magna) dignissimum hoc mutuae inter nos caritatis
pignore iudicabamus; sed quod erudiendo Getae tuo,
cuius prima aetas manifestum iam ingenii lumen
ostendit, non inutiles fore libri videbantur, quos ab
ipsis dicendi velut incunabulis, per omnes, quae
modo aliquid oratori futuro conferant, artis ad sum-
7 mam eius operis perducere destinabamus; atque eo
magis, quod duo iam sub nomine meo libri fereban-
tur artis rhetoricae neque editi a me neque in hoc
comparati. Namque alterum sermonem per biduum
habitum pueri, quibus id praestabatur, exceperant;
alterum pluribus sane diebus, quantum notando consequi potuerant, interceptum boni iuvenes, sed
nimium amantes mei, temerario editionis honore
8 vulgaverant. Quare in his quoque libris erunt eadem
aliqua, multa mutata, plurima adiecta, omnia vero
compositiora et, quantum nos poterimus, elaborata.

9   Oratorem autem instituimus illum perfectum, qui
esse nisi vir bonus non potest; ideoque non dicendi
modo eximiam in eo facultatem sed omnes animi

to you, Marcellus Victorius. You have been the truest of friends to me and you have shown a passionate enthusiasm for literature. But good as these reasons are, they are not the only reasons that lead me to regard you as especially worthy of such a pledge of our mutual affection. There is also the consideration that this book should prove of service in the education of your son Geta, who, young though he is, already shows clear promise of real talent. It has been my design to lead my reader from the very cradle of speech through all the stages of education which can be of any service to our budding orator till we have reached the very summit of the art. I 7 have been all the more desirous of so doing because two books on the art of rhetoric are at present circulating under my name, although never published by me or composed for such a purpose. One is a two days' lecture which was taken down by the boys who were my audience. The other consists of such notes as my good pupils succeeded in taking down from a course of lectures on a somewhat more extensive scale: I appreciate their kindness, but they showed an excess of enthusiasm and a certain lack of discretion in doing my utterances the honour of publication. Consequently in the present work 8 although some passages remain the same, you will find many alterations and still more additions, while the whole theme will be treated with greater system and with as great perfection as lies within my power.

My aim, then, is the education of the perfect 9 orator. The first essential for such an one is that he should be a good man, and consequently we demand of him not merely the possession of exceptional

10 virtutes exigimus. Neque enim hoc concesserim,
rationem rectae honestaeque vitae (ut quidam putaverunt) ad philosophos relegandam, cum vir ille
vere civilis et publicarum privatarumque rerum
administrationi accommodatus, qui regere consiliis
urbes, fundare legibus, emendare iudiciis possit,
11 non alius sit profecto quam orator. Quare, tametsi
me fateor usurum quibusdam, quae philosophorum
libris continentur, tamen ea iure vereque contenderim esse operis nostri proprieque ad artem
12 oratoriam pertinere. An, si frequentissime de
iustitia, fortitudine, temperantia ceterisque similibus disserendum est, adeo ut vix ulla possit causa
reperiri in quam non aliqua ex his incidat quaestio,
eaque omnia inventione atque elocutione sunt ex-
plicanda, dubitabitur, ubicunque vis ingenii et copia
dicendi postulatur, ibi partes oratoris esse prae-
13 cipuas? Fueruntque haec, ut Cicero apertissime
colligit, quemadmodum iuncta natura sic officio
quoque copulata, ut iidem sapientes atque elo-
quentes haberentur. Scidit deinde se studium,
atque inertia factum est, ut artes esse plures viderentur. Nam ut primum lingua esse coepit in quaestu
institutumque eloquentiae bonis male uti, curam

---

[1] *de Or.* iii. 15.

gifts of speech, but of all the excellences of character as well.   For I will not admit that the principles of 10 upright and honourable living should, as some have held, be regarded as the peculiar concern of philosophy. The man who can really play his part as a citizen and is capable of meeting the demands both of public and private business, the man who can guide a state by his counsels, give it a firm basis by his legislation and purge its vices by his decisions as a judge, is assuredly no other than the orator of our quest. Wherefore, although I admit I shall make 11 use of certain of the principles laid down in philosophical textbooks, I would insist that such principles have a just claim to form part of the subject-matter of this work and do actually belong to the art of oratory. I shall frequently be compelled to speak of 12 such virtues as courage, justice, self-control; in fact scarcely a case comes up in which some one of these virtues is not involved; every one of them requires illustration and consequently makes a demand on the imagination and eloquence of the pleader.   I ask you then, can there be any doubt that, wherever imaginative power and amplitude of diction are required, the orator has a specially important part to play? These two branches of knowledge were, as 13 Cicero has clearly shown,[1] so closely united, not merely in theory but in practice, that the same men were regarded as uniting the qualifications of orator and philosopher. Subsequently this single branch of study split up into its component parts, and thanks to the indolence of its professors was regarded as consisting of several distinct subjects. As soon as speaking became a means of livelihood and the practice of making an evil use of the

14 morum, qui diserti habebantur, reliquerunt. Ea
vero destituta infirmioribus ingeniis velut praedae
fuit. Inde quidam, contempto bene dicendi labore,
ad formandos animos statuendasque vitae leges
regressi partem quidem potiorem, si dividi posset,
retinuerunt; nomen tamen sibi insolentissimum
arrogaverunt, ut soli studiosi sapientiae vocarentur,
quod neque summi imperatores neque in consiliis
rerum maximarum ac totius administratione rei
publicae clarissime versati sibi unquam vindicare
sunt ausi. Facere enim optima quam promittere
15 maluerunt. Ac veterum quidem sapientiae professorum multos et honesta praecepisse et, ut praece-
perint, etiam vixisse, facile concesserim; nostris
vero temporibus sub hoc nomine maxima in plerisque vitia latuerunt. Non enim virtute ac studiis,
ut haberentur philosophi, laborabant, sed vultum et
tristitiam et dissentientem a ceteris habitum pes-
16 simis moribus praetendebant. Haec autem, quae
velut propria philosophiae asseruntur, passim tractamus omnes. Quis enim non de iusto, aequo ac
bono, modo non et vir pessimus, loquitur? quis
non etiam rusticorum aliqua de causis naturalibus
quaerit? nam verborum proprietas ac differentia
omnibus, qui sermonem curae habent, debet esse

blessings of eloquence came into vogue, those who had a reputation for eloquence ceased to study moral philosophy, and ethics, thus abandoned by the 14 orators, became the prey of weaker intellects. As a consequence certain persons, disdaining the toil of learning to speak well, returned to the task of forming character and establishing rules of life and kept to themselves what is, if we *must* make a division, the better part of philosophy, but presumptuously laid claim to the sole possession of the title of philosopher, a distinction which neither the greatest generals nor the most famous statesmen and administrators have ever dared to claim for themselves. For they preferred the performance to the promise of great deeds. I am ready to admit that 15 many of the old philosophers inculcated the most excellent principles and practised what they preached. But in our own day the name of philosopher has too often been the mask for the worst vices. For their attempt has not been to win the name of philosopher by virtue and the earnest search for wisdom; instead they have sought to disguise the depravity of their characters by the assumption of a stern and austere mien accompanied by the wearing of a garb differing from that of their fellow men. Now as a matter of fact we all of us frequently 16 handle those themes which philosophy claims for its own. Who, short of being an utter villain, does not speak of justice, equity and virtue? Who (and even common country-folk are no exception) does not make some inquiry into the causes of natural phenomena? As for the special uses and distinctions of words, they should be a subject of study common to all who give any thought to the meaning of language.

17 communis. Sed ea et sciet optime et eloquetur orator; qui si fuisset aliquando perfectus, non a philosophorum scholis virtutis praecepta peterentur. Nunc necesse est ad eos aliquando auctores recurrere, qui desertam, ut dixi, partem oratoriae artis, meliorem praesertim, occupaverunt, et velut nostrum reposcere; non ut nos illorum utamur inventis, sed

18 ut illos alienis usos esse doceamus. Sit igitur orator vir talis, qualis vere sapiens appellari possit; nec moribus modo perfectus (nam id mea quidem opinione, quanquam sunt qui dissentiant, satis non est) sed etiam scientia et omni facultate dicendi,

19 qualis fortasse nemo adhuc fuerit; sed non ideo minus nobis ad summa tendendum est; quod fecerunt plerique veterum, qui, etsi nondum quemquam sapientem repertum putabant, praecepta tamen

20 sapientiae tradiderunt. Nam est certe aliquid consummata eloquentia, neque ad eam pervenire natura humani ingenii prohibet. Quod si non contingat, altius tamen ibunt, qui ad summa nitentur, quam qui, praesumpta desperatione quo velint evadendi, protinus circa ima substiterint.

21 Quo magis impetranda erit venia, si ne minora quidem illa, verum operi, quod instituimus, necessaria praeteribo. Nam liber primus ea, quae sunt

But it is surely the orator who will have the greatest 17
mastery of all such departments of knowledge and
the greatest power to express it in words. And if ever
he had reached perfection, there would be no need
to go to the schools of philosophy for the precepts of
virtue. As things stand, it is occasionally necessary
to have recourse to those authors who have, as I
said above, usurped the better part of the art of
oratory after its desertion by the orators and to
demand back what is ours by right, not with a view
to appropriating their discoveries, but to show them
that they have appropriated what in truth belonged
to others. Let our ideal orator then be such as to 18
have a genuine title to the name of philosopher: it
is not sufficient that he should be blameless in point
of character (for I cannot agree with those who hold
this opinion): he must also be a thorough master of
the science and the art of speaking, to an extent
that perhaps no orator has yet attained. Still we 19
must none the less follow the ideal, as was done by
not a few of the ancients, who, though they refused
to admit that the perfect sage had yet been found,
none the less handed down precepts of wisdom for
the use of posterity. Perfect eloquence is assuredly 20
a reality, which is not beyond the reach of human
intellect. Even if we fail to reach it, those whose
aspirations are highest, will attain to greater heights
than those who abandon themselves to premature
despair of ever reaching the goal and halt at the
very foot of the ascent.

I have therefore all the juster claim to indulgence, 21
if I refuse to pass by those minor details which are
none the less essential to my task. My first book
will be concerned with the education preliminary to

ante officium rhetoris, continebit. Secundo prima
apud rhetorem elementa et quae de ipsa rhetorices
22 substantia quaeruntur tractabimus. Quinque deinceps inventioni (nam huic et dispositio subiungitur), quattuor elocutioni, in cuius partem memoria
ac pronuntiatio veniunt, dabuntur. Unus accedet,
in quo nobis orator ipse informandus est, ubi,[1] qui
mores eius, quae in suscipiendis, discendis, agendis
causis ratio, quod eloquentiae genus, quis agendi
debeat esse finis, quae post finem studia, quantum
23 nostra valebit infirmitas, disseremus. His omnibus
admiscebitur, ut quisque locus postulabit, docendi
ratio, quae non eorum modo scientia, quibus solis
quidam nomen artis dederunt, studiosos instruat et
(ut sic dixerim) ius ipsum rhetorices interpretetur,
sed alere facundiam, vires augere eloquentiae possit.
24 Nam plerumque nudae illae artes nimia subtilitatis
adfectatione frangunt atque concidunt quidquid est
in oratione generosius, et omnem sucum ingenii
bibunt et ossa detegunt : quae ut esse et adstringi
nervis suis debent, sic corpore operienda sunt.
25 Ideoque nos non particulam illam, sicut plerique,
sed quidquid utile ad instituendum oratorem putabamus, in hos duodecim libros contulimus breviter

---

[1] ubi . . . disseremus, *Spalding* : ut . . . disseramus, *MSS.*

the duties of the teacher of rhetoric. My second will deal with the rudiments of the schools of rhetoric and with problems connected with the essence of rhetoric itself. The next five will be concerned 22 with Invention, in which I include Arrangement. The four following will be assigned to Eloquence, under which head I include Memory and Delivery. Finally there will be one book in which our complete orator will be delineated; as far as my feeble powers permit, I shall discuss his character, the rules which should guide him in undertaking, studying and pleading cases, the style of his eloquence, the time at which he should cease to plead cases and the studies to which he should devote himself after such cessation. In the course of these 23 discussions I shall deal in its proper place with the method of teaching by which students will acquire not merely a knowledge of those things to which the name of art is restricted by certain theorists, and will not only come to understand the laws of rhetoric, but will acquire that which will increase their powers of speech and nourish their eloquence. For as a rule the result of the dry text- 24 books on the art of rhetoric is that by straining after excessive subtlety they impair and cripple all the nobler elements of style, exhaust the lifeblood of the imagination and leave but the bare bones, which, while it is right and necessary that they should exist and be bound each to each by their respective ligaments, require a covering of flesh as well. I shall therefore avoid the precedent set 25 by the majority and shall not restrict myself to this narrow conception of my theme, but shall include in my twelve books a brief demonstration of everything

omnia demonstraturi. Nam si quantum de quaque re dici potest persequamur, finis operis non reperietur.

26 Illud tamen in primis testandum est, nihil praecepta atque artes valere nisi adiuvante natura. Quapropter ei, cui deerit ingenium, non magis haec scripta sint quam de agrorum cultu sterilibus terris.

27 Sunt et alia ingenita cuique adiumenta, vox, latus patiens laboris, valetudo, constantia, decor; quae si modica obtigerunt, possunt ratione ampliari, sed nonnunquam ita desunt, ut bona etiam ingenii studiique corrumpant; sicut et haec ipsa sine doctore perito, studio pertinaci, scribendi, legendi, dicendi multa et continua exercitatione per se nihil prosunt.

I. Igitur nato filio pater spem de illo primum quam optimam capiat, ita diligentior a principiis fiet. Falsa enim est querela, paucissimis hominibus vim percipiendi, quae tradantur, esse concessam, plerosque vero laborem ac tempora tarditate ingenii perdere. Nam contra plures reperias et faciles in excogitando et ad discendum promptos. Quippe id est homini naturale; ac sicut aves ad volatum, equi ad cursum, ad saevitiam ferae gignuntur; ita

which may seem likely to contribute to the education of an orator. For if I were to attempt to say
all that might be said on each subject, the book
would never be finished.

There is however one point which I must em- 26
phasise before I begin, which is this. Without
natural gifts technical rules are useless. Consequently the student who is devoid of talent will
derive no more profit from this work than barren
soil from a treatise on agriculture. There are, it is 27
true, other natural aids, such as the possession of a
good voice and robust lungs, sound health, powers of
endurance and grace, and if these are possessed only
to a moderate extent, they may be improved by
methodical training. In some cases, however, these
gifts are lacking to such an extent that their absence
is fatal to all such advantages as talent and study
can confer, while, similarly, they are of no profit in
themselves unless cultivated by skilful teaching, per-
sistent study and continuous and extensive practice
in writing, reading and speaking.

I. I would, therefore, have a father conceive the
highest hopes of his son from the moment of his
birth. If he does so, he will be more careful about
the groundwork of his education. For there is
absolutely no foundation for the complaint that but
few men have the power to take in the knowledge
that is imparted to them, and that the majority are
so slow of understanding that education is a waste
of time and labour. On the contrary you will find
that most are quick to reason and ready to learn.
Reasoning comes as naturally to man as flying to
birds, speed to horses and ferocity to beasts of prey:

nobis propria est mentis agitatio atque sollertia,
2 unde origo animi caelestis creditur. Hebetes vero
et indociles non magis secundum naturam homines
eduntur quam prodigiosa corpora et monstris in-
signia, sed hi pauci admodum fuerunt. Argumentum quod in pueris elucet spes plurimorum,
quae cum emoritur aetate, manifestum est, non
naturam defecisse sed curam. Praestat tamen in-
3 genio alius alium. Concedo; sed plus efficiet aut
minus; nemo reperitur, qui sit studio nihil consecutus. Hoc qui perviderit, protinus ut erit parens
factus, acrem quam maxime curam spei futuri oratoris impendat.

4   Ante omnia ne sit vitiosus sermo nutricibus, quas
si fieri posset sapientes Chrysippus optavit, certe
quantum res pateretur optimas eligi voluit. Et
morum quidem in his haud dubie prior ratio est,
5 recte tamen etiam loquantur. Has primum audiet
puer, harum verba effingere imitando conabitur. Et
natura tenacissimi sumus eorum, quae rudibus animis
percepimus; ut sapor, quo nova imbuas, durat, nec
lanarum colores, quibus simplex ille candor mutatus
est, elui possunt. Et haec ipsa magis pertinaciter
haerent, quo deteriora sunt. Nam bona facile mutantur in peius; num quando in bonum verteris

our minds are endowed by nature with such activity
and sagacity that the soul is believed to proceed
from heaven.   Those who are dull and unteachable 2
are as abnormal as prodigious births and monstrosi-
ties, and are but few in number.   A proof of what
I say is to be found in the fact that boys commonly
show promise of many accomplishments, and when
such promise dies away as they grow up, this is
plainly due not to the failure of natural gifts, but to
lack of the requisite care.   But, it will be urged,
there are degrees of talent.   Undoubtedly, I reply, 3
and there will be a corresponding variation in actual
accomplishment: but that there are any who gain
nothing from education, I absolutely deny.   The
man who shares this conviction, must, as soon as he
becomes a father, devote the utmost care to fostering the promise shown by the son whom he destines
to become an orator.

Above all see that the child's nurse speaks 4
correctly.   The ideal, according to Chrysippus,
would be that she should be a philosopher: failing
that he desired that the best should be chosen, as
far as possible.   No doubt the most important point
is that they should be of good character: but they
should speak correctly as well.   It is the nurse that 5
the child first hears, and her words that he will first
attempt to imitate.   And we are by nature most
tenacious of childish impressions, just as the flavour
first absorbed by vessels when new persists, and the
colour imparted by dyes to the primitive whiteness
of wool is indelible.   Further it is the worst
impressions that are most durable.   For, while what
is good readily deteriorates, you will never turn vice

vitia? Non assuescat ergo, ne dum infans quidem
est, sermoni qui dediscendus sit.

6 In parentibus vero quam plurimum esse eruditionis optaverim, nec de patribus tantum loquor.
Nam Gracchorum eloquentiae multum contulisse accepimus Corneliam matrem, cuius doctissimus sermo
in posteros quoque est epistolis traditus : et Laelia
C. filia reddidisse in loquendo paternam elegantiam
dicitur, et Hortensiae Q. filiae oratio apud Trium-
viros habita legitur non tantum in sexus honorem.

7 Nec tamen ii, quibus discere ipsis non contigit,
minorem curam docendi liberos habeant; sed sint
propter hoc ipsum ad cetera magis diligentes.

8 De pueris, inter quos educabitur ille huic spei
destinatus, idem quod de nutricibus dictum sit. De
paedagogis hoc amplius, ut aut sint eruditi plene,
quam primam esse curam velim, aut se non esse
eruditos sciant. Nihil est peius iis, qui paulum
aliquid ultra primas litteras progressi falsam sibi
scientiae persuasionem induerunt. Nam et cedere
praecipiendi partibus indignantur et velut iure
quodam potestatis, quo fere hoc hominum genus
intumescit, imperiosi atque interim saevientes stul-

---

[1] There is no translation for *paedagogus*, the slave-tutor.
"Tutor," "guardian," "governor," and similar terms are
all misleading. He had the general supervision of the boy,
escorted him to school and elsewhere, and saw that he
did not get into mischief, but did not, as a rule, direct his
studies.

into virtue. Do not therefore allow the boy to
become accustomed even in infancy to a style of
speech which he will subsequently have to unlearn.

As regards parents, I should like to see them as 6
highly educated as possible, and I do not restrict this
remark to fathers alone. We are told that the
eloquence of the Gracchi owed much to their
mother Cornelia, whose letters even to-day testify to
the cultivation of her style. Laelia, the daughter
of Gaius Laelius, is said to have reproduced the
elegance of her father's language in her own speech,
while the oration delivered before the triumvirs by
Hortensia, the daughter of Quintus Hortensius, is
still read and not merely as a compliment to her sex.
And even those who have not had the fortune to 7
receive a good education should not for that reason
devote less care to their son's education; but should
on the contrary show all the greater diligence in
other matters where they can be of service to their
children.

As regards the boys in whose company our budding 8
orator is to be brought up, I would repeat what
I have said about nurses. As regards his *paedagogi*,[1]
I would urge that they should have had a thorough
education, or if they have not, that they should be
aware of the fact. There are none worse than
those, who as soon as they have progressed beyond
a knowledge of the alphabet delude themselves
into the belief that they are the possessors of real
knowledge. For they disdain to stoop to the
drudgery of teaching, and conceiving that they
have acquired a certain title to authority—a frequent
source of vanity in such persons—become imperious
or even brutal in instilling a thorough dose of their

9 titiam suam perdocent. Nec minus error eorum
nocet moribus; siquidem Leonides Alexandri paedagogus, ut a Babylonio Diogene traditur, quibusdam
eum vitiis imbuit, quae robustum quoque et iam
maximum regem ab illa institutione puerili sunt
persecuta.

10 Si cui multa videor exigere, cogitet oratorem
institui, rem arduam, etiam cum ei formando nihil
defuerit; praeterea plura ac difficiliora superesse.
Nam et studio perpetuo et praestantissimis praecep-

11 toribus et plurimis disciplinis opus est. Quapropter
praecipienda sunt optima; quae si quis gravabitur,
non rationi defuerint sed homini. Si tamen non
continget, quales maxime velim nutrices, pueros,
paedagogos habere, at unus certe sit assiduus loquendi non imperitus, qui, si qua erunt ab his
praesente alumno dicta vitiose, corrigat protinus nec
insidere illi sinat; dum tamen intelligatur, id, quod
prius dixi, bonum esse, hoc remedium.

12 A sermone Graeco puerum incipere malo, quia
Latinum, qui pluribus in usu est, vel nobis nolen-
tibus perbibet, simul quia disciplinis quoque Graecis
prius instituendus est, unde et nostrae fluxerunt.

24

own folly. Their misconduct is no less prejudicial 9
to morals. We are, for instance, told by Diogenes
of Babylon, that Leonides, Alexander's *paedagogus*,
infected his pupil with certain faults, which as a
result of his education as a boy clung to him even in
his maturer years when he had become the greatest
of kings.

If any of my readers regards me as somewhat 10
exacting in my demands, I would ask him to reflect
that it is no easy task to create an orator, even
though his education be carried out under the most
favourable circumstances, and that further and
greater difficulties are still before us. For continuous application, the very best of teachers and
a variety of exercises are necessary. Therefore the 11
rules which we lay down for the education of our
pupil must be of the best. If anyone refuses to be
guided by them, the fault will lie not with the
method, but with the individual. Still if it should
prove impossible to secure the ideal nurse, the ideal
companions, or the ideal *paedagogus*, I would insist
that there should be one person at any rate attached
to the boy who has some knowledge of speaking
and who will, if any incorrect expression should be
used by nurse or *paedagogus* in the presence of
the child under their charge, at once correct the
error and prevent its becoming a habit. But it must
be clearly understood that this is only a remedy, and
that the ideal course is that indicated above.

I prefer that a boy should begin with Greek, 12
because Latin, being in general use, will be picked
up by him whether we will or no; while the fact
that Latin learning is derived from Greek is a
further reason for his being first instructed in the

13 Non tamen hoc adeo superstitiose fieri velim, ut diu tantum Graece loquatur aut discat, sicut plerisque moris est. Hoc enim accidunt et oris plurima vitia in peregrinum sonum corrupti et sermonis ; cui cum Graecae figurae assidua consuetudine haeserunt, in diversa quoque loquendi ratione pertinacissime

14 durant. Non longe itaque Latina subsequi debent et cito pariter ire. Ita fiet, ut, cum aequali cura linguam utramque tueri coeperimus, neutra alteri officiat.

15 Quidam litteris instituendos, qui minores septem annis essent, non putaverunt, quod illa primum aetas et intellectum disciplinarum capere et laborem pati posset. In qua sententia Hesiodum esse plurimi tradunt qui ante grammaticum Aristophanen fuerunt ; nam is primus ὑποθήκας, in quo libro scriptum

16 hoc invenitur, negavit esse huius poëtae. Sed alii quoque auctores, inter quos Eratosthenes, idem praeceperunt. Melius autem, qui nullum tempus vacare cura volunt, ut Chrysippus. Nam is, quamvis nutricibus triennium dederit, tamen ab illis quoque iam formandam quam optimis institutis mentem

17 infantium iudicat. Cur autem non pertineat ad litteras aetas, quae ad mores iam pertinet ? Neque ignoro, toto illo, de quo loquor, tempore vix tantum effici, quantum conferre unus postea possit annus ;

---

[1] *Admonitions*, a lost didactic poem. Aristophanes of Byzantium, 257–180 B.C., the famous Alexandrian critic.

latter. I do not however desire that this principle 13
should be so superstitiously observed that he should
for long speak and learn only Greek, as is done in the
majority of cases. Such a course gives rise to many
faults of language and accent; the latter tends to
acquire a foreign intonation, while the former
through force of habit becomes impregnated with
Greek idioms, which persist with extreme obstinacy
even when we are speaking another tongue. The 14
study of Latin ought therefore to follow at no great
distance and in a short time proceed side by side
with Greek. The result will be that, as soon as we
begin to give equal attention to both languages,
neither will prove a hindrance to the other.

Some hold that boys should not be taught to 15
read till they are seven years old, that being the
earliest age at which they can derive profit from
instruction and endure the strain of learning. Most
of them attribute this view to Hesiod, at least such
as lived before the time of Aristophanes the grammarian, who was the first to deny that the *Hy-
pothecae*,[1] in which this opinion is expressed, was the
work of that poet. But other authorities, among 16
them Eratosthenes, give the same advice. Those
however who hold that a child's mind should not be
allowed to lie fallow for a moment are wiser.
Chrysippus, for instance, though he gives the nurses
a three years' reign, still holds the formation of
the child's mind on the best principles to be a part
of their duties. Why, again, since children are 17
capable of moral training, should they not be
capable of literary education? I am well aware
that during the whole period of which I am speaking
we can expect scarcely the same amount of progress

sed tamen mihi, qui dissenserunt, videntur non tam discentibus in hac parte quam docentibus pepercisse.

18 Quid melius alioqui facient, ex quo loqui poterunt? Faciant enim aliquid necesse est. Aut cur hoc, quantulumcunque est, usque ad septem annos lucrum fastidiamus? Nam certe quamlibet parvum sit, quod contulerit aetas prior, maiora tamen aliqua discet puer ipso illo anno, quo minora didicisset.

19 Hoc per singulos prorogatum in summam proficit, et quantum in infantia praesumptum est temporis, adolescentiae adquiritur. Idem etiam de sequentibus annis praeceptum sit, ne, quod cuique discendum est, sero discere incipiat. Non ergo perdamus primum statim tempus, atque eo minus, quod initia litterarum sola memoria constant, quae non modo iam est in parvis sed tum etiam tenacissima est.

20 Nec sum adeo aetatum imprudens, ut instandum protinus teneris acerbe putem exigendamque plane operam. Nam id in primis cavere oportebit, ne studia, qui amare nondum potest, oderit et amaritudinem semel perceptam etiam ultra rudes annos reformidet. Lusus hic sit; et rogetur et laudetur et numquam non fecisse se gaudeat, aliquando ipso nolente doceatur alius, cui invideat; contendat

that one year will effect afterwards. Still those who disagree with me seem in taking this line to spare the teacher rather than the pupil. What better 18 occupation can a child have so soon as he is able to speak? And he must be kept occupied somehow or other. Or why should we despise the profit to be derived before the age of seven, small though it be? For though the knowledge absorbed in the previous years may be but little, yet the boy will be learning something more advanced during that year, in which he would otherwise have been occupied with something more elementary. Such progress each suc- 19 cessive year increases the total, and the time gained during childhood is clear profit to the period of youth. Further as regards the years which follow I must emphasise the importance of learning what has to be learnt in good time. Let us not therefore waste the earliest years: there is all the less excuse for this, since the elements of literary training are solely a question of memory, which not only exists even in small children, but is specially retentive at that age.

I am not however so blind to differences of age 20 as to think that the very young should be forced on prematurely or given real work to do. Above all things we must take care that the child, who is not yet old enough to love his studies, does not come to hate them and dread the bitterness which he has once tasted, even when the years of infancy are left behind. His studies must be made an amuse- ment: he must be questioned and praised and taught to rejoice when he has done well; sometimes too, when he refuses instruction, it should be given to some other to excite his envy, at times also he

29

interim et saepius vincere se putet ; praemiis etiam,
quae capit illa aetas, evocetur.

21 Parva docemus oratorem instituendum professi,
sed est sua etiam studiis infantia ; et ut corporum
mox fortissimorum educatio a lacte cunisque initium
ducit, ita futurus eloquentissimus edidit aliquando
vagitum et loqui primum incerta voce temptavit
et haesit circa formas litterarum. Nec si quid
22 discere satis non est, ideo nec necesse est. Quodsi
nemo reprehendit patrem, qui haec non negligenda
in suo filio putet, cur improbetur, si quis ea, quae
domi suae recte faceret, in publicum promit ? Atque
eo magis, quod minora etiam facilius minores
percipiunt, et ut corpora ad quosdam membrorum
flexus formari nisi tenera non possunt, sic animos
23 quoque ad pleraque duriores robur ipsum facit. An
Philippus Macedonum rex Alexandro filio suo prima
litterarum elementa tradi ab Aristotele, summo eius
aetatis philosopho, voluisset, aut ille suscepisset hoc
officium, si non studiorum initia et a perfectissimo
quoque optime tractari et pertinere ad summam

must be engaged in competition and should be allowed to believe himself successful more often than not, while he should be encouraged to do his best by such rewards as may appeal to his tender years.

These instructions may seem but trivialities in 21 view of the fact that I am professing to describe the education of an orator. But studies, like men, have their infancy, and as the training of the body which is destined to grow to the fulness of strength begins while the child is in his cradle and at his mother's breast, so even the man who is destined to rise to the heights of eloquence was once a squalling babe, tried to speak in stammering accents and was puzzled by the shapes of letters. Nor does the fact that capacity for learning is inadequate, prove that it is not necessary to learn anything. No 22 one blames a father because he thinks that such details should on no account be neglected in the case of his own son. Why then should he be criticised who sets down for the benefit of the public what he would be right to put into practice in his own house? There is this further reason why he should not be blamed. Small children are better adapted for taking in small things, and just as the body can only be trained to certain flexions of the limbs while it is young and supple, so the acquisition of strength makes the mind offer greater resistance to the acquisition of most subjects of knowledge. Would Philip of Macedon have wished that his son 23 Alexander should be taught the rudiments of letters by Aristotle, the greatest philosopher of that age, or would the latter have undertaken the task, if he had not thought that even the earliest instruction is best given by the most perfect teacher and has real

24 credidisset? Fingamus igitur Alexandrum dari
nobis impositum gremio, dignum tanta cura in-
fantem (quanquam suus cuique dignus est): pu-
deatne me in ipsis statim elementis etiam brevia
docendi monstrare compendia?

Neque enim mihi illud saltem placet, quod fieri
in plurimis video, ut litterarum nomina et contextum
25 prius quam formas parvuli discant. Obstat hoc
agnitioni earum non intendentibus mox animum ad
ipsos ductus, dum antecedentem memoriam sequuntur. Quae causa est praecipientibus, ut etiam,
cum satis adfixisse eas pueris recto illo quo primum
scribi solent contextu videntur, retro agant rursus et
varia permutatione turbent, donec litteras qui in-
stituuntur facie norint non ordine. Quapropter
optime sicut hominum pariter et habitus et nomina
26 edocebuntur. Sed quod in litteris obest, in syllabis
non nocebit. Non excludo autem, id quod est inventum [1] irritandae ad discendum infantiae gratia
eburneas etiam litterarum formas in lusum offerre;
vel si quid aliud, quo magis illa aetas gaudeat,
inveniri potest, quod tractare, intueri, nominare
iucundum sit.

27 Cum vero iam ductus sequi coeperit, non inutile
erit eas tabellae quam optime insculpi, ut per illos

---

[1] inventum, *Heindorf*: notum, *MSS.*

reference to the whole of education? Let us assume 24
therefore that Alexander has been confided to our
charge and that the infant placed in our lap deserves
no less attention than he—though for that matter
every man's child deserves equal attention. Would
you be ashamed even in teaching him the alphabet
to point out some brief rules for his education?

At any rate I am not satisfied with the course
(which I note is usually adopted) of teaching small
children the names and order of the letters before
their shapes. Such a practice makes them slow 25
to recognise the letters, since they do not pay
attention to their actual shape, preferring to be
guided by what they have already learned by
rote. It is for this reason that teachers, when
they think they have sufficiently familiarised their
young pupils with the letters written in their
usual order, reverse that order or rearrange it in
every kind of combination, until they learn to know
the letters from their appearance and not from
the order in which they occur. It will be best
therefore for children to begin by learning their
appearance and names just as they do with men.
The method, however, to which we have objected in 26
teaching the alphabet, is unobjectionable when
applied to syllables. I quite approve on the other
hand of a practice which has been devised to
stimulate children to learn by giving them ivory
letters to play with, as I do of anything else that
may be discovered to delight the very young, the
sight, handling and naming of which is a pleasure.

As soon as the child has begun to know the 27
shapes of the various letters, it will be no bad thing
to have them cut as accurately as possible upon a

velut sulcos ducatur stilus. Nam neque errabit,
quemadmodum in ceris (continebitur enim utrinque
marginibus neque extra praescriptum egredi poterit)
et celerius ac saepius sequendo certa vestigia fir-
mabit articulos, neque egebit adiutorio manum suam
28 manu superimposita regentis. Non est aliena res,
quae fere ab honestis negligi solet, cura bene ac
velociter scribendi. Nam cum sit in studiis praecipuum, quoque solo verus ille profectus et altis
radicibus nixus paretur, scribere ipsum, tardior stilus
cogitationem moratur, rudis et confusus intellectu
caret; unde sequitur alter dictandi, quae trans-
29 ferenda sunt, labor. Quare cum semper et ubique
tum praecipue in epistolis secretis et familiaribus
delectabit ne hoc quidem neglectum reliquisse.

30   Syllabis nullum compendium est; perdiscendae
omnes nec, ut fit plerumque, difficillima quaeque
earum differenda, ut in nominibus scribendis depre-
31 hendantur. Quin immo ne primae quidem memoriae
temere credendum; repetere et diu inculcare fuerit
utilius, et in lectione quoque non properare ad con-
tinuandam eam vel accelerandam, nisi cum inoffensa
atque indubitata litterarum inter se coniunctio
suppeditare sine ulla cogitandi saltem mora poterit.

board, so that the pen may be guided along the
grooves. Thus mistakes such as occur with wax
tablets will be rendered impossible; for the pen
will be confined between the edges of the letters
and will be prevented from going astray. Further
by increasing the frequency and speed with which
they follow these fixed outlines we shall give steadi-
ness to the fingers, and there will be no need to
guide the child's hand with our own. The art of 28
writing well and quickly is not unimportant for our
purpose, though it is generally disregarded by persons
of quality. Writing is of the utmost importance
in the study which we have under consideration and
by its means alone can true and deeply rooted
proficiency be obtained. But a sluggish pen delays
our thoughts, while an unformed and illiterate hand
cannot be deciphered, a circumstance which necessitates another wearisome task, namely the dic-
tation of what we have written to a copyist. We shall 29
therefore at all times and in all places, and above all
when we are writing private letters to our friends,
find a gratification in the thought that we have not
neglected even this accomplishment.

As regards syllables, no short cut is possible: they 30
must all be learnt, and there is no good in putting
off learning the most difficult; this is the general
practice, but the sole result is bad spelling. Further 31
we must beware of placing a blind confidence in a
child's memory. It is better to repeat syllables and
impress them on the memory and, when he is
reading, not to press him to read continuously or
with greater speed, unless indeed the clear and
obvious sequence of letters can suggest itself without
its being necessary for the child to stop to think.

Tunc ipsis syllabis verba complecti et his sermonem
32 connectere incipiat. Incredibile est, quantum morae
lectioni festinatione adiiciatur. Hinc enim accidit
dubitatio, intermissio, repetitio plus quam possunt
audentibus, deinde, cum errarunt, etiam iis quae iam
33 sciunt diffidentibus. Certa sit ergo in primis lectio,
deinde coniuncta et diu lentior, donec exercitatione
34 contingat emendata velocitas. Nam prospicere in
dextrum (quod omnes praecipiunt) et providere, non
rationis modo sed usus quoque est; quoniam sequentia intuenti priora dicenda sunt, et, quod difficillimum est, dividenda intentio animi, ut aliud
voce aliud oculis agatur. Illud non poenitebit
curasse, cum scribere nomina puer (quemadmodum
moris est) coeperit, ne hanc operam in vocabulis
35 vulgaribus et forte occurrentibus perdat. Protinus
enim potest interpretationem linguae secretioris,
quas Graeci γλώσσας vocant, dum aliud agitur,
ediscere et inter prima elementa consequi rem
postea proprium tempus desideraturam. Et quoniam
circa res adhuc tenues moramur, ii quoque versus,
qui ad imitationem scribendi proponentur, non
otiosas velim sententias habeant sed honestum ali-
36 quid monentes. Prosequitur haec memoria in
senectutem et impressa animo rudi usque ad mores
proficiet. Etiam dicta clarorum virorum et electos

The syllables once learnt, let him begin to construct words with them and sentences with the words. You will hardly believe how much reading is delayed 32 by undue haste. If the child attempts more than his powers allow, the inevitable result is hesitation, interruption and repetition, and the mistakes which he makes merely lead him to lose confidence in what he already knows. Reading must therefore first be 33 sure, then connected, while it must be kept slow for a considerable time, until practice brings speed unaccompanied by error. For to look to the right, 34 which is regularly taught, and to look ahead depends not so much on precept as on practice ; since it is necessary to keep the eyes on what follows while reading out what precedes, with the resulting difficulty that the attention of the mind must be divided, the eyes and voice being differently engaged. It will be found worth while, when the boy begins to write out words in accordance with the usual practice, to see that he does not waste his labour in writing out common words of everyday occurrence. He can readily learn the explanations 35 or *glosses*, as the Greeks call them, of the more obscure words by the way and, while he is still engaged on the first rudiments, acquire what would otherwise demand special time to be devoted to it. And as we are still discussing minor details, I would urge that the lines, which he is set to copy, should not express thoughts of no significance, but convey some sound moral lesson. He will remember such 36 aphorisms even when he is an old man, and the impression made upon his unformed mind will contribute to the formation of his character. He may also be entertained by learning the sayings of famous men

ex poëtis maxime (namque eorum cognitio parvis gratior est) locos ediscere inter lusum licet. Nam et maxime necessaria est oratori (sicut suo loco dicam) memoria, et ea praecipue firmatur atque alitur exercitatione, et in his, de quibus nunc loquimur, aetatibus, quae nihildum ipsae generare ex se queunt, prope sola est, quae iuvari cura do-
37 centium possit. Non alienum fuerit exigere ab his aetatibus, quo sit absolutius os et expressior sermo, ut nomina quaedam versusque adfectatae difficultatis ex pluribus et asperrime coëuntibus inter se syllabis catenatos et velut confragosos quam citatissime volvant; χαλινοὶ Graece vocantur. Res modica dictu, qua tamen omissa multa linguae vitia, nisi primis eximuntur annis, inemendabili in posterum pravitate durantur.

II. Sed nobis iam paulatim adcrescere puer et exire de gremio et discere serio incipiat. Hoc igitur potissimum loco tractanda quaestio est, utiliusne sit domi atque intra privatos parietes studentem continere an frequentiae scholarum et velut publicis
2 praeceptoribus tradere. Quod quidem cum iis, a quibus clarissimarum civitatium mores sunt instituti, tum eminentissimis auctoribus video placuisse. Non est tamen dissimulandum, esse nonnullos, qui ab hoc prope publico more privata quadam persuasione dissentiant. Hi duas praecipue rationes sequi videntur: unam, quod moribus magis consulant fugiendo turbam hominum eius aetatis, quae sit ad

and above all selections from the poets, poetry being more attractive to children. For memory is most necessary to an orator, as I shall point out in its proper place, and there is nothing like practice for strengthening and developing it. And at the tender age of which we are now speaking, when originality is impossible, memory is almost the only faculty which can be developed by the teacher. It will be worth 37 while, by way of improving the child's pronunciation and distinctness of utterance, to make him rattle off a selection of names and lines of studied difficulty: they should be formed of a number of syllables which go ill together and should be harsh and rugged in sound : the Greeks call them "gags." This sounds a trifling matter, but its omission will result in numerous faults of pronunciation, which, unless removed in early years, will become a perverse and incurable habit and persist through life.

II. But the time has come for the boy to grow up little by little, to leave the nursery and tackle his studies in good earnest. This therefore is the place to discuss the question as to whether it is better to have him educated privately at home or hand him over to some large school and those whom I may call public instructors. The latter course has, I 2 know, won the approval of most eminent authorities and of those who have formed the national character of the most famous states. It would, however, be folly to shut our eyes to the fact that there are some who disagree with this preference for public education owing to a certain prejudice in favour of private tuition. These persons seem to be guided in the main by two principles. In the interests of morality they would avoid the society of a number of human

vitia maxime prona, unde causas turpium factorum
saepe extitisse utinam falso iactaretur; alteram,
quod, quisquis futurus est ille praeceptor, liberalius
tempora sua impensurus uni videtur, quam si eadem
3 in plures partiatur. Prior causa prorsus gravis.
Nam si studiis quidem scholas prodesse, moribus
autem nocere constaret, potior mihi ratio vivendi
honeste quam vel optime dicendi videretur. Sed
mea quidem sententia iuncta ista atque indiscreta
sunt. Neque enim esse oratorem nisi bonum virum
iudico, et fieri etiamsi potest nolo. De hac re
igitur prius.

4 Corrumpi mores in scholis putant; nam et cor-
rumpuntur interim, sed domi quoque, et sunt multa
eius rei exempla tam hercule quam conservatae
sanctissime utrobique opinionis. Natura cuiusque
totum curaque distat. Da mentem ad peiora fa-
cilem, da negligentiam formandi custodiendique in
aetate prima pudoris: non minorem flagitiis occasionem secreta praebuerint. Nam et potest turpis
esse domesticus ille praeceptor, nec tutior inter
servos malos quam ingenuos parum modestos con-
5 versatio est. At si bona ipsius indoles, si non caeca
ac sopita parentum socordia est, et praeceptorem
eligere sanctissimum quemque (cuius rei praecipua

beings at an age that is specially liable to acquire serious faults : I only wish I could deny the truth of the view that such education has often been the cause of the most discreditable actions. Secondly they hold that whoever is to be the boy's teacher, he will devote his time more generously to one pupil than if he has to divide it among several. The first 3 reason certainly deserves serious consideration. If it were proved that schools, while advantageous to study, are prejudicial to morality, I should give my vote for virtuous living in preference to even supreme excellence of speaking. But in my opinion the two are inseparable. I hold that no one can be a true orator unless he is also a good man and, even if he could be, I would not have it so. I will therefore deal with this point first.

It is held that schools corrupt the morals. It is 4 true that this is sometimes the case. But morals may be corrupted at home as well. There are numerous instances of both, as there are also of the preservation of a good reputation under either circumstance. The nature of the individual boy and the care devoted to his education make all the difference. Given a natural bent toward evil or negligence in developing and watching over modest behaviour in early years, privacy will provide equal opportunity for sin. The teacher employed at home may be of bad character, and there is just as much danger in associating with bad slaves as there is with immodest companions of good birth. On the 5 other hand if the natural bent be towards virtue, and parents are not afflicted with a blind and torpid indifference, it is possible to choose a teacher of the highest character (and those who are wise will make

prudentibus cura est) et disciplinam, quae maxime severa fuerit, licet, et nihilominus amicum gravem virum aut fidelem libertum lateri filii sui adiungere, cuius assiduus comitatus etiam illos meliores faciat, qui timebantur.

6 Facile erat huius metus remedium. Utinam liberorum nostrorum mores non ipsi perderemus. Infantiam statim deliciis solvimus. Mollis illa educatio, quam indulgentiam vocamus, nervos omnes mentis et corporis frangit. Quid non adultus concupiscet, qui in purpuris repit? Nondum prima verba exprimit, iam coccum intelligit, iam conchylium poscit. Ante palatum eorum quam os 7 instituimus. In lecticis crescunt; si terram attigerint, e manibus utrinque sustinentium pendent. Gaudemus, si quid licentius dixerint: verba ne Alexandrinis quidem permittenda deliciis risu et osculo excipimus. Nec mirum: nos docuimus, ex 8 nobis audiunt. Nostras amicas, nostros concubinos vident, omne convivium obscenis canticis strepit, pudenda dictu spectantur. Fit ex his consuetudo, inde natura. Discunt haec miseri, antequam sciant vitia esse; inde soluti ac fluentes non accipiunt ex scholis mala ista sed in scholas adferunt.

9 Verum in studiis magis vacabit unus uni. Ante omnia nihil prohibet esse illum nescio quem unum

this their first object), to adopt a method of education of the strictest kind and at the same time to attach some respectable man or faithful freedman to their son as his friend and guardian, that his unfailing companionship may improve the character even of those who gave rise to apprehension.

Yet how easy were the remedy for such fears. **6** Would that we did not too often ruin our children's character ourselves! We spoil them from the cradle. That soft upbringing, which we call kindness, saps all the sinews both of mind and body. If the child crawls on purple, what will he not desire when he comes to manhood? Before he can talk he can distinguish scarlet and cries for the very best brand of purple. We train their palates before we teach their lips to speak. They grow up in litters: **7** if they set foot to earth, they are supported by the hands of attendants on either side. We rejoice if they say something over-free, and words which we should not tolerate from the lips even of an Alexandrian page are greeted with laughter and a kiss. We have no right to be surprised. It was we that taught them: they hear us use such words, they see **8** our mistresses and minions; every dinner party is loud with foul songs, and things are presented to their eyes of which we should blush to speak. Hence springs habit, and habit in time becomes second nature. The poor children learn these things before they know them to be wrong. They become luxurious and effeminate, and far from acquiring such vices at schools, introduce them themselves.

I now turn to the objection that one master can **9** give more attention to one pupil. In the first place there is nothing to prevent the principle of " one

etiam cum eo, qui in scholis eruditur. Sed etiamsi
iungi utrumque non posset, lumen tamen illud
conventus honestissimi tenebris ac solitudini praetu-
lissem. Nam optimus quisque praeceptor frequentia
10 gaudet ac maiore se theatro dignum putat. At
fere minores ex conscientia suae infirmitatis haerere
singulis et officio fungi quodammodo paedagogorum
non indignantur.

11 Sed praestat alicui vel gratia vel pecunia vel
amicitia, ut doctissimum atque incomparabilem
magistrum domi habeat: num tamen ille totum
in uno diem consumpturus est? aut potest esse
ulla tam perpetua discentis intentio, quae non
ut visus oculorum obtutu continuo fatigetur? cum
praesertim multo plus secreti temporis studia
12 desiderent. Neque enim scribenti, ediscenti, cogi-
tanti praeceptor adsistit, quorum aliquid agentibus cuiuscunque interventus impedimento est.
Lectio quoque non omnis nec semper praeeunte
vel interpretante eget. Quando enim tot auctorum notitia contingeret? Modicum ergo tempus
est, quo in totum diem velut opus ordinetur,
ideoque per plures ire possunt etiam quae singulis
13 tradenda sunt. Pleraque vero hanc condicionem
habent, ut eadem voce ad omnes simul perferantur.
Taceo de partitionibus et declamationibus rhetorum,

teacher, one boy" being combined with school education. And even if such a combination should prove impossible, I should still prefer the broad daylight of a respectable school to the solitude and obscurity of a private education. For all the best teachers pride themselves on having a large number of pupils and think themselves worthy of a bigger audience. On the other hand in the case of in- 10 ferior teachers a consciousness of their own defects not seldom reconciles them to being attached to a single pupil and playing the part—for it amounts to little more—of a mere *paedagogus*.

But let us assume that influence, money or friend- 11 ship succeed in securing a paragon of learning to teach the boy at home. Will he be able to devote the whole day to one pupil? Or can we demand such continuous attention on the part of the learner? The mind is as easily tired as the eye, if given no relaxation. Moreover by far the larger proportion of the learner's time ought to be devoted to private study. The teacher does not stand over him while 12 he is writing or thinking or learning by heart. While he is so occupied the intervention of anyone, be he who he may, is a hindrance. Further, not all reading requires to be first read aloud or interpreted by a master. If it did, how would the boy ever become acquainted with all the authors required of him? A small time only is required to give purpose and direction to the day's work, and consequently individual instruction can be given to more than one pupil. There are moreover a large number of 13 subjects in which it is desirable that instruction should be given to all the pupils simultaneously. I say nothing of the analyses and declamations of

quibus certe quantuscunque numerus adhibeatur,
14 tamen unusquisque totum feret. Non enim vox
illa praeceptoris ut cena minus pluribus sufficit, sed
ut sol universis idem lucis calorisque largitur. Grammaticus quoque si de loquendi ratione disserat, si
quaestiones explicet, historias exponat, poëmata
15 enarret, tot illa discent quot audient. At enim
emendationi praelectionique numerus obstat. Sit
incommodum, (nam quid fere undique placet?) mox
illud comparabimus commodis.

Nec ego tamen eo mitti puerum volo, ubi negli-
gatur. Sed neque praeceptor bonus maiore se turba,
quam ut sustinere eam possit, oneraverit; et in
primis ea habenda cura est, ut is omni modo fiat nobis
familiariter amicus, nec officium in docendo spectet
16 sed adfectum. Ita nunquam erimus in turba. Nec
sane quisquam litteris saltem leviter imbutus eum,
in quo studium ingeniumque perspexerit, non in
suam quoque gloriam peculiariter fovebit. Sed ut
fugiendae sint magnae scholae (cui ne ipsi quidem
rei adsentior, si ad aliquem merito concurritur), non
tamen hoc eo valet, ut fugiendae sint omnino
scholae. Aliud est enim vitare eas, aliud eligere.

17 Et si refutavimus quae contra dicuntur, iam

the professors of rhetoric : in such cases there is no
limit to the number of the audience, as each individual pupil will in any case receive full value.
The voice of a lecturer is not like a dinner which 14
will only suffice for a limited number ; it is like the
sun which distributes the same quantity of light and
heat to all of us. So too with the teacher of
literature. Whether he speak of style or expound
disputed passages, explain stories or paraphrase
poems, everyone who hears him will profit by his
teaching. But, it will be urged, a large class is 15
unsuitable for the correction of faults or for explanation. It may be inconvenient : one cannot hope for
absolute perfection ; but I shall shortly contrast the
inconvenience with the obvious advantages.

Still I do not wish a boy to be sent where he will
be neglected. But a good teacher will not burden
himself with a larger number of pupils than he can
manage, and it is further of the very first importance that he should be on friendly and intimate
terms with us and make his teaching not a duty
but a labour of love. Then there will never be
any question of being swamped by the number of
our fellow-learners. Moreover any teacher who has 16
the least tincture of literary culture will devote
special attention to any boy who shows signs of
industry and talent; for such a pupil will redound
to his own credit. But even if large schools are to
be avoided, a proposition from which I must dissent
if the size be due to the excellence of the teacher,
it does not follow that all schools are to be avoided.
It is one thing to avoid them, another to select the
best.

Having refuted these objections, let me now 17

18 explicemus, quid ipsi sequamur. Ante omnia
futurus orator, cui in maxima celebritate et in media
rei publicae luce vivendum est, adsuescat iam a
tenero non reformidare homines neque illa solitaria
et velut umbratica vita pallescere. Excitanda mens
et adtollenda semper est, quae in eiusmodi secretis
aut languescit et quendam velut in opaco situm
ducit, aut contra tumescit inani persuasione; necesse
est enim nimium tribuat sibi, qui se nemini com-
19 parat. Deinde cum proferenda sunt studia, caligat
in sole et omnia nova offendit, ut qui solus didicerit
20 quod inter multos faciendum est. Mitto amicitias,
quae ad senectutem usque firmissime durant religiosa
quadam necessitudine imbutae. Neque enim est
sanctius sacris iisdem quam studiis initiari. Sensum
ipsum, qui communis dicitur, ubi discet, cum se a
congressu, qui non hominibus solum sed mutis
21 quoque animalibus naturalis est, segregarit? Adde
quod domi ea sola discere potest, quae ipsi praeci-
pientur, in schola etiam quae aliis. Audiet multa
cotidie probari, multa corrigi; proderit alicuius
obiurgata desidia, proderit laudata industria, ex-
22 citabitur laude aemulatio, turpe ducet cedere pari,

explain my own views. It is above all things ne- 18
cessary that our future orator, who will have to live
in the utmost publicity and in the broad daylight of
public life, should become accustomed from his
childhood to move in society without fear and
habituated to a life far removed from that of the
pale student, the solitary and recluse. His mind
requires constant stimulus and excitement, whereas
retirement such as has just been mentioned induces
languor and the mind becomes mildewed like things
that are left in the dark, or else flies to the opposite
extreme and becomes puffed up with empty conceit;
for he who has no standard of comparison by which
to judge his own powers will necessarily rate them
too high. Again when the fruits of his study have 19
to be displayed to the public gaze, our recluse is
blinded by the sun's glare, and finds everything new
and unfamiliar, for though he has learnt what is required to be done in public, his learning is but the
theory of a hermit. I say nothing of friendships 20
which endure unbroken to old age having acquired
the binding force of a sacred duty: for initiation
in the same studies has all the sanctity of initiation
in the same mysteries of religion. And where shall
he acquire that instinct which we call common
feeling, if he secludes himself from that intercourse
which is natural not merely to mankind but even to
dumb animals? Further, at home he can only learn 21
what is taught to himself, while at school he will
learn what is taught others as well. He will hear
many merits praised and many faults corrected every
day: he will derive equal profit from hearing the
indolence of a comrade rebuked or his industry
commended. Such praise will incite him to emu- 22

49

pulchrum superasse maiores. Accendunt omnia
haec animos, et licet ipsa vitium sit ambitio, frequen-
23 ter tamen causa virtutum est. Non inutilem scio
servatum esse a praeceptoribus meis morem, qui,
cum pueros in classes distribuerant, ordinem dicendi
secundum vires ingenii dabant; et ita superiore loco
quisque declamabat, ut praecedere profectu videbatur.
24 Huius rei iudicia praebebantur; ea nobis ingens
palma, ducere vero classem multo pulcherrimum.
Nec de hoc semel decretum erat; tricesimus dies
reddebat victo certaminis potestatem. Ita nec
superior successu curam remittebat et dolor victum
25 ad depellendam ignominiam concitabat. Id nobis
acriores ad studia dicendi faces subdidisse quam exhortationem docentium, paedagogorum custodiam,
vota parentum, quantum animi mei coniectura colli-
26 gere possum, contenderim. Sed sicut firmiores in litteris profectus alit aemulatio, ita incipientibus atque
adhuc teneris condiscipulorum quam praeceptoris
iucundior hoc ipso quod facilior imitatio est. Vix
enim se prima elementa ad spem tollere effingendae,
quam summam putant, eloquentiae audebunt; proxima amplectentur magis, ut vites arboribus applicitae
inferiores prius apprehendendo ramos in cacumina

lation, he will think it a disgrace to be outdone by
his contemporaries and a distinction to surpass his
seniors. All such incentives provide a valuable
stimulus, and though ambition may be a fault in
itself, it is often the mother of virtues. I remember 23
that my own masters had a practice which was not
without advantages. Having distributed the boys
in classes, they made the order in which they were
to speak depend on their ability, so that the boy
who had made most progress in his studies had the
privilege of declaiming first. The performances 24
on these occasions were criticised. To win com-
mendation was a tremendous honour, but the prize
most eagerly coveted was to be the leader of the
class. Such a position was not permanent. Once a
month the defeated competitors were given a fresh
opportunity of competing for the prize. Consequently success did not lead the victor to relax his
efforts, while the vexation caused by defeat served
as an incentive to wipe out the disgrace. I will 25
venture to assert that to the best of my memory
this practice did more to kindle our oratorical am-
bitions than all the exhortations of our instructors,
the watchfulness of our *paedagogi* and the prayers of
our parents. Further while emulation promotes 26
progress in the more advanced pupils, beginners who
are still of tender years derive greater pleasure from
imitating their comrades than their masters, just
because it is easier. For children still in the elementary stages of education can scarce dare hope to
reach that complete eloquence which they understand to be their goal : their ambition will not soar
so high, but they will imitate the vine which has to
grasp the lower branches of the tree on which it is

51

27 evadunt. Quod adeo verum est, ut ipsius etiam
magistri, si tamen ambitiosis utilia praeferet, hoc
opus sit, cum adhuc rudia tractabit ingenia, non
statim onerare infirmitatem discentium, sed tem-
perare vires suas et ad intellectum audientis
28 descendere. Nam ut vascula oris angusti super-
fusam humoris copiam respuunt, sensim autem
influentibus vel etiam instillatis complentur, sic
animi puerorum quantum excipere possint videndum
est. Nam maiora intellectu velut parum apertos
29 ad percipiendum animos non subibunt. Utile igitur
habere, quos imitari primum, mox vincere velis. Ita
paulatim et superiorum spes erit. His adiicio, praeceptores ipsos non idem mentis ac spiritus in dicendo posse concipere singulis tantum praesentibus
quod illa celebritate audientium instinctos.

30   Maxima enim pars eloquentiae constat animo.
Hunc adfici, hunc concipere imagines rerum et trans-
formari quodammodo ad naturam eorum, de quibus
loquimur, necesse est. Is porro, quo generosior
celsiorque est, hoc maioribus velut organis com-
movetur; ideoque et laude crescit et impetu augetur
31 et aliquid magnum agere gaudet. Est quaedam
tacita dedignatio, vim dicendi tantis comparatam

trained before it can reach the topmost boughs.   So 27
true is this that it is the master's duty as well, if he
is engaged on the task of training unformed minds
and prefers practical utility to a more ambitious
programme, not to burden his pupils at once with
tasks to which their strength is unequal, but to curb
his energies and refrain from talking over the heads
of his audience.   Vessels with narrow mouths will 28
not receive liquids if too much be poured into them
at a time, but are easily filled if the liquid is admitted in a gentle stream or, it may be, drop by
drop; similarly you must consider how much a
child's mind is capable of receiving : the things
which are beyond their grasp will not enter their
minds, which have not opened out sufficiently to
take them in.   It is a good thing therefore that a 29
boy should have companions whom he will desire
first to imitate and then to surpass : thus he will be
led to aspire to higher achievement.   I would add
that the instructors themselves cannot develop the
same intelligence and energy before a single listener
as they can when inspired by the presence of a
numerous audience.

For eloquence depends in the main on the state 30
of the mind, which must be moved, conceive images
and adapt itself to suit the nature of the subject
which is the theme of speech.   Further the loftier
and the more elevated the mind, the more powerful
will be the forces which move it : consequently
praise gives it growth and effort increase, and the
thought that it is doing something great fills it with
joy.   The duty of stooping to expend that power of 31
speaking which has been acquired at the cost of such
effort upon an audience of one gives rise to a silent

laboribus ad unum auditorem demittere: pudet
supra modum sermonis attolli. Et sane concipita
quis mente vel declamantis habitum vel orantis
vocem, incessum, pronuntiationem, illum denique
animi et corporis motum, sudorem, ut alia prae-
teream, et fatigationem, audiente uno: nonne
quiddam pati furori simile videatur? Non esset in
rebus humanis eloquentia, si tantum cum singulis
loqueremur.

III. Tradito sibi puero docendi peritus ingenium
eius in primis naturamque perspiciet. Ingenii signum
in parvis praecipuum memoria est. Eius duplex
virtus, facile percipere et fideliter continere. Proximum imitatio; nam id quoque est docilis naturae,
sic tamen, ut ea quae discit effingat, non habitum
forte et ingressum et si quid in peius notabile est.

2 Non dabit mihi spem bonae indolis, qui hoc imi-
tandi studio petet, ut rideatur. Nam probus quoque
in primis erit ille vere ingeniosus; alioqui non peius
duxerim tardi esse ingenii quam mali. Probus
autem ab illo segni et iacente plurimum aberit.

3 Hic meus quae tradentur non difficulter accipiet,
quaedam etiam interrogabit, sequetur tamen magis
quam praecurret. Illud ingeniorum velut praecox
genus non temere unquam pervenit ad frugem.

4 Hi sunt, qui parva facile faciunt et audacia provecti,

feeling of disdain, and the teacher is ashamed to raise his voice above the ordinary conversational level. Imagine the air of a declaimer, or the voice of an orator, his gait, his delivery, the movements of his body, the emotions of his mind, and, to go no further, the fatigue of his exertions, all for the sake of one listener! Would he not seem little less than a lunatic? No, there would be no such thing as eloquence, if we spoke only with one person at a time.

III. The skilful teacher will make it his first care, as soon as a boy is entrusted to him, to ascertain his ability and character. The surest indication in a child is his power of memory. The characteristics of a good memory are twofold: it must be quick to take in and faithful to retain impressions of what it receives. The indication of next importance is the power of imitation: for this is a sign that the child is teachable: but he must imitate merely what he is taught, and must not, for example, mimic someone's gait or bearing or defects. For I have no hope that a child will turn 2 out well who loves imitation merely for the purpose of raising a laugh. He who is really gifted will also above all else be good. For the rest, I regard slowness of intellect as preferable to actual badness. But a good boy will be quite unlike the dullard and the sloth. My ideal pupil will absorb 3 instruction with ease and will even ask some questions; but he will follow rather than anticipate his teacher. Precocious intellects rarely produce sound fruit. By the precocious I mean those who 4 perform small tasks with ease and, thus emboldened, proceed to display all their little accomplishments

quidquid illud possunt, statim ostendunt. Possunt autem id demum, quod in proximo est; verba continuant, haec vultu interrito, nulla tardati verecundia proferunt. Non multum praestant sed
5 cito. Non subest vera vis nec penitus immissis radicibus nititur; ut, quae summo solo sparsa sunt semina, celerius se effundunt, et imitatae spicas herbulae inanibus aristis ante messem flavescunt. Placent haec annis comparata; deinde stat profectus, admiratio decrescit.

6 Haec cum animadverterit, perspiciat deinceps, quonam modo tractandus sit discentis animus. Sunt quidam, nisi institeris, remissi, quidam imperia indignantur, quosdam continet metus, quosdam debilitat, alios continuatio extundit, in aliis plus im-
7 petus facit. Mihi ille detur puer, quem laus excitet, quem gloria iuvet, qui victus fleat. Hic erit alendus ambitu, hunc mordebit obiurgatio, hunc honor excitabit, in hoc desidiam nunquam verebor.

8 Danda est tamen omnibus aliqua remissio; non solum quia nulla res est, quae perferre possit continuum laborem, atque ea quoque, quae sensu et anima carent, ut servare vim suam possint, velut quiete alterna retenduntur; sed quod studium dis-
9 cendi voluntate, quae cogi non potest, constat. Itaque

without being asked : but their accomplishments are
only of the most obvious kind : they string words together and trot them out boldly and undeterred by
the slightest sense of modesty. Their actual achievement is small, but what they can do they perform with
ease. They have no real power and what they have 5
is but of shallow growth : it is as when we cast
seed on the surface of the soil : it springs up too
rapidly, the blade apes the loaded ear, and yellows
ere harvest time, but bears no grain. Such tricks
please us when we contrast them with the per-
former's age, but progress soon stops and our admiration withers away.

Such indications once noted, the teacher must next 6
consider what treatment is to be applied to the mind
of his pupil. There are some boys who are slack,
unless pressed on ; others again are impatient of
control : some are amenable to fear, while others are
paralysed by it : in some cases the mind requires
continued application to form it, in others this result
is best obtained by rapid concentration. Give me
the boy who is spurred on by praise, delighted by
success and ready to weep over failure. Such an 7
one must be encouraged by appeals to his ambition ;
rebuke will bite him to the quick ; honour will be a
spur, and there is no fear of his proving indolent.

Still, all our pupils will require some relaxation, 8
not merely because there is nothing in this world
that can stand continued strain and even unthinking
and inanimate objects are unable to maintain their
strength, unless given intervals of rest, but because
study depends on the good will of the student, a
quality that cannot be secured by compulsion.
Consequently if restored and refreshed by a holiday 9

et virium plus adferunt ad discendum renovati ac
recentes et acriorem animum, qui fere necessitatibus
10 repugnat. Nec me offenderit lusus in pueris ; est
et hoc signum alacritatis ; neque illum tristem
semperque demissum sperare possim erectae circa
studia mentis fore, cum in hoc quoque maxime
11 naturali aetatibus illis impetu iaceat. Modus tamen
sit remissionibus, ne aut odium studiorum faciant
negatae aut otii consuetudinem nimiae. Sunt
etiam nonnulli acuendis puerorum ingeniis non
inutiles lusus, cum positis invicem cuiusque generis
12 quaestiunculis aemulantur. Mores quoque se inter
ludendum simplicius detegunt ; modo nulla videatur
aetas tam infirma, quae non protinus quid rectum
pravumque sit discat, tum vel maxime formanda,
cum simulandi nescia est et praecipientibus facillime
cedit. Frangas enim citius quam corrigas, quae in
13 pravum induruerunt. Protinus ergo, ne quid cupide,
ne quid improbe, ne quid impotenter faciat, mo-
nendus est puer ; habendumque in animo semper
illud Vergilianum :

Adeo in teneris consuescere multum est.

Caedi vero discentes, quamlibet et receptum sit
et Chrysippus non improbet, minime velim. Primum,
14 quia deforme atque servile est et certe, (quod con-

they will bring greater energy to their learning and
approach their work with greater spirit of a kind
that will not submit to be driven. I approve of play 10
in the young; it is a sign of a lively disposition; nor
will you ever lead me to believe that a boy who is
gloomy and in a continual state of depression is ever
likely to show alertness of mind in his work, lacking
as he does the impulse most natural to boys of his
age. Such relaxation must not however be un- 11
limited: otherwise the refusal to give a holiday will
make boys hate their work, while excessive indulgence will accustom them to idleness. There are
moreover certain games which have an educational
value for boys, as for instance when they compete
in posing each other with all kinds of questions
which they ask turn and turn about. Games 12
too reveal character in the most natural way, at
least that is so if the teacher will bear in mind
that there is no child so young as to be unable to
learn to distinguish between right and wrong, and
that the character is best moulded, when it is still
guiltless of deceit and most susceptible to instruction: for once a bad habit has become engrained,
it is easier to break than bend. There must be no 13
delay, then, in warning a boy that his actions must
be unselfish, honest, self-controlled, and we must
never forget the words of Virgil,

"So strong is custom formed in early years." [1]

I disapprove of flogging, although it is the regular
custom and meets with the acquiescence of Chrysippus, because in the first place it is a disgraceful
form of punishment and fit only for slaves, and is in 14

[1] *Georg.* ii. 272.

venit, si aetatem mutes), iniuria est; deinde, quod,
si cui tam est mens illiberalis, ut obiurgatione non
corrigatur, is etiam ad plagas ut pessima quaeque
mancipia durabitur : postremo, quod ne opus erit
quidem hac castigatione, si assiduus studiorum
15 exactor astiterit. Nunc fere negligentia paedagogorum sic emendari videtur, ut pueri non facere,
quae recta sunt, cogantur sed cur non fecerint
puniantur. Denique cum parvulum verberibus
coegeris, quid iuveni facias, cui nec adhiberi potest
16 hic metus et maiora discenda sunt ? Adde, quod
multa vapulantibus dictu deformia et mox vere-
cundiae futura saepe dolore vel metu acciderunt,
qui pudor frangit animum et abiicit atque ipsius
17 lucis fugam et taedium dictat. Iam si minor in
eligendis custodum vel praeceptorum moribus fuit
cura, pudet dicere, in quae probra nefandi homines
isto caedendi iure abutantur, quam det aliis quoque
nonnunquam occasionem hic miserorum metus. Non
morabor in parte hac; nimium est quod intelligitur.
Quare hoc dixisse satis est ; in aetatem infirmam et
iniuriae obnoxiam nemini debet nimium licere.
18 Nunc quibus instituendus sit artibus, qui sic forma-
bitur, ut fieri possit orator, et quae in quaque aetate
inchoanda, dicere ingrediar.

IV. Primus in eo, qui scribendi legendique

any case an insult, as you will realise if you imagine
its infliction at a later age. Secondly if a boy is so
insensible to instruction that reproof is useless, he
will, like the worst type of slave, merely become
hardened to blows. Finally there will be absolutely no
need of such punishment if the master is a thorough
disciplinarian. As it is, we try to make amends for 15
the negligence of the boy's *paedagogus*, not by
forcing him to do what is right, but by punishing
him for not doing what is right. And though you
may compel a child with blows, what are you
to do with him when he is a young man no longer
amenable to such threats and confronted with tasks
of far greater difficulty? Moreover when children 16
are beaten, pain or fear frequently have results of
which it is not pleasant to speak and which are
likely subsequently to be a source of shame, a shame
which unnerves and depresses the mind and leads
the child to shun and loathe the light. Further if in- 17
adequate care is taken in the choices of respectable
governors and instructors, I blush to mention the
shameful abuse which scoundrels sometimes make
of their right to administer corporal punishment or
the opportunity not infrequently offered to others
by the fear thus caused in the victims. I will not
linger on this subject; it is more than enough if I
have made my meaning clear. I will content myself
with saying that children are helpless and easily
victimised, and that therefore no one should be given
unlimited power over them. I will now proceed to 18
describe the subjects in which the boy must be
trained, if he is to become an orator, and to indicate
the age at which each should be commenced.

IV. As soon as the boy has learned to read and

adeptus erit facultatem, grammatici est locus. Nec
refert, de Graeco an de Latino loquar, quanquam
2 Graecum esse priorem placet. Utrique eadem via
est. Haec igitur professio, cum brevissime in duas
partes dividatur, recte loquendi scientiam et poetarum enarrationem, plus habet in recessu quam
3 fronte promittit. Nam et scribendi ratio coniuncta cum loquendo est, et enarrationem praecedit
emendata lectio, et mixtum his omnibus iudicium
est; quo quidem ita severe sunt usi veteres grammatici, ut non versus modo censoria quadam virgula
notare et libros, qui falso viderentur inscripti, tanquam subditos summovere familia permiserint sibi,
sed auctores alios in ordinem redegerint, alios
4 omnino exemerint numero. Nec poetas legisse
satis est: excutiendum omne scriptorum genus
non propter historias modo sed verba, quae frequenter ius ab auctoribus sumunt. Tum neque
citra musicen grammatice potest esse perfecta, cum
ei de metris rhythmisque dicendum sit, nec, si
rationem siderum ignoret, poetas intelligat, qui (ut
alia omittam) totiens ortu occasuque signorum in
declarandis temporibus utantur; nec ignara philosophiae, cum propter plurimos in omnibus fere
carminibus locos ex intima naturalium quaestionum
subtilitate repetitos, tum vel propter Empedoclea
in Graecis, Varronem ac Lucretium in Latinis, qui

---

[1] *grammaticus* is the teacher of literature and languages;
at times it is necessary to restrict its meaning to "grammar."

write without difficulty, it is the turn for the teacher [1] of literature. My words apply equally to Greek and Latin masters, though I prefer that a start should be made with a Greek: in either case the method 2 is the same. This profession may be most briefly considered under two heads, the art of speaking correctly and the interpretation of the poets; but there is more beneath the surface than meets the eye. For the art of writing is combined with that of 3 speaking, and correct reading precedes interpretation, while in each of these cases criticism has its work to perform. The old school of teachers indeed carried their criticism so far that they were not content with obelising lines or rejecting books whose titles they regarded as spurious, as though they were expelling a supposititious child from the family circle, but also drew up a canon of authors, from which some were omitted altogether. Nor is it 4 sufficient to have read the poets only; every kind of writer must be carefully studied, not merely for the subject matter, but for the vocabulary; for words often acquire authority from their use by a particular author. Nor can such training be regarded as complete if it stop short of music, for the teacher of literature has to speak of metre and rhythm: nor again if he be ignorant of astronomy, can he understand the poets; for they, to mention no further points, frequently give their indications of time by reference to the rising and setting of the stars. Ignorance of philosophy is an equal drawback, since there are numerous passages in almost every poem based on the most intricate questions of natural philosophy, while among the Greeks we have Empedocles and among our own poets Varro and Lucretius, all of

5 praecepta sapientiae versibus tradiderunt. Eloquentia quoque non mediocri est opus, ut de una-
quaque earum, quas demonstravimus, rerum dicat
proprie et copiose. Quo minus sunt ferendi, qui
hanc artem ut tenuem atque ieiunam cavillantur,
quae nisi oratoris futuri fundamenta fideliter iecit,
quidquid superstruxeris, corruet; necessaria pueris,
iucunda senibus, dulcis secretorum comes et quae
vel sola in omni studiorum genere plus habeat
operis quam ostentationis.

6 Ne quis igitur tanquam parva fastidiat grammatices elementa, non quia magnae sit operae con-
sonantes a vocalibus discernere ipsasque eas in
semivocalium numerum mutarumque partiri, sed
quia interiora velut sacri huius adeuntibus apparebit
multa rerum subtilitas, quae non modo acuere ingenia puerilia sed exercere altissimam quoque
7 eruditionem ac scientiam possit. An cuiuslibet
auris est exigere litterarum sonos? non hercule
magis quam nervorum. At grammatici saltem
omnes in hanc descendent rerum tenuitatem,
desintne aliquae nobis necessariae litterarum, non
cum Graeca scribimus (tum enim ab iisdem duas
8 mutuamur) sed propriae, in Latinis, ut in his *seruus*
et *uulgus* Aeolicum digammon desideratur, et

---

[1] Y and Z.

whom have expounded their philosophies in verse.
No small powers of eloquence also are required to 5
enable the teacher to speak appropriately and
fluently on the various points which have just been
mentioned.   For this reason those who criticise the
art of teaching literature as trivial and lacking in
substance put themselves out of court.   Unless the
foundations of oratory are well and truly laid by
the teaching of literature, the superstructure will
collapse.   The study of literature is a necessity for
boys and the delight of old age, the sweet companion of our privacy and the sole branch of study
which has more solid substance than display.

The elementary stages of the teaching of litera- 6
ture must not therefore be despised as trivial.   It is
of course an easy task to point out the difference
between vowels and consonants, and to subdivide the
latter into semivowels and mutes.   But as the pupil
gradually approaches the inner shrine of the sacred
place, he will come to realise the intricacy of the subject, an intricacy calculated not merely to sharpen the
wits of a boy, but to exercise even the most profound
knowledge and erudition.   It is not every ear that 7
can appreciate the correct sound of the different
letters.   It is fully as hard as to distinguish the
different notes in music.   But all teachers of literature will condescend to such minutiae : they
will discuss for instance whether certain necessary
letters are absent from the alphabet, not indeed
when we are writing Greek words (for then we
borrow two letters [1] from them), but in the case of
genuine Latin words : for example in words such as 8
seruus and *uulgus* we feel the lack of the Aeolic
digamma ; there is also a sound intermediate between

medius est quidam V et I litterae sonus; non enim
sic *optimum* dicimus ut *opimum,* et in *here* neque E
9 plane neque I auditur; an rursus aliae redundent,
praeter notam aspirationis, (quae si necessaria est,
etiam contrariam sibi poscit) ut K, quae et ipsa
quorundam nominum nota est, et Q, cuius similis
effectu specieque, nisi quod paulum a nostris obli-
quatur, Coppa apud Graecos nunc tantum in numero
manet, et nostrarum ultima, qua tam carere po-
10 tuimus quam ψ non quaerimus? Atque etiam in
ipsis vocalibus grammatici est videre, an aliquas pro
consonantibus usus acceperit, quia *iam* sicut *etiam*
scribitur et *uos* ut *tuos.*[1] At quae ut vocales iun-
guntur aut unam longam faciunt, ut veteres scripserunt qui geminatione earum velut apice utebantur,
aut duas; nisi quis putat etiam ex tribus vocalibus
syllabam fieri, si non aliquae officio consonantium
11 fungantur. Quaeret hoc etiam, quomodo duabus
demum vocalibus in se ipsas coeundi natura sit, cum
consonantium nulla nisi alteram frangat. Atqui
littera I sibi insidit, *coniicit* enim est ab illo *iacit,* et
V, quomodo nunc scribitur *uulgus* et *seruus.* Sciat
etiam Ciceroni placuisse *aiio Maiiam*que geminata I
scribere; quod si est, etiam iungetur ut consonans.

[1] etiam ... uos ... tuos, *Ritschl*: tam ... quos ... cos,
MSS.

---

[1] *K* = Kaeso, Kalendae, Karthago, Kaput, Kalumnia, etc.
The *q*-sound can be expressed by *c. Koppa* (Ϙ) as a numeral
= 90.

u and *i*, for we do not pronounce *optimum* as we do *opimum*, while in *here* the sound is neither exactly *e* or *i*. Again there is the question whether certain letters 9 are not superfluous, not to mention the mark of the aspirate, to which, if it is required at all, there should be a corresponding symbol to indicate the opposite: for instance *k*, which is also used as an abbreviation for certain nouns, and *q*, which, though slanted slightly more by us, resembles both in sound and shape the Greek *koppa*, now used by the Greeks solely as a numerical sign [1]: there is also *x*, the last letter of our own alphabet, which we could dispense with as easily as with *psi*. Again the teacher of 10 literature will have to determine whether certain vowels have not been consonantalised. For instance *iam* and *etiam* are both spelt with an *i*, *uos* and *tuos* both with a *u*. Vowels, however, when joined as vowels, either make one long vowel (compare the obsolete method of indicating a long vowel by doubling it as the equivalent of the circumflex), or a diphthong, though some hold that even three vowels can form a single syllable; this however is only possible if one or more assume the role of consonants. He will also inquire why it is that 11 there are two vowels which may be repeated, while a consonant can only be followed and modified by a different consonant.[2] But *i* can follow *i* (for *coniicit* is derived from *iacit*[3]): so too does *u*, witness the modern spelling of *seruus* and *uulgus*. He should also know that Cicero preferred to write *aiio* and *Maiiam* with a double *i*; in that case one

[2] The two vowels are *i* and *u*. A consonant cannot be duplicated within one syllable.

[3] The derivation is mentioned to show that two *i*'s, not one, are found in the second syllable of *coniicit*.

12 **Quare** discat puer, quid in litteris proprium, quid commune, quae cum quibus cognatio; nec miretur, cur ex *scamno* fiat *scabillum* aut a *pinno* (quod est acutum) securis utrinque habens aciem *bipennis*; ne illorum sequatur errorem, qui, quia a pennis duabus hoc esse nomen existimant, *pennas* avium dici volunt.

13 Neque has modo noverit mutationes, quas adferunt declinatio aut praepositio, ut *secat secuit, cadit excidit, caedit excidit, calcat exculcat* (et fit a *lavando lotus* et inde rursus *inlotus* et mille talia), sed quae rectis quoque casibus aetate transierunt. Nam ut *Valesii Fusii* in *Valerios Furios*que venerunt: ita *arbos, labos, vapos* etiam et *clamos* ac *lases* fuerunt.

14 Atque haec ipsa S littera ab his nominibus exclusa in quibusdam ipsa alteri successit, nam *mertare* atque *pultare* dicebant, quin *fordeum faedos*que pro aspiratione F velut simili littera utentes; nam contra Graeci aspirare F ut ϕ solent, ut pro Fundanio Cicero testem, qui primam eius litteram dicere non

15 possit, irridet. Sed B quoque in locum aliarum dedimus aliquando, unde *Burrus* et *Bruges* et *Belena*. Nec non eadem fecit ex *duello bellum*, unde *Duelios*

16 quidam dicere *Belios* ausi. Quid *stlocum stlites*que? Quid T litterae cum D quaedam cognatio? Quare

---

[1] *i.e.* of *lares.*   [2] For *mersare* and *pulsare.*
[3] *i.e.* Pyrrus, Phryges, Helena.

of them is consonantalised. A boy therefore must 12
learn both the peculiarities and the common characteristics of letters and must know how they are
related to each other. Nor must he be surprised
that *scabillum* is formed from *scamnus* or that a
double-edged axe should be called *bipennis* from
pinnus, "sharp": for I would not have him fall into
the same error as those who, supposing this word to
be derived from *bis* and *pennae*, think that it is a
metaphor from the wings of birds.

He must not be content with knowing only those 13
changes introduced by conjugation and prefixes,
such as *secat secuit, cadit excĭdit, caedit excīdit, calcat
exculcat,* to which might be added *lotus* from *lauare*
and again *inlotus* with a thousand others. He must
learn as well the changes that time has brought
about even in nominatives. For just as names like
Valesius and *Fusius* have become *Valerius* and *Furius,*
so *arbos, labos, vapos* and even *clamos* and *lases*[1]
were the original forms. And this same letter *s*, 14
which has disappeared from these words, has itself
in some cases taken the place of another letter. For
our ancestors used to say *mertare* and *pultare*.[2] They
also said *fordeum* and *faedi*, using *f* instead of the
aspirate as being a kindred letter. For the Greeks
unlike us aspirate *f* like their own *phi*, as Cicero
bears witness in the *pro Fundanio*, where he laughs at
a witness who is unable to pronounce the first letter
of that name. In some cases again we have substi- 15
tuted *b* for other letters, as with *Burrus, Bruges,*
and *Belena*.[3] The same letter too has turned *duellum*
into *bellum*, and as a result some have ventured to
call the *Duelii Belii*. What of *stlocus* and *stlites*? 16
What of the connexion between *t* and *d*, a connexion

minus mirum, si in vetustis operibus urbis nostrae et
celebribus templis legantur *Alexanter* et *Cassantra*.
Quid O atque V permutatae invicem, ut *Hecoba* et
notrix, *Culcides* et *Pulixena* scriberentur, ac, ne in
Graecis id tantum notetur, *dederont* ac *probaveront*?
Sic Ὀδυσσεύς, quem Ὑλυσσέα fecerant Aeolis, ad
17 *Ulixen* deductus est. Quid? non E quoque I loco
fuit? *Menerva* et *leber* et *magester* et *Diove Victore*
non *Diovi Victori*? Sed mihi locum signare satis est,
non enim doceo, sed admoneo docturos. Inde in
syllabas cura transibit, de quibus in orthographia
pauca adnotabo.

Tum videbit, ad quem hoc pertinet, quot et quae
partes orationis; quanquam de numero parum
18 convenit. Veteres enim, quorum fuerunt Aristoteles
quoque atque Theodectes, verba modo et nomina et
convinctiones tradiderunt; videlicet quod in verbis
vim sermonis, in nominibus materiam (quia alterum
est quod loquimur, alterum de quo loquimur), in
convinctionibus autem complexus eorum esse iudicaverunt: quas coniunctiones a plerisque dici scio,
sed haec videtur ex συνδέσμῳ magis propria trans-
19 latio. Paulatim a philosophis ac maxime Stoicis
auctus est numerus, ac primum convinctionibus
articuli adiecti, post praepositiones, nominibus ap-

which makes it less surprising that on some of
the older buildings of Rome and certain famous
temples we should find the names *Alexanter* and
Cassantra? What again of the interchange of *o*
and *u*, of which examples may be found in *Hecoba*,
notrix, *Culcides* and *Pulixena*, or to take purely Latin
words *dederont* and *probaueront*? So too *Odysseus*,
which the Aeolian dialect turned into *Ulysseus*, has
been transformed by us into *Ulixes*. Similarly *e* in 17
certain cases held the place that is now occupied
by *i*, as in *Menerua*, *leber*, *magester*, and *Dioue victore*
in place of *Dioui victori*. It is sufficient for me to
give a mere indication as regards these points, for I
am not teaching, but merely advising those who
have got to teach. The next subject to which attention must be given is that of syllables, of which I will
speak briefly, when I come to deal with orthography.

Following this the teacher concerned will note
the number and nature of the parts of speech,
although there is some dispute as to their number.
Earlier writers, among them Aristotle himself and 18
Theodectes, hold that there are but three, *verbs,
nouns* and *convinctions*. Their view was that the
force of language resided in the verbs, and the
matter in the nouns (for the one is what we speak,
the other that which we speak about), while the
duty of the convinctions was to provide a link
between the nouns and the verbs. I know that
conjunction is the term in general use. But *convinction*
seems to me to be the more accurate translation of
the Greek σύνδεσμός. Gradually the number was 19
increased by the philosophers, more especially by
the Stoics: *articles* were first added to the *convinctions*, then *prepositions*: to nouns *appellations* were

QUINTILIAN

pellatio, deinde pronomen, deinde mixtum verbo
participium, ipsis verbis adverbia. Noster sermo
articulos non desiderat, ideoque in alias partes
20 orationis sparguntur. Sed accedit superioribus inter-
iectio. Alii tamen ex idoneis dumtaxat auctoribus
octo partes secuti sunt ut Aristarchus et aetate
nostra Palaemon, qui vocabulum sive appellationem
nomini subiecerunt tanquam speciem eius. At ii,
qui aliud nomen aliud vocabulum faciunt, novem.
Nihilominus fuerunt, qui ipsum adhuc vocabulum
ab appellatione deducerent, ut esset vocabulum
corpus visu tactuque manifestum, *domus, lectus,*
appellatio, cui vel alterum deesset vel utrumque,
ventus, caelum, deus, virtus. Adiiciebant et assevera-
tionem ut *eheu,* et tractationem ut *fasciatim*; quae
21 mihi non approbantur. Vocabulum an appellatio
dicenda sit προσηγορία et subiicienda nomini necne,
quia parvi refert, liberum opinaturis relinquo.

22 Nomina declinare et verba in primis pueri sciant,
neque enim aliter pervenire ad intellectum sequentium possunt; quod etiam monere supervacuum
erat, nisi ambitiosa festinatione plerique a posterioribus inciperent et, dum ostentare discipulos circa

---

¹ Generally interpreted *collective*: but see Colson, *Class.
Quart.* x. 1, p. 17 ; *fasciatim* = in bundles (from *fascis*).

added, then the *pronoun* and finally the *participle*,
which holds a middle position between the verb
and the noun. To the verb itself was added the
adverb. Our own language dispenses with the
articles, which are therefore distributed among the
other parts of speech. But *interjections* must be 20
added to those already mentioned. Others however follow good authority in asserting that there
are eight parts of speech. Among these I may
mention Aristarchus and in our own day Palaemon,
who classified the *vocable* or *appellation* as a species
of the genus noun. Those on the other hand who
distinguish between the noun and the vocable, make
nine parts of speech. But yet again there are
some who differentiate between the vocable and the
appellation, saying that the *vocable* indicates concrete
objects which can be seen and touched, such as a
" house " or " bed," while an *appellation* is something
imperceptible either to sight or touch or to both,
such as the " wind," " heaven," or " virtue." They
added also the *asseveration*, such as "alas" and the
derivative [1] such as *fasciatim*. But of these classifica-
tions I do not approve. Whether we should trans- 21
late προσηγορία by *vocable* or *appellation*, and whether
it should be regarded as a species of noun, I leave
to the decision of such as desire to express their
opinion : it is a matter of no importance.

Boys should begin by learning to decline nouns 22
and conjugate verbs : otherwise they will never be
able to understand the next subject of study. This
admonition would be superfluous but for the fact
that most teachers, misled by a desire to show rapid
progress, begin with what should really come at the
end : their passion for displaying their pupils' talents

23 speciosiora malunt, compendio morarentur. Atqui si
quis et didicerit satis et (quod non minus deesse
interim solet) voluerit docere quae didicit, non erit
contentus tradere in nominibus tria genera et quae
24 sunt duobus omnibusve communia. Nec statim
diligentem putabo, qui promiscua, quae ἐπίκοινα
dicuntur, ostenderit, in quibus sexus uterque per
alterum apparet; aut quae feminina positione mares
aut neutrali feminas significant, qualia sunt *Murena*
25 et *Glycerium.* Scrutabitur ille praeceptor acer atque
subtilis origines nominum, quae ex habitu corporis
*Rufos Longos*que fecerunt; ubi erit aliud secretius,
Sullae, Burri, Galbae, Plauti, Pansae, Scauri taliaque;
et ex casu nascentium; hic *Agrippa* et *Opiter* et
Cordus et *Postumus* erunt; et ex iis, quae post natos
eveniunt, unde *Vopiscus.* Iam *Cottae, Scipiones,*
26 *Laenates, Serani* sunt ex variis causis. Gentes quoque ac loca et alia multa reperias inter nominum
causas. In servis iam intercidit illud genus, quod
ducebatur a domino, unde *Marcipores Publipores*que.
Quaerat etiam, sitne apud Graecos vis quaedam

---

¹ Sulla = ? spindleshanks (*surula*). Burrus = red. Galba
= caterpillar. Plautus = flat-footed. Pansa = splay-footed.
Scaurus = with swollen ankles. Agrippa = born feet fore-
most. Opiter = one whose father died while his grandfather
still lived. Cordus = late-born. Postumus = last-born, or
born after the father's death. Vopiscus = a twin born alive

in connexion with the more imposing aspects of
their work serves but to delay progress and their
short cut to knowledge merely lengthens the
journey. And yet a teacher who has acquired 23
sufficient knowledge himself and is ready to teach
what he has learned—and such readiness is all too
rare—will not be content with stating that nouns
have three genders or with mentioning those which
are common to two or all three together. Nor 24
again shall I be in a hurry to regard it as a proof of
real diligence, if he points out that there are irregular nouns of the kind called *epicene* by the Greeks,
in which one gender implies both, or which in spite
of being feminine or neuter in form indicate males
or females respectively, as for instance *Muraena*
and *Glycerium*. A really keen and intelligent teacher 25
will inquire into the origin of names derived from
physical characteristics, such as *Rufus* or *Longus*,
whenever their meaning is obscure, as in the case of
Sulla, Burrus, Galba, Plautus, Pansa, Scaurus and the
like; of names derived from accidents of birth such
as *Agrippa, Opiter, Cordus* and *Postumus*, and again of
names given after birth such as *Vopiscus*. Then there
are names such as *Cotta, Scipio, Laenas* or *Seranus*,[1]
which originated in various ways. It will also be found 26
that names are frequently derived from races, places
and many other causes. Further there are obsolete
slave-names such as *Marcipor* or *Publipor*[2] derived
from the names of their owners. The teacher must
also inquire whether there is not room for a sixth

after the premature birth and death of the other. Scipio =
staff. Laenas from *laena* (cloak). Seranus = the sower.
Cotta uncertain.

[2] *i.e. Marcipuer, Publipuer.*

sexti casus et apud nos quoque septimi. Nam cum
dico *hasta percussi,* non utor ablativi natura; nec, si
27 idem Graece dicam, dativi. Sed in verbis quoque
quis est adeo imperitus, ut ignoret genera et
qualitates et personas et numeros? Litterarii paene
ista sunt ludi et trivialis scientiae. Iam quosdam illa
turbabunt, quae declinationibus non tenentur. Nam
et quaedam participia an verba an appellationes
sint, dubitari potest, quia aliud alio loco valent, ut
28 *lectum* et *sapiens* et quaedam verba appellationibus
similia, ut *fraudator, nutritor.* Iam *itur in antiquam
silvam* nonne propriae cuiusdam rationis est? nam
quod initium eius invenias? cui simile *fletur.* Accipimus aliter, ut *panditur interea domus omnipotentis
Olympi,* aliter ut *totis usque adeo turbatur agris.* Est
etiam quidam tertius modus, ut *urbs habitatur,* unde
29 et *campus curritur, mare navigatur. Pransus* quoque
ac *potus* diversum valet quam indicat. Quid? quod
multa verba non totum declinationis ordinem ferunt?
Quaedam etiam mutantur ut *fero* in praeterito,
quaedam tertiae demum personae figura dicuntur ut

---

[1] *lectum* may be acc. of *lectus,* "bed," or supine or past
part. pass. of *legere,* "to read"; *sapiens* may be pres. part.
of *sapere,* "to know," or an adj. = "wise"; *fraudator* and
nutritor are 2nd and 3rd pers. sing. fut. imper. pass. of
fraudo and *nutrio.*

[2] *Aen.* vi. 179: "They go into the ancient wood."

case in Greek and a seventh in Latin. For when I
say "wounded by a spear," the case is not a true
ablative in Latin nor a true dative in Greek. Again 27
if we turn to verbs, who is so ill-educated as not to
be familiar with their various kinds and qualities,
their different persons and numbers. Such subjects belong to the elementary school and the
rudiments of knowledge. Some, however, will
find points undetermined by inflexion somewhat
perplexing. For there are certain participles, about
which there may be doubts as to whether they are
really nouns or verbs, since their meaning varies
with their use, as for example *lectum* and *sapiens,*
while there are other verbs which resemble nouns, 28
such as *fraudator* and *nutritor.*[1] Again *itur in antiquam
silvam*[2] is a peculiar usage. For there is no subject
to serve as a starting point : *fletur* is a similar example.
The passive may be used in different ways as for
instance in

> *panditur interea domus omnipotentis Olympi*[3]

and in

> *totis usque adeo turbatur agris.*[4]

Yet a third usage is found in *urbs habitatur,* whence
we get phrases such as *campus curritur* and *mare navigatur. Pransus* and *potus*[5] have a meaning which does 29
not correspond to their form. And what of those
verbs which are only partially conjugated? Some
(as for instance *fero*) even suffer an entire change in
the perfect. Others are used only in the third

[3] *Aen.* x. 1 : "Meanwhile the house of almighty Olympus
is opened."

[4] *Ecl.* i. 11 : "There is such confusion in all the fields."

[5] "Having dined," "having drunk." Active in sense,
passive in form.

licet, piget, quaedam simile quiddam patiuntur
vocabulis quae in adverbium transeunt? Nam ut
noctu et *diu* ita *dictu factu*que. Sunt enim haec
quoque verba participialia quidem, non tamen qualia
*dicto facto*que.

V. Iam cum omnis oratio tris habeat virtutes, ut
emendata, ut dilucida, ut ornata sit (quia dicere
apte, quod est praecipuum, plerique ornatui subiiciunt), totidem vitia, quae sunt supra dictis contraria, emendate loquendi regulam, quae gram-
2 matices prior pars est, examinet. Haec exigitur
verbis aut singulis aut pluribus. *Verba* nunc generaliter accipi volo, nam duplex eorum intellectus
est; alter, qui omnia per quae sermo nectitur
significat, ut apud Horatium: *verbaque provisam rem
non invita sequentur;* alter, in quo est una pars
orationis, *lego, scribo.* Quam vitantes ambiguitatem
quidam dicere maluerunt *voces, locutiones, dictiones.*
3 Singula sunt aut nostra aut peregrina, aut simplicia
aut composita, aut propria aut translata, aut usitata
aut ficta.

Uni verbo vitium saepius quam virtus inest.
Licet enim dicamus aliquod proprium, speciosum,
sublime: nihil tamen horum nisi in complexu loquendi serieque contingit; laudamus enim verba
4 rebus bene accommodata. Sola est, quae notari

person, such as *licet* and *piget,* while some resemble
nouns tending to acquire an adverbial meaning; for
we say *dictu* and *factu*[1] as we say *noctu* and *diu,*
since these words are participial though quite different
from *dicto* and *facto.*

V. Style has three kinds of excellence, correctness, lucidity and elegance (for many include the
all-important quality of appropriateness under the
heading of elegance). Its faults are likewise threefold, namely the opposites of these excellences. The
teacher of literature therefore must study the rules
for correctness of speech, these constituting the
first part of his art. The observance of these rules 2
is concerned with either one or more words. I must
now be understood to use *verbum* in its most general
sense. It has of course two meanings; the one covers
all the parts of which language is composed, as in
the line of Horace :

> " Once supply the thought,
> And words will follow swift as soon as sought ";[2]

the other restricts it to a part of speech such as
lego and *scribo.* To avoid this ambiguity, some
authorities prefer the terms *voces, locutiones, dictiones.*
Individual words will either be native or imported, 3
simple or compound, literal or metaphorical, in
current use or newly-coined.

A single word is more likely to be faulty than
to possess any intrinsic merit. For though we
may speak of a word as appropriate, distinguished
or sublime, it can possess none of these properties
save in relation to connected and consecutive speech ;
since when we praise words, we do so because they
suit the matter. There is only one excellence that 4

---

[1] Supines.   [2] *Ars Poetica,* 311.

possit velut *vocalitas*, quae εὐφωνία dicitur; cuius
in eo delectus est, ut inter duo, quae idem significant ac tantundem valent, quod melius sonet malis.

5   Prima barbarismi ac soloecismi foeditas absit. Sed
quia interim excusantur haec vitia aut consuetudine
aut auctoritate aut vetustate aut denique vicinitate
virtutum (nam saepe a figuris ea separare difficile
est), ne qua tam lubrica observatio fallat, acriter se
in illud tenue discrimen grammaticus intendat, de
quo nos latius ibi loquemur, ubi de figuris orationis
6 tractandum erit.   Interim vitium, quod fit in singulis verbis, sit barbarismus.   Occurrat mihi forsan
aliquis, quid hic promisso tanti operis dignum? aut
quis hoc nescit, alios barbarismos scribendo fieri
alios loquendo;—quia, quod male scribitur, male
etiam dici necesse est; quae vitiose dixeris, non
utique et scripto peccant—illud prius adiectione,
detractione, immutatione, transmutatione, hoc secundum divisione, complexione, aspiratione, sono
7 contineri? Sed ut parva sint haec, pueri docentur
adhuc, et grammaticos officii sui commonemus.   Ex
quibus si quis erit plane impolitus et vestibulum
modo artis huius ingressus, intra haec, quae pro-

---

[1] *cp.* § 40.

can be isolated for consideration, namely euphony, the Greek term for our *uocalitas* : that is to say that, when we are confronted with making a choice between two exact synonyms, we must select that which sounds best.

In the first place *barbarisms* and *solecisms* must not **5** be allowed to intrude their offensive presence. These blemishes are however pardoned at times, because we have become accustomed to them or because they have age or authority in their favour or are near akin to positive excellences, since it is often difficult to distinguish such blemishes from figures of speech.[1] The teacher therefore, that such slippery customers may not elude detection, must seek to acquire a delicate discrimination ; but of this I will speak later when I come to discuss figures of speech. For the present **6** I will define *barbarism* as an offence occurring in connexion with single words. Some of my readers may object that such a topic is beneath the dignity of so ambitious a work. But who does not know that some *barbarisms* occur in writing, others in speaking ? For although what is incorrect in writing will also be incorrect in speech, the converse is not necessarily true, inasmuch as mistakes in writing are caused by addition or omission, substitution or transposition, while mistakes in speaking are due to separation or combination of syllables, to aspiration or other errors of sound. Trivial as these **7** points may seem, our boys are still at school and I am reminding their instructors of their duty. And if one of our teachers is lacking in education and has done no more than set foot in the outer courts of his art, he will have to confine himself to the rules published in the elementary text-books : the

fitentium commentariolis vulgata sunt, consistet,
doctiores multa adiicient, vel hoc primum, quod
8 barbarismum pluribus modis accipimus.   Unum
gente, quale est, si quis Afrum vel Hispanum
Latinae orationi nomen inserat, ut ferrum, quo
rotae vinciuntur, dici solet *cantus*, quanquam eo
tanquam recepto utitur Persius ; sicut Catullus
ploxenum circa Padum invenit, et in oratione La-
bieni (sive illa Cornelii Galli est) in Pollionem
casamo adsectator e Gallia ductum est ; nam *mas-
trucam*, quod Sardum est, irridens Cicero ex in-
9 dustria dixit.   Alterum genus barbarismi accipimus,
quod fit animi natura, ut is, a quo insolenter quid
aut minaciter aut crudeliter dictum sit, barbare
10 locutus existimatur. Tertium est illud vitium barbarismi, cuius exempla vulgo sunt plurima, sibi etiam
quisque fingere potest, ut verbo, cui libebit, adiiciat
litteram syllabamve vel detrahat, aut aliam pro alia
11 aut eandem alio quam rectum est loco ponat.   Sed
quidam fere in iactationem eruditionis sumere illa ex
poetis solent et auctores quos praelegunt criminantur.   Scire autem debet puer, haec apud scriptores
carminum aut venia digna aut etiam laude duci,
12 potiusque illa docendi erunt minus vulgata.   Nam
duos in uno nomine faciebat barbarismos Tinga
Placentinus (si reprehendenti Hortensio credimus)
preculam pro *pergula* dicens, et immutatione cum
c pro *g* uteretur, et transmutatione cum *r* prae-
poneret *e* antecedenti.   At in eiusdem vitii gemina-

more learned teacher on the other hand will be in a
position to go much further: first of all, for example,
he will point out that there are many different kinds
of *barbarism*. One kind is due to race, such as the 8
insertion of a Spanish or African term ; for instance
the iron tire of a wheel is called *cantus*,[1] though
Persius uses it as established in the Latin language ;
Catullus picked up *ploxenum*[2] (a box) in the valley
of the Po, while the author of the *in Pollionem*, be
he Labienus or Cornelius Gallus, imported *casamo*
from Gaul in the sense of "follower." As for
mastruca,[3] which is Sardinian for a "rough coat," it
is introduced by Cicero merely as an object of deri-
sion. Another kind of barbarism proceeds from the 9
speaker's temper : for instance, we regard it as barbarous if a speaker use cruel or brutal language.
A third and very common kind, of which anyone 10
may fashion examples for himself, consists in the
addition or omission of a letter or syllable, or in the
substitution of one for another or in placing one
where it has no right to be. Some teachers however, 11
to display their learning, are in the habit of picking
out examples of *barbarism* from the poets and attacking the authors whom they are expounding for
using such words. A boy should however realize
that in poets such peculiarities are pardonable or
even praiseworthy, and should therefore be taught
less common instances. For Tinga of Placentia, if 12
we may believe Hortensius who takes him to task for
it, committed two *barbarisms* in one word by saying
precula for *pergula* : that is to say he substituted *c*
for *g*, and transposed *r* and *e*. On the other hand

---

[1] Pers. v. 71.   Usually, though wrongly, spelt *oanthus*.
[2] Cat. xcvii. 6.   [3] In *Or. pro Scauro.*

QUINTILIAN

tione *Mettoeoque Fufetioeo*[1] dicens Ennius poetico
13 iure defenditur.   Sed in prosa quoque est quaedam
iam recepta immutatio.   Nam Cicero *Canopitarum*
exercitum dicit, ipsi *Canobon* vocant; et *Trasu-*
mennum pro *Tarsumenno* multi auctores, etiamsi est
in eo transmutatio, vindicaverunt.   Similiter alia;
nam sive est *adsentior*, Sisenna dixit *adsentio* mul-
tique et hunc et analogian secuti, sive illud verum
14 est, haec quoque pars consensu defenditur.   At ille
pexus pinguisque doctor aut illic detractionem aut
hic adiectionem putabit.   Quid quod quaedam, quae
singula procul dubio vitiosa sunt, iuncta sine repre-
15 hensione dicuntur?   Nam et *dua* et *tre* [et *pondo*]
diversorum generum sunt barbarismi; at *duapondo*
et *trepondo* usque ad nostram aetatem ab omnibus
16 dictum est, et recte dici Messala confirmat.   Ab-
surdum forsitan videatur dicere, barbarismum, quod
est unius verbi vitium, fieri per numeros aut genera
sicut soloecismum : *scala* tamen et *scopa* contraque
hordea et *mulsa,* licet litterarum mutationem, detractionem, adiectionem habeant, non alio vitiosa sunt,
quam quod pluralia singulariter et singularia plu-

---

[1] Mettoeoque Fufetioeo, *Skutsch* : mettioeo et furetioeo, *A,*
the other MSS. giving similar corruptions.

---

[1] The barbarism lies in the use of the old Greek termination -oeo in the genitive.
[2] Two and three pounds in weight.

when Ennius writes *Mettoeoque Fufetioeo*,[1] where
the *barbarism* is twice repeated, he is defended on
the plea of poetic licence. Substitution is however 13
sometimes admitted even in prose, as for instance
when Cicero speaks of the army of *Canopus* which is
locally styled *Canobus*, while the number of authors
who have been guilty of transposition in writing
Trasumennus for *Tarsumennus* has succeeded in stan-
dardising the error. Similar instances may be quoted.
If *adsentior* be regarded as the correct form, we must
remember that Sisenna said *adsentio*, and that many
have followed him on the ground of analogy: on
the other hand, if *adsentio* is the correct form, we
must remember that *adsentior* has the support of
current usage. And yet our fat fool, the fashionable 14
schoolmaster, will regard one of these forms as an
example of omission or the other as an instance
of addition. Again there are words which when
used separately are undoubtedly incorrect, but
when used in conjunction excite no unfavourable
comment. For instance *dua* and *tre* are *barbarisms* 15
and differ in gender, but the words *duapondo*
and *trepondo*[2] have persisted in common parlance
down to our own day, and Messala shows that the
practice is correct. It may perhaps seem absurd to 16
say that a *barbarism*, which is an error in a single
word, may be made, like a *solecism*, by errors in
connexion with number or gender. But take on the
one hand *scala* (stairs) and *scopa* (which literally
means a twig, but is used in the sense of broom)
and on the other hand *hordea* (barley) and *mulsa*
(mead): here we have substitution, omission and
addition of letters, but the blemish consists in the
former case merely in the use of singular for plural,

QUINTILIAN

raliter efferuntur ; et *gladia* qui dixerunt, genere
17 exciderunt. Sed hoc quoque notare contentus sum,
ne arti culpa quorundam pervicacium perplexae
videar et ipse quaestionem addidisse.

Plus exigunt subtilitatis quae accidunt in dicendo
vitia, quia exempla eorum tradi scripto non possunt,
nisi cum in versus inciderunt, ut divisio *Europaï
Asiaï*, et ei contrarium vitium, quod συναίρεσιν et
συναλοιφὴν Graeci vocant, nos complexionem dicamus, qualis est apud P. Varronem *tum te flagranti
18 deiectum fulmine Phaethon.* Nam si esset prosa
oratio, easdem litteras enuntiare veris syllabis
licebat. Praeterea quae fiunt spatio, sive cum syllaba correpta producitur, ut *Italiam fato profugus,*
seu longa corripitur, ut *unius ob noxam et furias,*
extra carmen non deprehendas ; sed nec in carmine
19 vitia dicenda sunt. Illa vero nonnisi aure exi-
guntur, quae fiunt per sonos ; quanquam per aspira-
tionem, sive adiicitur vitiose sive detrahitur, apud
nos potest quaeri an in scripto sit vitium, si *h*
littera est, non nota. Cuius quidem ratio mutata
20 cum temporibus est saepius. Parcissime ea veteres
usi etiam in vocalibus, cum *aedos ircos*que dicebant ;
diu deinde servatum, ne consonantibus aspirarent,

---

[1] The archaic genitive as used by epic poets.
[2] *Phæthon* for *Phaëthon.*   [3] *Aen.* i. 6.   [4] *Aen.* i. 45.

in the latter of plural for singular. Those on the other hand who have used the word *gladia* are guilty of a mistake in gender. I merely mention these as 17 instances: I do not wish anyone to think that I have added a fresh problem to a subject into which the obstinacy of pedants has already introduced confusion.

The faults which arise in the course of actual speaking require greater penetration on the part of the critic, since it is impossible to cite examples from writing, except in cases where they occur in poetry, as when the diphthong is divided into two syllables in *Europai* and *Asiai*[1]; or when the opposite fault occurs, called *synaeresis* or *synaloephe* by the Greeks and *complexio* by ourselves: as an example I may quote the line of Publius Varro:

tum te flagranti deiectum fulmine Phaethon.[2]

If this were prose, it would be possible to give 18 the letters their true syllabic value. I may mention as further anomalies peculiar to poetry the lengthening of a short syllable as in *Italiam fato profugus,*[3] or the shortening of a long such as *unius ob noxam et furias* ;[4] but in poetry we cannot label these as actual faults. Errors in sound on the other hand 19 can be detected by the ear alone; although in Latin, as regards the addition or omission of the aspirate, the question may be raised whether this is an error when it occurs in writing; for there is some doubt whether *h* is a letter or merely a breathing, practice having frequently varied in different ages. Older 20 authors used it but rarely even before vowels, saying *aedus* or *ircus*, while its conjunction with consonants was for a long time avoided, as in words such as

ut in *Graccis* et in *triumpis* ; erupit brevi tempore
nimius usus, ut *choronae, chenturiones, praechones*
adhuc quibusdam in inscriptionibus maneant, qua
21 de re Catulli nobile epigramma est.   Inde durat
ad nos usque *vehementer* et *comprehendere* et *mihi*,
nam *mehe* quoque pro *me* apud antiquos tragoediarum
praecipue scriptores in veteribus libris invenimus.

22   Adhuc difficilior observatio est per tenores (quos
quidem ab antiquis dictos *tonores* comperi videlicet
declinato a Graecis verbo, qui τόνους dicunt), vel
accentus, quas Graeci προσῳδίας vocant, cum acuta
et gravis alia pro alia ponuntur, ut in hoc *Camillus*,
23 si acuitur prima : aut gravis pro flexa, ut *Cethegus*,
et hic prima acuta (nam sic media mutatur) ; aut
flexa pro gravi, ut *Appi* [1] circumducta sequenti, quam
ex duabus syllabis in unam cogentes et deinde
24 flectentes dupliciter peccant.   Sed id saepius in
Graecis nominibus accidit, ut *Atrei*, quem nobis
iuvenibus doctissimi senes acuta prima dicere solebant, ut necessario secunda gravis esset, item *Nerei
Terei*que.   Haec de accentibus tradita.

[1] aut Appi, *Spalding* : aut apice, *A* : ut, *B*.

---

[1] Cat. lxxxi.

[2] The Roman accent was a stress, while the Greek was a
pitch accent, though by the Christian era tending to change
into stress.   Roman grammarians borrow the Greek termin-
ology and speak of accents in terms of pitch.   The explanation of this is probably that the Roman stress accent was

Graccus or *triumpus*. Then for a short time it broke
out into excessive use, witness such spelling as *chorona,
chenturia* or *praecho,* which may still be read in certain
inscriptions : the well-known epigram of Catullus [1]
will be remembered in this connexion. The spellings 21
vehementer, comprehendere and *mihi* have lasted to our
own day : and among early writers, especially of
tragedy, we actually find *mehe* for *me* in the older MSS.

It is still more difficult to detect errors of *tenor* or 22
tone (I note that old writers spell the word *tonor,*
as derived from the Greek τόνος), or of accent, styled
prosody by the Greeks, such as the substitution of
the acute accent for the grave or the grave for the
acute : such an example would be the placing of the
acute accent on the first syllable of *Camíllus,* or the 23
substitution of the grave for the circumflex in *Cethêgus,*
an error which results in the alteration of the
quantity of the middle syllable, since it means
making the first syllable acute ; or again the substitution of the circumflex for the grave on the
second syllable of *Appi,* where the contraction of
two syllables into one circumflexed syllable involves
a double error. This, however, occurs far more fre- 24
quently in Greek words such as *Atrei,* which in our
young days was pronounced by the most learned of
our elders with an acute accent on the first syllable,
necessitating a grave accent on the second ; the
same remark applies to *Nerei* and *Terei.* Such has
been the tradition as regards accents. [2]

accompanied by an elevation of the pitch. Here the acute
accent certainly implies stress ; the grave implies a drop in
pitch and the absence of stress. The circumflex means that
the voice rises slightly and then falls slightly, but implies
stress. See Lindsay, *Latin Language,* pp. 148-153.

25 Ceterum scio iam quosdam eruditos, nonnullos
etiam grammaticos sic docere ac loqui, ut propter
quaedam vocum discrimina verbum interim acuto
26 sono finiant, ut in illis *quae circum littora, circum
piscosos scopulos,* ne, si gravem posuerint secundam,
circus dici videatur non *circuitus.* Itemque cum
quale interrogantes gravi, comparantes acuto tenore
concludunt; quod tamen in adverbiis fere solis ac
pronominibus vindicant, in ceteris veterem legem
27 sequuntur. Mihi videtur condicionem mutare, quod
his locis verba coniungimus. Nam cum dico *circum
litora,* tanquam unum enuntio dissimulata distinc-
tione, itaque tanquam in una voce una est acuta,
quod idem accidit in illo *Troiae qui primus ab oris.*
28 Evenit, ut metri quoque condicio mutet accentum,
ut *Pecudes pictaeque volucres;* nam volucres media
acuta legam, quia, etsi natura brevis, tamen positione longa est, ne faciat iambum, quem non recipit
29 versus herous. Separata vero haec a praecepto non
recedent, aut si consuetudo vicerit, vetus lex

---

[1] *Aen.* iv. 254.
[2] *i.e.* that *circum* is the acc. of *circus,* and not the adverb
indicating circuit.
[3] *Aen.* i. 1: *qui* coalesces with *primus, ab* with *oris.*
[4] *Georg.* iii. 243.

Still I am well aware that certain learned men 25
and some professed teachers of literature, to ensure
that certain words may be kept distinct, sometimes
place an acute accent on the last syllable, both when
they are teaching and in ordinary speech : as, for
instance, in the following passage :

> *quae circum litora, circum*
> *piscosos scopulos,*[1]

where they make the last syllable of *circum* acute on 26
the ground that, if that syllable were given the grave
accent, it might be thought that they meant *circus*
not *circuitus*.[2] Similarly when *quale* is interrogative,
they give the final syllable a grave accent, but when
using it in a comparison, make it acute. This practice,
however, they restrict almost entirely to adverbs
and pronouns ; in other cases they follow the old
usage. Personally I think that in such phrases 27
as these the circumstances are almost entirely altered
by the fact that we join two words together. For
when I say *circum litora* I pronounce the phrase as
one word, concealing the fact that it is composed of
two, consequently it contains but one acute accent,
as though it were a single word. The same thing
occurs in the phrase *Troiae qui primus ab oris.*[3] It 28
sometimes happens that the accent is altered by
the metre as in *pecudes pictaeque volucres*[4] ; for I shall
read *volucres* with the acute on the middle syllable,
because, although that syllable is short by nature, it
is long by position : else the last two syllables
would form an iambus, which its position in the
hexameter does not allow. But these same words, 29
if separated, will form no exception to the rule : or
if the custom under discussion prevails, the old law

sermonis abolebitur; cuius difficilior apud Graecos
observatio est, quia plura illis loquendi genera, quas
διαλέκτους vocant, et quod alia vitiosum interim alia
rectum est; apud nos vero brevissima ratio.
30 Namque in omni voce acuta intra numerum trium
syllabarum continetur, sive eae sunt in verbo solae
sive ultimae, et in iis aut proxima extremae aut ab
ea tertia. Trium porro, de quibus loquor, media
longa aut acuta aut flexa erit; eodem loco brevis
utique gravem habebit sonum, ideoque positam ante
31 se id est ab ultima tertiam acuet. Est autem in
omni voce utique acuta sed nunquam plus una
nec unquam ultima ideoque in dissyllabis prior.
Praeterea nunquam in eadem flexa et acuta,
quoniam est in flexa et acuta, itaque neutra
claudet vocem Latinam. Ea vero, quae sunt
syllabae unius, erunt acuta aut flexa, ne sit aliqua
32 vox sine acuta. Et illa per sonos accidunt, quae
demonstrari scripto non possunt, vitia oris et linguae:
ἰωτακισμοὺς et λαμβδακισμοὺς et ἰσχνότητας et
πλατειασμοὺς feliciores fingendis nominibus Graeci
vocant, sicut κοιλοστομίαν, cum vox quasi in recessu
33 oris auditur. Sunt etiam proprii quidam et inen-
arrabiles soni, quibus nonnunquam nationes reprehen-
dimus. Remotis igitur omnibus, de quibus supra

---

[1] Iotacism = doubling the *i* sound, *e.g. Troiia* for *Troia*;
lambdacism = doubling the *l*.

of the language will disappear. (This law is more difficult for the Greeks to observe, because they have several dialects, as they call them, and what is wrong in one may be right in another.) But with us the rule is simplicity itself. For in every word 30 the acute accent is restricted to three syllables, whether these be the only syllables in the word or the three last, and will fall either on the penultimate or the antepenultimate. The middle of the three syllables of which I speak will be acute or circumflexed, if long, while if it be short, it will have a grave accent and the acute will be thrown back to the preceding syllable, that is to say the antepenultimate. Every word has an acute accent, but 31 never more than one. Further the acute never falls on the last syllable and therefore in dissyllabic words marks the first syllable. Moreover the acute accent and the circumflex are never found in one and the same word, since the circumflex itself contains an acute accent. Neither the circumflex nor the acute, therefore, will ever be found in the last syllable of a Latin word, with this exception, that monosyllables must either be acute or circumflexed; otherwise we should find words without an acute accent at all. There are also faults of sound, which we cannot repro- 32 duce in writing, as they spring from defects of the voice and tongue. The Greeks who are happier in inventing names than we are call them iotacisms, lambdacisms,[1] ἰσχνότητες (attenuations) and πλατεια-σμοί (broadenings); they also use the term κοιλοστομία, when the voice seems to proceed from the depths of the mouth. There are also certain peculiar and 33 indescribable sounds for which we sometimes take whole nations to fault. To sum up then, if all the faults of which we have just spoken be avoided,

dixi, vitiis erit illa quae vocatur ὀρθοέπεια, id est
emendata cum suavitate vocum explanatio : nam sic
accipi potest recta.

34 Cetera vitia omnia ex pluribus vocibus sunt,
quorum est soloecismus, quanquam circa hoc quoque
disputatum est. Nam etiam qui complexu orationis
accidere eum confitentur, quia tamen unius emenda-
tione verbi corrigi possit, in verbo esse vitium non in
35 sermone contendunt ; cum, sive *amarae corticis* seu
medio cortice per genus facit soloecismum (quorum
neutrum quidem reprehendo, cum sit utriusque Vergilius auctor ; sed fingamus utrumlibet non recte
dictum), mutatio vocis alterius, in qua vitium erat,
rectam loquendi rationem sit redditura, ut *amarı*
corticis fiat vel *media cortice*. Quod manifestae
calumniae est ; neutrum enim vitiosum est separa-
tum, sed compositione peccatur, quae iam sermonis
36 est. Illud eruditius quaeritur, an in singulis quoque
verbis possit fieri soloecismus, uti si unum quis ad se
vocans dicat *venite,* aut si plures a se dimittens ita
loquatur *abi* aut *discede.* Nec non cum responsum
ab interrogante dissentit, ut si dicenti *Quem video ?*
ita occurras *Ego.* In gestu etiam nonnulli putant
idem vitium inesse, cum aliud voce aliud nutu vel
37 manu demonstratur. Huic opinioni neque omnino

---

[1] *Ecl.* vi. 62.   [2] *Georg.* ii. 74.

we shall be in possession of the Greek ὀρθοέπεια, that is to say, an exact and pleasing articulation; for that is what we mean when we speak of correct pronunciation.

All other faults in speaking are concerned with 34 more words than one; among this class of faults is the *solecism*, although there have been controversies about this as well. For even those who acknowledge that it occurs in connected speech, argue that, since it can be corrected by the alteration of one word, the fault lies in the word and not in the phrase or sentence. For example whether *amarae corticis*[1] or 35 *medio cortice*[2] contains a solecism in gender (and personally I object to neither, as Vergil is the author of both; however, for the sake of argument let us assume that one of the two is incorrect), still whichever phrase is incorrect, it can be set right by the alteration of the word in which the fault lies: that is to say we can emend either to *amari corticis* or *media cortice*. But it is obvious that these critics misrepresent the case. For neither word is faulty in itself; the error arises from its association with another word. The fault therefore lies in the phrase. Those who raise the question as to whether 36 a *solecism* can arise in a single word show greater intelligence. Is it for instance a *solecism* if a man when calling a single person to him says *uenite*, or in dismissing several persons says *abi* or *discede*? Or again if the answer does not correspond to the question: suppose, for example, when someone said to you "Whom do I see?", you were to reply "I." Some too think it a *solecism* if the spoken word is contradicted by the motion of hand or head. I do 37 not entirely concur with this view nor yet do I

accedo neque plane dissentio. Nam id fateor accidere voce una non tamen aliter, quam si sit aliquid, quod vim alterius vocis obtineat, ad quod vox illa referatur, ut soloecismus ex complexu fiat eorum, quibus res significantur et voluntas osten-
38 ditur. Atque ut omnem effugiam cavillationem, sit aliquando in uno verbo nunquam in solo verbo. Per quot autem et per quas accidat species, non satis convenit. Qui plenissime, quadripertitam volunt esse rationem nec aliam quam barbarismi, ut fiat adiectione *nam enim, de susum, in Alexandriam;*
39 detractione *ambulo viam, Aegypto venio, ne hoc fecit;* transmutatione, qua ordo turbatur, *quoque ego, enim hoc voluit, autem non habuit.* Ex quo genere an sit *igitur* initio sermonis positum, dubitari potest, quia maximos auctores in diversa fuisse opinione video, cum apud alios sit etiam frequens, apud alios
40 nunquam reperiatur. Haec tria genera quidam deducunt a soloecismo, et adiectionis vitium πλεονα_σμόν, detractionis ἔλλειψιν, inversionis ἀναστροφὴν vocant, quae si in speciem soloecismi cadat, ὑπερβατὸν
41 quoque eodem appellari modo posse. Immutatio sine controversia est, cum aliud pro alio ponitur. Id per omnes orationis partes deprehendimus, frequentissime in verbo, quia plurima huic accidunt;

---

[1] *i.e. nam* cannot be coupled with *enim*; *de* being a pre-position cannot govern an adverb ("from above"); *in* is not required with *Alexandriam*, which is the name of a

wholly dissent. I admit that a *solecism* may occur in a single word, but with this proviso: there must be something else equivalent to another word, to which the word, in which the error lies, can be referred, so that the *solecism* arises from the faulty connexion of those symbols by which facts are expressed and purpose indicated. To avoid all sus- 38 picion of quibbling, I will say that a *solecism* may occur in one word, but never in a word in isolation. There is, however, some controversy as to the number and nature of the different kinds of *solecism.* Those who have dealt with the subject most fully make a fourfold division, identical with that which is made in the case of *barbarisms : solecisms* are brought about by addition, for instance in phrases such as *nam enim, de susum, in Alexandriam*; by 39 omission, in phrases such as *ambulo viam, Aegypto venio,* or *ne hoc fecit*: and by transposition as in *quoque ego, enim hoc voluit, autem non habuit.*[1] Under this last head comes the question whether *igitur* can be placed first in a sentence : for I note that authors of the first rank disagree on this point, some of them frequently placing it in that position, others never. Some distinguish these three classes of 40 error from the *solecism,* styling addition a *pleonasm,* omission an *ellipse,* and transposition *anastrophe*: and they assert that if *anastrophe* is a solecism, *hyperbaton* might also be so called. About substitution, that is 41 when one word is used instead of another, there is no dispute. It is an error which we may detect in connexion with all the parts of speech, but most frequently in the verb, because it has greater variety

town. *Quoque, enim* and *autem* cannot come first in a sentence. *Ambulo per viam, ab Aegypto venio, ne hoc quidem fecit* would be the correct Latin.

ideoque in eo fiunt soloecismi per genera, tempora, personas, modos, sive cui *status* eos dici seu *qualitates* placet, vel sex vel, ut alii volunt, octo;—nam totidem vitiorum erunt formae, in quot species eorum quidque, de quibus supra dictum est, diviseris—

42 praeterea numeros, in quibus nos singularem ac pluralem habemus Graeci et δυϊκόν. Quanquam fuerunt, qui nobis quoque adiicerent dualem *scripsere, legere;* quod evitandae asperitatis gratia mollitum est, ut apud veteres pro *male mereris, male merere.* Ideoque quod vocant *dualem,* in illo solo genere consistit, cum apud Graecos et in verbi tota fere ratione et in nominibus deprehendatur, et sic quoque raris-

43 simus eius sit usus, apud nostrorum vero neminem haec observatio reperiatur, quin e contrario *devenere locos* et *conticuere omnes* et *consedere duces* aperte nos doceant, nihil horum ad duos pertinere; *dixere* quoque, quamquam id Antonius Rufus ex diverso ponit exemplum, de pluribus patronis praeco pro-

44 nuntiet. Quid? non Livius circa initia statim primi libri, *Tenuere,* inquit, *arcem Sabini?* et mox, *in adversum Romani subiere?* Sed quem potius ego quam M. Tullium sequar? qui in Oratore, *Non*

---

[1] *Aen.* i. 369: "They came to the places."
[2] *Aen.* ii. 1: "All were silent."
[3] Ovid, *Met.* xiii. 1: "The chiefs sat them down."
[4] *Dixere,* "they have spoken," was said when the advocates had finished their pleading.

than any other : consequently in connexion with the
verb we get *solecisms* of gender, tense, person and
mood (or "states" or "qualities" if you prefer either
of these terms), be these types of error six in number,
as some assert, or eight as is insisted by others (for
the number of the forms of solecism will depend on
the number of subdivisions which you assign to the
parts of speech of which we have just spoken).
Further there are solecisms of number; now Latin 42
has two numbers, singular and plural, while Greek
possesses a third, namely the dual.   There have
however been some who have given us a dual as
well in words such as *scripsere* and *legere,* in which
as a matter of fact the final syllable has been
softened to avoid harshness, just as in old writers
we find *male merere* for *male mereris.*   Consequently
what they assert to be a dual is concerned solely
with this one class of termination, whereas in Greek
it is found throughout the whole structure of the
verb and in nouns as well, though even then it is
but rarely used.   But we find not a trace of such a 43
usage in any Latin author.   On the contrary phrases
such as *devenere locos,*[1] *conticuere omnes,*[2] and
consedere duces[3] clearly prove that they have nothing to do with the dual.   Moreover *dixere,*[4] although Antonius Rufus cites it as proof to the
contrary, is often used by the usher in the courts to
denote more than two advocates.   Again, does not 44
Livy near the beginning of his first book write
tenuere arcem Sabini[5] and later *in adversum Romani
subiere ?*   But I can produce still better authority.
For Cicero in his *Orator* says, "I have no objection

[5] Liv. i. xii.: "The Sabines held the citadel." "The
Romans marched up the slope against them."

reprehendo, inquit, *scripsere ; scripserunt esse verius*
45 *sentio.* Similiter in vocabulis et nominibus fit soloecismus genere, numero, proprie autem casibus,
quidquid horum alteri succedet. Huic parti subiun-
gatur licet per comparationes et superlationes,
itemque in quibus patrium pro possessivo dicitur vel
46 contra. Nam vitium, quod fit per quantitatem ut
magnum peculiolum, erunt qui soloecismum putent
quia pro nomine integro positum sit deminutum.
Ego dubito, an id improprium potius appellem, sig-
nificatione enim deerrat ; soloecismi porro vitium non
47 est in sensu sed in complexu. In participio per
genus et casum, ut in vocabulo, per tempora, ut in
verbo, per numerum, ut in utroque, peccatur. Pronomen quoque genus, numerum, casus habet, quae
48 omnia recipiunt huiusmodi errorem. Fiunt soloecismi et quidem plurimi per partes orationis ; sed
id tradere satis non est, ne ita demum vitium esse
credat puer, si pro alia ponatur alia, ut verbum, ubi
nomen esse debuerit, vel adverbium, ubi pronomen,
49 et similia. Nam sunt quaedam cognata, ut dicunt,
id est eiusdem generis, in quibus, qui alia specie
quam oportet utetur, non minus quam ipso genere
50 permutato deliquerit. Nam et *an* et *aut* coniunctiones sunt, male tamen interroges, *hic aut ille sit ;*

---

[1] *Orat.* xlvii. 157.
[2] Lit. "A great little fortune."
[3] *e.g. intus* for *intro,* the *genus* being adverbs of place.

to the form *scripsere,* though I regard *scripserunt* as
the more correct." [1]   Similarly in vocables and 45
nouns *solecisms* occur in connexion with gender,
number and more especially case, by substitution
of one for another. To these may be added
solecisms in the use of comparatives and superlatives,
or the employment of patronymics instead of
possessives and *vice versa.* As for *solecisms* connected 46
with expressions of quantity, there are some who
will regard phrases such as *magnum peculiolum* [2] as a
solecism, because the diminutive is used instead of
the ordinary noun, which implies no diminution.   I
think I should call it a misuse of the diminutive rather
than a *solecism* ; for it is an error of sense, whereas
solecisms are not errors of sense, but rather faulty
combinations of words. As regards participles, 47
solecisms occur in case and gender as with nouns, in
tense as with verbs, and in number as in both.
The pronoun admits of *solecisms* in gender, number
and case.   *Solecisms* also occur with great fre- 48
quency in connexion with parts of speech : but
a bare statement on this point is not sufficient,
as it may lead a boy to think that such error
consists only in the substitution of one part of
speech for another, as for instance if a verb is
placed where we require a noun, or an adverb takes
the place of a pronoun and so on. For there are 49
some nouns which are cognate, that is to say of the
same *genus,* and he who uses the wrong *species* [3] in
connexion with one of these will be guilty of the
same offence as if he were to change the *genus.*
Thus *an* and *aut* are conjunctions, but it would be 50
bad Latin to say in a question *hic aut ille sit* [4]; *ne* and

---

[4] For *hic an ille sit ?*

et *ne* ac *non* adverbia; qui tamen dicat pro illo "*ne
feceris*" "*non feceris*," in idem incidat vitium, quia
alterum negandi est alterum vetandi.   Hoc amplius
intro et *intus* loci adverbia, *eo* tamen *intus* et *intro*
51 *sum* soloecismi sunt.   Eadem in diversitate prono-
minum, interiectionum, praepositionum accident;
est etiam soloecismus in oratione comprehensionis
unius sequentium ac priorum inter se inconveniens
52 positio.   Quaedam tamen et faciem soloecismi
habent et dici vitiosa non possunt, ut *tragoedia
Thyestes* et *ludi Floralia* ac *Megalensia,* quanquam
haec sequenti tempore interciderunt nunquam aliter
a veteribus dicta.   Schemata igitur nominabuntur,
frequentiora quidem apud poetas sed oratoribus
53 quoque permissa.   Verum schema fere habebit
aliquam rationem, ut docebimus eo, quem paulo
ante promisimus, loco.   Sed id quoque, quod
schema vocatur, si ab aliquo per imprudentiam
54 factum erit, soloecismi vitio non carebit.   In eadem
specie sunt sed schemate carent, ut supra dixi,
nomina feminina, quibus mares utuntur, et neutralia,
quibus feminae.   Hactenus de soloecismo.   Neque
enim artem grammaticam componere aggressi sumus,
sed cum in ordinem incurreret, inhonoratam transire
noluimus.
55   Hoc amplius, ut institutum ordinem sequar, verba

---

[1] The meaning of this passage is uncertain, but the
solecism in question is probably an anacoluthon.

non are adverbs : but he who says *non feceris* in lieu of *ne feceris,* is guilty of a similar mistake, since one negative denies, while the other forbids. Further *intro* and *intus* are adverbs of place, but *eo intus* and *intro sum* are solecisms. Similar errors may be 51 committed in connexion with the various kinds of pronouns, interjections and prepositions. It is also a *solecism*[1] if there is a disagreement between what precedes and what follows within the limits of a single clause. Some phrases have all the appearance 52 of a *solecism* and yet cannot be called faulty ; take for instance phrases such as *tragoedia Thyestes* or *ludi Floralia* and *Megalensia*[2] : although these are never found in later times, they are the rule in ancient writers. We will therefore style them *figures* and, though their use is more frequent in poets, will not deny their employment even to orators. Figures however will generally have some justification, 53 as I shall show in a later portion of this work, which I promised you a little while back.[3] I must however point out that a figure, if used unwittingly, will be a *solecism.* In the same class, though they 54 cannot be called figures, come errors such as the use of masculine names with a female termination and feminine names with a neuter termination. I have said enough about *solecisms* ; for I did not set out to write a treatise on grammar, but was unwilling to slight the science by passing it by without salutation, when it met me in the course of my journey.

I therefore resume the path which I prescribed 55 for myself and point out that words are either

[2] Where strict grammar would require *tragoedia Thyestis, ludi Florales, Megalenses.* The normal usage would be simply to say *Thyestes, Floralia, Megalensia.*

[3] I. iv. 24. The promise is fulfilled in Book IX.

aut Latina aut peregrina sunt. Peregrina porro ex
omnibus prope dixerim gentibus ut homines, ut in-
56 stituta etiam multa venerunt. Taceo de Tuscis et
Sabinis et Praenestinis quoque; nam ut eorum sermone utentem Vettium Lucilius insectatur, quemadmodum Pollio reprehendit in Livio Patavinitatem,
57 licet omnia Italica pro Romanis habeam. Plurima
Gallica evaluerunt ut *raeda* ac *petorritum,* quorum
altero tamen Cicero altero Horatius utitur. Et
mappam circo quoque usitatum nomen Poeni sibi vindicant, et *gurdos,* quos pro stolidis accipit vulgus, ex
58 Hispania duxisse originem audivi. Sed haec divisio
mea ad Graecum sermonem praecipue pertinet, nam
et maxima ex parte Romanus inde conversus est et
confessis quoque Graecis utimur verbis, ubi nostra
desunt, sicut illi a nobis nonnunquam mutuantur.
Inde illa quaestio exoritur, an eadem ratione per
59 casus duci externa qua nostra conveniat. Ac si
reperias grammaticum veterum amatorem, neget
quidquam ex Latina ratione mutandum, quia, cum
sit apud nos casus ablativus, quem illi non habent,
parum conveniat uno casu nostro quinque Graecis
60 uti; quin etiam laudet virtutem eorum, qui poten-
tiorem facere linguam Latinam studebant, nec
alienis egere institutis fatebantur. Inde *Castorem*
media syllaba producta pronuntiarunt, quia hoc
omnibus nostris nominibus accidebat, quorum prima

native or foreign.   Foreign words, like our population
and our institutions, have come to us from practically
every nation upon earth.   I pass by words of Tuscan, 56
Sabine and Praenestine origin; for though Lucilius
attacks Vettius for using them, and Pollio reproves
Livy for his lapses into the dialect of Padua, I may be
allowed to regard all such words as of native origin.
Many Gallic words have become current coin, such 57
as *raeda* (chariot) and *petorritum* (four-wheeled
wagon) of which Cicero uses the former and Horace
the latter.   *Mappa* (napkin) again, a word familiar
in connexion with the circus, is claimed by the
Carthaginians, while I have heard that *gurdus*, which
is colloquially used in the sense of "stupid," is
derived from Spain.   But this distinction between 58
native and foreign words has reference chiefly to
Greek.   For Latin is largely derived from that
language, and we use words which are admittedly
Greek to express things for which we have no Latin
equivalent.   Similarly they at times borrow words
from us.   In this connexion the problem arises
whether foreign words should be declined according
to their language or our own.   If you come across 59
an archaistic grammarian, he will insist on absolute
conformity to Latin practice, because, since we have
an ablative and the Greeks have not, it would be
absurd in declining a word to use five Greek
cases and one Latin.   He will also praise the 60
patriotism of those who aimed at strengthening the
Latin language and asserted that we had no need
of foreign practices.   They, therefore, pronounced
Castorem with the second syllable long to bring it
into conformity with all those Latin nouns which
have the same termination in the nominative as

positio in easdem quas *Castor* litteras exit; et ut
Palaemo ac *Telamo* et *Plato* (nam sic eum Cicero
quoque appellat) dicerentur, retinuerunt, quia
Latinum, quod *o* et *n* litteris finiretur, non reperie-
61 bant. Ne in *a* quidem atque *s* litteras exire temere
masculina Graeca nomina recto casu patiebantur,
ideoque et apud Caelium legimus *Pelia cincinnatus* et
apud Messalam *bene fecit Euthia* et apud Ciceronem
Hermagora, ne miremur, quod ab antiquorum pleris-
62 que *Aenea* ut *Anchisa* sit dictus. Nam si ut *Maecenas*,
Sufenas, *Asprenas* dicerentur, genitivo casu non *e*
littera, sed *tis* syllaba terminarentur. Inde *Olympo*
et *tyranno* acutam syllabam mediam dederunt, quia
duabus longis insequentibus primam brevem acui
63 noster sermo non patitur. Sic genitivus *Ulixi* et
Achilli fecit, sic alia plurima. Nunc recentiores
instituerunt Graecis nominibus Graecas declinationes
potius dare, quod tamen ipsum non semper fieri
potest. Mihi autem placet Latinam rationem sequi,
quousque patitur decor. Neque enim iam *Calypsonem* dixerim ut *Iunonem*, quanquam secutus antiquos,
64 C. Caesar utitur hac ratione declinandi. Sed
auctoritatem consuetudo superavit. In ceteris,
quae poterunt utroque modo non indecenter efferri,
qui Graecam figuram sequi malet, non Latine quidem
sed tamen citra reprehensionem loquetur.
65 Simplices voces prima positione id est natura sua

Castor. They also insisted on the forms *Palaemo,
Telamo,* and *Plato* (the last being adopted by Cicero),
because they could not find any Latin nouns ending
in *-on.* They were reluctant even to permit 61
masculine Greek nouns to end in *-as* in the nominative case, and consequently in Caelius we find *Pelia
cincinnatus* and in Messala *bene fecit Euthia,* and in
Cicero *Hermagora.*[1] So we need not be surprised
that the majority of early writers said *Aenea* and
Anchisa. For, it was urged, if such words are spelt 62
like *Maecenas, Sufenas* and *Asprenas,* the genitive
should terminate in *-tis* not in *-e.* On the same
principle they placed an acute accent on the middle
syllable of *Olympus* and *tyrannus,* because Latin does
not allow an acute accent on the first syllable if it is
short and is followed by two long syllables. So too 63
we get the Latinised genitives *Ulixi* and *Achilli* together with many other analogous forms. More recent
scholars have instituted the practice of giving Greek
nouns their Greek declension, although this is not
always possible. Personally I prefer to follow the
Latin method, so far as grace of diction will permit.
For I should not like to say *Calypsonem* on the analogy
of *Iunonem,* although Gaius Caesar in deference to
antiquity does adopt this way of declining it. Current
practice has however prevailed over his authority. In 64
other words which can be declined in either way
without impropriety, those who prefer it can employ
the Greek form: they will not be speaking Latin,
but will not on the other hand deserve censure.

Simple words are what they are in the nomin- 65
ative, that is, their essential nature. Compound

[1] This form does not actually occur in Cicero, MSS.
evidently wrongly giving *Hermagoras.*

constant, compositae aut praepositionibus subiun-
guntur ut *innocens* (dum ne pugnantibus inter se
duabus, quale est *imperterritus;* alioqui possunt
aliquando continuari duae ut *incompositus, reconditus*
et quo Cicero utitur *subabsurdum*), aut e duobus quasi
66 corporibus coalescunt, ut *maleficus.* Nam ex tribus
nostrae utique linguae non concesserim; quamvis
capsis Cicero dicat compositum esse ex *cape si vis,* et
inveniantur qui *Lupercalia* aeque tres partes orationis
67 esse contendant, quasi *luere per caprum;* nam *Solitaurilia* iam persuasum est esse *Suovetaurilia,* et sane
ita se habet sacrum, quale apud Homerum quoque
est. Sed haec non tam ex tribus quam ex particulis
trium coeunt. Ceterum etiam ex praepositione et
duobus vocabulis dure videtur struxisse Pacuvius
68 *Nerei repandirostrum, incurvicervicum pecus.* Iun-
guntur autem aut ex duobus Latinis integris ut
superfui, subterfugi (quanquam ex integris an composita sint quaeritur), aut ex integro et corrupto ut

---

[1] Quintilian regards the negative *in* as a preposition. His
objection to *imperterritus* (which is used by Vergil) seems
to lie in the fact that while *interritus* is a natural way of
expressing "unterrified," it is unreasonable to negative *per-
territus,* which means "thoroughly terrified." The presence
of the intensifying *per* conflicts with the force of the
negative *in.* [2] *Orat.* xlv. 154.

[3] As in *Od.* xi. 130. The word means sacrifices of a pig,
sheep and bull.

words are formed by the prefix of a preposition as
in *innocens,* though care must be taken that two
conflicting prepositions are not prefixed as in
imperterritus[1]: if this be avoided they may in certain
cases have a double prefix as in *incompositus* or
reconditus or the Ciceronian *subabsurdum.* They may
also be formed by what I might term the combination of two independent units, as in *maleficus.*
For I will not admit that the combination of three 66
is possible at any rate in Latin, although Cicero
asserts that *capsis*[2] is compounded of *cape si vis,* and
there are to be found scholars who contend that
Lupercalia likewise is a compound of three parts of
speech, namely *luere per caprum.* As for *Solitaurilia* 67
it is by now universally believed to stand for
Suovetaurilia, a derivation which corresponds to the
actual sacrifice, which has its counterpart in Homer[3]
as well. But these compounds are formed not so
much from three words as from the fragments of
three. On the other hand Pacuvius seems to have
formed compounds of a preposition and two vocables
(*i.e.* nouns) as in

Nerei repandirostrum incurvicervicum pecus :

" The flock
Of Nereus snout-uplifted, neck-inarched " :

the effect is unpleasing. Compounds are however 68
formed from two complete Latin words, as for instance *superfui* and *subterfugi ;* though in this case
there is some question as to whether the words from
which they are formed are complete.[4] They may
also be formed of one complete and one incomplete

[4] *i.e.* if both elements are complete in themselves is the
word a true compound ?

malevolus, aut **ex** corrupto et integro ut *noctivagus,*
aut ex duobus corruptis ut *pedisecus,* aut ex nostro
et peregrino ut *biclinium,* aut contra ut *epilogium* et
Anticato, aliquando et ex duobus peregrinis ut *epiraedium.*   Nam cum sit praepositio Graeca, *raeda*
Gallicum : neque Graecus tamen neque Gallus utitur
composito ; Romani suum ex alieno utroque fecerunt.

69 Frequenter autem praepositiones quoque compositio
ista corrumpit : inde *abstulit, aufugit, amisit,* cum
praepositio sit *ab* sola ; et *coit,* cum sit praepositio
70 *con ;* sic *ignavi* et *erepublica* et similia.   Sed res tota
magis Graecos decet, nobis minus succedit, nec id
fieri natura puto, sed alienis favemus ; ideoque cum
κυρταύχενα mirati simus, *incurvicervicum* vix a risu
defendimus.

71   Propria sunt verba, cum id significant, in quod
primo denominata sunt ; translata, cum alium natura
intellectum alium loco praebent.   Usitatis tutius
utimur, nova non sine quodam periculo fingimus.
Nam si recepta sunt, modicam laudem adferunt
72 orationi, repudiata etiam in iocos exeunt.   Auden-
dum **tamen** ; namque, ut Cicero ait, etiam quae
primo dura visa sunt, usu molliuntur.   Sed minime
nobis concessa est ὀνοματοποιΐα ; quis enim ferat, si

---

[1] Sometimes written as one word.
[2] *de Nat. deorum,* I. xxxiv. 95.

word, as in the case of *malevolus,* or of one incomplete and one complete, such as *noctivagus,* or of two incomplete words as in *pedisecus* (footman), or from one Latin and one foreign word as in *biclinium* (a dining-couch for two), or in the reverse order as in *epitogium* (an upper garment) or *Anticato,* and sometimes even from two foreign words as in *epiraedium* (a thong attaching the horse to the raeda). For in this last case the preposition is Greek, while *raeda* is Gallic, while the compound is employed neither by Greek nor Gaul, but has been appropriated by Rome from the two foreign tongues. In 69 the case of prepositions they are frequently changed by the act of compounding: as a result we get *abstulit, aufugit, amisit,* though the preposition is *ab,* and *coit,* though the preposition is *con.* The same is true of *ignauus* and *erepublica.*[1] But compounds are 70 better suited to Greek than to Latin, though I do not think that this is due to the nature of our language: the reason rather is that we have a preference for foreign goods, and therefore receive κυρταύχην with applause, whereas we can scarce defend *incurvicervicus* from derisive laughter.

Words are *proper* when they bear their original 71 meaning; *metaphorical,* when they are used in a sense different from their natural meaning. *Current* words are safest to use: there is a spice of danger in coining *new.* For if they are adopted, our style wins but small glory from them; while if they are rejected, they become a subject for jest. Still we 72 must make the venture; for as Cicero[2] says, use softens even these words which at first seemed harsh. On the other hand the power of *onomatopoeia* is denied us. Who would tolerate an attempt to imitate

quid simile illis merito laudatis λίγξε βιός et σίζεν
ὀφθαλμός fingere audeamus? Nam ne *balare* quidem
aut *hinnire* fortiter diceremus, nisi iudicio vetustatis
niterentur.

VI. Est etiam sua loquentibus observatio, sua
scribentibus. Sermo constat ratione vel vetustate,
auctoritate, consuetudine. Rationem praestat praecipue analogia, nonnunquam et etymologia. Vetera
maiestas quaedam et, ut sic dixerim, religio com-
2 mendat. Auctoritas ab oratoribus vel historicis peti
solet; nam poetas metri necessitas excusat, nisi
si quando nihil impediente in utroque modulatione
pedum alterum malunt, qualia sunt, *imo de stirpe
recisum*, et *aëriae quo congessere palumbes* et *silice in
nuda* et similia; cum summorum in eloquentia
virorum iudicium pro ratione, et velut error honestus
3 est magnos duces sequentibus. Consuetudo vero
certissima loquendi magistra, utendumque plane
sermone ut nummo, cui publica forma est. Omnia
tamen haec exigunt acre iudicium, analogia praecipue, quam proxime ex Graeco transferentes in
4 Latinum proportionem vocaverunt. Eius haec vis
est, ut id quod dubium est ad aliquid simile, de quo
non quaeritur, referat et incerta certis probet.
Quod efficitur duplici via: comparatione similium
in extremis maxime syllabis, propter quod ea quae

---

[1] Homer, *Il.* iv. 125.   [2] *Od.* ix. 394.
[3] *Aen.* xii. 208 : "cut away from the lowest root." *Ecl.* iii.
69 : "where airy doves have made their nest." *Ecl.* i. 15 :
"on the naked rock." *Stirps, palumbes* and *silex* are usually
masculine.

phrases like the much praised λίγξε βιός,[1] "the
bow twanged," and σίζεν ὀφθαλμός,[2] "the eye
hissed"? We should even feel some qualms about
using *balare* "to baa," and *hinnire*, "to whinny," if
we had not the sanction of antiquity to support us.

VI. There are special rules which must be observed both by speakers and writers. Language is
based on reason, antiquity, authority and usage.
Reason finds its chief support in analogy and sometimes in etymology. As for antiquity, it is commended to us by the possession of a certain majesty, I
might almost say sanctity. Authority as a rule we **2**
derive from orators and historians. For poets, owing
to the necessities of metre, are allowed a certain
licence except in cases where they deliberately
choose one of two expressions, when both are metri-
cally possible, as for instance in *imo de stirpe recisum*
and *aeriae quo congessere palumbes* or *silice in nuda*[3]
and the like. The judgment of a supreme orator
is placed on the same level as reason, and even error
brings no disgrace, if it result from treading in the
footsteps of such distinguished guides. Usage **3**
however is the surest pilot in speaking, and we
should treat language as currency minted with
the public stamp. But in all these cases we have
need of a critical judgment, especially as regards
analogy (a Greek term for which a Latin equivalent
has been found in *proportion*). The essence of *analogy* **4**
is the testing of all subjects of doubt by the application of some standard of comparison about which
there is no question, the proof that is to say of the
uncertain by reference to the certain. This can be
done in two different ways: by comparing similar
words, paying special attention to their final syllables

sunt e singulis negantur debere rationem, et demi-
5 nutione.   Comparatio   in   nominibus   aut   genus
deprehendit aut declinationem; genus, ut si quaeratur, *funis* masculinum sit an femininum, simile illi
sit *panis*; declinationem, ut si veniat in dubium,
hac domu dicendum sit an *hac domo* et *domuum* an
6 *domorum :* similia sint [domus] *anus, manus.* Demi-
nutio genus modo detegit, et, ne ab eodem exemplo
recedam, *funem* masculinum esse *funiculus* ostendit.
7 Eadem in verbis quoque ratio comparationis, ut, si
quis antiquos secutus *fervere* brevi media syllaba
dicat, deprehendatur vitiose loqui, quod omnia, quae
e et *o* litteris fatendi modo terminantur, eadem, si
infinitis *e* litteram media syllaba acceperunt, utique
productam habent: *prandeo pendeo spondeo, prandere*
8 *pendere spondere.* At quae *o* solam habent, dummodo
per eandem litteram in infinito exeant, brevia fiunt:
lego dico curro, legere dicere currere; etiamsi est apud
Lucilium *Fervit aqua et fervet, fervit nunc, fervet ad*
9 *annum.* Sed, pace dicere hominis eruditissimi liceat,
si *fervit* putat illi simile *currit* et *legit, fervo* dicetur
ut *lego* et *curro,* quod nobis inauditum est. Sed non
est haec vera comparatio; nam *fervit* est illi simile

---

¹ *sc.* because two monosyllables, unless identical, cannot
have the same final syllable.   **²** In Book IX.

(hence monosyllables are asserted to lie outside the domain of *analogy*[1]) and by the study of diminutives. Comparison of nouns will reveal either their gender 5 or their declension: in the first case, supposing the question is raised as to whether *funis* be masculine or feminine, *panis* will supply a standard of comparison: in the second case, supposing we are in doubt as to whether we should say *hac domu* or *hac domo*, *domuum* or *domorum*, the standard of comparison will be found in words such as *anus* or *manus*. Diminutives 6 merely reveal the gender: for instance, to return to a word previously used as an illustration, *funiculus* proves that *funis* is masculine. The same standard 7 may be applied in the case of verbs. For instance if it should be asserted that the middle syllable of *fervere* is short, we can prove this to be an error, because all verbs which in the indicative terminate in *-eo*, make the middle syllable of the infinitive long, if that syllable contain an *e*: take as examples such verbs as *prandeo, pendeo, spondeo* with infinitives *prandēre, pendēre, spondēre*. Those verbs, however, 8 which terminate in *-o* alone, if they form the infinitive in *e*, have the *e* short; compare *lego, dico, curro*, with the infinitives, *legĕre, dicĕre, currĕre*. I admit that in Lucilius we find—

fervit aqua et fervet: fervit nunc fervet ad annum. [2]

"The water boils and boil it will; it boils and for a year will boil."

But with all due respect to so learned a man, if he regards *fervit* as on the same footing as *currit* and *legit*, we shall say *fervo* as we say *lego* and *curro*: 9 but such a form has never yet come to my ears. But this is not a true comparison: for *fervit* re-

servit, quam proportionem sequenti dicere necesse est
10 *fervire* ut *servire*. Prima quoque aliquando positio ex
obliquis invenitur, ut memoria repeto convictos a me,
qui reprehenderant, quod hoc verbo usus essem,
pepigi; nam id quidem dixisse summos auctores con-
fitebantur, rationem tamen negabant permittere,
quia prima positio *paciscor,* cum haberet naturam
patiendi, faceret tempore praeterito *pactus sum.*
11 Nos praeter auctoritatem oratorum atque historicorum analogia quoque dictum hoc tuebamur. Nam
cum legeremus in XII tabulis *ni ita pacunt,* invenie-
bamus simile huic *cadunt,* inde prima positio, etiamsi
vetustate exoleverat, apparebat *paco* ut *cado,* unde
12 non erat dubium sic *pepigi* nos dicere ut *cecidi.* Sed
meminerimus non per omnia duci analogiae posse
rationem, cum et sibi ipsa plurimis in locis repugnet.
Quaedam sine dubio conantur eruditi defendere, ut,
cum deprehensum est, *lepus* et *lupus* similia positione
quantum casibus numerisque dissentiant: ista re-
spondent non esse paria, quia *lepus* epicoenon sit,
lupus masculinum; quanquam Varro in eo libro, quo
initia Romanae urbis enarrat, *lupum feminam* dicit
13 Ennium Pictoremque Fabium secutus. Illi autem
iidem, cum interrogantur, cur *aper apri* et *pater patris*
faciat, illud nomen positum, hoc ad aliquid esse
contendunt. Praeterea quoniam utrumque a Graeco

sembles *servit*, and on this analogy we should say *fervire* like *servire*. It is also possible in certain 10 cases to discover the present indicative of a verb from the study of its other tenses. I remember, for instance, refuting certain scholars who criticised me for using the word *pepigi*: for, although they admitted that it had been used by some of the best authors, they asserted that it was an irrational form because the present indicative *paciscor*, being passive in form, made *pactus sum* as its perfect. I in addition 11 to quoting the authority of orators and historians maintained that I was also supported by analogy. For when I found *ni ita pacunt* in the Twelve Tables, I noted that *cadunt* provided a parallel: it was clear therefore that the present indicative, though now obsolete, was *paco* on the analogy of *cado*, and it was further obvious that we say *pepigi* for just the same reason that we say *cecidi*. But we must 12 remember that *analogy* cannot be universally applied, as it is often inconsistent with itself. It is true indeed that scholars have attempted to justify certain apparent anomalies: for example, when it is noted to what an extent *lepus* and *lupus*, which resemble each other closely in the nominative, differ in the plural and in the other cases, they reply that they are not true parallels, since *lepus* is *epicene*, while *lupus* is masculine, although Varro in the book in which he narrates the origins of Rome, writes *lupus femina*, following the precedent of Ennius and Fabius Pictor. The same scholars, however, when 13 asked why *aper* became *apri* in the genitive, but *pater patris*, asserted that *aper* was an absolute, *pater* a relative noun. Further since both words derive from the Greek, they took refuge in the fact

ductum sit, ad eam rationem recurrunt, ut πατρὸς
14 patris, κάπρου apri faciat. Illa tamen quomodo
effugient, ut, nomina quamvis feminina singulari
nominativo us litteris finita nunquam genitivo casu
ris syllaba terminentur, faciat tamen Venus Veneris?
item cum es litteris finita per varios exeant genitivos,
nunquam tamen eadem ris syllaba terminatos, Ceres
15 cogat dici Cereris? Quid vero? quod tota positionis
eiusdem in diversos flexus eunt? cum Alba faciat
Albanos et Albenses, volo volui et volavi. Nam praeterito quidem tempore varie formari verba prima
persona o littera terminata, ipsa analogia confiteatur;
siquidem facit cado cecidi, spondeo spopondi, pingo pinxi,
16 lego legi, pono posui, frango fregi, laudo laudavi. Non
enim, cum primum fingerentur homines, analogia
demissa caelo formam loquendi dedit, sed inventa
est postquam loquebantur, et notatum in sermone
quid quomodo caderet. Itaque non ratione nititur
sed exemplo, nec lex est loquendi sed observatio, ut
ipsam analogiam nulla res alia fecerit quam consuetudo.
17 Inhaerent tamen ei quidam molestissima diligentiae
perversitate, ut audaciter potius dicant quam audacter,
licet omnes oratores aliud sequantur, et emicavit non
emicuit et conire non coire. His permittamus et
audivisse et scivisse et tribunale et faciliter dicere;
frugalis quoque sit apud illos non frugi, nam quo alio
18 modo fiet frugalitas? Iidem centum milia nummum et
fidem Deum ostendant duplices quoque soloecismos

---

[1] i.e. nummum and deum should, strictly speaking, be
accus. singular.

that πατρός provides a parallel to *patris* and κάπρου
to *apri*. But how will they evade the difficulty 14
that feminine nouns whose nominative singular
ends in -*us* never make the genitive end in -*ris*,
and yet the genitive of *Venus* is *Veneris*: again
nouns ending in -*es* have various genitive terminations, but never end in -*ris*, but yet we have
no choice but to make the genitive of *Ceres Cereris*?
Again what of those words which, although identi- 15
cal in the form of the nominative or present indicative, develop the utmost variety in their inflections.
Thus from *Alba* we get both *Albanus* and *Albensis*,
from *volo* both *volui* and *volavi*. Analogy itself
admits that verbs whose present indicative ends in
-*o* have a great variety of perfect formations, as
for instance *cado cecidi, spondeo spopondi, pingo pinxi,
lego legi, pono posui, frango fregi, laudo laudavi*. For 16
analogy was not sent down from heaven at the
creation of mankind to frame the rules of language,
but was discovered after they began to speak and to
note the terminations of words used in speech. It
is therefore based not on reason but on example,
nor is it a law of language, but rather a practice
which is observed, being in fact the offspring of
usage. Some scholars, however, are so perverse and 17
obstinate in their passion for analogy, that they say
audaciter in preference to *audacter*, the form preferred
by all orators, and *emicavit* for *emicuit*, and *conire*
for *coire*. We may permit them to say *audivisse,
scivisse, tribunale* and *faciliter*, nor will we deprive
them of *frugalis* as an alternative for *frugi*: for
from what else can *frugalitas* be formed? They may 18
also be allowed to point out that phrases such as
centum milia nummum and *fidem deum*[1] involve a

esse, quando et casum mutant et numerum; nescie-
bamus enim ac non consuetudini et decori servie-
bamus, sicut in plurimis, quae M. Tullius in Oratore
19 divine ut omnia exequitur. Sed Augustus quoque
in epistulis ad C. Caesarem scriptis emendat, quod is
calidum dicere quam *caldum* malit, non quia id non
sit Latinum sed quia sit odiosum et, ut ipse Graeco
20 verbo significavit, περίεργον. Atqui hanc quidam
ὀρθοέπειαν solam putant, quam ego minime excludo.
Quid enim tam necessarium quam recta locutio?
Immo inhaerendum ei iudico, quoad licet, diu etiam
mutantibus repugnandum; sed abolita atque abrogata
retinere insolentiae cuiusdam est et frivolae in parvis
21 iactantiae. Multum enim litteratus, qui sine aspiratione et producta secunda syllaba salutarit (*avere* est
enim) et *calefacere* dixerit potius, quam quod dicimus,
et *conservavisse,* his adiiciat *face* et *dice* et similia.
22 Recta est haec via; quis negat? sed adiacet et
mollior et magis trita. Ego tamen non alio magis
angor, quam quod obliquis casibus ducti etiam primas
sibi positiones non invenire sed mutare permittunt:
ut cum *ebur* et *robur,* ita dicta ac scripta summis
auctoribus, in *o* litteram secundae syllabae trans-
ferunt, quia sit *roboris* et *eboris, sulpur* autem et
guttur u litteram in genitivo servent; ideoque *iecur*
23 etiam et *femur* controversiam fecerunt. Quod non

---

[1] xlvi. 155.
[2] For *havĕ, calfacere, conservasse.*

double solecism, since they change both case and
number. Of course we were in blank ignorance
of the fact and were not simply conforming to usage
and the demands of elegance, as in the numerous
cases, with which Cicero deals magnificently, as
always, in his *Orator*.[1] Augustus again in his letters 19
to Gaius Caesar corrects him for preferring *calidus*
to *caldus*, not on the ground that the former is not
Latin, but because it is unpleasing and as he himself
puts it in Greek περίεργον (affected). Some hold 20
that this is just a question of ὀρθοέπεια or correctness
of speech, a subject to which I am far from being
indifferent. For what can be more necessary than
that we should speak correctly? Nay, I even think
that, as far as possible, we should cling to correct
forms and resist all tendencies to change. But to
attempt to retain forms long obsolete and extinct
is sheer impertinence and ostentatious pedantry.
I would suggest that the ripe scholar, who says "*ave*" 21
without the aspirate and with a long *e* (for it comes
from *avēre*), and uses *calefacere* and *conservavisse* in
preference to the usual forms,[2] should also add *face*,
dice and the like to his vocabulary. His way is the 22
right way. Who doubts it? But there is an easier
and more frequented path close by. There is,
however, nothing which annoys me more than their
habit not merely of inferring the nominative from
the oblique cases, but of actually altering it. For
instance in *ebur* and *robur*, the forms regularly used
both in writing and speech by the best authors,
these gentlemen change their second syllable to *o*,
because their genitives are *roboris* and *eboris*, and because *sulpur* and *guttur* keep the *u* in the genitive. So
too *femur* and *iecur* give rise to similar controversy.

minus est licentiosum, quam si *sulpuri* et *gutturi*
subiicerent in genitivo litteram *o* mediam, quia esset
eboris et *roboris*; sicut Antonius Gnipho, qui *robur*
quidem et *ebur* atque etiam *marmur* fatetur esse,
verum fieri vult ex his *robura, ebura, marmura.*

24 Quodsi animadverterent litterarum adfinitatem,
scirent sic ab eo, quod est *robur, roboris* fieri, quomodo ab eo, quod est *miles limes, militis limitis, iudex
vindex, iudicis vindicis,* et quae supra iam attigi.

25 Quid vero quod, ut dicebam, similes positiones in
longe diversas figuras per obliquos casus exeunt, ut
virgo Iuno, fusus lusus, cuspis puppis et mille alia?
cum illud etiam accidat, ut quaedam pluraliter non
dicantur, quaedam contra singulari numero, quaedam
casibus careant, quaedam a primis statim positionibus

26 tota mutentur, ut *Iuppiter.* Quod verbis etiam
accidit ut illi *fero,* cuius praeteritum perfectum et
ulterius non invenitur. Nec plurimum refert, nulla
haec an praedura sint. Nam quid *progenies* genitivo
singulari, quid plurali *spes* faciet? Quomodo autem
quire et *ruere* vel in praeterita patiendi modo vel in

27 participia transibunt? Quid de aliis dicam, cum
senatus *senati* an *senatus* faciat, incertum sit? Quare
mihi non invenuste dici videtur, aliud esse Latine
aliud grammatice loqui. Ac de analogia nimium.

28 Etymologia, quae verborum originem inquirit, a

Their proceedings are just as arbitrary as if they 23
were to substitute an *o* in the genitives of *sulpur*
and *guttur* on the analogy of *eboris* and *roboris*.
Thus Antonius Gnipho while admitting *robur, ebur*
and even *marmur* to be correct, would have their
plurals to be *ebura, robura* and *marmura*. If they 24
would only pay attention to the affinities existing
between letters, they would realize that *robur* makes
its genitive *roboris* in precisely the same way that
limes, miles, iudex and *uindex* make their genitives
militis, limitis, iudicis and *uindicis*, not to mention other
words to which I have already referred. Do not nouns 25
which are similar in the nominative show, as I have
already observed, quite different terminations in the
oblique cases? Compare *uirgo* and *Iuno, lusus* and
fusus, cuspis and *puppis* and a thousand others.
Again some nouns are not used in the plural, while
others are not used in the singular, some are inde-
clinable, while others, like *Jupiter,* in the oblique
cases entirely abandon the form of the nominative. 26
The same is true of verbs: for instance *fero* dis-
appears in the perfect and subsequent tenses. Nor
does it matter greatly whether such forms are non-
existent or too harsh to use. For what is the genitive singular of *progenies* or the genitive plural of *spes*?
Or how will *quire* and *ruere* form a perfect passive or
passive participles. Why should I mention other 27
words when it is even doubtful whether the genitive
of *senatus* is *senati* or *senatus*? In view of what I
have said, it seems to me that the remark, that it
is one thing to speak Latin and another to speak
grammar, was far from unhappy. So much for
analogy, of which I have said more than enough.

Etymology inquires into the origin of words, and 28

Cicerone dicta est notatio, quia nomen eius apud
Aristotelem invenitur σύμβολον, quod est nota; nam
verbum ex verbo ductum, id est veriloquium, ipse
Cicero, qui finxit, reformidat. Sunt qui vim potius
29 intuiti originationem vocent. Haec habet aliquando
usum necessarium, quotiens interpretatione res, de
qua quaeritur, eget, ut M. Caelius se esse hominem
frugi vult probare, non quia abstinens sit (nam
id ne ementiri quidem poterat), sed quia utilis
multis, id est fructuosus, unde sit ducta *frugalitas*.
Ideoque in definitionibus assignatur etymologiae
30 locus. Nonnunquam etiam barbara ab emendatis
conatur discernere, ut cum, *Triquetram* dici Siciliam
an *Triquedram, meridiem* an *medidiem* oporteat quae-
31 ritur, aliaque quae consuetudini serviunt. Continet
autem in se multam eruditionem, sive ex Graecis
orta tractemus, quae sunt plurima, praecipueque
Aeolica ratione (cui est sermo noster simillimus)
declinata, sive ex historiarum veterum notitia nomina
hominum, locorum, gentium, urbium requiramus,
unde *Bruti, Publicolae, Pythici*? cur *Latium, Italia,
Beneventum*? quae *Capitolium* et collem *Quirinalem* et
Argiletum appellandi ratio?
32 Iam illa minora, in quibus maxime studiosi eius

---

1 *Top.* viii. 35.   2 περὶ ἑρμ. 2.
3 For derivations see Index of Names at end.

was called *notation* by Cicero,[1] on the ground that
the term used by Aristotle[2] is σύμβολον, which may
be translated by *nota*. A literal rendering of ἐτυμολογία
would be *ueriloquium*, a form which even Cicero, its
inventor, shrinks from using. Some again, with an
eye to the meaning of the word, call it *origination*.
Etymology is sometimes of the utmost use, when- 29
ever the word under discussion needs interpretation.
For instance Marcus Caelius wishes to prove that he
is *homo frugi*, not because he is abstemious (for he
could not even pretend to be that), but because he
is useful to many, that is *fructuosus*, from which
frugalitas is derived. Consequently we find room
for etymology when we are concerned with definitions. Sometimes again this science attempts to 30
distinguish between correct forms and *barbarisms*, as
for instance when we are discussing whether we
should call Sicily *Triquetra* or *Triquedra*, or say
meridies or *medidies*, not to mention other words
which depend on current usage. Such a science 31
demands profound erudition, whether we are dealing with the large number of words which are
derived from the Greek, more especially those
inflected according to the practice of the Aeolic
dialect, the form of Greek which most nearly
resembles Latin; or are using ancient historians as
a basis for inquiry into the origin of names of men,
places, nations and cities. For instance what is the
origin of names such as *Brutus, Publicola*, or *Pythicus*?
Why do we speak of *Latium, Italia* or *Beneventum*?
What is the reason for employing such names as
Capitolium, collis Quirinalis or *Argiletum*?[3]

I now turn to minor points concerning which 32
enthusiasts for etymology give themselves an

rei fatigantur, qui verba paulum declinata varie et
multipliciter ad veritatem reducunt aut correptis aut
porrectis, aut adiectis aut detractis, aut permutatis
litteris syllabisve.   Inde pravis ingeniis ad foedissima
usque ludibria labuntur.   Sit enim *Consul* a consu-
lendo vel a iudicando; nam et hoc *consulere* veteres
vocaverunt, unde adhuc remanet illud *rogat boni*
33 *consulas,* id est bonum iudices.   *Senatui* nomen
dederit aetas (nam iidem *Patres* sunt), et *rex rector*
et alia plurima indubitata; nec abnuerim *tegulae*
*regulae*que et similium his rationem.   Iam sit et
classis a calando et *lepus levipes* et *vulpes volipes*:
34 etiamne a contrariis aliqua sinemus trahi, ut *lucus,*
quia umbra opacus parum luceat, et *ludus,* quia sit
longissime a lusu, et *Ditis,* quia minime *dives?*
etiamne *hominem* appellari, quia sit *humo* natus (quasi
vero non omnibus animalibus eadem origo, aut illi
primi mortales ante nomen imposuerint terrae quam
35 sibi), et *verba* ab aere *verberato?*   Pergamus: sic
perveniemus eo usque, ut *stella* luminis *stilla* credatur,

infinity of trouble, restoring to their true form words
which have become slightly altered : the methods
which they employ are varied and manifold : they
shorten them or lengthen them, add, remove, or
interchange letters and syllables as the case may be.
As a result perverseness of judgment leads to the
most hideous absurdities.   I am ready to admit that
consul may be derived from *consulere* in the sense of
consulting or judging ; for the ancients used *consulere* in the latter sense, and it still survives in the
phrase *rogat boni consulas,* that is *bonum iudices,* "judge
fit."   Again *senatus* may well be derived from old 33
age (for the senators are called "the fathers") :
I concur in the derivations assigned to *rex rector*
to say nothing of many other words where there
can be no doubt, and do not refuse to accept those
suggested for *tegula, regula* and the like : let *classis*
be from *calare* (call out, summon), *lepus* be a contraction of *levipes* and *vulpes* of *volipes.*   But are we 34
also to admit the derivation of certain words from
their opposites, and accept *lucus a non lucendo,* since
a grove is dark with shade, *ludus* in the sense of
school as being so called because it is quite the
reverse of "play" and *Dis, Ditis* from *diues,* because
Pluto is far from being rich ?   Are we to assent to
the view that *homo* is derived from *humus,* because
man sprang from the earth, as though all other
living things had not the same origin or as if
primitive man gave the earth a name before giving
one to himself ?   Or again can *verbum* be derived
from *aer verberatus,* "beaten air"?   Let us go a 35
little further and we shall find that *stella* is believed
to be *stilla luminis* "a drop of light," a derivation
whose author is so famous in literature that it would

cuius etymologiae auctorem clarum sane in litteris
nominari in ea parte, qua a me reprehenditur, inhu-
36 manum est. Qui vero talia libris complexi sunt,
nomina sua ipsi inscripserunt; ingenioseque visus
est Gavius *caelibes* dicere veluti *caelites,* quod onere
gravissimo vacent, idque Graeco argumento iuvit,
ἠίθεους enim eadem de causa dici affirmat. Nec ei
cedit Modestus inventione, nam, quia *Caelo* Saturnus
genitalia absciderit, hoc nomine appellatos, qui
uxore careant, ait; Aelius *pituitam,* quia *petat vitam.*
37 Sed cui non post Varronem sit venia, qui *agrum,* quia
in eo *agatur* aliquid, et *graculos,* quia *gregatim* volent,
dictos Ciceroni persuadere voluit (ad eum enim
scribit), cum alterum ex Graeco sit manifestum duci,
38 alterum ex vocibus avium? Sed hoc tanti fuit
vertere, ut *merula,* quia sola volat, quasi *mera volans*
nominaretur. Quidam non dubitaverunt etymologiae
subiicere omnem nominis causam: ut ex habitu,
quemadmodum dixi, *Longos* et *Rufos,* ex sono *strepere,
murmurare;* etiam derivata, ut a *velocitate* dicitur
velox, et composita pluraque his similia, quae sine
dubio aliunde originem ducunt, sed arte non

---

[1] *de Lingua Lat.* v. 34 and 76.

[2] The above makes Quintilian derive *velox* from *velocitas,*
as Varro (*L.L.* viii. 15) derives *prudens* from *prudentia.*
Those who regard this as incredible must with Colson
transpose *ut . . . velox* to follow *Rufos* making *Velox* a cognomen, or with Meister read *velo* for *velocitate,* or *velo citato*
(Colson).

be unkind to mention his name in connexion with a
point where he comes in for censure. But those 36
who collected such derivations in book form, put
their names on the title page; and Gavius thought
himself a perfect genius when he identified *caelibes,*
"bachelors," with *caelites,* "gods," on the ground
that they are free from a heavy load of care, and
supported this opinion by a Greek analogy: for he
asserted that ἠίθεοι, "young men," had a precisely
similar origin. Modestus is not his inferior in
inventive power: for he asserts that *caelibes,* that is
to say unmarried men, are so called because Saturn
cut off the genital organs of *Caelus.* Aelius asserts
that *pituita,* "phlegm," is so called *quia petat uitam,*
because it attacks life. But we may pardon anyone 37
after the example set by Varro.[1] For he tried to
persuade Cicero, to whom he dedicated his work,
that a field was called *ager* because something is
done in it (*agitur*), and jackdaws *graculos* because
they fly in flocks (*gregatim*), in spite of the obvious
fact that the first word is derived from the Greek,
the latter from the cry of the bird in question.
But Varro had such a passion for derivations that he 38
derived the name *merula* "a blackbird" from *mera
uolans* on the ground that it flies alone! Some
scholars do not hesitate to have recourse to *etymology*
for the origin of every word, deriving names such as
Rufus or *Longus* from the appearance of their
possessor, verbs such as *strepere* or *murmurare* from
the sounds which they represent, and even ex-
tending this practice to certain derivatives, making
uelox for instance find its origin in *uelocitas,*[2] as well
as to compounds and the like: now although such
words doubtless have an origin, no special science is

egent, cuius in hoc opere non est usus nisi in dubiis.

39   Verba a vetustate repetita non solum magnos assertores habent sed etiam adferunt orationi maiestatem aliquam non sine delectatione; nam et auctoritatem antiquitatis habent et, quia intermissa

40   sunt, gratiam novitati similem parant. Sed opus est modo, ut neque crebra sint haec neque manifesta, quia nihil est odiosius adfectatione, nec utique ab ultimis et iam oblitteratis repetita temporibus, qualia sunt *topper* et *antegerio* et *exanclare* et *prosapia* et Saliorum carmina vix sacerdotibus suis satis

41   intellecta. Sed illa mutari vetat religio et consecratis utendum est; oratio vero, cuius summa virtus est perspicuitas, quam sit vitiosa, si egeat interprete? Ergo, ut novorum optima erunt maxime vetera, ita veterum maxime nova.

42   Similis circa auctoritatem ratio. Nam etiamsi potest videri nihil peccare, qui utitur iis verbis, quae summi auctores tradiderunt, multum tamen refert non solum, quid dixerint, sed etiam quid persuaserint. Neque enim *tuburchinabundum* et *lurchinabundum* iam in nobis quisquam ferat, licet Cato sit auctor, nec *hos lodices*, quanquam id Pollioni placet, nec *gladiola*, atqui Messala dixit, nec *par-*

required to detect it, since it is only doubtful cases
that demand the intervention of the etymologist.

Archaic words not only enjoy the patronage of 39
distinguished authors, but also give style a certain
majesty and charm.   For they have the authority of
age behind them, and for the very reason that they
have fallen into desuetude, produce an attractive
effect not unlike that of novelty.   But such words 40
must be used sparingly and must not thrust themselves upon our notice, since there is nothing more
tiresome than affectation, nor above all must they be
drawn from remote and forgotten ages : I refer to
words such as *topper*, " quite," *antegerio*, " exceed-
ingly," *exanclare*, " to exhaust," *prosapia*, " a race "
and the language of the Salian Hymns now scarcely
understood by its own priests.   Religion, it is true, 41
forbids us to alter the words of these hymns and
we must treat them as sacred things.   But what a
faulty thing is speech, whose prime virtue is clearness, if it requires an interpreter to make its meaning
plain !   Consequently in the case of old words the
best will be those that are newest, just as in the
case of new words the best will be the oldest.

The same arguments apply to authority.   For 42
although the use of words transmitted to us by the
best authors may seem to preclude the possibility
of error, it is important to notice not merely what
they said, but what words they succeeded in sanction-
ing.   For no one to-day would introduce words such
as *tuburchinabundus*, " voracious," or *lurchinabundus*,
" guzzling," although they have the authority of
Cato ;   nor make *lodices*, " blankets," masculine,
though Pollio preferred that gender; nor say *gladiola*, " small swords," though Messala used this plural,

ricidatum, quod in Caelio vix tolerabile videtur, nec *collos* mihi Calvus persuaserit; quae nec ipsi iam dicerent.

43 Superest igitur consuetudo; nam fuerit paene ridiculum malle sermonem, quo locuti sint homines, quam quo loquantur. Et sane quid est aliud vetus sermo quam vetus loquendi consuetudo? Sed huic ipsi necessarium est iudicium, constituendumque in primis id ipsum quid sit, quod consuetudinem 44 vocemus. Quae si ex eo, quod plures faciunt, nomen accipiat, periculosissimum dabit praeceptum, non orationi modo sed (quod maius est) vitae. Unde enim tantum boni, ut pluribus quae recta sunt placeant? Igitur ut velli et comam in gradus frangere et in balneis perpotare, quamlibet haec invaserint civitatem, non erit consuetudo, quia nihil horum caret reprehensione; at lavamur et tondemur et convivimus ex consuetudine: sic in loquendo, non si quid vitiose multis insederit, pro 45 regula sermonis accipiendum erit. Nam, ut transeam, quemadmodum vulgo imperiti loquantur, tota saepe theatra et omnem circi turbam exclamasse barbare scimus. Ergo consuetudinem sermonis vocabo consensum eruditorum, sicut vivendi consensum bonorum.

nor *parricidatus* for parricide, a form which can scarcely be tolerated even in Caelius, nor will Calvus persuade me to speak of *collos*, "necks." Indeed, were these authors alive to-day, they would never use such words.

Usage remains to be discussed. For it would be 43 almost laughable to prefer the language of the past to that of the present day, and what is ancient speech but ancient usage of speaking? But even here the critical faculty is necessary, and we must make up our minds what we mean by usage. If it 44 be defined merely as the practice of the majority, we shall have a very dangerous rule affecting not merely style but life as well, a far more serious matter. For where is so much good to be found that what is right should please the majority? The practices of depilation, of dressing the hair in tiers, or of drinking to excess at the baths, although they may have thrust their way into society, cannot claim the support of usage, since there is something to blame in all of them (although we have usage on our side when we bathe or have our hair cut or take our meals together). So too in speech we must not accept as a rule of language words and phrases that have become a vicious habit with a number of persons. To say nothing of the 45 language of the uneducated, we are all of us well aware that whole theatres and the entire crowd of spectators will often commit *barbarisms* in the cries which they utter as one man. I will therefore define usage in speech as the agreed practice of educated men, just as where our way of life is concerned I should define it as the agreed practice of all good men.

VII. Nunc, quoniam diximus, quae sit loquendi
regula, dicendum, quae scribentibus custodienda,
quod Graeci ὀρθογραφίαν vocant; hoc nos recte scribendi scientiam nominemus. Cuius ars non in hoc
posita est, ut noverimus, quibus quaeque syllaba litteris
constet (nam id quidem infra grammatici officium
est), sed totam, ut mea fert opinio, subtilitatem in
2 dubiis habet. Ut longis syllabis omnibus apponere
apicem ineptissimum est, quia plurimae natura ipsa
verbi quod scribitur patent, sed interim necessarium,
cum eadem littera alium atque alium intellectum,
prout correpta vel producta est, facit; ut *malus*
arborem significat an hominem non bonum apice
3 distinguitur, *palus* aliud priore syllaba longa aliud
sequenti significat, et cum eadem littera nominativo
casu brevis, ablativo longa est, utrum sequamur,
4 plerumque hac nota monendi sumus. Similiter
putaverunt illa quoque servanda discrimina, ut *ex*
praepositionem, si verbum sequeretur *specto,* adiecta
secundae syllabae *s* littera, si *pecto,* remota scribere-
5 mus. Illa quoque servata est a multis differentia,
ut *ad,* cum esset praepositio, *d* litteram, cum autem
coniunctio, *t* acciperet, itemque *cum,* si tempus signi-
ficaret, per *qu,* si comitem, per *c* ac duas sequentes
6 scriberetur. Frigidiora his alia, ut *quidquid c* quartam haberet, ne interrogare bis videremur; et

VII. Having stated the rules which we must follow in speaking, I will now proceed to lay down the rules which must be observed when we write. Such rules are called *orthography* by the Greeks; let us style it the science of writing correctly. This science does not consist merely in the knowledge of the letters composing each syllable (such a study is beneath the dignity of a teacher of grammar), but, in my opinion, develops all its subtlety in connexion with doubtful points. For instance, while it 2 is absurd to place a circumflex over all long syllables since the quantity of most syllables is obvious from the very nature of the word which is written, it is all the same occasionally necessary, since the same letter involves a different meaning according as it is long or short. For example we determine whether *malus* is to mean an "apple tree" or a "bad man" by the use of the circumflex; *palus* means a "stake," if 3 the first syllable is long, a "marsh," if it be short; again when the same letter is short in the nominative and long in the ablative, we generally require the circumflex to make it clear which quantity to understand. Similarly it has been held that we should 4 observe distinctions such as the following: if the preposition *ex* is compounded with *specto*, there will be an *s* in the second syllable, while there will be no *s* if it is compounded with *pecto*. Again the follow- 5 ing distinction has frequently been observed: *ad* is spelt with a *d* when it is a preposition, but with a *t* when it is a conjunction, while *cum* is spelt *quum* when it denotes time, but *cum* when it denotes accompaniment. Still more pedantic are the practices 6 of making the fourth letter of *quidquid* a *c* to avoid the appearance of repeating a question, and of writing

quotidie non *cotidie*, ut sit *quot diebus*. Verum haec
iam etiam inter ipsas ineptias evanuerunt.

7   Quaeri solet, in scribendo praepositiones sonum
quem iunctae efficiunt, an quem separatae, observare
conveniat : ut, cum dico *optinuit* (secundam enim *b*
8 litteram ratio poscit, aures magis audiunt *p*) et
immunis, illud enim, quod veritas exigit, sequentis
9 syllabae sono victum *m* gemina commutatur. Est
et in dividendis verbis observatio, mediam litteram
consonantem priori an sequenti syllabae adiungas :
haruspex enim, quia pars eius posterior a *spectando*
est, *s* litteram tertiae dabit; *abstemius*, quia ex
abstinentia temeti composita vox est, primae re-
10 linquet.   Nam *k* quidem in nullis verbis utendum
puto, nisi quae significat, etiam ut sola ponatur.
Hoc eo non omisi, quod quidam eam, quotiens
a sequatur, necessariam credunt, cum sit *c* littera,
quae ad omnes vocales vim suam perferat.

11 Verum orthographia quoque consuetudini servit,
ideoque saepe mutata est.   Nam illa vetustissima
transeo tempora, quibus et pauciores litterae nec
similes his nostris earum formae fuerunt et vis
quoque diversa, sicut apud Graecos *o* litterae, quae
interim longa ac brevis ut apud nos, interim pro

---

[1] *K* may stand for *Kalendae, Kaeso, Karthago, Kalumnia, Kaput.*
[2] The original alphabet consisted of twenty-one letters,
and was increased to twenty-three by the addition of *y*
and *z*.

quotidie instead of *cotidie* to show that it stands for *quot diebus*. But such practices have disappeared into the limbo of absurdities.

It is often debated whether in our spelling of 7 prepositions we should be guided by their sound when compounded, or separate. For instance when I say *optinuit*, logic demands that the second letter should be a *b*, while to the ear the sound is rather that of *p*: or again take the case of *immunis*: 8 the letter *n*, which is required by strict adherence to fact, is forced by the sound of the *m* which follows to change into another *m*. We must also note when 9 analysing compound words, whether the middle consonant adheres to the preceding syllable or to that which follows. For example since the latter part of *haruspex* is from *spectare*, the *s* must be assigned to the third syllable. In *abstemius* on the other hand it will go with the first syllable since the word is derived from *abstinentia temeti*, "abstention from wine." As for *k* my view is that it should not 10 be used at all except in such words as may be indicated by the letter standing alone as an abbreviation.[1] I mention the fact because some hold that *k* should be used whenever the next letter is an *a*, despite the existence of the letter *c* which maintains its force in conjunction with all the vowels.

Orthography, however, is also the servant of usage 11 and therefore undergoes frequent change. I make no mention of the earliest times when our alphabet contained fewer letters [2] and their shapes differed from those which we now use, while their values also were different. For instance in Greek the letter *o* was sometimes long and short, as it is with us, and again was sometimes used to express the syllable

12 syllaba quam nomine suo exprimit posita est; ut *a*[1]
Latinis veteribus *d* plurimis in verbis adiectam
ultimam, quod manifestum est etiam ex columna
rostrata, quae est Duilio in foro posita; interim *g*
quoque, ut in pulvinari Solis, qui colitur iuxta aedem
13 Quirini, *vesperug*, quod *vesperuginem* accipimus. De
mutatione etiam litterarum, de qua supra dixi, nihil
repetere hic necesse est, fortasse enim sicut scribe-
14 bant etiam loquebantur. Semivocales geminare diu
non fuit usitatissimi moris, atque e contrario usque
ad Accium et ultra porrectas syllabas geminis, ut
15 dixi, vocalibus scripserunt. Diutius duravit, ut *e* et
i iungendis eadem ratione qua Graeci ει uterentur;
ea casibus numerisque discreta est, ut Lucilius praecipit: *Iam puerei venere, e postremum facito atque i,*
Ut pueri plures fiant; ac deinceps idem: *Mendaci*
16 *furique addes e, cum dare furi Iusseris.* Quod quidem
cum supervacuum est, quia *i* tam longae quam brevis
naturam habet, tum incommodum aliquando. Nam
in iis, quae proximam ub ultima litteram *e* habebunt
et *i* longa terminabuntur, illam rationem sequentes
utemur *e* gemina, qualia sunt haec *aurei*, *argentei* et
17 his similia. Idque iis praecipue, qui ad lectionem
instituentur, etiam impedimento erit; sicut in

---

[1] *i.e.* the interjection O !
[2] The ablative originally terminated in *d*; *e.g. pugnandod,*
marid, navaled, praedad, etc., on the base of the column of
Duilius.
[3] I. iv. 12–17. [4] *e.g. iusi* was written for *iussi.*

which is identical with its name.[1] And in Latin 12
ancient writers ended a number of words with *d*, as
may be seen on the column adorned with the beaks
of ships, which was set up in the forum in honour
of Duilius.[2] Sometimes again they gave words a
final *g*, as we may still see in the shrine of the Sun,
close to the temple of Quirinus, where we find the
word *uesperug*, which we write *uesperugo* (evening
star). I have already spoken of the interchange 13
of letters [3] and need not repeat my remarks here:
perhaps their pronunciation corresponded with their
spelling. For a long time the doubling of semi- 14
vowels was avoided,[4] while down to the time of
Accius and beyond, long syllables were indicated by
repetition of the vowel. The practice of joining *e* 15
and *i* as in the Greek diphthong ει lasted longer: it
served to distinguish cases and numbers, for which
we may compare the instructions of Lucilius:

> The boys are come: why then, their names must
>   end
> With *e* and *i* to make them more than one;

and later—

> If to a thief and liar (*mendaci furique*) you would
>   give,
> In *e* and *i* your thief must terminate.

But this addition of *e* is quite superfluous, since ι 16
can be long no less than short: it is also at times
inconvenient. For in those words which end in *i*
and have *e* as their last letter but one, we shall on
this principle have to write *e* twice : I refer to words
such as *aurei* or *argentei* and the like. Now such a 17
practice will be an actual hindrance to those who are
learning to read. This difficulty occurs in Greek as

Graecis accidit adiectione ι litterae, quam non solum
dativis casibus in parte ultima ascribunt sed quibusdam etiam interponunt, ut in ΛΗΙΣΤΗΙ, quia
etymologia ex divisione in tris syllabas facta desideret
18 eam litteram. *Ae* syllabam, cuius secundam nunc *e*
litteram ponimus, varie per *a* et *i* efferebant; quidam
semper ut Graeci, quidam singulariter tantum, cum
in dativum vel genitivum casum incidissent, unde
pictai vestis et *aquai* Vergilius amantissimus vetustatis
19 carminibus inseruit. In iisdem plurali numero *e*
utebantur, *hi Syllae, Galbae*. Est in hac quoque
parte Lucilii praeceptum, quod quia pluribus explicatur versibus, si quis parum credet, apud ipsum in
20 nono requirat. Quid quod Ciceronis temporibus
paulumque infra, fere quotiens *s* littera media
vocalium longarum vel subiecta longis esset, gemina-
batur, ut *caussae, cassus, divissiones?* quomodo et
ipsum et Vergilium quoque scripsisse manus eorum
21 docent. Atqui paulum superiores etiam illud, quod
nos gemina dicimus *iussi*, una dixerunt. Iam *optimus
maximus*, ut mediam *i* litteram, quae veteribus *u*
fuerat, acciperent, Gai primum Caesaris inscriptione
22 traditur factum. *Here* nunc *e* littera terminamus, at
veterum comicorum adhuc libris invenio *Heri ad me
venit;* quod idem in epistolis Augusti, quas sua manu
23 scripsit aut emendavit, deprehenditur. Quid? non
Cato Censorius *dicam* et *faciam dicem* et *faciem* scrip-

---

[1] The noun being formed from λῃίζω. ΛΗΙΣΤΗΙ in the text
is dative after *in*. The trisyllable to which Q. refers is the
nominative.   [2] *Aen.* ix. 26 and vii. 464.

well in connexion with the addition of an *iota*, which
is employed not merely in the termination of the
dative, but is sometimes found in the middle of
words as in λῃστής, for the reason that the analysis
applied by etymology shows the word to be a trisyllable[1] and requires the addition of that letter.
The diphthong *ae* now written with an *e*, was pro- 18
nounced in old days as *ai*; some wrote *ai* in all cases,
as in Greek, others confined its use to the dative and
genitive singular; whence it comes that Vergil,[2]
always a passionate lover of antiquity, inserted *pictai
uestis* and *aquai* in his poems. But in the plural they 19
used *e* and wrote *Syllae, Galbae*. Lucilius has given
instructions on this point also; his instructions
occupy quite a number of verses, for which the
incredulous may consult his ninth book. Again in 20
Cicero's days and a little later, it was the almost
universal practice to write a double *s*, whenever that
letter occurred between two long vowels or after a
long vowel, as for example in *caussae, cassus, diuissiones*.
That he and Vergil both used this spelling is shown
by their own autograph manuscripts. And yet at 21
a slightly earlier date *iussi* which we write with a
double *s* was spelt with only one. Further *optimus
maximus*, which older writers spelt with a *u*, appear for the first time with an *i* (such at any rate
is the tradition) in an inscription of Gaius Caesar.[3]
We now write *here*, but I still find in manuscripts of 22
the old comic poets phrases such as *heri ad me uenit*,[4]
and the same spelling is found in letters of Augustus
written or corrected by his own hand. Again did 23
not Cato the censor spell *dicam* and *faciam* as *dicem*

[3] Caligula, the first of the Caesars to adopt this title.
[4] Ter. *Phorm.* 36.

sit, eundemque in ceteris, quae similiter cadunt,
modum tenuit, quod et ex veteribus eius libris manifestum est et a Messala in libro de *s* littera positum?
24 *Sibe* et *quase* scriptum in multorum libris est, sed an
hoc voluerint auctores, nescio; T. Livium ita his
usum ex Pediano comperi, qui et ipse eum seque-
25 batur; haec nos *i* littera finimus. Quid dicam
vortices et *vorsus* ceteraque ad eundem modum, quae
primus Scipio Africanus in *e* litteram secundam
26 vertisse dicitur? Nostri praeceptores *seruum ceru-
um*que *u* et *o* litteris scripserunt, quia subiecta sibi
vocalis in unum sonum coalescere et confundi
nequiret; nunc *u* gemina scribuntur ea ratione,
quam reddidi; neutro sane modo vox, quam sen-
timus, efficitur. Nec inutiliter Claudius Aeolicam
27 illam ad hos usus litteram adiecerat. Illud nunc
melius, quod *cui* tribus, quas praeposui, litteris
enotamus; in quo pueris nobis ad pinguem sane
sonum *qu* et *oi* utebantur, tantum ut ab illo *qui*
distingueretur.
28 Quid? quae scribuntur aliter quam enuntiantur?
Nam et *Gaius C* littera significatur, quae inversa
mulierem declarat; quia tam *Gaias* esse vocitatas
quam *Gaios* etiam ex nuptialibus sacris apparet.
29 Nec *Gnaeus* eam litteram in praenominis nota accipit,
quae sonat; et *columnam* et *consules* exempta *n* littera

---

[1] *cp.* I. iv. 8.
[2] The bride used the formula *ubi tu Gaius, ibi ego Gaia.*

and *faciem* and observe the same practice in words of similar termination? This is clear from old manuscripts of his works and is recorded by Messala in his treatise on the letter *s*. *Sibe* and *quase* are found 24 in many books, but I cannot say whether the authors wished them to be spelt thus: I learn from Pedianus that Livy, whose precedent he himself adopted, used this spelling: to-day we make these words end with an *i*. What shall I say of *uortices*, 25 *uorsus* and the like, which Scipio Africanus is said to have been the first to spell with an *e*? My own 26 teachers spelt *seruus* and *ceruus* with a *uo*, in order that the repetition of the vowel might not lead to the coalescence and confusion of the two sounds: to-day however we write these words with a double *u* on the principle which I have already stated: neither spelling however exactly expresses the pronunciation. It was not without reason that Claudius introduced the Aeolic *digamma* to represent this sound.[1] It is a distinct improvement that to-day we 27 spell *cui* as I have written it: when I was a boy it used to be spelt *quoi*, giving it a very full sound, merely to distinguish it from *qui*.

Again, what of words whose spelling is at variance 28 with their pronunciation? For instance *C* is used as an abbreviation for Gaius, and when inverted stands for a woman, for as we know from the words of the marriage service women used to be called *Gaiae*, just as men were called *Gaii*.[2] *Gnaeus* too in the 29 abbreviation indicating the *praenomen* is spelt in a manner which does not agree with its pronunciation. We also find *columna*[3] and *consul* spelt without an *n*,

---

[3] *columa* is mentioned by the grammarian Pompeius as a barbarism in the fifth century. *cp.* dimin. *columella*. *Consul* is abbreviated *cos.*

legimus; et *Subura*, cum tribus litteris notatur, *c*
tertiam ostendit. Multa sunt generis huius; sed
haec quoque vereor ne modum tam parvae quaestionis
excesserint.

30   Iudicium autem suum grammaticus interponat his
omnibus; nam hoc valere plurimum debet. Ego
(nisi quod consuetudo obtinuerit) sic scribendum
31 quidque iudico, quomodo sonat. Hic enim est usus
litterarum, ut custodiant voces et velut depositum
reddant legentibus, itaque id exprimere debent quod
32 dicturi sumus. Hae fere sunt emendate loquendi
scribendique partes; duas reliquas significanter
ornateque dicendi non equidem grammaticis aufero,
sed cum mihi officia rhetoris supersint, maiori operi
reservo.

33   Redit autem illa cogitatio, quosdam fore, qui haec
quae diximus parva nimium et impedimenta quoque
maius aliquid agentibus putent. Nec ipse ad ex-
tremam usque anxietatem et ineptas cavillationes
descendendum atque iis ingenia concidi et comminui
34 credo. Sed nihil ex grammatice nocuerit, nisi quod
supervacuum est. An ideo minor est M. Tullius
orator, quod idem artis huius diligentissimus fuit et
in filio (ut epistolis apparet) recte loquendi asper
quoque exactor? aut vim C. Caesaris fregerunt editi
35 de analogia libri? aut ideo minus Messala nitidus,

---

[1] The original name was *Sucusa*.

while *Subura* when indicated by three letters is spelt
Suc.[1] I could quote many other examples of this,
but I fear that I have already said too much on so
trivial a theme.

On all such subjects the teacher must use his own 30
judgment; for in such matters it should be the
supreme authority. For my own part, I think that,
within the limits prescribed by usage, words should
be spelt as they are pronounced. For the use of 31
letters is to preserve the sound of words and to
deliver them to readers as a sacred trust : consequently they ought to represent the pronunciation
which we are to use. These are the more important 32
points in connexion with writing and speaking
correctly. I do not go so far as to deny to the
teacher of literature all part in the two remaining departments of speaking and writing with
elegance and significance, but I reserve these for a
more important portion of this work, as I have still
to deal with the duties of the teacher of rhetoric.

I am however haunted by the thought that some 33
readers will regard what I have said as trivial details
which are only likely to prove a hindrance to those
who are intent upon a greater task ; and I myself
do not think that we should go so far as to lose our
sleep of nights or quibble like fools over such
minutiae ; for such studies make mincemeat of the
mind. But it is only the superfluities of grammar 34
that do any harm. I ask you, is Cicero a less great
orator for having given this science his diligent
attention or for having, as his letters show, demanded
rigid correctness of speech from his son ? Or was the
vigour of Gaius Caesar's eloquence impaired by the
publication of a treatise on Analogy ? Or the polish 35

quia quosdam totos libellos non verbis modo singulis sed etiam litteris dedit? Non obstant hae
disciplinae per illas euntibus sed circa illas
haerentibus.

VIII. Superest lectio, in qua puer ut sciat, ubi
suspendere spiritum debeat, quo loco versum distinguere, ubi claudatur sensus, unde incipiat, quando
attollenda vel summittenda sit vox, quo quidque flexu,
quid lentius, celerius, concitatius, lenius dicendum,
2 demonstrari nisi in opere ipso non potest. Unum
est igitur, quod in hac parte praecipiam : ut omnia
ista facere possit, intelligat. Sit autem in primis
lectio virilis et cum suavitate quadam gravis et non
quidem prosae similis, quia et carmen est et se
poetae canere testantur; non tamen in canticum
dissoluta nec plasmate (ut nunc a plerisque fit)
effeminata; de quo genere optime C. Caesarem
praetextatum adhuc accepimus dixisse : *Si cantas,*
3 *male cantas ; si legis, cantas.* Nec prosopopoeias, ut
quibusdam placet, ad comicum morem pronuntiari
velim; esse tamen flexum quendam, quo distingu-
antur ab iis, in quibus poeta persona sua utetur.
4 Cetera admonitione magna egent, in primis, ut
tenerae mentes tracturaeque altius, quidquid rudibus

of Messala dimmed by the fact that he devoted whole books to the discussion not merely of single words, but of single letters? Such studies do no harm to those who but pass through them: it is only the pedantic stickler who suffers.

VIII. Reading remains for consideration. In this connexion there is much that can only be taught in actual practice, as for instance when the boy should take breath, at what point he should introduce a pause into a line, where the sense ends or begins, when the voice should be raised or lowered, what modulation should be given to each phrase, and when he should increase or slacken speed, or speak with greater or less energy. In 2 this portion of my work I will give but one golden rule: to do all these things, he must understand what he reads. But above all his reading must be manly, combining dignity and charm; it must be different from the reading of prose, for poetry is song and poets claim to be singers. But this fact does not justify degeneration into sing-song or the effeminate modulations now in vogue: there is an excellent saying on this point attributed to Gaius Caesar while he was still a boy: "If you are singing, you sing badly: if you are reading, you sing." Again I do not, like some teachers, wish character 3 as revealed by speeches to be indicated as it is by the comic actor, though I think that there should be some modulation of the voice to distinguish such passages from those where the poet is speaking in person. There are other points where there is much 4 need of instruction: above all, unformed minds which are liable to be all the more deeply impressed by what they learn in their days of childish

et omnium ignaris insederit, non modo quae diserta
sed vel magis quae honesta sunt, discant.

5 Ideoque optime institutum est, ut ab Homero
atque Vergilio lectio inciperet, quanquam ad intelli-
gendas eorum virtutes firmiore iudicio opus est; sed
huic rei superest tempus, neque enim semel legentur.
Interim et sublimitate heroi carminis animus adsurgat
et ex magnitudine rerum spiritum ducat et optimis
6 imbuatur.   Utiles tragoediae, alunt et lyrici; si
tamen in his non auctores modo sed etiam partes
operis elegeris, nam et Graeci licenter multa et
Horatium nolim in quibusdam interpretari.   Elegia
vero, utique quae amat, et hendecasyllabi, qui sunt
commata Sotadeorum (nam de Sotadeis ne praecipiendum quidem est) amoveantur, si fieri potest,
si minus, certe ad firmius aetatis robur reserventur.
7 Comoediae, quae plurimum conferre ad eloquentiam
potest, cum per omnes et personas et adfectus eat,
quem usum in pueris putem, paulo post suo loco
dicam; nam cum mores in tuto fuerint, inter praecipua legenda erit.   De Menandro loquor, nec tamen
8 excluserim alios.   Nam Latini quoque auctores
adferent utilitatis aliquid.   Sed pueris, quae maxime

---

[1] One form of Sotadean is _ ᵕ _ ᵕ _ _ _ ᵕ ᵕ _ ᵕ _ _ .
The Hendecasyllable runs ᵕ _ _ _ ᵕ ᵕ _ ᵕ _ ᵕ _ _ , = the
Sotadean minus the first three syllables. Both metres were
frequently used for indecent lampoons. For Sotades see
index.
[2] *sc.* ch. xi.

ignorance, must learn not merely what is eloquent; it is even more important that they should study what is morally excellent.

It is therefore an admirable practice which now 5 prevails, to begin by reading Homer and Vergil, although the intelligence needs to be further developed for the full appreciation of their merits: but there is plenty of time for that since the boy will read them more than once. In the meantime let his mind be lifted by the sublimity of heroic verse, inspired by the greatness of its theme and imbued with the loftiest sentiments. The reading of tragedy 6 also is useful, and lyric poets will provide nourishment for the mind, provided not merely the authors be carefully selected, but also the passages from their works which are to be read. For the Greek lyric poets are often licentious and even in Horace there are passages which I should be unwilling to explain to a class. Elegiacs, however, more especially erotic elegy, and hendecasyllables, which are merely sections of Sotadean verse [1] (concerning which latter I need give no admonitions), should be entirely banished, if possible; if not absolutely banished, they should be reserved for pupils of a less impressionable age. As to comedy, whose contribution to eloquence may be of 7 no small importance, since it is concerned with every kind of character and emotion, I will shortly point out in its due place [2] what use can in my opinion be made of it in the education of boys. As soon as we have no fear of contaminating their morals, it should take its place among the subjects which it is specially desirable to read. I speak of Menander, though I would not exclude others. For Latin 8 authors will also be of some service. But the

ingenium alant atque animum augeant, praelegenda ;
ceteris, quae ad eruditionem modo pertinent, longa
aetas spatium dabit. Multum autem veteres etiam
Latini conferunt, (quanquam plerique plus ingenio
quam arte valuerunt) in primis copiam verborum,
quorum in tragoediis gravitas, in comoediis elegantia

9 et quidam velut ἀττικισμός inveniri potest. Oeconomia quoque in iis diligentior quam in plerisque
novorum erit, qui omnium operum solam virtutem
sententias putaverunt. Sanctitas certe et, ut sic
dicam, virilitas ab iis petenda est, quando nos in
omnia deliciarum vitia dicendi quoque ratione de-

10 fluximus. Denique credamus summis oratoribus,
qui veterum poemata vel ad fidem causarum vel
ad ornamentum eloquentiae adsumunt. Nam prae-

11 cipue quidem apud Ciceronem frequenter tamen apud
Asinium etiam et ceteros, qui sunt proximi, videmus
Enni, Acci, Pacuvi, Lucili, Terenti, Caecili et aliorum
inseri versus summa non eruditionis modo gratia sed
etiam iucunditatis, cum poeticis voluptatibus aures a

12 forensi asperitate respirent. Quibus accedit non
mediocris utilitas, cum sententiis eorum velut quibusdam testimoniis quae proposuere confirment. Verum
priora illa ad pueros magis, haec sequentia ad robusti-

subjects selected for lectures to boys should be those
which will enlarge the mind and provide the greatest nourishment to the intellect. Life is quite long
enough for the subsequent study of those other subjects which are concerned with matters of interest
solely to learned men. But even the old Latin poets
may be of great value, in spite of the fact that their
strength lies in their natural talent rather than in
their art: above all they will contribute richness
of vocabulary: for the vocabulary of the tragedians
is full of dignity, while in that of the comedians
there is a certain elegance and Attic grace. They 9
are, too, more careful about dramatic structure than
the majority of moderns, who regard epigram as the
sole merit of every kind of literary work. For
purity at any rate and manliness, if I may say so,
we must certainly go to these writers, since to-day
even our style of speaking is infected with all the
faults of modern decadence. Finally we may derive 10
confidence from the practice of the greatest orators
of drawing upon the early poets to support their
arguments or adorn their eloquence. For we find, 11
more especially in the pages of Cicero, but frequently in Asinius and other orators of that period, quotations from Ennius, Accius, Pacuvius, Lucilius, Terence,
Caecilius and others, inserted not merely to show
the speaker's learning, but to please his hearers
as well, since the charms of poetry provide a pleasant relief from the severity of forensic eloquence.
Such quotations have the additional advantage of 12
helping the speaker's case, for the orator makes use
of the sentiments expressed by the poet as evidence
in support of his own statements. But while my
earlier remarks have special application to the
education of boys, those which I have just made

ores pertinebunt, cum grammatices amor et usus
lectionis non scholarum temporibus, sed vitae spatio
terminentur.

13   In praelegendo grammaticus et illa quidem minora
praestare debebit, ut partes orationis reddi sibi soluto
versu desideret et pedum proprietates, quae adeo
debent esse notae in carminibus, ut etiam in oratoria
compositione desiderentur. Deprehendat, quae
barbara, quae impropria, quae contra leges loquendi
14 sint posita; non ut ex iis utique improbentur
poetae (quibus, quia plerumque servire metro
coguntur, adeo ignoscitur, ut vitia ipsa aliis in carmine appellationibus nominentur; metaplasmos[1]
enim et schematismos et schemata, ut dixi, vocamus,
et laudem virtutis necessitati damus), sed ut com-
15 moneat artificialium et memoriam agitet. Id quoque
inter prima rudimenta non inutile demonstrare,
quot quaeque verba modis intelligenda sint. Circa
glossemata etiam, id est voces minus usitatas, non
16 ultima eius professionis diligentia est. Enimvero
iam maiore cura doceat tropos omnes, quibus praecipue non poema modo sed etiam oratio ornatur;
schemata utraque, id est figuras, quaeque λέξεως
quaeque διανοίας vocantur, quorum ego sicut tro-

---

[1] The formation of cases of nouns and tenses of verbs from
a non-existent nom. or pres.: or more generally any change
in the forms of a word.

[2] *schematismus* and *schemata* both seem to mean the same,
sc. figures.   [3] See Book VIII. chap. vi.

apply rather to persons of riper years; for the love of letters and the value of reading are not confined to one's schooldays, but end only with life.

In lecturing the teacher of literature must give 13 attention to minor points as well: he will ask his class after analysing a verse to give him the parts of speech and the peculiar features of the feet which it contains: these latter should be so familiar in poetry as to make their presence desired even in the prose of oratory. He will point out what words are barbarous, what improperly used, and what are contrary to the laws of language. He will not do 14 this by way of censuring the poets for such peculiarities, for poets are usually the servants of their metres and are allowed such licence that faults are given other names when they occur in poetry: for we style them *metaplasms*,[1] *schematisms* and *schemata*,[2] as I have said, and make a virtue of necessity. Their aim will rather be to familiarise the pupil with the artifices of style and to stimulate his memory. Further in the elementary stages of such 15 instruction it will not be unprofitable to show the different meanings which may be given to each word. With regard to *glossemata*, that is to say words not in common use, the teacher must exercise no ordinary diligence, while still greater care is required in 16 teaching all the tropes[3] which are employed for the adornment more especially of poetry, but of oratory as well, and in making his class acquainted with the two sorts of *schemata* or figures known as *figures of speech* and *figures of thought*.[4] I shall however post-

[4] See Book IX. chaps. i. and ii. A trope is an expression used in a sense which it cannot strictly bear. A figure is a form of speech differing from the ordinary method of expression; see IX i. 4.

porum tractatum in eum locum differo, quo mihi de
17 ornatu orationis dicendum erit. Praecipue vero illa
infigat animis, quae in oeconomia virtus, quae in
decore rerum, quid personae cuique convenerit, quid
in sensibus laudandum, quid in verbis, ubi copia
probabilis, ubi modus.

18 His accedet enarratio historiarum, diligens quidem
illa non tamen usque ad supervacuum laborem occupata. Nam receptas aut certe claris auctoribus
memoratas exposuisse satis est. Persequi quidem,
quid quis unquam vel contemptissimorum hominum
dixerit, aut nimiae miseriae aut inanis iactantiae est
et detinet atque obruit ingenia melius aliis vacatura.
19 Nam qui omnes etiam indignas lectione scidas ex-
cutit, anilibus quoque fabulis accommodare operam
potest. Atqui pleni sunt huiusmodi impedimentis
grammaticorum commentarii, vix ipsis qui compo-
20 suerunt satis noti. Nam Didymo, quo nemo plura
scripsit, accidisse compertum est, ut, cum historiae
cuidam tanquam vanae repugnaret, ipsius proferretur
21 liber, qui eam continebat. Quod evenit praecipue
in fabulosis usque ad deridicula quaedam, quaedam
etiam pudenda; unde improbissimo cuique pleraque
fingendi licentia est, adeo ut de libris totis et aucto-

pone discussion of *tropes* and *figures* till I come to
deal with the various ornaments of style. Above 17
all he will impress upon their minds the value of
proper arrangement, and of graceful treatment of
the matter in hand : he will show what is appropriate
to the various characters, what is praiseworthy in the
thoughts or words, where copious diction is to be
commended and where restraint.

In addition to this he will explain the various 18
stories that occur : this must be done with care,
but should not be encumbered with superfluous
detail. For it is sufficient to set forth the version
which is generally received or at any rate rests upon
good authority. But to ferret out everything that
has ever been said on the subject even by the most
worthless of writers is a sign of tiresome pedantry
or empty ostentation, and results in delaying and
swamping the mind when it would be better
employed on other themes. The man who pores 19
over every page even though it be wholly unworthy
of reading, is capable of devoting his attention
to the investigation of old wives' tales. And yet
the commentaries of teachers of literature are full
of such encumbrances to learning and strangely
unfamiliar to their own authors. It is, for instance, 20
recorded that Didymus, who was unsurpassed for
the number of books which he wrote, on one occasion
objected to some story as being absurd, whereupon
one of his own books was produced which contained
the story in question. Such abuses occur chiefly in 21
connexion with fabulous stories and are sometimes
carried to ludicrous or even scandalous extremes :
for in such cases the more unscrupulous commentator
has such full scope for invention, that he can tell lies

ribus, ut succurrit, mentiantur tuto, quia inveniri qui
nunquam fuere non possunt: nam in notioribus
frequentissime deprehenduntur a curiosis. Ex quo
mihi inter virtutes grammatici habebitur aliqua
nescire.

IX. Et finitae quidem sunt partes duae, quas haec
professio pollicetur, id est ratio loquendi et enarratio
auctorum, quarum illam *methodicen* hanc *historicen*
vocant. Adiiciamus tamen eorum curae quaedam
dicendi primordia, quibus aetates nondum rhetorem
2 capientes instituant. Igitur Aesopi fabellas, quae
fabulis nutricularum proxime succedunt, narrare sermone puro et nihil se supra modum extollente,
deinde eandem gracilitatem stilo exigere condiscant;
versus primo solvere, mox mutatis verbis interpretari,
tum paraphrasi audacius vertere, qua et breviare
quaedam et exornare salvo modo poetae sensu
3 permittitur. Quod opus etiam consummatis pro-
fessoribus difficile qui commode tractaverit, cuicunque discendo sufficiet. Sententiae quoque et chriae
et ethologiae subiectis dictorum rationibus apud
grammaticos scribantur, quia initium ex lectione
ducunt; quorum omnium similis est ratio, forma
diversa, quia sententia universalis est vox, ethologia

---

[1] The meaning of *ethologia* is doubtful, but probably means
a simple character-sketch of some famous man.

to his heart's content about whole books and authors without fear of detection : for what never existed can obviously never be found, whereas if the subject is familiar the careful investigator will often detect the fraud. Consequently I shall count it a merit in a teacher of literature that there should be some things which he does not know.

IX. I have now finished with two of the departments, with which teachers of literature profess to deal, namely the art of speaking correctly and the interpretation of authors ; the former they call *methodicē*, the latter *historicē*. We must however add to their activities instruction in certain rudiments of oratory for the benefit of those who are not yet ripe for the schools of rhetoric. Their pupils should 2 learn to paraphrase Aesop's fables, the natural successors of the fairy stories of the nursery, in simple and restrained language and subsequently to set down this paraphrase in writing with the same simplicity of style : they should begin by analysing each verse, then give its meaning in different language, and finally proceed to a freer paraphrase in which they will be permitted now to abridge and now to embellish the original, so far as this may be done without losing the poet's meaning. This is no 3 easy task even for the expert instructor, and the pupil who handles it successfully will be capable of learning everything. He should also be set to write *aphorisms, moral essays (chriae)* and *delineations of character (ethologiae)*,[1] of which the teacher will first give the general scheme, since such themes will be drawn from their reading. In all of these exercises the general idea is the same, but the form differs : *aphorisms* are general propositions, while *ethologiae*

4 personis continetur. Chriarum plura genera traduntur: unum simile sententiae, quod est positum
in voce simplici, *Dixit ille,* aut, *Dicere solebat;*
alterum, quod est in respondendo, *Interrogatus ille,*
vel, *cum hoc ei dictum esset, respondit;* tertium huic
non dissimile, *cum quis dixisset aliquid, vel fecisset.*

5 Etiam in ipsorum factis esse chriam putant, ut
*Crates, cum indoctum puerum vidisset, paedagogum eius
percussit;* et aliud paene par ei, quod tamen eodem
nomine appellare non audent sed dicunt χρειῶδες, ut
Milo, quem vitulum assueverat ferre, taurum ferebat.
In his omnibus et declinatio per eosdem ducitur
casus, et tam factorum quam dictorum ratio est.

6 Narratiunculas a poetis celebratas notitiae causa non
eloquentiae tractandas puto. Cetera maioris operis
ac spiritus Latini rhetores relinquendo necessaria
grammaticis fecerunt; Graeci magis operum suorum
et onera et modum norunt.

X. Haec de Grammatice, quam brevissime potui,
non ut omnia dicerem sectatus, quod infinitum erat,
sed ut maxime necessaria; nunc de ceteris artibus,
quibus instituendos, priusquam rhetori tradantur,

---

[1] The sense is not clear: it appears to refer to the stereo-
typed form in which the *chria* was couched.

are concerned with persons. Of *moral essays* there **4**
are various forms : some are akin to *aphorisms* and
commence with a simple statement " he said " or " he
used to say " : others give the answer to a question
and begin " on being asked " or " in answer to this
he replied," while a third and not dissimilar type
begins, " when someone has said or done something."
Some hold that a *moral essay* may take some action **5**
as its text; take for example the statement " Crates
on seeing an ill-educated boy, beat his *paedagogus*," or
a very similar example which they do not venture
actually to propose as a theme for a *moral essay*, but
content themselves with saying that it is of the
nature of such a theme, namely " Milo, having
accustomed himself to carrying a calf every day,
ended by carrying it when grown to a bull." All
these instances are couched in the same gram-
matical form [1] and deeds no less than sayings may
be presented for treatment. Short stories from the **6**
poets should in my opinion be handled not with
a view to style but as a means of increasing knowledge. Other more serious and ambitious tasks
have been also imposed on teachers of literature by
the fact that Latin rhetoricians will have nothing to
do with them : Greek rhetoricians have a better
comprehension of the extent and nature of the tasks
placed on their shoulders.

X. I have made my remarks on this stage of
education as brief as possible, making no attempt to
say everything, (for the theme is infinite), but confining myself to the most necessary points. I will
now proceed briefly to discuss the remaining arts in
which I think boys ought to be instructed before
being handed over to the teacher of rhetoric : for it

pueros existimo, strictim subiungam, ut efficiatur
orbis ille doctrinae, quem Graeci ἐγκύκλιον παιδείαν
vocant.

2 Nam iisdem fere annis aliarum quoque disciplinarum studia ingredienda sunt, quae, quia et ipsae
artes sunt et esse perfectae sine orandi scientia
possunt nec rursus ad efficiendum oratorem satis
valent solae, an sint huic operi necessariae quae-

3 ritur. Nam quid, inquiunt, ad agendam causam
dicendamve sententiam pertinet, scire, quemadmodum data linea constitui triangula aequis lateribus
possint? Aut quo melius vel defendet reum vel
reget consilia, qui citharae sonos nominibus et spatiis

4 distinxerit? Enumerent etiam fortasse multos
quamlibet utiles foro, qui nec geometren audierint
nec musicos nisi hac communi voluptate aurium
intelligant. Quibus ego primum hoc respondeo,
quod M. Cicero scripto ad Brutum libro frequentius
testatur, non eum a nobis institui oratorem, qui sit
aut fuerit, sed imaginem quandam concepisse nos

5 animo perfecti illius et nulla parte cessantis. Nam
et sapientem formantes eum, qui sit futurus consummatus undique et, ut dicunt, mortalis quidam
deus, non modo cognitione caelestium vel mortalium
putant instruendum, sed per quaedam parva sane,
si ipsa demum aestimes, ducunt sicut exquisitas
interim ambiguitates; non quia *ceratinae* aut *croco-*

is by such studies that the course of education described by the Greeks as ἐγκύκλιος παιδεία or general education will be brought to its full completion.

For there are other subjects of education which 2 must be studied simultaneously with literature. These being independent studies are capable of completion without a knowledge of oratory, while on the other hand they cannot by themselves produce an orator. The question has consequently been raised as to whether they are necessary for this purpose. What, say some, has the knowledge of the way to 3 describe an equilateral triangle on a given straight line got to do with pleading in the law-courts or speaking in the senate? Will an acquaintance with the names and intervals of the notes of the lyre help an orator to defend a criminal or direct the policy of his country? They will perhaps produce a long 4 list of orators who are most effective in the courts but have never sat under a geometrician and whose understanding of music is confined to the pleasure which their ears, like those of other men, derive from it. To such critics I reply, and Cicero frequently makes the same remark in his Orator, that I am not describing any orator who actually exists or has existed, but have in my mind's eye an ideal orator, perfect down to the smallest detail. For when the 5 philosophers describe the ideal sage who is to be consummate in all knowledge and a very god incarnate, as they say, they would have him receive instruction not merely in the knowledge of things human and divine, but would also lead him through a course of subjects, which in themselves are comparatively trivial, as for instance the elaborate subtleties of formal logic: not that acquaintance

QUINTILIAN

dilinae possint facere sapientem, sed quia illum ne
6 in minimis quidem oporteat falli. Similiter oratorem, qui debet esse sapiens, non geometres faciet
aut musicus quaeque his alia subiungam, sed hae
quoque artes, ut sit consummatus, iuvabunt. Nisi
forte antidotos quidem atque alia, quae oculis aut
vulneribus medentur, ex multis atque interim contrariis quoque inter se effectibus componi videmus,
quorum ex diversis fit una illa mixtura, quae nulli
earum similis est, ex quibus constat, sed proprias vires
7 ex omnibus sumit; et muta animalia mellis illum
inimitabilem humanae rationi saporem vario florum
ac sucorum genere perficiunt: nos mirabimur, si
oratio, qua nihil praestantius homini dedit providentia, pluribus artibus egeat, quae, etiam cum se
non ostendunt in dicendo nec proferunt, vim tamen
occultam suggerunt et tacitae quoque sentiuntur?
8 "Fuit aliquis sine iis disertus": sed ego oratorem
volo. "Non multum adiiciunt": sed aeque non
erit totum, cui vel parva deerunt; et optimum
quidem hoc esse conveniet; cuius etiamsi in arduo
spes est, nos tamen praecipiamus omnia, ut saltem
plura fiant. Sed cur deficiat animus? Natura enim
perfectum oratorem esse non prohibet, turpiterque
desperatur quidquid fieri potest.

---

[1] You have what you have not lost: you have not lost
horns : therefore you have horns.

[2] A crocodile, having seized a woman's son, said that he
would restore him, if she would tell him the truth. She
replied, " You will not restore him." Was it the crocodile's
duty to give him up?

with the so called " horn "¹ or " crocodile"² problems
can make a man wise, but because it is important that he should never trip even in the
smallest trifles. So too the teacher of geometry, 6
music or other subjects which I would class with
these, will not be able to create the perfect orator
(who like the philosopher ought to be a wise man),
but none the less these arts will assist in his perfection. I may draw a parallel from the use of antidotes
and other remedies applied to the eyes or to wounds.
We know that these are composed of ingredients
which produce many and sometimes contrary effects,
but mixed together they make a single compound
resembling no one of its component parts, but
deriving its peculiar properties from all : so too dumb 7
insects produce honey, whose taste is beyond the
skill of man to imitate, from different kinds of flowers
and juices. Shall we marvel then, if oratory, the
highest gift of providence to man, needs the assistance
of many arts, which, although they do not reveal or
intrude themselves in actual speaking, supply hidden
forces and make their silent presence felt ? " But " 8
it will be urged "men have proved fluent without
their aid." Granted, but I am in quest of an orator.
"Their contribution is but small." Yes, but we shall
never attain completeness, if minor details be
lacking. And it will be agreed that though our
ideal of perfection may dwell on a height that is hard
to gain, it is our duty to teach all we know, that
achievement may at least come somewhat nearer
the goal. But why should our courage fail ? The
perfect orator is not contrary to the laws of nature,
and it is cowardly to despair of anything that is
within the bounds of possibility.

9   Atque ego vel iudicio veterum poteram esse
contentus. Nam quis ignorat musicen (ut de hac
primum loquar) tantum iam illis antiquis temporibus
non studii modo verum etiam venerationis habuisse,
ut iidem musici et vates et sapientes iudicarentur
(mittam alios) Orpheus et Linus ; quorum utrumque
dis genitum, alterum vero, quia rudes quoque atque
agrestes animos admiratione mulceret, non feras
modo sed saxa etiam silvasque duxisse posteritatis
10 memoriae traditum est.   Itaque et Timagenes auctor
est, omnium in litteris studiorum antiquissimam
musicen extitisse, et testimonio sunt clarissimi
poetae, apud quos inter regalia convivia laudes
heroum ac deorum ad citharam canebantur. Iopas
vero ille Vergilii nonne *canit errantem lunam solisque
labores* et cetera? Quibus certe palam confirmat
auctor eminentissimus, musicen cum divinarum
11 etiam rerum cognitione esse coniunctam. Quod si
datur, erit etiam oratori necessaria, siquidem (ut
diximus) haec quoque pars, quae ab oratoribus relicta
a philosophis est occupata, nostri operis fuit, ac sine
omnium talium scientia non potest esse perfecta
12 eloquentia. Atque claros nomine sapientiae viros,
nemo dubitaverit, studiosos musices fuisse, cum
Pythagoras atque eum secuti acceptam sine dubio
antiquitus opinionem vulgaverint, mundum ipsum
ratione esse compositum, quam postea sit lyra

---

[1] *Aen.* i. 742.

For myself I should be ready to accept the verdict 9
of antiquity. Who is ignorant of the fact that
music, of which I will speak first, was in ancient
times the object not merely of intense study but of
veneration : in fact Orpheus and Linus, to mention
no others, were regarded as uniting the roles of musician, poet and philosopher. Both were of divine
origin, while the former, because by the marvel of
his music he soothed the savage breast, is recorded
to have drawn after him not merely beasts of the
wild, but rocks and trees. So too Timagenes 10
asserts that music is the oldest of the arts related to
literature, a statement which is confirmed by the testi-
mony of the greatest of poets in whose songs we read
that the praise of heroes and of gods were sung to
the music of the lyre at the feasts of kings. Does not
Iopas, the Vergilian bard, sing

" The wandering moon and labours of the Sun " [1]

and the like ? whereby the supreme poet mani-
fests most clearly that music is united with the
knowledge even of things divine. If this be admit- 11
ted, music will be a necessity even for an orator,
since those fields of knowledge, which were annexed
by philosophy on their abandonment by oratory,
once were ours and without the knowledge of all
such things there can be no perfect eloquence.
There can in any case be no doubt that some of 12
those men whose wisdom is a household word have
been earnest students of music : Pythagoras for
instance and his followers popularised the belief,
which they no doubt had received from earlier
teachers, that the universe is constructed on the
same principles which were afterwards imitated in

imitata, nec illa modo contenti dissimilium con-
cordia, quam vocant ἁρμονίαν, sonum quoque iis
13 motibus dederint. Nam Plato, cum in aliis quibusdam tum praecipue in Timaeo, ne intelligi
quidem nisi ab iis, qui hanc quoque partem disciplinae diligenter perceperint, potest. De philosophis loquor, quorum fons ipse Socrates iam senex
14 institui lyra non erubescebat? Duces maximos et
fidibus et tibiis cecinisse traditum et exercitus
Lacedaemoniorum musicis accensos modis. Quid
autem aliud in nostris legionibus cornua ac tubae
faciunt? quorum concentus quanto est vehementior,
tantum Romana in bellis gloria ceteris praestat.
15 Non igitur frustra Plato civili viro, quem πολιτικὸν
vocat, necessariam musicen credidit. Et eius
sectae, quae aliis severissima aliis asperrima videtur,
principes in hac fuere sententia, ut existimarent
sapientium aliquos nonnullam operam his studiis
accommodaturos. Et Lycurgus, durissimarum Lace-
daemoniis legum auctor, musices disciplinam pro-
16 bavit. Atque eam natura ipsa videtur ad tolerandos
facilius labores velut muneri nobis dedisse, si quidem
et remigem cantus hortatur; nec solum in iis
operibus, in quibus plurium conatus praeeunte aliqua
iucunda voce conspirat, sed etiam singulorum fatigatio quamlibet se rudi modulatione solatur.
17 Laudem adhuc dicere artis pulcherrimae videor,

---

[1] The music of the spheres: *cp.* the vision of Er in Plato
(*Rep.* 10) and the *Somnium Scipionis* of Cicero. The
sounds produced by the heavenly bodies correspond to the
notes of the heptachord.

the construction of the lyre, and not content merely
with emphasising that concord of discordant elements
which they style harmony attributed a sound to the
motions of the celestial bodies.[1] As for Plato, there 13
are certain passages in his works, more especially in
the *Timaeus*,[2] which are quite unintelligible to those
who have not studied the theory of music. But
why speak only of the philosophers, whose master,
Socrates, did not blush to receive instruction in playing the lyre even when far advanced in years? It is 14
recorded that the greatest generals played on the
lyre and the pipe, and that the armies of Sparta were
fired to martial ardour by the strains of music. And
what else is the function of the horns and trumpets
attached to our legions? The louder the concert of
their notes, the greater is the glorious supremacy of
our arms over all the nations of the earth. It was 15
not therefore without reason that Plato regarded the
knowledge of music as necessary to his ideal statesman or politician, as he calls him; while the leaders
even of that school, which in other respects is the
strictest and most severe of all schools of philosophy,[3]
held that the wise man might well devote some of
his attention to such studies. Lycurgus himself, the
founder of the stern laws of Sparta, approved of the
training supplied by music. Indeed nature itself 16
seems to have given music as a boon to men to lighten
the strain of labour: even the rower in the galleys
is cheered to effort by song. Nor is this function of
music confined to cases where the efforts of a number
are given union by the sound of some sweet voice
that sets the tune, but even solitary workers find
solace at their toil in artless song. So far I have 17
attempted merely to sound the praises of the noblest

[2] *Tim.* p. 47.   [3] *sc.* the Stoics.

nondum eam tamen oratori coniungere. Transeamus igitur id quoque, quod grammatice quondam
ac musice iunctae fuerunt; siquidem Archytas atque
Euenus etiam subiectam grammaticen musicae putaverunt, et eosdem utriusque rei praeceptores fuisse
cum Sophron ostendit, mimorum quidem scriptor
sed quem Plato adeo probavit, ut suppositos capiti
18 libros eius, cum moreretur, habuisse credatur, tum
Eupolis, apud quem Prodamus et musicen et litteras
docet, et Maricas, qui est Hyperbolus, nihil se ex
musice scire nisi litteras confitetur. Aristophanes
quoque non uno libro sic institui pueros antiquitus
solitos esse demonstrat, et apud Menandrum in
Hypobolimaeo senex, qui reposcenti filium patri
velut˙ rationem impendiorum, quae in educationem
contulerit, exponens, psaltis se et geometris multa
19 dicit dedisse. Unde etiam ille mos, ut in conviviis
post cenam circumferretur lyra; cuius cum se
imperitum Themistocles confessus esset, ut verbis
20 Ciceronis utar, *est habitus indoctior*. Sed veterum
quoque Romanorum epulis fides ac tibias adhibere
moris fuit. Versus quoque Saliorum habent carmen.
Quae cum omnia sint a Numa rege instituta, faciunt
manifestum, ne illis quidem, qui rudes ac bellicosi
videntur, cura musices, quantum illa recipiebat aetas,
21 defuisse. Denique in proverbium usque Graecorum

---

[1] *Knights*, 188.
[2] *Tusc. Disp.* I. ii. 4.

of arts without bringing it into connexion with the
education of an orator. I will therefore pass by the
fact that the art of letters and that of music were
once united : indeed Archytas and Euenus held
that the former was subordinate to the latter, while
we know that the same instructors were employed
for the teaching of both from Sophron, a writer of
farces, it is true, but so highly esteemed by Plato,
that he is believed to have had Sophron's works
under his pillow on his deathbed : the same fact is 18
proved by the case of Eupolis, who makes Prodamus
teach both music and literature, and whose Maricas,
who was none other than Hyperbolus in disguise,
asserts that he knows nothing of music but letters.
Aristophanes [1] again in more than one of his plays
shows that boys were trained in music from remote
antiquity, while in the *Hypobolimaeus* of Menander
an old man, when a father claims his son from him,
gives an account of all expenses incurred on behalf
of the boy's education and states that he has paid
out large sums to musicians and geometricians.
From the importance thus given to music also origi- 19
nated the custom of taking a lyre round the company
after dinner, and when on such an occasion Themistocles confessed that he could not play, his education
was (to quote the words of Cicero) " regarded as im-
perfect." [2] Even at the banquets of our own forefathers 20
it was the custom to introduce the pipe and lyre, and
even the hymn of the Salii has its tune. These
practices were instituted by King Numa and clearly
prove that not even those whom we regard as rude
warriors, neglected the study of music, at least in so
far as the resources of that age allowed. Finally 21
there was actually a proverb among the Greeks,

celebratum est, indoctos a Musis atque a Gratiis
22 abesse. Verum quid ex ea proprie petat futurus
orator, disseramus.

Numeros musice duplices habet in vocibus et in
corpore, utriusque enim rei aptus quidam modus
desideratur. Vocis rationem Aristoxenus musicus
dividit in ῥυθμὸν et μέλος, quorum alterum modulatione, alterum canore ac sonis constat. Num igitur
non haec omnia oratori necessaria? quorum unum
ad gestum, alterum ad collocationem verborum,
tertium ad flexus vocis, qui sunt in agendo quoque
23 plurimi, pertinet : nisi forte in carminibus tantum et
in canticis exigitur structura quaedam et inoffensa
copulatio vocum, in agendo supervacua est ; aut non
compositio et sonus in oratione quoque varie pro
24 rerum modo adhibetur sicut in musice. Namque et
voce et modulatione grandia elate, iucunda dulciter,
moderata leniter canit, totaque arte consentit cum
25 eorum quae dicuntur adfectibus. Atqui in orando
quoque intentio vocis, remissio, flexus pertinet ad
movendos audientium adfectus, aliaque et colloca-
tionis et vocis (ut eodem utar verbo) modulatione
concitationem iudicis, alia misericordiam petimus ;
cum etiam organis, quibus sermo exprimi non potest,
26 adfici animos in diversum habitum sentiamus. Cor-

---

[1] Music includes dancing.

that the uneducated were far from the company of
the Muses and Graces.   But let us discuss the 22
advantages which our future orator may reasonably
expect to derive from the study of Music.

Music has two modes of expression in the voice
and in the body;[1] for both voice and body require
to be controlled by appropriate rules.   Aristoxenus
divides music, in so far as it concerns the voice, into
rhythm and *melody*, the one consisting in measure,
the latter in sound and song.   Now I ask you whether
it is not absolutely necessary for the orator to be
acquainted with all these methods of expression
which are concerned firstly with gesture, secondly
with the arrangement of words and thirdly with the
inflexions of the voice, of which a great variety are
required in pleading.   Otherwise we must assume 23
that structure and the euphonious combination of
sounds are necessary only for poetry, lyric and otherwise, but superfluous in pleading, or that unlike
music, oratory has no interest in the variation of
arrangement and sound to suit the demands of the
case.   But eloquence does vary both tone and rhythm, 24
expressing sublime thoughts with elevation, pleasing
thoughts with sweetness, and ordinary with gentle
utterance, and in every expression of its art is in
sympathy with the emotions of which it is the mouth-
piece.   It is by the raising, lowering or inflexion of 25
the voice that the orator stirs the emotions of his
hearers, and the measure, if I may repeat the term,
of voice or phrase differs according as we wish
to rouse the indignation or the pity of the judge.
For, as we know, different emotions are roused even
by the various musical instruments, which are
incapable of reproducing speech.   Further the 26

poris quoque aptus et decens motus, qui dicitur
εὐρυθμία, et est necessarius nec aliunde peti potest;
in quo pars actionis non minima consistit, qua de
27 re sepositus nobis est locus.   Age, non habebit
imprimis curam vocis orator?   Quid tam musices
proprium?   Sed ne haec quidem praesumenda pars
est.   Uno interim contenti simus exemplo C.
Gracchi, praecipui suorum temporum oratoris, cui
contionanti consistens post eum musicus fistula,
quam τονάριον vocant, modos, quibus deberet intendi,
28 monstrabat.   Haec ei cura inter turbidissimas
actiones vel terrenti optimates vel iam timenti fuit.
Libet propter quosdam imperitiores etiam crassiore,
ut vocant, Musa dubitationem huius utilitatis
29 eximere.   Nam poetas certe legendos oratori futuro
concesserint: num igitur hi sine musice? ac si quis
tam caecus animi est, ut de aliis dubitet, illos certe,
qui carmina ad lyram composuerunt.   Haec diutius
forent dicenda, si hoc studium velut novum praeci-
30 perem.   Cum vero antiquitus usque a Chirone atque
Achille ad nostra tempora apud omnes, qui modo
legitimam disciplinam non sint perosi, duraverit,

---

[1] Book XI. chap. iii.

motion of the body must be suitable and becoming,
or as the Greeks call it *eurythmic*, and this can only
be secured by the study of music. This is a most
important department of eloquence, and will receive
separate treatment in this work.[1] To proceed, an 27
orator will assuredly pay special attention to his
voice, and what is so specially the concern of music
as this? Here too I must not anticipate a later
section of this work, and will content myself by
citing the example of Gaius Gracchus, the leading
orator of his age, who during his speeches had a
musician standing behind him with a pitchpipe, or
tonarion as the Greeks call it, whose duty it was to
give him the tones in which his voice was to be
pitched. Such was the attention which he paid to 28
this point even in the midst of his most turbulent
speeches, when he was terrifying the patrician party
and even when he had begun to fear their power.
I should like for the benefit of the uninstructed,
those " creatures of the heavier Muse," as the saying
is, to remove all doubts as to the value of music.
They will at any rate admit that the poets should be 29
read by our future orator. But can they be read
without some knowledge of music? Or if any of
my critics be so blind as to have some doubts about
other forms of poetry, can the lyric poets at any
rate be read without such knowledge? If there
were anything novel in my insistence on the study
of music, I should have to treat the matter at
greater length. But in view of the fact that the 30
study of music has, from those remote times when
Chiron taught Achilles down to our own day, continued to be studied by all except those who
have a hatred for any regular course of study, it

non est committendum, ut illa dubia faciam defensi-
31 onis sollicitudine.   Quamvis autem satis iam ex
ipsis, quibus sum modo usus, exemplis credam esse
manifestum, quae mihi et quatenus musice placeat,
apertius tamen profitendum puto, non hanc a me
praecipi, quae nunc in scenis effeminata et impudicis
modis fracta non ex parte minima, si quid in nobis
virilis roboris manebat, excidit, sed qua laudes
fortium canebantur, quaque ipsi fortes canebant;
nec psalteria et spadicas, etiam virginibus probis
recusanda, sed cognitionem rationis, quae ad movendos leniendosque adfectus plurimum valet.
32 Nam et Pythagoran accepimus concitatos ad vim
pudicae domui adferendam iuvenes, iussa mutare in
spondeum modos tibicina, composuisse; et Chrysippus etiam nutricum illi, quae adhibetur infantibus,
33 adlectationi suum quoddam carmen assignat.   Est
etiam non inerudite ad declamandum ficta materia,
in qua ponitur tibicen, qui sacrificanti Phrygium
cecinerat, acto illo in insaniam et per praecipitia
delato accusari, quod causa mortis extiterit; quae
si dici debet ab oratore nec dici citra scientiam

would be a mistake to seem to cast any doubt upon
its value by showing an excessive zeal in its defence.
It will, however, I think be sufficiently clear from 31
the examples I have already quoted, what I regard
as the value and the sphere of music in the training
of an orator. Still I think I ought to be more
emphatic than I have been in stating that the music
which I desire to see taught is not our modern music,
which has been emasculated by the lascivious melo-
dies of our effeminate stage and has to no small
extent destroyed such manly vigour as we still
possessed. No, I refer to the music of old which was
employed to sing the praises of brave men and was
sung by the brave themselves. I will have none
of your psalteries and viols, that are unfit even for
the use of a modest girl. Give me the knowledge
of the principles of music, which have power to
excite or assuage the emotions of mankind. We 32
are told that Pythagoras on one occasion, when some
young men were led astray by their passions to
commit an outrage on a respectable family, calmed
them by ordering the piper to change her strain to a
spondaic measure, while Chrysippus selects a special
tune to be used by nurses to entice their little charges
to sleep. Further I may point out that among the 33
fictitious themes employed in declamation is one,
doing no little credit to its author's learning, in
which it is supposed that a piper is accused of manslaughter because he had played a tune in the Phry-
gian mode as an accompaniment to a sacrifice, with
the result that the person officiating went mad and
flung himself over a precipice. If an orator is
expected to declaim on such a theme as this, which
cannot possibly be handled without some knowledge

musices potest, quomodo non hanc quoque artem
necessariam esse operi nostro vel iniqui consentient?

34   In geometria partem fatentur esse utilem teneris
aetatibus.   Agitari namque animos et acui ingenia
et celeritatem percipiendi venire inde concedunt,
sed prodesse eam non ut ceteras artes, cum per-
ceptae sint, sed cum discatur, existimant: ea vulgaris

35 opinio est.   Nec sine causa summi viri etiam im-
pensam huic scientiae operam dederunt.   Nam
cum sit geometria divisa in numeros atque formas,
numerorum quidem notitia non oratori modo, sed
cuicunque saltem primis litteris erudito necessaria
est.   In causis vero vel frequentissime versari solet;
in quibus actor, non dico, si circa summas trepidat,
sed si digitorum saltem incerto aut indecoro gestu

36 a computatione dissentit, iudicatur indoctus.   Illa
vero linearis ratio et ipsa quidem cadit frequenter
in causas (nam de terminis mensurisque sunt lites),
sed habet maiorem quandam aliam cum arte oratoria

37 cognationem.   Iam primum ordo est geometriae
necessarius; nonne et eloquentiae?   Ex prioribus
geometria probat insequentia, ex certis incerta;
nonne id in dicendo facimus?   Quid? illa proposi-
tarum quaestionum conclusio non fere tota constat

---

[1] Geometry here includes all mathematics.
[2] There was a separate symbol for each number, depending
on the hand used and the position of the fingers.   See *Class.
Review*, 1911, p. 72.

of music, how can my critics for all their prejudice
fail to agree that music is a necessary element in
the education of an orator?

As regards geometry,[1] it is granted that portions of 34
this science are of value for the instruction of children:
for admittedly it exercises their minds, sharpens
their wits and generates quickness of perception.
But it is considered that the value of geometry
resides in the process of learning, and not as with
other sciences in the knowledge thus acquired.
Such is the general opinion. But it is not without 35
good reason that some of the greatest men have
devoted special attention to this science. Geometry
has two divisions; one is concerned with numbers,
the other with figures. Now knowledge of the former
is a necessity not merely to the orator, but to any
one who has had even an elementary education.
Such knowledge is frequently required in actual
cases, in which a speaker is regarded as de-
ficient in education, I will not say if he hesitates
in making a calculation, but even if he contradicts
the calculation which he states in words by making
an uncertain or inappropriate gesture with his fingers.[2]
Again linear geometry is frequently required in 36
cases, as in lawsuits about boundaries and measurements. But geometry and oratory are related in a
yet more important way than this. In the first 37
place logical development is one of the necessities
of geometry. And is it not equally a necessity for
oratory? Geometry arrives at its conclusions from
definite premises, and by arguing from what is certain
proves what was previously uncertain. Is not this
just what we do in speaking? Again are not the
problems of geometry almost entirely solved by the

syllogismis? Propter quod plures invenias, qui
dialecticae similem quam qui rhetoricae fateantur
hanc artem. Verum et orator etiamsi raro non
38 tamen nunquam probabit dialectice. Nam et syllogismo, si res poscet, utetur et certe enthymemate,
qui rhetoricus est syllogismus. Denique probationum quae sunt potentissimae γραμμικαὶ ἀποδείξεις
vulgo dicuntur: quid autem magis oratio quam
39 probationem petit? Falsa quoque veris similia
geometrica ratione deprehendit. Fit hoc et in
numeris per quasdam, quas ψευδογραφίας vocant,
quibus pueri ludere solebamus. Sed alia maiora
sunt. Nam quis non ita proponenti credat?
"Quorum locorum extremae lineae eandem mensuram
colligunt, eorum spatium quoque, quod iis lineis
40 continetur, par sit necesse est." At id falsum est.
Nam plurimum refert, cuius sit formae ille circuitus;
reprehensique a geometris sunt historici, qui mag-
nitudinem insularum satis significari navigationis
ambitu crediderunt. Nam ut quaeque forma per-
41 fectissima ita capacissima est. Ideoque illa circum-
currens linea si efficiet orbem, quae forma est in
planis maxime perfecta, amplius spatium complec-
tetur quam si quadratum paribus oris efficiat, rursus
quadrata triangulis, triangula ipsa plus aequis lateri-
42 bus quam inaequalibus. Sed alia forsitan obscuriora;

---

[1] See v. xiv. 1 for an example from the *Pro Ligario*.
"The cause was then doubtful, as there were arguments on
both sides. Now, however, we must regard that cause as the
better, to which the gods have given their approval."

syllogistic method, a fact which makes the majority
assert that geometry bears a closer resemblance to
logic than to rhetoric? But even the orator will
sometimes, though rarely, prove his point by formal
logic. For, if necessary, he will use the syllogism, 38
and he will certainly make use of the enthymeme
which is a rhetorical form of syllogism.[1] Further
the most absolute form of proof is that which is
generally known as linear demonstration. And what
is the aim of oratory if not proof? Again oratory 39
sometimes detects falsehoods closely resembling the
truth by the use of geometrical methods. An
example of this may be found in connexion with
numbers in the so-called pseudographs, a favourite
amusement in our boyhood.[2] But there are more
important points to be considered. Who is there
who would not accept the following proposition?
"When the lines bounding two figures are equal in
length, the areas contained within those lines are
equal." But this is false, for everything depends on 40
the shape of the figure formed by these lines, and
historians have been taken to task by geometricians
for believing the time taken to circumnavigate an
island to be a sufficient indication of its size. For
the space enclosed is in proportion to the perfection
of the figure. Consequently if the bounding line 41
to which we have referred form a circle, the most
perfect of all plane figures, it will contain a greater
space than if the same length of line took the form
of a square, while a square contains a greater space
than a triangle having the same total perimeter, and
an equilateral triangle than a scalene triangle. But 42
there are other points which perhaps present greater

[2] It is not known to what Quintilian refers.

nos facillimum etiam imperitis sequamur experimentum. Iugeri mensuram ducentos et quadraginta longitudinis pedes esse dimidioque in latitudinem patere, non fere quisquam est qui ignoret, et qui sit circuitus et quantum campi claudat, colligere expedi-
43 tum. At centeni et octogeni in quamque partem pedes idem spatium extremitatis sed multo amplius clausae quattuor lineis areae faciunt. Id si computare quem piget, brevioribus numeris idem discat. Nam deni in quadram pedes, quadraginta per oram, intra centum erunt. At si quini deni per latera, quini in fronte sint, ex illo, quod amplectuntur,
44 quartam deducent eodem circumductu. Si vero porrecti utrinque undeviceni singulis distent, non plures intus quadratos habebunt, quam per quot longitudo ducetur; quae circumibit autem linea, eiusdem spatii erit, cuius ea quae centum continet. Ita quidquid formae quadrati detraxeris, amplitudini
45 quoque peribit. Ergo etiam id fieri potest, ut maiore circuitu minor loci amplitudo claudatur. Haec in planis. Nam in collibus vallibusque etiam
46 imperito patet plus soli esse quam caeli. Quid quod se eadem geometria tollit ad rationem usque mundi? in qua, cum siderum certos constitutosque cursus numeris docet, discimus nihil esse inordinatum atque fortuitum; quod ipsum nonnunquam pertinere ad oratorem potest.
47 tinere ad oratorem potest. An vero, cum Pericles

difficulty. I will take an example which is easy
even for those who have no knowledge of geometry.
There is scarcely anyone who does not know that
the Roman acre is 240 feet long and 120 feet
broad, and its total perimeter and the area enclosed
can easily be calculated. But a square of 180 feet 43
gives the same perimeter, yet contains a much
larger area within its four sides. If the calculation
prove irksome to any of my readers, he can learn the
same truth by employing smaller numbers. Take a
ten foot square: its perimeter is forty feet and it
contains 100 square feet. But if the dimensions be
fifteen feet by five, while the perimeter is the same,
the area enclosed is less by a quarter. On the other 44
hand if we draw a parallelogram measuring nineteen
feet by one, the number of square feet enclosed will
be no greater than the number of linear feet making
the actual length of the parallelogram, though the
perimeter will be exactly as that of the figure which
encloses an area of 100 square feet. Consequently the
area enclosed by four lines will decrease in proportion
as we depart from the form of a square. It further 45
follows that it is perfectly possible for the space
enclosed to be less, though the perimeter be greater.
This applies to plane figures only : for even one who
is no mathematician can see that, when we have to
consider hills or valleys, the extent of ground enclosed
is greater than the sky over it. But geometry soars 46
still higher to the consideration of the system of
the universe : for by its calculations it demonstrates
the fixed and ordained courses of the stars, and
thereby we acquire the knowledge that all things
are ruled by order and destiny, a consideration
which may at times be of value to an orator. When 47

Athenienses solis obscuratione territos redditis eius
rei causis metu liberavit, aut cum Sulpicius ille
Gallus in exercitu L. Paulli de lunae defectione
disseruit, ne velut prodigio divinitus facto militum
animi terrerentur, non videtur usus esse oratoris
48 officio ? Quod si Nicias in Sicilia scisset, non eodem
confusus metu pulcherrimum Atheniensium exercitum perdidisset; sicut Dion, cum ad destruendam
Dionysii tyrannidem venit, non est tali casu deter-
ritus. Sint extra licet usus bellici, transeamusque,
quod Archimedes unus obsidionem Syracusarum in
49 longius traxit. Illud utique iam proprium ad efficiendum quod intendimus, plurimas quaestiones,
quibus difficilior alia ratione explicatio est, ut de
ratione dividendi, de sectione in infinitum, de cele-
ritate augenda, linearibus illis probationibus solvi
solere ; ut, si est oratori (quod proximus demonstra-
bit liber) de omnibus rebus dicendum, nullo modo
sine geometria esse possit orator.

XI. Dandum aliquid comoedo quoque, dum eate-
nus, qua pronuntiandi scientiam futurus orator
desiderat. Non enim puerum, quem in hoc instituimus, aut femineae vocis exilitate frangi volo aut
2 seniliter tremere. Nec vitia ebrietatis effingat

---

[1] Quintilian is perhaps referring to the measurement of
the area of an irregular figure by dividing it into a number
of small equal and regular figures the size of which was
calculable.

Pericles dispelled the panic caused at Athens by the eclipse of the sun by explaining the causes of the phenomenon, or Sulpicius Gallus discoursed on the eclipse of the moon to the army of Lucius Paulus to prevent the soldiers being seized with terror at what they regarded as a portent sent by heaven, did not they discharge the function of an orator? If Nicias 48 had known this when he commanded in Sicily, he would not have shared the terror of his men nor lost the finest army that Athens ever placed in the field. Dion for instance when he came to Syracuse to over-throw the tyranny of Dionysius, was not frightened away by the occurrence of a similar phenomenon. However we are not concerned with the uses of geometry in war and need not dwell upon the fact that Archimedes singlehanded succeeded in appreci-ably prolonging the resistance of Syracuse when it was besieged. It will suffice for our purpose that 49 there are a number of problems which it is difficult to solve in any other way, which are as a rule solved by these linear demonstrations, such as the method of division, section to infinity,[1] and the ratio of in-crease in velocity. From this we may conclude that, if as we shall show in the next book an orator has to speak on every kind of subject, he can under no circumstances dispense with a knowledge of geometry.

XI. The comic actor will also claim a certain amount of our attention, but only in so far as our future orator must be a master of the art of delivery. For I do not of course wish the boy, whom we are training to this end, to talk with the shrillness of a woman or in the tremulous accents of old age. Nor 2 for that matter must he ape the vices of the

neque servili vernilitate imbuatur nec amoris, avaritiae, metus discat adfectum ; quae neque oratori sunt necessaria et mentem, praecipue in aetate prima
3 teneram adhuc et rudem, inficiunt. Nam frequens imitatio transit in mores. Ne gestus quidem omnis ac motus a comoedis petendus est. Quanquam enim utrumque eorum ad quendam modum praestare debet orator, plurimum tamen aberit a scenico, nec vultu nec manu nec excursionibus nimius. Nam si qua in his ars est dicentium, ea prima est, ne ars esse videatur.

4 Quod est igitur huius doctoris officium? In primis vitia si qua sunt oris emendet, ut expressa sint verba, ut suis quaeque litterae sonis enuntientur. Quarundam enim vel exilitate vel pinguitudine nimia laboramus, quasdam velut acriores parum efficimus et aliis non dissimilibus sed quasi hebetioribus per-
5 mutamus. Quippe et Rho litterae, qua Demosthenes quoque laboravit, Labda succedit (quarum vis est apud nos quoque); et cum *c* ac similiter *g* non
6 evaluerunt, in *t* ac *d* molliuntur. Ne illas quidem circa *s* litteram delicias hic magister feret, nec verba in faucibus patietur audiri nec oris inanitate resonare

---

[1] The mis-spelling of *flagro* as *fraglo* exemplifies the confusion to which Quintilian refers. A similar, though correct, substitution is found in *lavacrum* for *lavaclum*, etc. See Lindsay, *Lat. Langu.*, pp. 92 ff.

drunkard, or copy the cringing manners of a slave, or learn to express the emotions of love, avarice or fear. Such accomplishments are not necessary to an orator and corrupt the mind, especially while it is still pliable and unformed. For repeated imita- 3 tion passes into habit. Nor yet again must we adopt all the gestures and movements of the actor. Within certain limits the orator must be a master of both, but he must rigorously avoid staginess and all extravagance of facial expression, gesture and gait. For if an orator does command a certain art in such matters, its highest expression will be in the concealment of its existence.

What then is the duty of the teacher whom 4 we have borrowed from the stage? In the first place he must correct all faults of pronunciation, and see that the utterance is distinct, and that each letter has its proper sound. There is an unfortunate tendency in the case of some letters to pronounce them either too thinly or too fully, while some we find too harsh and fail to pronounce sufficiently, substituting others whose sound is similar but somewhat duller. For instance, 5 *lambda* is substituted for *rho*, a letter which was always a stumbling-block to Demosthenes; our *l* and *r* have of course the same value.[1] Similarly when *c* and *g* are not given their full value, they are softened into *t* and *d*. Again our teacher must 6 not tolerate the affected pronunciation of *s*[2] with which we are painfully familiar, nor suffer words to be uttered from the depths of the throat or

---

[2] Quintilian perhaps alludes to the habit of prefixing *i* to initial *st*, *sp*, *sc* found in inscriptions of the later Empire. See Lindsay, *op. cit.* p. 102.

nec, quod minime sermoni puro conveniat, simplicem
vocis naturam pleniore quodam sono circumliniri,
7 quod Graeci καταπεπλασμένον dicunt. Sic appellatur
cantus tibiarum, quae praeclusis quibus clarescunt
foraminibus, recto modo exitu graviorem spiritum
8 reddunt. Curabit etiam, ne extremae syllabae in-
tercidant, ut par sibi sermo sit, ut, quotiens exclamandum erit, lateris conatus sit ille non capitis, ut
gestus ad vocem, vultus ad gestum accommodetur.
9 Observandum erit etiam, ut recta sit facies dicentis,
ne labra distorqueantur, ne immodicus hiatus rictum
discindat, ne supinus vultus, ne deiecti in terram
oculi, ne inclinata utrolibet cervix. Nam frons pluri-
10 bus generibus peccat. Vidi multos, quorum super-
cilia ad singulos vocis conatus adlevarentur, aliorum
constricta, aliorum etiam dissidentia, cum alterum in
verticem tenderent, altero paene oculus ipse preme-
11 retur. Infinitum autem, ut mox dicemus, in his
quoque rebus momentum est; et nihil potest placere
quod non decet.

12   Debet etiam docere comoedus, quomodo narrandum, qua sit auctoritate suadendum, qua concitatione
consurgat ira, qui flexus deceat miserationem. Quod
ita optime faciet, si certos ex comoediis elegerit

rolled out hollow-mouthed, or permit the natural sound of the voice to be over-laid with a fuller sound, a fault fatal to purity of speech; the Greeks give this peculiarity the name καταπε- 7 πλασμένον (plastered over), a term applied to the tone produced by a pipe, when the stops which produce the treble notes are closed, and a bass note is produced through the main aperture only. He 8 will also see that final syllables are not clipped, that the quality of speech is continuously maintained, that when the voice is raised, the strain falls upon the lungs and not the mouth, and that gesture and voice are mutually appropriate. He will also insist 9 that the speaker faces his audience, that the lips are not distorted nor the jaws parted to a grin, that the face is not thrown back, nor the eyes fixed on the ground, nor the neck slanted to left or right. For there are a variety of faults of facial expression. I have seen many, who raised their brows whenever 10 the voice was called upon for an effort, others who wore a perpetual frown, and yet others who could not keep their eyebrows level, but raised one towards the top of the head and depressed the other till it almost closed the eye. These are 11 details, but as I shall shortly show, they are of enormous importance, for nothing that is unbecoming can have a pleasing effect.

Our actor will also be required to show how a 12 narrative should be delivered, and to indicate the authoritative tone that should be given to advice, the excitement which should mark the rise of anger, and the change of tone that is characteristic of pathos. The best method of so doing is to select special passages from comedy appropriate for the

locos et ad hoc maxime idoneos, id est, actionibus
13 similes. Iidem autem non ad pronuntiandum modo
utilissimi verum ad augendam quoque eloquentiam
14 maxime accommodati erunt. Et haec, dum infirma
aetas maiora non capiet; ceterum, cum legere orationes oportebit, cum virtutes earum iam sentiet,
tum mihi diligens aliquis ac peritus adsistat, neque
solum lectionem formet, verum ediscere etiam electa
ex iis cogat et ea dicere stantem clare et quemadmodum agere oportebit, ut protinus pronuntiationem,
vocem, memoriam exerceat.

15 Ne illos quidem reprehendendos puto, qui paulum
etiam palaestricis vacaverunt. Non de his loquor,
quibus pars vitae in oleo, pars in vino consumitur,
qui corporum cura mentem obruerunt (hos enim
abesse ab eo quem instituimus quam longissime
16 velim); sed nomen est idem iis, a quibus gestus
motusque formantur, ut recta sint brachia, ne in-
doctae rusticae manus, ne status indecorus, ne qua
in proferendis pedibus inscitia, ne caput oculique ab
17 alia corporis inclinatione dissideant. Nam neque
haec esse in parte pronuntiationis negaverit quisquam, neque ipsam pronuntiationem ab oratore
secernet, et certe, quod facere oporteat, non indig-
nandum est discere, cum praesertim haec chironomia,
quae est, ut nomine ipso declaratur, lex gestus, et
ab illis temporibus heroicis orta sit et a summis

purpose, that is to say, resembling the speeches of
a pleader. These are not only most useful in train- 13
ing the delivery, but are admirably adapted to
increase a speaker's eloquence. These are the 14
methods to be employed while the pupil is too young
to take in more advanced instruction; but when
the time has come for him to read speeches, and as
soon as he begins to appreciate their merits, he
should have a careful and efficient teacher at his
side not merely to form his style of reading aloud,
but to make him learn select passages by heart and
declaim them standing in the manner which actual
pleading would require : thus he will simultaneously
train delivery, voice and memory.

I will not blame even those who give a certain 15
amount of time to the teacher of gymnastics. I am
not speaking of those, who spend part of their life
in rubbing themselves with oil and part in wine-
bibbing, and kill the mind by over-attention to the
body : indeed, I would have such as these kept
as far as possible from the boy whom we are
training. But we give the same name to those who 16
form gesture and motion so that the arms may be
extended in the proper manner, the management of
the hands free from all trace of rusticity and
inelegance, the attitude becoming, the movements
of the feet appropriate and the motions of the head
and eyes in keeping with the poise of the body. No 17
one will deny that such details form a part of the
art of delivery, nor divorce delivery from oratory ;
and there can be no justification for disdaining to
learn what has got to be done, especially as
chironomy, which, as the name shows, is *the law of
gesture,* originated in heroic times and met with the

Graeciae viris atque ipso etiam Socrate probata, a
Platone quoque in parte civilium posita virtutum et
a Chrysippo in praeceptis de liberorum educatione
18 compositis non omissa.   Nam Lacedaemonios quidem
etiam saltationem quandam tanquam ad bella quoque utilem habuisse inter exercitationes accepimus.
Neque id veteribus Romanis dedecori fuit; argumentum est sacerdotum nomine ac religione durans
ad hoc tempus saltatio, et illa in tertio Ciceronis de
Oratore libro verba Crassi, quibus praecipit, ut orator
utatur *laterum inclinatione forti ac virili, non a scena et
histrionibus sed ab armis aut etiam a palaestra;* cuius
disciplinae usus in nostram usque aetatem sine re-
19 prehensione descendit.   A me tamen nec ultra
pueriles annos retinebitur nec in his ipsis diu.
Neque enim gestum oratoris componi ad similitudi-
nem saltationis volo, sed subesse aliquid ex hac
exercitatione puerili, unde nos non id agentes furtim
decor ille discentibus traditus prosequatur.

XII. Quaeri solet, an, etiamsi discenda sint haec,
eodem tempore tamen tradi omnia et percipi possint.
Negant enim quidam, quia confundatur animus ac
fatigetur tot disciplinis in diversum tendentibus, ad
quas nec mens nec corpus nec dies ipse sufficiat, et

---

[1] lix. 220.

approval of the greatest Greeks, not excepting
Socrates himself, while it was placed by Plato among
the virtues of a citizen and included by Chrysippus
in his instructions relative to the education of
children. We are told that the Spartans even 18
regarded a certain form of dance as a useful
element in military training. Nor again did the
ancient Romans consider such a practice as disgraceful: this is clear from the fact that priestly and
ritual dances have survived to the present day, while
Cicero in the third book of his *de Oratore*[1] quotes the
words of Crassus, in which he lays down the
principle that the orator "should learn to move his
body in a bold and manly fashion derived not from
actors or the stage, but from martial and even from
gymnastic exercises." And such a method of training has persisted uncensured to our own time. In my 19
opinion, however, such training should not extend
beyond the years of boyhood, and even boys should
not devote too much time to it. For I do not wish
the gestures of oratory to be modelled on those
of the dance. But I do desire that such boyish
exercises should continue to exert a certain influence, and that something of the grace which we
acquired as learners should attend us in after life
without our being conscious of the fact.

XII. The question is not infrequently asked, as
to whether, admitting that these things ought to
be learned, it is possible for all of them to be
taught and taken in simultaneously. There are
some who say that this is impossible on the ground
that the mind is confused and tired by application
to so many studies of different tendencies: neither
the intelligence nor the physique of our pupils, nor

si maxime patiatur hoc aetas robustior, pueriles
2 annos onerari non oporteat. Sed non satis perspi-
ciunt, quantum natura humani ingenii valeat; quae
ita est agilis ac velox, sic in omnem partem, ut ita
dixerim, spectat, ut ne possit quidem aliquid agere
tantum unum, in plura vero non eodem die modo,
sed eodem temporis momento vim suam intendat.
3 An vero citharoedi non simul et memoriae et sono
vocis et plurimis flexibus serviunt, cum interim alios
nervos dextra percurrunt, alios laeva trahunt, continent, praebent, ne pes quidem otiosus certam
legem temporum servat, et haec pariter omnia?
4 Quid? nos agendi subita necessitate deprehensi
nonne alia dicimus, alia providemus, cum pariter
inventio rerum, electio verborum, compositio, gestus,
pronuntiatio, vultus, motus desiderentur? Quae si
velut sub uno conatu tam diversa parent simul, cur
non pluribus curis horas partiamur? cum praesertim
reficiat animos ac reparet varietas ipsa, contraque sit
aliquanto difficilius in labore uno perseverare. Ideo
et stilus lectione requiescit, et ipsius lectionis
5 taedium vicibus levatur. Quamlibet multa egeri-
mus, quodam tamen modo recentes sumus ad id quod
incipimus. Quis non obtundi potest, si per totum
diem cuiuscunque artis unum magistrum ferat?
Mutatione recreabitur sicut in cibis, quorum diversi-

the time at our disposal are sufficient, they say, and
even though older boys may be strong enough, it is
a sin to put such a burden on the shoulders of childhood. These critics show an insufficient appre- 2
ciation of the capacities of the human mind, which
is so swift and nimble and versatile, that it cannot
be restricted to doing one thing only, but insists on
devoting its attention to several different subjects not
merely in one day, but actually at one and the
same time. Do not harpists simultaneously exert 3
the memory and pay attention to the tone and
inflexions of the voice, while the right hand runs
over certain strings and the left plucks, stops or
releases others, and even the foot is employed in
beating time, all these actions being performed at
the same moment? Again, do not we ourselves, 4
when unexpectedly called upon to plead, speak
while we are thinking what we are to say next,
invention of argument, choice of words, rhythm,
gesture, delivery, facial expression and movement all
being required simultaneously? If all these things
can be done with one effort in spite of their
diversity, why should we not divide our hours among
different branches of study? We must remember
that variety serves to refresh and restore the mind,
and that it is really considerably harder to work at
one subject without intermission. Consequently we
should give the pen a rest by turning to read, and
relieve the tedium of reading by changes of subject.
However manifold our activities, in a certain sense 5
we come fresh to each new subject. Who can
maintain his attention, if he has to listen for a
whole day to one teacher harping on the same
subject, be it what it may? Change of studies is

tate reficitur stomachus et pluribus minore fastidio
6 alitur. Aut dicant isti mihi, quae sit alia ratio
discendi. Grammatico soli deserviamus, deinde
geometrae tantum, omittamus interim quod didici-
mus? mox transeamus ad musicum, excidant priora?
et cum Latinis studebimus litteris, non respiciamus
ad Graecas, et, ut semel finiam, nihil faciamus nisi
7 novissimum? Cur non idem suademus agricolis, ne
arva simul et vineta et oleas et arbustum colant, ne
pratis et pecoribus et hortis et alvearibus avibusque
accommodent curam? Cur ipsi aliquid forensibus
negotiis, aliquid desideriis amicorum, aliquid rationibus domesticis, aliquid curae corporis, nonnihil
voluptatibus cotidie damus? quarum nos una res
quaelibet nihil intermittentes fatigaret. Adeo
facilius est multa facere quam diu.

8   Illud quidem minime verendum est, ne laborem
studiorum pueri difficilius tolerent, neque enim ulla
aetas minus fatigatur. Mirum sit forsitan, sed ex-
9 perimentis deprehendas. Nam et dociliora sunt
ingenia, priusquam obduruerunt. Id vel hoc argumento patet, quod intra biennium, quam verba recte
formare potuerunt, quamvis nullo instante, omnia
fere loquuntur; at noviciis nostris per quot annos

like change of foods: the stomach is refreshed by
their variety and derives greater nourishment from
variety of viands. If my critics disagree, let them 6
provide me with an alternative method. Are we
first to deliver ourselves up to the sole service of
the teacher of literature, and then similarly to the
teacher of geometry, neglecting under the latter
what was taught us by the former? And then are
we to go on to the musician, forgetting all that we
learned before? And when we study Latin literature, are we to do so to the exclusion of Greek? In
fine, to have done with the matter once and for all,
are we to do nothing except that which last comes
to our hand? On this principle, why not advise 7
farmers not to cultivate corn, vines, olives and
orchard trees at the same time? or from devoting
themselves simultaneously to pastures, cattle, gardens, bees and poultry? Why do we ourselves daily
allot some of our time to the business of the courts,
some to the demands of our friends, some to our
domestic affairs, some to the exercise of the body,
and some even to our pleasures? Any one of these
occupations, if pursued without interruption, would
fatigue us. So much easier is it to do many things
than to do one thing for a long time continuously.

We need have no fear at any rate that boys will 8
find their work too exhausting: there is no age more
capable of enduring fatigue. The fact may be surprising, but it can be proved by experiment. For
the mind is all the easier to teach before it is set. This 9
may be clearly proved by the fact that within two
years after a child has begun to form words correctly,
he can speak practically all without any pressure
from outside. On the other hand how many years

sermo Latinus repugnat. Magis scias, si quem iam
robustum instituere litteris coeperis, non sine causa
dici παιδομαθεῖς eos, qui in sua quidque arte optime
10 faciant. Et patientior est laboris natura pueris
quam iuvenibus. Videlicet, ut corpora infantium
nec casus, quo in terram totiens deferuntur, tam
graviter adfligit nec illa per manus et genua reptatio
nec post breve tempus continui lusus et totius diei
discursus, quia pondus illis abest nec sese ipsi
gravant: sic animī quoque, credo, quia minore
conatu moventur nec suo nisu studiis insistunt, sed
formandos se tantummodo praestant, non similiter
11 fatigantur. Praeterea secundum aliam aetatis illius
facilitatem velut simplicius docentes sequuntur nec
quae iam egerint metiuntur. Abest illis adhuc
etiam laboris iudicium. Porro, ut frequenter experti
sumus, minus adficit sensus fatigatio quam cogitatió.
12 Sed ne temporis quidem unquam plus erit, quia
his aetatibus omnis in audiendo profectus est. Cum
ad stilum secedet, cum generabit ipse aliquid atque
componet, tum inchoare haec studia vel non vacabit
13 vel non libebit. Ergo cum grammaticus totum
occupare diem non possit nec debeat, ne discentis
animum taedio avertat, quibus potius studiis haec
14 temporum velut subsiciva donabimus? Nam nec
ego consumi studentem in his artibus volo, nec

it takes for our newly-imported slaves to become familiar with the Latin language. Try to teach an adult to read and you will soon appreciate the force of the saying applied to those who do everything connected with their art with the utmost skill " he started young !" Moreover boys stand the strain of 10 work better than young men. Just as small children suffer less damage from their frequent falls, from their crawling on hands and knees and, a little later, from their incessant play and their running about from morn till eve, because they are so light in weight and have so little to carry, even so their minds are less susceptible of fatigue, because their activity calls for less effort and application to study demands no exertion of their own, since they are merely so much plastic material to be moulded by the teacher. And further owing to the general 11 pliability of childhood, they follow their instructors with greater simplicity and without attempting to measure their own progress : for as yet they do not even appreciate the nature of their work. Finally, as I have often noticed, the senses are less affected by mere hard work than they are by hard thinking.

Moreover there will never be more time for such 12 studies, since at this age all progress is made through listening to the teacher. Later when the boy has to write by himself, or to produce and compose something out of his own head, he will neither have the time nor the inclination for the exercises which we have been discussing. Since, then, the teacher of literature 13 neither can nor ought to occupy the whole day, for fear of giving his pupil a distaste for work, what are the studies to which the spare time should preferably be devoted ? For I do not wish the student to wear 14

moduletur aut musicis notis cantica excipiat, nec
utique ad minutissima usque geometriae opera de-
scendat, non comoedum in pronuntiando nec salta-
torem in gestu facio; quae si omnia exigerem,
suppeditabat tamen tempus.   Longa est enim, quae
discit, aetas, et ego non de tardis ingeniis loquor.

15 Denique cur in his omnibus, quae discenda oratori
futuro puto, eminuit Plato? qui non contentus
disciplinis, quas praestare poterant Athenae, non
Pythagoreorum, ad quos in Italiam navigaverat,
Aegypti quoque sacerdotes adiit atque eorum arcana
perdidicit.

16   Difficultatis patrocinia praeteximus segnitiae.
Neque enim nobis operis amor est, nec, quia sit
honesta ac rerum pulcherrima eloquentia, petitur
ipsa, sed ad venalem usum et sordidum lucrum

17 accingimur.   Dicant sine his in foro multi et
adquirant, dum sit locupletior aliquis sordidae mercis
negotiator et plus voci suae debeat praeco.   Nec
velim quidem lectorem dari mihi quid studia

18 referant computaturum.   Qui vero imaginem ipsam
eloquentiae divina quadam mente conceperit, quique
illam (ut ait non ignobilis tragicus) *reginam rerum
orationem* ponet ante oculos, fructumque non ex
stipe advocationum sed ex animo suo et contempla-

---

[1] Pacuvius (Ribbeck, 177).

himself out in such pursuits: I would not have him sing or learn to read music or dive deep into the minuter details of geometry, nor need he be a finished actor in his delivery or a dancer in his gesture: if I did demand all these accomplishments, there would yet be time for them; the period allotted to education is long, and I am not speaking of duller wits. Why did 15 Plato bear away the palm in all these branches of knowledge which in my opinion the future orator should learn? I answer, because he was not merely content with the teaching which Athens was able to provide or even with that of the Pythagoreans whom he visited in Italy, but even approached the priests of Egypt and made himself thoroughly acquainted with all their secret lore.

The plea of the difficulty of the subject is put 16 forward merely to cloak our indolence, because we do not love the work that lies before us nor seek to win eloquence for our own because it is a noble art and the fairest thing in all the world, but gird up our loins for mercenary ends and for the winning of filthy lucre. Without such accomplishments many may 17 speak in the courts and make an income; but it is my prayer that every dealer in the vilest merchandise may be richer than they and that the public crier may find his voice a more lucrative possession. And I trust that there is not one even among my readers who would think of calculating the monetary value of such studies. But he that has enough of the 18 divine spark to conceive the ideal eloquence, he who, as the great tragic poet [1] says, regards " oratory " as "the queen of all the world" and seeks not the transitory gains of advocacy, but those stable and lasting rewards which his own soul and knowledge and

tione ac scientia petet perpetuum illum nec fortunae subiectum, facile persuadebit sibi, ut tempora, quae spectaculis, campo, tesseris, otiosis denique sermonibus, ne dicam somno et conviviorum mora conteruntur, geometrae potius ac musico impendat, quanto plus delectationis habiturus quam ex illis

19 ineruditis voluptatibus. Dedit enim hoc providentia hominibus munus, ut honesta magis iuvarent. Sed nos haec ipsa dulcedo longius duxit. Hactenus ergo de studiis, quibus, antequam maiora capiat, puer instituendus est ; proximus liber velut novum sumet exordium et ad rhetoris officia transibit.

contemplation can give, *he* will easily persuade himself to spend his time not, like so many, in the theatre or in the Campus Martius, in dicing or in idle talk, to say naught of the hours that are wasted in sleep or long drawn banqueting, but in listening rather to the geometrician and the teacher of music. For by this he will win a richer harvest of delight than can ever be gathered from the pleasures of the ignorant, since among the many gifts of providence to man not the least is this that the highest pleasure is the child of virtue. But the attractions of my theme 19 have led me to say overmuch. Enough of those studies in which a boy must be instructed, while he is yet too young to proceed to greater things! My next book will start afresh and will pass to the consideration of the duties of the teacher of rhetoric.

BOOK II

LIBER II

I. TENUIT consuetudo, quae cotidie magis invalescit, ut praeceptoribus eloquentiae, Latinis quidem semper sed etiam Graecis interim, discipuli serius quam ratio postulat, traderentur. Eius rei duplex causa est, quod et rhetores utique nostri suas partes omiserunt et grammatici alienas occupaverunt. 2 Nam et illi declamare modo et scientiam declamandi ac facultatem tradere officii sui ducunt, idque intra deliberativas iudicialesque materias (nam cetera ut professione sua minora despiciunt), et hi non satis credunt excepisse, quae relicta erant, (quo nomine gratia quoque iis habenda est), sed ad prosopopoeïas usque ac suasorias, in quibus onus dicendi vel 3 maximum est, irrumpunt. Hinc ergo accidit, ut, quae alterius artis prima erant opera, facta sint alterius novissima, et aetas altioribus iam disciplinis debita in schola minore subsidat ac rhetoricen apud grammaticos exerceat. Ita, quod est maxime ridiculum, non ante ad declamandi magistrum mittendus videtur puer quam declamare sciat.

---

¹ *suasoriae* are declamations on deliberative themes (*e.g.* Hannibal deliberates whether he should cross the Alps).

BOOK II

I. THE custom has prevailed and is daily growing commoner of sending boys to the schools of rhetoric much later than is reasonable : this is always the case as regards Latin rhetoric and occasionally applies to Greek as well. The reason for this is twofold : the rhetoricians, more especially our own, have abandoned certain of their duties and the teachers of literature have undertaken tasks which rightly belong to others. For the rhetorician con- 2 siders that his duty is merely to declaim and give instruction in the theory and practice of declamation and confines his activities to deliberative and judicial themes, regarding all others as beneath the dignity of his profession ; while the teacher of literature is not satisfied to take what is left him (and we owe him a debt of gratitude for this), but even presumes to handle declamations in character and deliberative themes,[1] tasks which impose the very heaviest burden on the speaker. Consequently subjects which once 3 formed the first stages of rhetoric have come to form the final stages of a literary education, and boys who are ripe for more advanced study are kept back in the inferior school and practise rhetoric under the direction of teachers of literature. Thus we get the absurd result that a boy is not regarded as fit to go on to the schools of declamation till he knows how to declaim.

4   Nos suum cuique professioni modum demus. Et
grammatice (quam in Latinum transferentes littera-
turam vocaverunt) fines suos norit, praesertim
tantum ab hac appellationis suae paupertate, intra
quam primi illi constitere, provecta; nam tenuis a
fonte assumptis historicorum criticorumque viribus
pleno iam satis alveo fluit, cum praeter rationem
recte loquendi non parum alioqui copiosam prope
omnium maximarum artium scientiam amplexa sit;
5 et rhetorice, cui nomen vis eloquendi dedit, officia
sua non detrectet nec occupari gaudeat pertinentem
ad se laborem, quae, dum opere cedit, iam paene
6 possessione depulsa est. Neque infitiabor, aliquem
ex his, qui grammaticen profiteantur, eo usque
scientiae progredi posse, ut ad haec quoque tradenda
sufficiat; sed cum id aget, rhetoris officio fungetur
non suo.
7   Nos porro quaerimus, quando iis, quae rhetorice
praecipit, percipiendis puer maturus esse videatur.
In quo quidem non id est aestimandum, cuius quisque sit aetatis, sed quantum in studiis iam effecerit.
Et ne diutius disseram, quando sit rhetori tradendus,
8 sic optime finiri credo; cum poterit. Sed hoc ipsum
ex superiore pendet quaestione. Nam si grammatices munus usque ad suasorias prorogatur, tardius

The two professions must each be assigned their 4
proper sphere. *Grammatice*, which we translate as
the science of letters, must learn to know its own
limits, especially as it has encroached so far beyond
the boundaries to which its unpretentious name
should restrict it and to which its earlier professors
actually confined themselves. Springing from a tiny
fountain-head, it has gathered strength from the
historians and critics and has swollen to the dimensions of a brimming river, since, not content with the
theory of correct speech, no inconsiderable subject,
it has usurped the study of practically all the highest
departments of knowledge. On the other hand 5
rhetoric, which derives its name from the power of
eloquence, must not shirk its peculiar duties nor rejoice to see its own burdens shouldered by others.
For the neglect of these is little less than a surrender
of its birthright. I will of course admit that there 6
may be a few professors of literature who have
acquired sufficient knowledge to be able to teach rhetoric as well ; but when they do so, they are perform-
ing the duties of the rhetorician, not their own.

A further point into which we must enquire con- 7
cerns the age at which a boy may be considered
sufficiently advanced to profit by the instructions of
the rhetorician. In this connexion we must consider
not the boy's actual age, but the progress he has
made in his studies. To put it briefly, I hold that
the best answer to the question " When should a
boy be sent to the school of rhetoric ? " is this,
" When he is fit." But this question is really depen- 8
dent on that previously raised. For if the duties of
the teacher of literature are prolonged to include
instruction in deliberative declamation, this will

rhetore opus est. At si rhetor prima officia operis
sui non recusat, a narrationibus statim et laudandi
9 vituperandique opusculis cura eius desideratur. An
ignoramus antiquis hoc fuisse ad augendam eloquentiam genus exercitationis, ut theses dicerent et
communes locos et cetera citra complexum rerum
personarumque, quibus verae fictaeque controversiae
continentur? Ex quo palam est, quam turpiter
deserat eam partem rhetorices institutio, quam et
10 primam habuit et diu solam. Quid autem est ex iis,
de quibus supra dixi, quod non cum in alia, quae
sunt propria rhetorum, tum certe in illud iudiciale
causae genus incidat? An non in foro narrandum
11 est? qua in parte nescio an sit vel plurimum. Non
laus ac vituperatio certaminibus illis frequenter in-
seritur? Non communes loci, sive qui sunt in vitia
derecti, quales legimus a Cicerone compositos, seu
quibus quaestiones generaliter tractantur, quales
sunt editi a Quinto quoque Hortensio: ut, *Sitne
parvis argumentis credendum,* et pro testibus et in
12 testes, in mediis litium medullis versantur? Arma
sunt haec quodammodo praeparanda semper, ut iis,
cum res poscet, utare. Quae qui pertinere ad ora-

---

[1] *communes loci* = passages dealing with some general
principle or theme. For *theses* see II. iv. 24.

[2] *controversiae* are declamations on controversial or judicial
themes. A general rule or law is stated: then a special case,
which has to be solved in accordance with the law. An
abbreviated *controversia* is to be found in I. x. 33, and they
occur frequently hereafter (cp. esp. III. vi. 96).

postpone the need for the rhetorician. On the other hand if the rhetorician does not refuse to undertake the first duties of his task, his instruction will be required from the moment the boy begins to compose narratives and his first attempts at passages of praise or denunciation. We know that the orators of 9 earlier days improved their eloquence by declaiming themes and common-places [1] and other forms of rhetorical exercises not involving particular circumstances or persons such as provide the material for real or imaginary causes.[2] From this we can clearly see what a scandalous dereliction of duty it is for the schools of rhetoric to abandon this department of their work, which was not merely its first, but for a long time its sole task. What is there in 10 those exercises of which I have just spoken that does not involve matters which are the special concern of rhetoric and further are typical of actual legal cases? Have we not to narrate facts in the law-courts? Indeed I am not sure that this is not the most important department of rhetoric in actual practice. Are not eulogy and denunciation 11 frequently introduced in the course of the contests of the courts? Are not common-places frequently inserted in the very heart of lawsuits, whether, like those which we find in the works of Cicero, they are directed against vice, or, like those published by Quintus Hortensius, deal with questions of general interest such as "whether small points of argument should carry weight," or are employed to defend or impugn the credibility of witnesses? These are weapons which we should always have 12 stored in our armoury ready for immediate use as occasion may demand. The critic who denies that

tionem non putabit, is ne statuam quidem inchoari
credet, cum eius membra fundentur. Neque hanc
(ut aliqui putabunt) festinationem meam sic quisquam calumnietur, tanquam eum, qui sit rhetori
traditus, abducendum protinus a grammaticis putem.
13 Dabuntur et illis tum quoque tempora sua, neque
erit verendum, ne binis praeceptoribus oneretur
puer. Non enim crescet sed dividetur, qui sub uno
miscebatur, labor, et erit sui quisque operis magister
utilior; quod adhuc obtinent Graeci, a Latinis omis-
sum est, et fieri videtur excusate, quia sunt qui
labori isti successerint.

II. Ergo cum ad eas in studiis vires pervenerit
puer, ut, quae prima esse praecepta rhetorum
diximus, mente consequi possit, tradendus eius
artis magistris erit; quorum in primis inspici mores
2 oportebit. Quod ego non idcirco potissimum in hac
parte tractare sum aggressus, quia non in ceteris
quoque doctoribus idem hoc examinandum quam
diligentissime putem, sicut testatus sum libro priore;
sed quod magis necessariam eius rei mentionem
3 facit aetas ipsa discentium. Nam et adulti fere
pueri ad hos praeceptores transferuntur et apud eos
iuvenes etiam facti perseverant; ideoque maior

such matters concern an orator is one who will
refuse to believe that a statue is being begun
when its limbs are actually being cast. Some will
think that I am in too great a hurry, but let no one
accuse me of thinking that the pupil who has been
entrusted to the rhetorician should forthwith be
withdrawn from the teacher of literature. The latter 13
will still have certain hours allotted him, and there
is no reason to fear that a boy will be overloaded by
receiving instruction from two different masters. It
will not mean any increase of work, but merely the
division among two masters of the studies which
were previously indiscriminately combined under one :
and the efficiency of either teacher will be increased.
This method is still in vogue among the Greeks, but
has been abandoned by us, not perhaps without some
excuse, as there were others ready to step into the
rhetorician's shoes.

II. As soon therefore as a boy has made sufficient
progress in his studies to be able to follow what I
have styled the first stage of instruction in rhetoric,
he should be placed under a rhetorician. Our first
task must be to enquire whether the teacher is of
good character. The reason which leads me to deal 2
with this subject in this portion of my work is not
that I regard character as a matter of indifference
where other teachers are concerned, (I have already
shown how important I think it in the preceding
book), but that the age to which the pupil has now
attained makes the mention of this point especially
necessary. For as a rule boys are on the verge of 3
manhood when transferred to the teacher of rhetoric
and continue with him even when they are young
men: consequently we must spare no effort to secure

adhibenda tum cura est, ut et teneriores annos ab
iniuria sanctitas docentis custodiat et ferociores a
4 licentia gravitas deterreat. Neque vero sat est
summam praestare abstinentiam, nisi disciplinae
severitate convenientium quoque ad se mores
astrinxerit.

5 Sumat igitur ante omnia parentis erga discipulos
suos animum, ac succedere se in eorum locum, a
quibus sibi liberi tradantur, existimet. Ipse nec
habeat vitia nec ferat. Non austeritas eius tristis,
non dissoluta sit comitas, ne inde odium hinc contemptus oriatur. Plurimus ei de honesto ac bono
sermo sit; nam quo saepius monuerit, hoc rarius
castigabit. Minime iracundus, nec tamen eorum,
quae emendanda erunt, dissimulator, simplex in
docendo, patiens laboris, assiduus potius quam
6 immodicus. Interrogantibus libenter respondeat,
non interrogantes percontetur ultro. In laudandis
discipulorum dictionibus nec malignus nec effusus,
quia res altera taedium laboris, altera securitatem
7 parit. In emendando, quae corrigenda erunt, non
acerbus minimeque contumeliosus; nam id quidem
multos a proposito studendi fugat, quod quidam sic
8 obiurgant quasi oderint. Ipse aliquid immo multa
cotidie dicat, quae secum auditores referant. Licet
enim satis exemplorum ad imitandum ex lectione

that the purity of the teacher's character should preserve those of tenderer years from corruption, while its authority should keep the bolder spirits from breaking out into licence. Nor is it sufficient 4 that he should merely set an example of the highest personal self-control ; he must also be able to govern the behaviour of his pupils by the strictness of his discipline.

Let him therefore adopt a parental attitude to his 5 pupils, and regard himself as the representative of those who have committed their children to his charge. Let him be free from vice himself and refuse to tolerate it in others. Let him be strict but not austere, genial but not too familiar : for austerity will make him unpopular, while familiarity breeds contempt. Let his discourse continually turn on what is good and honourable ; the more he admonishes, the less he will have to punish. He must control his temper without however shutting his eyes to faults requiring correction : his instruction must be free from affectation, his industry great, his demands on his class continuous, but not extravagant. He 6 must be ready to answer questions and to put them unasked to those who sit silent. In praising the recitations of his pupils he must be neither grudging nor over-generous : the former quality will give them a distaste for work, while the latter will produce a complacent self-satisfaction. In correcting 7 faults he must avoid sarcasm and above all abuse : for teachers whose rebukes seem to imply positive dislike discourage industry. He should declaim 8 daily himself and, what is more, without stint, that his class may take his utterances home with them. For however many models for imitation he may

suppeditet, tamen viva illa, ut dicitur, vox alit plenius praecipueque eius praeceptoris, quem discipuli, si modo recte sunt instituti, et amant et verentur. Vix autem dici potest, quanto libentius imitemur eos, quibus favemus.

9 Minime vero permittenda pueris, ut fit apud plerosque, adsurgendi exultandique in laudando licentia; quin etiam iuvenum modicum esse, cum audient, testimonium debet. Ita fiet, ut ex iudicio praeceptoris discipulus pendeat, atque id se dixisse

10 recte, quod ab eo probabitur, credat. Illa vero vitiosissima, quae iam humanitas vocatur, invicem qualiacunque laudandi, cum est indecora et theatralis et severe institutis scholis aliena, tum studiorum perniciosissima hostis. Supervacua enim videntur cura ac labor, parata, quidquid effuderint,

11 laude. Vultum igitur praeceptoris intueri tam, qui audiunt, debent, quam ipse qui dicit; ita enim probanda atque improbanda discernet, si stilo facultas

12 continget, auditione iudicium. At nunc proni atque succincti ad omnem clausulam non exsurgunt modo verum etiam excurrunt et cum indecora exultatione conclamant. Id mutuum est et ibi declamationis

give them from the authors they are reading, it will still be found that fuller nourishment is provided by the living voice, as we call it, more especially when it proceeds from the teacher himself, who, if his pupils are rightly instructed, should be the object of their affection and respect. And it is scarcely possible to say how much more readily we imitate those whom we like.

I strongly disapprove of the prevailing practice of 9 allowing boys to stand up or leap from the seats in the expression of their applause. Young men, even when they are listening to others, should be temperate in manifesting their approval. If this be insisted upon, the pupil will depend on his instructor's verdict and will take his approval as a guarantee that he has spoken well. The worst 10 form of politeness, as it has come to be called, is that of mutual and indiscriminate applause, a practice which is unseemly, theatrical and unworthy of a decently disciplined school, in addition to being the worst foe to genuine study. For if every effusion is greeted with a storm of ready-made applause, care and industry come to be regarded as superfluous. The audience no less than the speaker should there- 11 fore keep their eyes fixed on their teacher's face, since thus they will learn to distinguish between what is praiseworthy and what is not: for just as writing gives facility, so listening begets the critical faculty. But in the schools of to-day we see boys 12 stooping forward ready to spring to their feet: at the close of each period they not merely rise, but rush forward with shouts of unseemly enthusiasm. Such compliments are mutual and the success of a declamation consists in this kind of applause. The

fortuna. Hinc tumor et vana de se persuasio usque
adeo, ut illo condiscipulorum tumultu inflati, si parum
a praeceptore laudentur, ipsi de illo male sentiant.

13 Sed se quoque praeceptores intente ac modeste
audiri velint; non enim iudicio discipulorum dicere
debet magister sed discipulus magistri. Quin, si
fieri potest, intendendus animus in hoc quoque, ut
perspiciat, quae quisque et quomodo laudet, et
placere, quae bene dicet, non suo magis quam eorum
nomine delectetur, qui recte iudicabunt.

14 Pueros adolescentibus permixtos sedere, non
placet mihi. Nam etiamsi vir talis, qualem esse
oportet studiis moribusque praepositum, modestam
habere potest etiam iuventutem, tamen vel infirmitas a robustioribus separanda est, et carendum non
solum crimine turpitudinis verum etiam suspicione.

15 Haec notanda breviter existimavi; nam ut absit
ab ultimis vitiis ipse ac schola, ne praecipiendum
quidem credo. Ac si quis est, qui flagitia manifesta
in eligendo filii praeceptore non vitet, iam hinc
sciat cetera quoque, quae ad utilitatem iuventutis
componere conamur, esse sibi hac parte omissa
supervacua.

III. Ne illorum quidem persuasio silentio transe-

result is vanity and empty self-sufficiency, carried to such an extent that, intoxicated by the wild enthusiasm of their fellow-pupils, they conceive a spite against their master, if his praise does not come up to their expectation. But teachers must also insist 13 on receiving an attentive and quiet hearing from the class when they themselves declaim. For the master should not speak to suit his pupil's standard, but they should speak to suit his. Further he should, if possible, keep his eyes open to note the points which each boy praises and observe the manner in which he expresses his approval, and should rejoice that his words give pleasure not only for his own sake, but for that of those who show sound judgment in their appreciation.

I do not approve of boys sitting mixed with young 14 men. For even if the teacher be such an one as we should desire to see in charge of the morals and studies of the young, and can keep his youthful pupils under proper control, it is none the less desirable to keep the weaker members separate from the more mature, and to avoid not only the actual charge of corruption but the merest suspicion of it. I have thought it worth while to put my views on 15 this subject quite briefly. For I do not think it necessary even to warn the teacher that both he and his school must be free from the grosser vices. And should there be any father who does not trouble to choose a teacher for his son who is free from the obvious taint of immorality, he may rest assured that all the other precepts, which I am attempting to lay down for the benefit of our youth, will be absolutely useless to him, if he neglects this.

III. I do not think that I should pass by in silence

unda est, qui, etiam cum idoneos rhetori pueros
putaverunt, non tamen continuo tradendos emi-
nentissimo credunt, sed apud minores aliquamdiu
detinent, tanquam instituendis artibus magis sit
apta mediocritas praeceptoris, cum ad intellectum
atque ad imitationem facilior tum ad suscipiendas

2 elementorum molestias minus superba. Qua in re
mihi non arbitror diu laborandum, ut ostendam,
quanto sit melius optimis imbui, quanta in eluendis
quae semel insederint vitiis difficultas consequatur,
cum geminatum onus succedentes premat et quidem

3 dedocendi gravius ac prius quam docendi. Propter
quod Timotheum clarum in arte tibiarum ferunt
duplices ab iis, quos alius instituisset, solitum exigere
mercedes, quam si rudes traderentur. Error tamen
est in re duplex: unus, quod interim sufficere illos
minores existimant, et bono sane stomacho contenti

4 sunt; quae quanquam est ipsa reprehensione digna
securitas, tamen esset utcunque tolerabilis, si eiusmodi praeceptores minus docerent non peius; alter
ille etiam frequentior, quod eos, qui ampliorem
dicendi facultatem sint consecuti, non putant ad
minora descendere, idque interim fieri, quia fas-
tidiant praestare hanc inferioribus curam, interim

5 quia omnino non possint. Ego porro eum qui nolit

even the opinion of those who, even when they regard boys as ripe for the rhetorician, still do not think that they should at once be placed under the most eminent teacher available, but prefer to keep them for a while under inferior masters, on the ground that in the elementary stages a mediocre instructor is easier to understand and to imitate, and less reluctant to undertake the tiresome task of teaching the rudiments as being beneath his notice. I do 2 not think that I need waste much time in pointing out how much better it is to absorb the best possible principles, or how hard it is to get rid of faults which have once become engrained; for it places a double burden on the shoulders of the later teacher and the preliminary task of unteaching is harder than that of teaching. It is for this reason that the 3 famous piper Timotheus is said to have demanded from those who had previously been under another master a fee double the amount which he charged for those who came to him untaught. The mistake to which I am referring is, however, twofold. First they regard these inferior teachers as adequate for the time being and are content with their instruction because they have a stomach that will swallow anything: this indifference, though blameworthy in 4 itself, would yet be tolerable, if the teaching provided by these persons were merely less in quantity and not inferior in quality as well. Secondly, and this is a still commoner delusion, they think that those who are blest with greater gifts of speaking will not condescend to the more elementary details, and that consequently they sometimes disdain to give attention to such inferior subjects of study and sometimes are incapable of so doing. For my part I regard the 5

in numero praecipientium non habeo, posse autem maxime, si velit, optimum quemque contendo: primum, quod eum, qui eloquentia ceteris praestet, illa quoque, per quae ad eloquentiam pervenitur,

6 diligentissime percepisse credibile est; deinde, quia plurimum in praecipiendo valet ratio, quae doctissimo cuique plenissima est; postremo, quia nemo sic in maioribus eminet, ut eum minora deficiant. Nisi forte Iovem quidem Phidias optime fecit, illa autem, quae in ornamentum operis eius accedunt, alius melius elaborasset, aut orator loqui nesciet aut leviores morbos curare non poterit praestantissimus medicus.

7 Quid ergo? non est quaedam eloquentia maior quam ut eam intellectu consequi puerilis infirmitas possit? Ego vero confiteor: sed hunc disertum praeceptorem prudentem quoque et non ignarum docendi esse oportebit summittentem se ad mensuram discentis; ut velocissimus quoque, si forte iter cum parvulo faciat, det manum et gradum suum minuat nec procedat ultra quam comes pos-

8 sit. Quid? si plerumque accidit ut faciliora sint ad intelligendum et lucidiora multo, quae a doctissimo quoque dicuntur? Nam et prima est eloquentiae virtus perspicuitas, et quo quis ingenio minus valet, hoc se magis attollere et dilatare conatur, ut statura breves in digitos eriguntur

teacher who is unwilling to attend to such details
as being unworthy of the name of teacher: and as
for the question of capacity, I maintain that it is the
most capable man who, given the will, is able to do
this with most efficiency. For in the first place it is a
reasonable inference that a man blest with abnormal
powers of eloquence will have made careful note of
the various steps by which eloquence is attained,
and in the second place the reasoning faculty, which 6
is specially developed in learned men, is all-important
in teaching, while finally no one is eminent in the
greater things of his art if he be lacking in the lesser.
Unless indeed we are asked to believe that while
Phidias modelled his Jupiter to perfection, the
decorative details of the statue would have been
better executed by another artist, or that an orator
does not know how to speak, or a distinguished
physician is incapable of treating minor ailments.

"Yes" it may be answered "but surely you do not 7
deny that there is a type of eloquence that is
too great to be comprehended by undeveloped
boys?" Of course there is. But this eloquent
teacher whom they fling in my face must be a
sensible man with a good knowledge of teaching and
must be prepared to stoop to his pupil's level, just as
a rapid walker, if walking with a small child, will
give him his hand and lessen his own speed and
avoid advancing at a pace beyond the powers of his
little companion. Again it frequently happens that 8
the more learned the teacher, the more lucid and
intelligible is his instruction. For clearness is the
first virtue of eloquence, and the less talented a man
is, the more he will strive to exalt and dilate himself,
just as short men tend to walk on tip-toe and weak

9 et plura infirmi minantur. Nam tumidos et corruptos et tinnulos et quocunque alio cacozeliae genere peccantes certum habeo non virium sed infirmitatis vitio laborare, ut corpora non robore sed valetudine inflantur et recto itinere lassi plerumque devertunt. Erit ergo etiam obscurior, quo quisque deterior.

10 Non excidit mihi, scripsisse me in libro priore, cum potiorem in scholis eruditionem esse quam domi dicerem, libentius se prima studia tenerosque profectus ad imitationem condiscipulorum, quae facilior esset, erigere; quod a quibusdam sic accipi potest, tanquam haec, quam nunc tueor, sententia priori

11 diversa sit. Id a me procul aberit; namque ea causa vel maxima est, cur optimo cuique praeceptori sit tradendus puer, quod apud eum discipuli quoque melius instituti aut dicent, quod inutile non sit imitari, aut si quid erraverint, statim corrigentur; at indoctus ille etiam probabit fortasse vitiosa et placere

12 audientibus iudicio suo coget. Sit ergo tam eloquentia quam moribus praestantissimus, qui ad Phoenicis Homerici exemplum dicere ac facere doceat.

men to use threats. As for those whose style is 9
inflated or vicious, and whose language reveals a
passion for high-sounding words or labours under
any other form of affectation, in my opinion they
suffer not from excess of strength but of weakness,
like bodies swollen not with the plumpness of
health but with disease, or like men who weary of
the direct road betake them to bypaths. Consequently the worse a teacher is, the harder he will
be to understand.

I have not forgotten that I stated in the preced- 10
ing book, when I urged that school was preferable
to home education, that pupils at the commencement of their studies, when progress is as yet
but in the bud, are more disposed to imitate their
schoolfellows than their masters, since such imitation
comes more easily to them. Some of my readers
may think that the view which I am now maintaining
is inconsistent with my previous statement. But I 11
am far from being inconsistent: for my previous
assertion affords the strongest reason for selecting the
very best teachers for our boys ; since pupils of a
first rate master, having received a better training,
will when they speak say something that may be
worthy of imitation, while if they commit some
mistake, they will be promptly corrected. But the
incompetent teacher on the other hand is quite
likely to give his approval to faulty work and by the
judgment which he expresses to force approval
on the audience. The teacher should therefore be 12
as distinguished for his eloquence as for his good
character, and like Phoenix in the *Iliad* be able to
teach his pupil both how to behave and how to
speak.

IV. Hinc iam, quas primas in docendo partes rhetorum putem, tradere incipiam, dilata parumper illa quae sola vulgo vocatur arte rhetorica. Ac mihi opportunus maxime videtur ingressus ab eo, cuius aliquid simile apud grammaticos puer didicerit.

2 Et quia narrationum, excepta qua in causis utimur, tres accepimus species, fabulam, quae versatur in tragoediis atque carminibus, non a veritate modo sed etiam a forma veritatis remota; argumentum, quod falsum sed vero simile comoediae fingunt; historiam, in qua est gestae rei expositio; grammaticis autem poeticas dedimus: apud rhetorem initium sit his-

3 torica, tanto robustior quanto verior. Sed narrandi quidem quae nobis optima ratio videatur, tum demonstrabimus, cum de iudiciali parte dicemus. Interim admonere illud satis est, ut sit ea neque arida prorsus atque ieiuna, (nam quid opus erat tantum studiis laboris impendere, si res nudas atque inornatas indicare satis videretur?) neque rursus sinuosa et arcessitis descriptionibus, in quas plerique imitatione poeticae licentiae ducuntur, lasciviat.

4 Vitium utrumque, peius tamen illud, quod ex inopia

---

[1] With special reference to the element of the miraculous. Ovid's *Metamorphoses* would give a good example.

[2] Book IV. chap. ii.

IV. I shall now proceed to indicate what I think should be the first subjects in which the rhetorician should give instruction, and shall postpone for a time our consideration of the art of rhetoric in the narrow sense in which that term is popularly used. For in my opinion it is most desirable that we should commence with something resembling the subjects already acquired under the teacher of literature.

Now there are three forms of narrative, without 2 counting the type used in actual legal cases. First there is the fictitious narrative as we get it in tragedies and poems, which is not merely not true but has little resemblance to truth.[1] Secondly, there is the realistic narrative as presented by comedies, which, though not true, has yet a certain verisimilitude. Thirdly there is the historical narrative, which is an exposition of actual fact. Poetic narratives are the property of the teacher of literature. The rhetorician therefore should begin with the historical narrative, whose force is in proportion to its truth. I will, however, postpone my demonstration 3 of what I regard as the best method of narration till I come to deal with narration as required in the courts.[2] In the meantime, it will be sufficient to urge that it should be neither dry nor jejune (for why spend so much labour over our studies if a bald and naked statement of fact is regarded as sufficiently expressive?); nor on the other hand must it be tortuous or revel in elaborate descriptions, such as those in which so many are led to indulge by a misguided imitation of poetic licence. Both 4 these extremes are faults; but that which springs from poverty of wit is worse than that which is due

quam quod ex copia venit. Nam in pueris oratio
perfecta nec exigi nec sperari potest; melior autem
indoles laeta generosique conatus et vel plura iusto
5 concipiens interim spiritus. Nec unquam me in his
discentis annis offendat, si quid superfuerit. Quin
ipsis quoque doctoribus hoc esse curae velim, ut
teneras adhuc mentes more nutricum mollius alant
et satiari velut quodam iucundioris disciplinae lacte
patiantur. Erit illud plenius interim corpus, quod
6 mox adulta aetas astringat. Hinc spes roboris.
Maciem namque et infirmitatem in posterum minari
solet protinus omnibus membris expressus infans.
Audeat haec aetas plura et inveniat et inventis
gaudeat, sint licet illa non satis sicca interim ac
severa. Facile remedium est ubertati; sterilia nullo
7 labore vincuntur. Illa mihi in pueris natura minimum spei dederit, in qua ingenium iudicio praesumi-
tur. Materiam esse primum volo vel abundantiorem
atque ultra quam oporteat fusam. Multum inde
decoquent anni, multum ratio limabit, aliquid velut
usu ipso deteretur, sit modo unde excidi possit et
quod exsculpi; erit autem, si non ab initio tenuem
nimium laminam duxerimus et quam caelatura altior
8 rumpat. Quod me de his aetatibus sentire minus

to imaginative excess. For we cannot demand or expect a perfect style from boys. But there is greater promise in a certain luxuriance of mind, in ambitious effort and an ardour that leads at times to ideas bordering on the extravagant. I have no ob- 5 jection to a little exuberance in the young learner. Nay, I would urge teachers too like nurses to be careful to provide softer food for still undeveloped minds and to suffer them to take their fill of the milk of the more attractive studies. For the time being the body may be somewhat plump, but maturer years will reduce it to a sparer habit. Such plumpness 6 gives hope of strength; a child fully formed in every limb is likely to grow up a puny weakling. The young should be more daring and inventive and should rejoice in their inventions, even though correctness and severity are still to be acquired. Exuberance is easily remedied, but barrenness is incurable, be your efforts what they may. To my 7 mind the boy who gives least promise is one in whom the critical faculty develops in advance of the imagination. I like to see the firstfruits of the mind copious to excess and almost extravagant in their profusion. The years as they pass will skim off much of the froth, reason will file away many excrescences, and something too will be removed by what I may perhaps call the wear and tear of life, so long as there is sufficient material to admit of cutting and chiselling away. And there will be sufficient, if only we do not draw the plate too thin to begin with, so that it runs the risk of being broken if the graver cut too deep. Those of my 8 readers who know their Cicero will not be surprised

227

mirabitur, qui apud Ciceronem legerit: *Volo enim se efferat in adolescente fecunditas.*

Quapropter in primis evitandus et in pueris praecipue magister aridus, non minus quam teneris adhuc plantis siccum et sine humore ullo solum.
9 Inde fiunt humiles statim et velut terram spectantes, qui nihil supra cotidianum sermonem attollere audeant. Macies illis pro sanitate et iudicii loco infirmitas est, et dum satis putant vitio carere, in id ipsum incidunt vitium, quod virtutibus carent. Quare mihi ne maturitas quidem ipsa festinet, nec musta in lacu statim austera sint; sic et annos ferent et vetustate proficient.

10 Ne illud quidem quod admoneamus indignum est, ingenia puerorum nimia interim emendationis severitate deficere; nam et desperant et dolent et novissime oderunt et, quod maxime nocet, dum
11 omnia timent, nihil conantur. Quod etiam rusticis notum est, qui frondibus teneris non putant adhibendam esse falcem, quia reformidare ferrum viden-
12 tur et nondum cicatricem pati posse. Iucundus ergo tum maxime debet esse praeceptor, ut remedia, quae alioqui natura sunt aspera, molli manu leniantur; laudare aliqua, ferre quaedam, mutare etiam, reddita cur id fiat ratione, illuminare interponendo

---

1 *de Or.* II. xxi. 88.
2 *cp.* Verg. *G.* ii. 369, *ante reformidant ferrum.*

that I take this view : for does he not say " I would
have the youthful mind run riot in the luxuriance of
its growth " ? [1]

We must, therefore, take especial care, above
all where boys are concerned, to avoid a dry
teacher, even as we avoid a dry and arid soil for
plants that are still young and tender. For with 9
such a teacher their growth is stunted and their
eyes are turned earthwards, and they are afraid to
rise above the level of daily speech. Their leanness
is regarded as a sign of health and their weakness as
a sign of sound judgment, and while they are content that their work should be devoid of faults they
fall into the fault of being devoid of merit. So let
not the ripeness of vintage come too soon nor the
must turn harsh while yet in the vat ; thus it will
last for years and mellow with age.

It is worth while too to warn the teacher that 10
undue severity in correcting faults is liable at times
to discourage a boy's mind from effort. He loses
hope and gives way to vexation, then last of all
comes to hate his work and fearing everything attempts nothing. This phenomenon is familiar to 11
farmers, who hold that the pruning-hook should not
be applied while the leaves are yet young, for they
seem to " shrink from the steel " [2] and to be unable
as yet to endure a scar. The instructor therefore 12
should be as kindly as possible at this stage ; remedies, which are harsh by nature, must be applied with
a gentle hand : some portions of the work must be
praised, others tolerated and others altered : the
reason for the alterations should however be given,
and in some cases the master will illumine an
obscure passage by inserting something of his own.

aliquid sui. Nonnunquam hoc quoque erit utile,
ipsum totas dictare materias, quas et imitetur puer
13 et interim tanquam suas amet. At si tam negligens
ei stilus fuerit, ut emendationem non recipiat;
expertus sum prodesse, quotiens eandem materiam
rursus a me tractatam scribere de integro iuberem;
posse enim adhuc eum melius, quatenus nullo magis
14 studia quam spe gaudent. Aliter autem alia aetas
emendanda est, et pro modo virium et exigendum
et corrigendum opus. Solebam ego dicere pueris
aliquid ausis licentius aut laetius, laudare illud me
adhuc, venturum tempus, quo idem non permit-
terem; ita et ingenio gaudebant et iudicio non
fallebantur.

15 Sed ut eo revertar, unde sum digressus: narra-
tiones stilo componi quanta maxima possit adhibita
diligentia volo. Nam ut primo, cum sermo institu-
itur, dicere quae audierint utile est pueris ad
loquendi facultatem, ideoque et retro agere exposi-
tionem et a media in utramque partem discurrere
sane merito cogantur, sed ad gremium praeceptoris,
et dum aliud [1] non possunt et dum res ac verba connectere incipiunt, ut protinus memoriam firment:
ita cum iam formam rectae atque emendatae ora-

---

[1] aliud, *added by Ed. Gryphiana.*

Occasionally again the teacher will find it useful to dictate whole themes himself that the boy may imitate them and for the time being love them as if they were his own. But if a boy's composition is so 13 careless as not to admit of correction, I have found it useful to give a fresh exposition of the theme and to tell him to write it again, pointing out that he was capable of doing better : for there is nothing like hope for making study a pleasure. Different 14 ages however demand different methods : the task set and the standard of correction must be proportioned to the pupil's strength. When boys ventured on something that was too daring or exuberant, I used to say to them that I approved of it for the moment, but that the time would come when I should no longer tolerate such a style. The result was that the consciousness of ability filled them with pleasure, without blinding their judgment.

However, to return to the point from which I had 15 digressed. Written narratives should be composed with the utmost care. It is useful at first, when a child has just begun to speak, to make him repeat what he has heard with a view to improving his powers of speech ; and for the same purpose, and with good reason, I would make him tell his story from the end back to the beginning or start in the middle and go backwards or forwards, but only so long as he is at his teacher's knee and while he is incapable of greater effort and is beginning to connect words and things, thereby strengthening the memory. Even so when he is beginning to understand the nature of correct and accurate speech, extempore effusions, improvised without waiting for thought to supply the matter or a moment's

tionis accipient, extemporalis garrulitas nec exspec-
tata cogitatio et vix surgendi mora circulatoriae
16 vere iactationis est. Hinc parentium imperitorum
inane gaudium, ipsis vero contemptus operis et in-
verecunda frons et consuetudo pessime dicendi et
malorum exercitatio et, quae magnos quoque profectus frequenter perdidit, arrogans de se persuasio
17 innascitur. Erit suum parandae facilitati tempus,
nec a nobis negligenter locus iste transibitur. Interim satis est, si puer omni cura et summo, quantum
illa aetas capit, labore aliquid probabile scripserit;
in hoc assuescat, huius sibi rei naturam faciat.
Ille demum in id, quod quaerimus, aut ei proximum
poterit evadere, qui ante discet recte dicere quam
cito.

18 Narrationibus non inutiliter subiungitur opus
destruendi confirmandique eas, quod ἀνασκευή et
κατασκευή vocatur. Id porro non tantum in fabulosis
et carmine traditis fieri potest, verum etiam in ipsis
annalium monumentis; ut, si quaeratur, an sit credibile super caput Valeri pugnantis sedisse corvum,
qui os oculosque hostis Galli rostro atque alis ever-
beraret, sit in utramque partem ingens ad dicendum
19 materia; aut de serpente, quo Scipio traditur genitus,
et lupa Romuli et Egeria Numae. Nam Graecis
historiis plerumque poeticae similis licentia est.

---

[1] See Aul. Gell. VII. i.

hesitation before rising to the feet, must not be permitted : they proceed from a passion for display that
would do credit to a common mountebank. Such 16
proceedings fill ignorant parents with senseless pride,
while the boys themselves lose all respect for their
work, adopt a conceited bearing, and acquire the
habit of speaking in the worst style and actually practising their faults, while they develop an arrogant conviction of their own talents which often proves fatal
even to the most genuine proficiency. There will be 17
a special time for acquiring fluency of speech and I
shall not pass the subject by unnoticed. For the meantime it will suffice if a boy, by dint of taking pains and
working as hard as his age will permit, manages to
produce something worthy of approval. Let him get
used to this until it becomes a second nature. It is
only he who learns to speak correctly before he can
speak with rapidity who will reach the heights that
are our goal or the levels immediately below them.

To narratives is annexed the task of refuting and 18
confirming them, styled *anaskeue* and *kataskeue,* from
which no little advantage may be derived. This may
be done not merely in connexion with fiction and
stories transmitted by the poets, but with the actual
records of history as well. For instance we may discuss the credibility of the story that a raven settled
on the head of Valerius in the midst of a combat and
with its wings and beak struck the eyes of the Gaul
who was his adversary, and a quantity of arguments
may be produced on either side : or we may discuss 19
the tradition that Scipio [1] was begotten by a serpent,
or that Romulus was suckled by the she-wolf, or the
story of Numa and Egeria. As regards Greek history, it allows itself something very like poetic

Saepe etiam quaeri solet de tempore, de loco quo gesta res dicitur, nonnunquam de persona quoque; sicut Livius frequentissime dubitat, et alii ab aliis historici dissentiunt.

20 Inde paulatim ad maiora tendere incipiet, laudare claros viros et vituperare improbos, quod non simplicis utilitatis opus est. Namque et ingenium exercetur multiplici variaque materia, et animus contemplatione recti pravique formatur, et multa inde cognitio rerum venit exemplisque, quae sunt in omni genere causarum potentissima, iam tum in-

21 struit, cum res poscet, usurum. Hinc illa quoque exercitatio subit comparationis, uter melior uterve deterior; quae quanquam versatur in ratione simili, tamen et duplicat materiam et virtutum vitiorumque non tantum naturam, sed etiam modum tractat. Verum de ordine laudis contraque, quoniam tertia haec rhetorices pars est, praecipiemus suo tempore.

22 Communes loci (de iis loquor, quibus citra personas in ipsa vitia moris est perorare, ut in adulterum, aleatorem, petulantem) ex mediis sunt iudiciis et, si reum adiicias, accusationes; quanquam hi quoque ab illo generali tractatu ad quasdam deduci species solent, ut si ponatur adulter caecus, aleator pauper, petulans senex. Habent autem

---

[1] Book III. chap. vii.

licence. Again the time and place of some particular occurrence and sometimes even the persons concerned often provide matter for discussion : Livy for instance is frequently in doubt as to what actually occurred and historians often disagree.

From this our pupil will begin to proceed to more 20 important themes, such as the praise of famous men and the denunciation of the wicked. Such tasks are profitable in more than one respect. The mind is exercised by the variety and multiplicity of the subject matter, while the character is moulded by the contemplation of virtue and vice. Further wide knowledge of facts is thus acquired, from which examples may be drawn if circumstances so demand, such illustrations being of the utmost value in every kind of case. It is but a step from this to practice 21 in the comparison of the respective merits of two characters. This is of course a very similar theme to the preceding, but involves a duplication of the subject matter and deals not merely with the nature of virtues and vices, but with their degree as well. But the method to be followed in panegyric and invective will be dealt with in its proper place, as it forms the third department of rhetoric.[1]

As to *commonplaces* (I refer to those in which 22 we denounce vices themselves such as adultery, gambling or profligacy without attacking particular persons), they come straight from the courts and, if we add the name of the defendant, amount to actual accusations. As a rule, however, the general character of a commonplace is usually given a special turn : for instance we make our adulterer blind, our gambler poor and our profligate far advanced in years. Sometimes too they entail

23 nonnunquam etiam defensionem. Nam et pro
luxuria et pro amore dicimus, et leno interim para-
situsque defenditur sic, ut non homini patrocinemur,
sed crimini.

24 Theses autem, quae sumuntur ex rerum comparatione, ut rusticane vita an urbana potior, iurisperiti
an militaris viri laus maior, mire sunt ad exercitationem dicendi speciosae atque uberes, quae vel ad
suadendi officium vel etiam ad iudiciorum discepta-
tionem iuvant plurimum. Nam posterior ex prae-
dictis locus in causa Murenae copiosissime a Cicerone

25 tractatur. Sunt et illae paene totae ad delibera-
tivum pertinentes genus, ducendane uxor, petendine
sint magistratus. Namque et hae personis modo
adiectis suasoriae erunt.

26 Solebant praeceptores mei neque inutili et nobis
etiam iucundo genere exercitationis praeparare nos
coniecturalibus causis, cum quaerere atque exsequi
iuberent, *Cur armata apud Lacedaemonios Venus,* et
*Quid ita crederetur Cupido puer atque volucer et sagittis
ac face armatus,* et similia, in quibus scrutabamur
voluntatem, cuius in controversiis frequens quaestio
est, quod genus chriae videri potest.

27 Nam locos quidem, quales sunt de testibus, sem-

---

[1] *Pro Mur.* ix. 21 *sqq.*
[2] The reason according to Lactantius (*Inst. Div.* i. 20) was
the bravery of the Spartan women in one of the Messenian
wars.

defence : for we may speak on behalf of luxury or 23
love, while a pimp or a parasite may be defended in
such a way that we appear as counsel not for the
character itself, but to rebut some specific charge
that is brought against him.

Theses on the other hand are concerned with 24
the comparison of things and involve questions such
as "Which is preferable, town or country life ?"
or "Which deserves the greatest praise, the lawyer
or the soldier ? " These provide the most attractive
and copious practice in the art of speaking, and are
most useful whether we have an eye to the duties
of deliberative oratory or the arguments of the
courts. For instance Cicero in his *pro Murena*[1] deals
very fully with the second of the two problems
mentioned above. Other *theses* too belong entirely 25
to the deliberative class of oratory, as for instance
the questions as to "Whether marriage is desirable " or "Whether a public career is a proper
object of ambition." Put such discussions into
the mouths of specific persons and they become
deliberative declamations at once.

My own teachers used to prepare us for conject- 26
ural cases by a form of exercise which was at once
useful and attractive : they made us discuss and
develop questions such as " Why in Sparta is Venus
represented as wearing armour ?"[2] or "Why is Cupid
believed to be a winged boy armed with arrows and
a torch ? " and the like. In these exercises our aim
was to discover the intention implied, a question
which frequently occurs in controversial declamations.
Such themes may perhaps be regarded as a kind of
chria or moral essay.

That certain topics such as the question as to 27

perne his credendum, et de argumentis, an habenda
etiam parvis fides, adeo manifestum est ad forenses
actiones pertinere, ut quidam neque ignobiles in
officiis civilibus scriptos eos memoriaeque diligentissime mandatos in promptu habuerint, ut quotiens
esset occasio, extemporales eorum dictiones his velut
28 emblematis exornarentur. Quo quidem (neque
enim eius rei iudicium differre sustineo) summam
videbantur mihi infirmitatem de se confiteri. Nam
quid ii possint in causis, quarum varia et nova semper
est facies, proprium invenire? quomodo propositis ex
parte adversa respondere, altercationibus velociter
occurrere, testem rogare? qui etiam in iis, quae
sunt communia et in plurimis causis tractantur, vul-
gatissimos sensus verbis nisi tanto ante praeparatis
29 prosequi nequeant. Necesse vero iis, cum eadem
iudiciis pluribus dicunt, aut fastidium moveant velut
frigidi et repositi cibi, aut pudorem deprehensa
totiens audientium memoria infelix supellex, quae
sicut apud pauperes ambitiosos pluribus et diversis
30 officiis conteratur: cum eo quidem quod vix ullus
est tam communis locus, qui possit cohaerere cum
causa nisi aliquo propriae quaestionis vinculo copu-

whether we should always believe a witness or
whether we should rely on circumstantial evidence,
are part and parcel of actual forensic pleading is so
obvious that certain speakers, men too who have
held civil office with no small distinction, have
written out passages dealing with such themes, committed them to memory and kept them ready for
immediate use, with a view to employing them when
occasion arose as a species of ornament to be inserted
into their extempore speeches.   This practice— 28
for I am not going to postpone expressing my judgment on it—I used to regard a confession of extreme weakness.   For how can such men find appropriate arguments in the course of actual cases which
continually present new and different features?
How can they answer the points that their opponents
may bring up? how deal a rapid counterstroke in
debate or cross-examine a witness? if, even in those
matters which are of common occurrence and crop
up in the majority of cases, they cannot give expression to the most familiar thoughts except in words
prepared so far in advance.   And when they produce 29
the same passage in a number of different cases, they
must come to loathe it like food that has grown cold
or stale, and they can hardly avoid a feeling of shame
at displaying this miserable piece of furniture to an
audience whose memory must have detected it so
many times already: like the furniture of the
ostentatious poor, it is sure to shew signs of wear
through being used for such a variety of different
purposes.   Also it must be remembered that there 30
is hardly a single commonplace of such universal
application that it will fit any actual case, unless
some special link is provided to connect it with

latus; appareat alioqui non tam insertum quam
31 adplicitum, vel quod dissimilis est ceteris vel quod
plerumque adsumi etiam parum apte solet, non quia
desideratur sed quia paratus est: ut quidam sen-
tentiarum gratia verbosissimos locos arcessunt, cum
32 ex locis debeat nasci sententia. Ita sunt autem
speciosa haec et utilia, si oriuntur ex causa; ceterum
quamlibet pulchra elocutio, nisi ad victoriam tendit,
utique supervacua, sed interim etiam contraria est.
Verum hactenus evagari satis fuerit.

33 Legum laus ac vituperatio iam maiores ac prope
summis operibus suffecturas vires desiderant; quae
quidem suasoriis an controversiis magis accommodata sit exercitatio, consuetudine et iure civitatium
differt. Apud Graecos enim lator earum ad iudicem
vocabatur, Romanis pro contione suadere ac dissua-
dere moris fuit. Utroque autem modo pauca de his
et fere certa dicuntur. Nam et genera sunt tria,
34 sacri, publici, privati iuris. Quae divisio ad laudem
magis spectat, si quis eam per gradus augeat, quod
lex, quod publica, quod ad religionem deum comparata sit. Ea quidem, de quibus quaeri solet,

---

[1] *i.e.* a court of *nomothetae* appointed by the Athenian
assembly, who examined the provisions of the proposed law.

the subject : otherwise it will seem to have been tacked on to the speech, not interwoven in its texture, either because it is out of keeping with the 31 circumstances or like most of its kind is inappropriately employed not because it is wanted, but because it is ready for use. Some speakers, for example, introduce the most long-winded commonplaces just for the sake of the sentiments they contain, whereas rightly the sentiments should spring from the context. Such 32 disquisitions are at once ornamental and useful, only if they arise from the nature of the case. But the most finished eloquence, unless it tend to the winning of the case, is to say the least superfluous and may even defeat its own purpose. However I must bring this digression to a close.

The praise or denunciation of laws requires greater 33 powers ; indeed they should almost be equal to the most serious tasks of rhetoric. The answer to the question as to whether this exercise is more nearly related to deliberative or controversial oratory depends on custom and law and consequently varies in different states. Among the Greeks the proposer of a law was called upon to set forth his case before a judge,[1] while in Rome it was the custom to urge the acceptance or rejection of a law before the public assembly. But in any case the arguments advanced in such cases are few in number and of a definite type. For there are only three kinds of law, *sacred*, *public* and *private*. This division is of rhetorical value 34 chiefly when a law is to be praised. For example the orator may advance from praise to praise by a series of gradations, praising an enactment first because it is *law*, secondly because it is *public*, and, finally, designed for the support of *religion*. As regards the questions

35 communia omnibus. Aut enim de iure dubitari
potest eius, qui rogat, ut de P. Clodi, qui non rite
creatus tribunus arguebatur; aut de ipsius roga-
tionis, quod est varium, sive non trino forte nundino
promulgata sive non idoneo die, sive contra inter-
cessionem vel auspicia aliudve quid, quod legitimis
obstet, dicitur lata esse vel ferri, sive alicui manen-
36 tium legum repugnare. Sed haec ad illas primas
exercitationes non pertinent; nam sunt hae citra
complexum personarum, temporum, causarum. Reliqua eadem fere vero fictoque huiusmodi certamine
37 tractantur. Nam vitium aut in verbis aut in rebus
est. In verbis quaeritur, an satis significent, an sit
in iis aliquid ambiguum; in rebus, an lex sibi ipsa
consentiat, an in praeteritum ferri debeat, an in
singulos homines. Maxime vero commune est
38 quaerere, an sit honesta, an utilis. Nec ignoro,
plures fieri a plerisque partes; sed nos iustum, pium,
religiosum, ceteraque his similia honesto complec-
timur. Iusti tamen species non simpliciter excuti
solent. Aut enim de re ipsa quaeritur, ut dignane

---

[1] Clodius was a patrician and got himself made a plebeian
by adoption to enable him to hold the tribunate. The
question of the legality of this procedure is discussed by
Cicero in the *de Domo*, 13–17.

[2] Lit. within the space of three market-days. *nundinum*
= 9 days, the second market-day being the ninth, and
forming the last day of the first *nundinum* and the first of

which generally arise, they are common to all cases.
Doubts may be raised as to whether the mover is 35
legally in a position to propose a law, as happened in
the case of Publius Clodius, whose appointment as
tribune of the plebs was alleged to be unconstitu-
tional.[1] Or the legality of the proposal itself may
be impugned in various ways ; it may for instance be
urged that the law was not promulgated within
seventeen [2] days, or was proposed, or is being proposed on an improper day, or in defiance of the
tribunicial veto or the auspices or any other legal
obstacle, or again that it is contrary to some existing law.   But such points are not suitable to 36
elementary rhetorical exercises, which are not concerned with persons, times or particular cases.
Other subjects, whether the dispute be real or fictitious, are generally treated on the following lines.
The fault must lie either in the words or the 37
matter. As regards the words, the question will
be whether they are sufficiently clear or contain
some ambiguity, and as regards the matter whether
the law is consistent with itself or should be retro-
spective or apply to special individuals. The point
however which is most commonly raised is the
question whether the law is right or expedient. I 38
am well aware that many rhetoricians introduce a
number of sub-divisions in connexion with this latter
enquiry. I however include under the term *right*
all such qualities as justice, piety and religion.
Justice is however usually discussed under various
aspects. A question may be raised about the acts
with which the law is concerned, as to whether they

the second. Similarly the third market-day is the last day
of the second *nundinum* and the first of the third.

poena vel praemio sit, aut de modo praemii poenae-
ve, qui tam maior quam minor culpari potest.
39 Utilitas quoque interim natura discernitur, interim
tempore.   Quaedam an obtineri possint, ambigi
solet.   Ne illud quidem ignorare oportet, leges
aliquando totas, aliquando ex parte reprehendi solere,
cum exemplum rei utriusque nobis claris orationibus
40 praebeatur.   Nec me fallit, eas quoque leges esse,
quae non in perpetuum rogentur, sed de honoribus
aut imperiis, qualis Manilia fuit, de qua Ciceronis
oratio est.   Sed de his nihil hoc loco praecipi potest;
constant enim propria rerum, de quibus agitur,
non communi qualitate.

41   His fere veteres facultatem dicendi exercuerunt
assumpta tamen a dialecticis argumentandi ratione.
Nam fictas ad imitationem fori consiliorumque
materias apud Graecos dicere circa Demetrium
42 Phalerea institutum fere constat.   An ab ipso id
genus exercitationis sit inventum, ut alio quoque
libro sum confessus, parum comperi; sed ne ii
quidem, qui hoc fortissime adfirmant, ullo satis
idoneo auctore nituntur.   Latinos vero dicendi
praeceptores extremis L. Crassi temporibus coepisse

---

[1] The *lex Manilia* proposed to give Pompey the command
against Mithridates.
[2] Probably the lost treatise on "The causes of the
decline of oratory" (*De causis corruptae eloquentiae*).

deserve punishment or reward or as to the degree of
punishment or reward that should be assigned, since
excess in either direction is open to criticism. Again 39
expediency is sometimes determined by the nature
of things, sometimes by the circumstances of the time.
Another common subject of controversy is whether
a law can be enforced, while one must not shut one's
eyes to the fact that exception is sometimes taken
to laws in their entirety, but sometimes only in
part, examples of both forms of criticism being
found in famous speeches. I am well aware, too, 40
that there are laws which are not proposed with
a view to perpetuity, but are concerned with tem-
porary honours or commands, such as the *lex Manilia*[1]
which is the subject of one of Cicero's speeches.
This however is not the place for instructions on
this topic, since they depend on the special circumstances of the matters under discussion, not on their
general characteristics.

Such were the subjects on which the ancients as 41
a rule exercised their powers of speaking, though
they called in the assistance of the logicians as well
to teach them the theory of argument. For it is
generally agreed that the declamation of fictitious
themes in imitation of the questions that arise in
the lawcourts or deliberative assemblies came into
vogue among the Greeks about the time of De-
metrius of Phalerum. Whether this type of exer- 42
cise was actually invented by him I have failed to
discover, as I have acknowledged in another work.[2]
But not even those who most strongly assert his
claim to be the inventor, can produce any adequate
authority in support of their opinion. As regards
Latin teachers of rhetoric, of whom Plotius was the

Cicero auctor est; quorum insignis maxime Plotius
fuit.

V. Sed de ratione declamandi post paulum.
Interim, quia prima rhetorices rudimenta tractamus,
non omittendum videtur id quoque, ut moneam,
quantum sit collaturus ad profectum discentium
rhetor, si, quemadmodum a grammaticis exigitur
poetarum enarratio, ita ipse quoque historiae atque
etiam magis orationum lectione susceptos a se discipulos instruxerit; quod nos in paucis, quorum id
aetas exigebat et parentes utile esse crediderant,
2 servavimus. Ceterum sentientibus iam tum optima
duae res impedimento fuerunt, quod et longa consuetudo aliter docendi fecerat legem, et robusti fere
iuvenes nec hunc laborem desiderantes exemplum
3 nostrum sequebantur. Nec tamen, etiamsi quid
novi vel sero invenissem, praecipere in posterum
puderet. Nunc vero scio id fieri apud Graecos sed
magis per adiutores, quia non videntur tempora
suffectura, si legentibus singulis praeire semper ipsi
4 velint. Et hercule praelectio, quae in hoc adhibetur, ut facile atque distincte pueri scripta oculis
sequantur, etiam illa, quae vim cuiusque verbi, si
quod minus usitatum incidat, docet, multum infra
5 rhetoris officium existimanda est. At demonstrare
virtutes vel, si quando ita incidat, vitia, id pro-

---

[1] See Cic. de Or. iii. 24, 93.

most famous, Cicero [1] informs us that they came into existence towards the end of the age of Crassus.

V. I will speak of the theory of declamation a little later. In the mean time, as we are discussing the elementary stages of a rhetorical education, I think I should not fail to point out how greatly the rhetorician will contribute to his pupils' progress, if he imitates the teacher of literature whose duty it is to expound the poets, and gives the pupils whom he has undertaken to train, instruction in the reading of history and still more of the orators. I myself have adopted this practice for the benefit of a few pupils of suitable age whose parents thought it would be useful. But though my intentions were 2 excellent, I found that there were two serious obstacles to success : long custom had established a different method of teaching, and my pupils were for the most part full-grown youths who did not require this form of teaching, but were taking my work as their model. However, the fact that I 3 have been somewhat late in making the discovery is not a reason why I should be ashamed to recommend it to those who come after me. I now know that this form of teaching is practised by the Greeks, but is generally entrusted to assistants, as the professors themselves consider that they have no time to give individual instruction to each pupil as he reads. And I admit that the form of lecture which this 4 requires, designed as it is to make boys follow the written word with ease and accuracy, and even that which aims at teaching the meaning of any rare words that may occur, are to be regarded as quite below the dignity of the teacher of rhetoric. On 5 the other hand it is emphatically part of his pro-

fessionis eius atque promissi, quo se magistrum
eloquentiae pollicetur, maxime proprium est, eo
quidem validius, quod non utique hunc laborem
docentium postulo, ut ad gremium revocatis cuius
6 quisque eorum velit libri lectione deserviant. Nam
mihi cum facilius tum etiam multo videtur magis
utile, facto silentio unum aliquem (quod ipsum im-
perari per vices optimum est) constituere lectorem,
ut protinus pronuntiationi quoque assuescant; tum
7 exposita causa, in quam scripta legetur oratio, (nam
sic clarius quae dicentur intelligi poterunt) nihil
otiosum pati, quodque in inventione quodque in
elocutione adnotandum erit, quae in prooemio
conciliandi iudicis ratio, quae narrandi lux, brevi-
tas, fides, quod aliquando consilium et quam occulta
8 calliditas (namque ea sola in hoc ars est, quae intelligi nisi ab artifice non possit); quanta deinceps
in dividendo prudentia, quam subtilis et crebra
argumentatio, quibus viribus inspiret, qua iucunditate permulceat, quanta in maledictis asperitas, in
iocis urbanitas, ut denique dominetur in adfectibus

fession and the undertaking which he makes in
offering himself as a teacher of eloquence, to point
out the merits of authors or, for that matter, any
faults that may occur: and this is all the more the
case, as I am not asking teachers to undertake the
task of recalling their pupils to stand at their knee once
more and of assisting them in the reading of whatever book they may select. It seems to me at once 6
an easier and more profitable method to call for
silence and choose some one pupil—and it will be
best to select them by turns—to read aloud, in
order that they may at the same time learn the
correct method of elocution. The case with which 7
the speech selected for reading is concerned should
then be explained, for if this be done they will
have a clearer understanding of what is to be read.
When the reading is commenced, no important
point should be allowed to pass unnoticed either
as regards the resourcefulness or the style shown
in the treatment of the subject: the teacher must
point out how the orator seeks to win the favour
of the judge in his *exordium*, what clearness, brevity
and sincerity, and at times what shrewd design and
well-concealed artifice is shown in the statement of
facts. For the only true art in pleading is that 8
which can only be understood by one who is a
master of the art himself. The teacher will proceed
further to demonstrate what skill is shown in the division into heads, how subtle and frequent are the thrusts
of argument, what vigour marks the stirring and
what charm the soothing passage, how fierce is the
invective and how full of wit the jests, and in
conclusion how the orator establishes his sway
over the emotions of his audience, forces his way

atque in pectora irrumpat animumque iudicum
9 similem iis, quae dicit, efficiat. Tum in ratione
eloquendi, quod verbum proprium, ornatum, sublime;
ubi amplificatio laudanda, quae virtus ei contraria,
quid speciose translatum, quae figura verborum,
quae levis et quadrata sed virilis tamen compositio.
10 Ne id quidem inutile, etiam corruptas aliquando
et vitiosas orationes, quas tamen plerique iudiciorum
pravitate mirantur, legi palam ostendique in his,
quam multa impropria, obscura, tumida, humilia,
sordida, lasciva, effeminata sint; quae non laudantur
modo a plerisque, sed, quod est peius, propter hoc
11 ipsum, quod sunt prava, laudantur. Nam sermo
rectus et secundum naturam enuntiatus nihil habere
ex ingenio videtur; illa vero, quae utcunque deflexa
sunt, tanquam exquisitiora miramur; non aliter
quam distortis et quocunque modo prodigiosis corporibus apud quosdam maius est pretium quam iis,
quae nihil ex communi habitu boni perdiderunt.
12 Atque etiam qui specie capiuntur, vulsis levatisque
et inustas comas acu comentibus et non suo colore
nitidis plus esse formae putant, quam possit tribuere
incorrupta natura, ut pulchritudo corporis venire
videatur ex malis morum.
13 Neque solum haec ipse debebit docere praeceptor

into their very hearts and brings the feelings of the jury into perfect sympathy with all his words. Finally as regards the style, he will emphasise the 9 appropriateness, elegance or sublimity of particular words, will indicate where the amplification of the theme is deserving of praise and where there is virtue in a diminuendo; and will call attention to brilliant metaphors, figures of speech and passages combining smoothness and polish with a general impression of manly vigour.

It will even at times be of value to read speeches 10 which are corrupt and faulty in style, but still meet with general admiration thanks to the perversity of modern tastes, and to point out how many expressions in them are inappropriate, obscure, high-flown, grovelling, mean, extravagant or effeminate, although they are not merely praised by the majority of critics, but, worse still, praised just because they are bad. For 11 we have come to regard direct and natural speech as incompatible with genius, while all that is in any way abnormal is admired as exquisite. Similarly we see that some people place a higher value on figures which are in any way monstrous or distorted than they do on those who have not lost any of the advantages of the normal form of man. There are 12 even some who are captivated by the shams of artifice and think that there is more beauty in those who pluck out superfluous hair or use depilatories, who dress their locks by scorching them with the curling iron and glow with a complexion that is not their own, than can ever be conferred by nature pure and simple, so that it really seems as if physical beauty depended entirely on moral hideousness.

It will, however, be the duty of the rhetorician 13

sed frequenter interrogare et iudicium discipulorum experiri. Sic audientibus securitas aberit nec quae dicentur superfluent aures, simulque ad id perducentur, quod ex hoc quaeritur, ut inveniant ipsi et intelligant. Nam quid aliud agimus docendo eos,

14 quam ne semper docendi sint? Hoc diligentiae genus ausim dicere plus collaturum discentibus quam omnes omnium artes, quae iuvant sine dubio multum; sed latiore quadam comprehensione per omnes quidem species rerum cotidie paene nascen-

15 tium ire qui possunt? Sicut de re militari, quanquam sunt tradita quaedam praecepta communia, magis tamen proderit scire, qua ducum quisque ratione, in quali re, tempore, loco sit sapienter usus aut contra. Nam in omnibus fere minus valent

16 praecepta quam experimenta. An vero declamabit quidem praeceptor, ut sit exemplo suis auditoribus; non plus contulerint lecti Cicero aut Demosthenes? Corrigetur palam, si quid in declamando discipulus erraverit; non potentius erit emendare orationem, quin immo etiam iucundius? Aliera enim vitia

17 reprehendi quisque mavult quam sua. Nec deerant plura, quae dicerem; sed neminem haec utilitas

not merely to teach these things, but to ask frequent
questions as well, and test the critical powers of his
class. This will prevent his audience from becoming
inattentive and will secure that his words do not fall
on deaf ears. At the same time the class will be led
to find out things for themselves and to use their
intelligence, which is after all the chief aim of this
method of training. For what else is our object in
teaching, save that our pupils should not always
require to be taught? I will venture to say that 14
this particular form of exercise, if diligently pursued,
will teach learners more than all the text-books of
all the rhetoricians: these are no doubt of very
considerable use, but being somewhat general in
their scope, it is quite impossible for them to deal
with all the special cases that are of almost daily
occurrence. The art of war will provide a parallel: 15
it is no doubt based on certain general principles,
but it will none the less be far more useful to know
the methods employed, whether wisely or the reverse, by individual generals under varying circumstances and conditions of time and place. For there
are no subjects in which, as a rule, practice is not
more valuable than precept. Is a teacher to declaim 16
to provide a model for his audience, and will not
more profit be derived from the reading of Cicero or
Demosthenes? Is a pupil to be publicly corrected
if he makes a mistake in declaiming, and will it not
be more useful, and more agreeable too, to correct
some actual speech? For everyone has a preference
for hearing the faults of others censured rather than
his own. I might say more on the subject. But 17
every one can see the advantages of this method.
Would that the reluctance to put it into practice

fugit, atque utinam tam non pigeat facere istud quam non displicebit.

18 Quod si potuerit obtineri, non ita difficilis supererit quaestio, qui legendi sint incipientibus. Nam quidam illos minores, quia facilior intellectus videbatur, probaverunt; alii floridius genus, ut ad alenda primarum aetatum ingenia magis accommodatum.

19 Ego optimos quidem et statim et semper sed tamen eorum candidissimum quemque et maxime expositum velim, ut Livium a pueris magis quam Sallustium, etsi hic historiae maior est auctor, ad quem

20 tamen intelligendum iam profectu opus sit. Cicero, ut mihi quidem videtur, et iucundus incipientibus quoque et apertus est satis, nec prodesse tantum sed etiam amari potest, tum (quemadmodum Livius praecipit) ut quisque erit Ciceroni simillimus.

21 Duo autem genera maxime cavenda pueris puto: unum, ne quis eos antiquitatis nimius admirator in Gracchorum Catonisque et aliorum similium lectione durescere velit; fient enim horridi atque ieiuni; nam neque vim eorum adhuc intellectu consequentur et elocutione, quae tum sine dubio erat optima, sed nostris temporibus aliena est, contenti, quod est

were not as great as the pleasure that would undoubtedly be derived from so doing!

This method once adopted, we are faced by the 18
comparatively easy question as to what authors
should be selected for our reading. Some have re-
commended authors of inferior merit on the ground
that they were easier to understand. Others on the
contrary would select the more florid school of writers
on the ground that they are likely to provide the
nourishment best suited to the minds of the young.
For my part I would have them read the best authors 19
from the very beginning and never leave them,
choosing those, however, who are simplest and most
intelligible. For instance, when prescribing for boys,
I should give Livy the preference over Sallust;
for, although the latter is the greater historian,
one requires to be well-advanced in one's studies
to appreciate him properly. Cicero, in my opinion, 20
provides pleasant reading for beginners and is sufficiently easy to understand : it is possible not only
to learn much from him, but to come to love him.
After Cicero I should, following the advice of Livy,
place such authors as most nearly resemble him.

There are two faults of taste against which boys 21
should be guarded with the utmost care. Firstly
no teacher suffering from an excessive admiration
of antiquity, should be allowed to cramp their
minds by the study of Cato and the Gracchi and
other similar authors. For such reading will give
them a harsh and bloodless style, since they will as
yet be unable to understand the force and vigour of
these authors, and contenting themselves with a
style which doubtless was admirable in its day, but
is quite unsuitable to ours, will come to think (and

pessimum, similes sibi magnis viris videbuntur
22 Alterum, quod huic diversum est, ne recentis huius
lasciviae flosculis capti voluptate prava deleniantur,
ut praedulce illud genus et puerilibus ingeniis hoc
23 gratius, quo propius est, adament. Firmis autem
iudiciis iamque extra periculum positis suaserim et
antiquos legere, ex quibus si assumatur solida ac
virilis ingenii vis, deterso rudis saeculi squalore, tum
noster hic cultus clarius enitescet, et novos, quibus
24 et ipsis multa virtus adest. Neque enim nos tardi-
tatis natura damnavit, sed dicendi mutavimus genus
et ultra nobis quam oportebat indulsimus; ita non
tam ingenio illi nos superarunt quam proposito.
Multa ergo licebit eligere; sed curandum erit, ne
25 iis, quibus permixta sunt, inquinentur. Quosdam
vero etiam, quos totos imitari oporteat, et fuisse
nuper et nunc esse, quidni libenter non modo con-
26 cesserim, verum etiam contenderim? Sed hi qui
sint, non cuiuscunque est pronuntiare. Tutius circa
priores vel erratur, ideoque hanc novorum distuli
lectionem, ne imitatio iudicium antecederet.

nothing could be more fatal) that they really resemble great men. Secondly the opposite extreme must 22 be equally avoided: they must not be permitted to fall victims to the pernicious allurements of the precious blooms produced by our modern euphuists, thus acquiring a passion for the luscious sweetness of such authors, whose charm is all the more attractive to boyish intellects because it is so easy of achievement. Once, however, the judgment is 23 formed and out of danger of perversion, I should strongly recommend the reading of ancient authors, since if, after clearing away all the uncouthness of those rude ages, we succeed in absorbing the robust vigour and virility of their native genius, our more finished style will shine with an added grace: I also approve the study of the moderns at this stage, since even they have many merits. For nature has not doomed us to be dullards, 24 but we have altered our style of oratory and indulged our caprices over much. It is in their ideals rather than their talents that the ancients show themselves our superiors. It will therefore be possible to select much that is valuable from modern writers, but we must take care that the precious metal is not debased by the dross with which it is so closely intermingled. Further I would not 25 merely gladly admit, but would even contend that we have recently had and still have certain authors who deserve imitation in their entirety. But it is 26 not for everyone to decide who these writers are. Error in the choice of earlier authors is attended with less danger, and I have therefore postponed the study of the moderns, for fear that we should imitate them before we are qualified to judge of their merits.

257

VI. Fuit etiam in hoc diversum praecipientium propositum, quod eorum quidam materias, quas discipulis ad dicendum dabant, non contenti divisione dirigere latius dicendo prosequebantur, nec solum 2 probationibus implebant sed etiam adfectibus. Alii, cum primas modo lineas duxissent, post declamationes, quid omisisset quisque, tractabant; quosdam vero locos non minore cura, quam cum ad dicendum ipsi surgerent, excolebant. Utile utrumque, et ideo neutrum ab altero separo; sed si facere tantum alterum necesse sit, plus proderit demonstrasse rectam protinus viam quam revocare ab errore iam 3 lapsos: primum quia emendationem auribus modo accipiunt, divisionem vero ad cogitationem etiam et stilum perferunt; deinde quod libentius praecipientem audiunt quam reprehendentem. Si qui vero paulo sunt vivaciores, in his praesertim moribus, etiam irascuntur admonitioni et taciti repugnant. 4 Neque ideo tamen minus vitia aperte coarguenda sunt. Habenda enim ratio ceterorum, qui recta esse, quae praeceptor non emendaverit, credent. Utraque autem ratio miscenda est et ita tractanda, 5 ut ipsae res postulabunt. Namque incipientibus

VI. I come now to another point in which the practice of teachers has differed. Some have not been content with giving directions as to the arrangement of the subjects set them as themes for declamation, but have developed them at some length themselves, supplying not merely the proofs, but the lines upon which the emotional passages should proceed. Others have merely suggested a 2 bare outline, and then when the declamations were over, have indicated the points missed by each speaker and worked up certain passages with no less care than they would have used, had they been going to stand up to speak themselves. Both practices have their advantages, and therefore I will not give either the pre-eminence. But if we must choose one of the two, it will be found more profitable to point out the right road at the outset, and not merely to recall the pupil from his error when he has already gone astray, since in the first place the correction 3 is only received by the ear, whereas when he is given a sketch of the various heads of the declamation, he has to take them down and think about them : secondly instruction is always more readily received than reproof. Indeed those of our pupils who have a lively disposition are liable in the present condition of manners to lose their temper when admonished and to offer silent resistance. That, however, is no reason for refraining from 4 the public correction of faults ; for we must take the rest of the class into account, who will believe that whatever has not been corrected by the master is right. The two methods should be employed conjointly and in such a way as circumstances may demand. Beginners must be given a subject 5

danda erit velut praeformata materia secundum cuiusque vires; at cum satis composuisse sese ad exemplum videbuntur, brevia quaedam demonstranda vestigia, quae persecuti iam suis viribus sine adminiculo progredi possint. Nonnunquam credi sibi ipsos oportebit, ne mala consuetudine semper alienum laborem sequendi nihil per se conari et quaerere sciant. Quodsi satis prudenter dicenda viderint, iam prope consummata fuerit praecipientis opera; at si quid erraverint adhuc, erunt ad ducem reducendi. Cui rei simile quiddam facientes aves cernimus, quae teneris infirmisque fetibus cibos ore suo collatos partiuntur; at cum visi sunt adulti, paulum egredi nidis et circumvolare sedem illam praecedentes ipsae docent, tum expertas vires libero caelo suaeque ipsorum fiduciae permittunt.

VII. Illud ex consuetudine mutandum prorsus existimo in iis, de quibus nunc disserimus, aetatibus, ne omnia quae scripserint ediscant et certa, ut moris est, die dicant; quod quidem maxime patres exigunt atque ita demum studere liberos suos, si quam frequentissime declamaverint, credunt, cum profectus

sketched out ready for treatment and suitable to
their respective powers. But when they show that
they have formed themselves sufficiently closely on
the models placed before them, it will be sufficient
to give them a few brief hints for their guidance
and to allow them to advance trusting in their own
strength and without external support. Sometimes 6
they should be left entirely to their own devices,
that they may not be spoilt by the bad habit of
always relying on another's efforts, and so prove incapable of effort and originality. But as soon as
they seem to have acquired a sound conception of
what they ought to say, the teacher's work will be
near completion: if they still make some mistakes,
they must be brought back under his guidance. We 7
may draw a lesson from the birds of the air, whom
we see distributing the food which they have collected in their bills among their weak and helpless
nestlings; but as soon as they are fledged, we see
them teaching their young to leave the nest and fly
round about it, themselves leading the way; finally,
when they have proved their strength, they are given
the freedom of the open sky and left to trust in
themselves.

VII. There is one practice at present in vogue
for boys of the age under discussion, which ought
in my opinion undoubtedly to be changed. They
should not be forced to commit all their own compositions to memory and to deliver them on an
appointed day, as is at present the custom. This
practice is especially popular with the boys' fathers,
who think that their sons are not really studying
unless they declaim on every possible occasion,
although as a matter of fact progress depends

2 praecipue diligentia constet. Nam ut scribere pueros plurimumque esse in hoc opere plane velim, sic ediscere electos ex orationibus vel historiis aliove quo genere dignorum ea cura voluminum locos, multo 3 magis suadeam. Nam et exercebitur acrius memoria aliena complectendo quam sua; et qui erunt in difficiliore huius laboris genere versati, sine molestia quae ipsi composuerint iam familiaria animo suo adfigent, et adsuescent optimis semperque habebunt intra se, quod imitentur; et iam non sentientes formam orationis illam, quam mente penitus acce-4 perint, expriment. Abundabunt autem copia verborum optimorum et compositione et figuris iam non quaesitis sed sponte et ex reposito velut thesauro se offerentibus. Accedit his et iucunda in sermone bene a quoque dictorum relatio et in causis utilis. Nam et plus auctoritatis adferunt ea, quae non praesentis gratia litis sunt comparata, et laudem saepe 5 maiorem quam si nostra sint conciliant. Aliquando tamen permittendum quae ipsi scripserint dicere, ut laboris sui fructum etiam ex illa quae maxime petitur laude plurium capiant. Verum id quoque tum fieri

mainly on industry. For though I strongly ap- 2
prove of boys writing compositions and would have
them spend as much time as possible over such
tasks, I had much rather that for the purpose of
learning by heart passages should be selected from
the orators or historians or any other works that
may be deserving of such attention. For it is a 3
better exercise for the memory to learn the words
of others than it is to learn one's own, and those
who have practised this far harder task will find
no difficulty in committing to memory their own
compositions with which they are already familiar.
Further they will form an intimate acquaintance
with the best writings, will carry their models
with them and unconsciously reproduce the style
of the speech which has been impressed upon the
memory. They will have a plentiful and choice 4
vocabulary and a command of artistic structure and
a supply of figures which will not have to be
hunted for, but will offer themselves spontane-
ously from the treasure-house, if I may so call it,
in which they are stored. In addition they will
be in the agreeable position of being able to
quote the happy sayings of the various authors, a
power which they will find most useful in the
courts. For phrases which have not been coined
merely to suit the circumstances of the lawsuit of
the moment carry greater weight and often win
greater praise than if they were our own. I 5
would however allow boys occasionally to declaim
their own compositions that they may reap the reward of their labours in the applause of a large
audience, that most coveted of all prizes. But this
should not be permitted until they have produced

oportebit, cum aliquid commodius elimaverint, ut eo
velut praemio studii sui donentur ac se meruisse ut
dicerent gaudeant.

VIII. Virtus praeceptoris haberi solet nec imme-
rito diligenter in iis, quos erudiendos susceperit,
notare discrimina ingeniorum et, quo quemque natura
maxime ferat, scire. Nam est in hoc incredibilis
quaedam varietas nec pauciores animorum paene
2 quam corporum formae. Quod intelligi etiam ex
ipsis oratoribus potest, qui tantum inter se distant
genere dicendi, ut nemo sit alteri similis, quamvis
plurimi se ad eorum quos probabant imitationem
3 composuerint. Utile deinde plerisque visum est ita
quemque instituere, ut propria naturae bona doctrina
foverent et in id potissimum ingenia, quo tenderent,
adiuvarentur; ut si quis palaestrae peritus, cum in
aliquod plenum pueris gymnasium venerit, expertus
eorum omni modo corpus animumque discernat, cui
4 quisque certamini praeparandus sit, ita praeceptorem eloquentiae, cum sagaciter fuerit intuitus, cuius
ingenium presso limatoque genere dicendi, cuius
acri, gravi, dulci, aspero, nitido, urbano maxime
gaudeat, ita se commodaturum singulis, ut in eo,
5 quo quisque eminet, provehatur; quod et adiuta
cura natura magis evalescat, et qui in diversa ducatur
neque in iis, quibus minus aptus est, satis possit
efficere et ea, in quae natus videtur, deserendo faciat
6 infirmiora. Quod mihi (libera enim vel contra re-

something more finished than usual : they will thus
be rewarded for their industry and rejoice in the
thought that the privilege accorded them is the
recompense of merit.

VIII. It is generally and not unreasonably regarded
as the sign of a good teacher that he should be able
to differentiate between the abilities of his respective
pupils and to know their natural bent. The gifts of
nature are infinite in their variety, and mind differs
from mind almost as much as body from body. This 2
is clear from a consideration of the orators themselves, who differ in style to such an extent that no
one is like another, in spite of the fact that numbers
have modelled their style on that of their favorite
authors. Many again think it useful to direct their 3
instruction to the fostering of natural advantages and
to guide the talents of their pupils along the lines
which they instinctively tend to follow. Just as an
expert gymnast, when he enters a gymnasium full of
boys, after testing body and mind in every way, is
able to decide for what class of athletic contest they
should be trained, even so, they say, a teacher of 4
oratory after careful observation of a boy's stylistic
preferences, be they for terseness and polish, energy,
dignity, charm, roughness, brilliance or wit, will so
adapt his instructions to individual needs that each
pupil will be pushed forward in the sphere for which
his talents seem specially to design him; for nature, 5
when cultivated, goes from strength to strength,
while he who runs counter to her bent is ineffective
in those branches of the art for which he is less
suited and weakens the talents which he seemed
born to employ. Now, since the critic who is 6
guided by his reason is free to dissent even from

ceptas persuasiones rationem sequenti sententia est)
in parte verum videtur.   Nam proprietates ingenio-
7 rum dispicere prorsus necessarium est. In his quoque
certum studiorum facere delectum nemo dissuaserit.
Namque erit alius historiae magis idoneus, alius compositus ad carmen, alius utilis studio iuris, ut nonnulli
rus fortasse mittendi.   Sic discernet haec dicendi
magister, quomodo palaestricus ille cursorem faciet
aut pugilem aut luctatorem aliudve quid ex iis, quae
8 sunt sacrorum certaminum.   Verum ei, qui foro
destinabitur, non in unam partem aliquam sed in
omnia, quae sunt eius operis, etiam si qua difficiliora
discenti videbuntur, elaborandum est.   Nam et
omnino supervacua erat doctrina, si natura suffi-
9 ceret.   An si quis ingenio corruptus ac tumidus, ut
plerique sunt, inciderit, in hoc eum ire patiemur?
aridum atque ieiunum non alemus et quasi ves-
tiemus?   Nam si quaedam detrahere necessarium
10 est, cur non sit adiicere concessum?   Neque ego
contra naturam pugno.   Non enim deserendum id
bonum, si quod ingenitum est, existimo, sed augen-
11 dum addendumque quod cessat.   An vero clarissimus ille praeceptor Isocrates, quem non magis libri
bene dixisse quam discipuli bene docuisse testantur,

received opinions, I must insist that to my thinking this view is only partially true. It is undoubtedly necessary to note the individual gifts of
each boy, and no one would ever convince me 7
that it is not desirable to differentiate courses of
study with this in view. One boy will be better
adapted for the study of history, another for poetry,
another for law, while some perhaps had better be
packed off to the country. The teacher of rhetoric
will distinguish such special aptitudes, just as our
gymnast will turn one pupil into a runner, another
into a boxer or wrestler or an expert at some other
of the athletic accomplishments for which prizes are
awarded at the sacred games. But on the other 8
hand, he who is destined for the bar must study not
one department merely, but must perfect himself in
all the accomplishments which his profession demands, even though some of them may seem too hard
for him when he approaches them as a learner. For if
natural talent alone were sufficient, education might
be dispensed with. Suppose we are given a pupil 9
who, like so many, is of depraved tastes and swollen
with his own conceit; shall we suffer him to go his
own sweet way? If a boy's disposition is naturally
dry and jejune, ought we not to feed it up or at any
rate clothe it in fairer apparel? For, if in some cases
it is necessary to remove certain qualities, surely
there are others where we may be permitted to add
what is lacking. Not that I would set myself against 10
the will of nature. No innate good quality should be
neglected, but defects must be made good and weak-
nesses made strong. When Isocrates, the prince of 11
instructors, whose works proclaim his eloquence no
less than his pupils testify to his excellence as a

cum de Ephoro atque Theopompo sic iudicaret, ut
alteri frenis alteri calcaribus opus esse diceret, aut
in illo lentiore tarditatem aut in illo paene praecipiti
concitationem adiuvandam docendo existimavit, cum
alterum alterius natura miscendum arbitraretur?

12   Imbecillis tamen ingeniis sane sic obsequendum
sit, ut tantum in id, quo vocat natura, ducantur; ita
enim, quod solum possunt, melius efficient. Si vero
liberalior materia contigerit et in qua merito ad
spem oratoris simus aggressi, nulla dicendi virtus
13 omittenda est.   Nam licet sit aliquam in partem
pronior, ut necesse est, ceteris tamen non repugna-
bit, atque ea cura paria faciet iis, in quibus eminebat;
sicut ille (ne ab eodem exemplo recedamus) exer-
cendi corpora peritus, non, si docendum pancratias-
ten susceperit, pugno ferire vel calce tantum aut
nexus modo atque in iis certos aliquos docebit, sed
omnia quae sunt eius certaminis. Erit qui ex his
aliqua non possit: in id maxime quod poterit in-
14 cumbet.   Nam sunt haec duo vitanda prorsus:
unum ne temptes quod effici non possit, alterum ne
ab eo, quod quis optime facit, in aliud, ad quod
minus est idoneus, transferas. At si fuerit qui

---

[1] The *pancration* was a mixture of wrestling and boxing.

teacher, gave his opinion of Ephorus and Theopompus
to the effect that the former needed the spur and the
latter the curb, what was his meaning? Surely not
that the sluggish temperament of the one and the
headlong ardour of the other alike required modification by instruction, but rather that each would gain
from an admixture of the qualities of the other.

In the case of weaker understandings however some 12
concession must be made and they should be directed
merely to follow the call of their nature, since thus
they will be more effective in doing the only thing
that lies in their power. But if we are fortunate
enough to meet with richer material, such as justifies
us in the hope of producing a real orator, we must
leave no oratorical virtue uncared for. For though he 13
will necessarily have a natural bent for some special
department of oratory, he will not feel repelled by
the others, and by sheer application will develop his
other qualities until they equal those in which he
naturally excels. The skilled gymnast will once again
provide us with a parallel: if he undertakes to train
a pancratiast,¹ he will not merely teach him how
to use his fists or his heels, nor will he restrict
his instructions to the holds in wrestling, giving
special attention to certain tricks of this kind,
but will train him in every department of the
science. Some will no doubt be incapable of attaining proficiency in certain exercises; these must
specialise on those which lie within their powers.
For there are two things which he must be most 14
careful to avoid: first, he must not attempt the impossible, secondly he must not switch off his pupil
from what he can do well to exercises for which he is
less well suited. But if his pupil is like the famous

docebitur ille, quem adolescentes senem vidimus,
Nicostratus, omnibus in eo docendi partibus similiter
utetur, efficietque illum, qualis hic fuit, luctando
pugnandoque, quorum utroque certamine iisdem
15 diebus coronabatur, invictum. Et quanto id magis
oratoris futuri magistro providendum erit? Non
enim satis est dicere presse tantum aut subtiliter aut
aspere, non magis quam phonasco acutis tantum aut
mediis aut gravibus sonis aut horum etiam particulis
excellere. Nam sicut cithara ita oratio perfecta non
est, nisi ab imo ad summum omnibus intenta nervis
consentiat.

IX. Plura de officio docentium locutus discipulos
id unum interim moneo, ut praeceptores suos non
minus quam ipsa studia ament, et parentes esse non
2 quidem corporum sed mentium credant. Multum
haec pietas conferet studio; nam ita et libenter
audient et dictis credent et esse similes concupiscent,
in ipsos denique coetus scholarum laeti alacresque
convenient, emendati non irascentur, laudati gaude-
3 bunt, ut sint carissimi, studio merebuntur. Nam ut
illorum officium est docere, sic horum praebere se
dociles; alioqui neutrum sine altero sufficit. Et
sicut hominis ortus ex utroque gignentium con-
fertur, et frustra sparseris semina, nisi illa prae-
mollitus foverit sulcus: ita eloquentia coalescere

Nicostratus, whom we saw when he was old and we were boys, he will train him equally in every department of the science and will make him a champion both in boxing and wrestling, like Nicostratus himself who won the prize for both contests within a few days of each other. And how much more important is the 15 employment of such methods where our future orator is concerned! It is not enough to be able to speak with terseness, subtlety or vehemence, any more than it would be for a singing master to excel in the upper, middle or lower register only, or in particular sections of these registers alone. Eloquence is like a harp and will never reach perfection, unless all its strings be taut and in tune.

IX. Though I have spoken in some detail of the duties of the teacher, I shall for the moment confine my advice to the learners to one solitary admonition, that they should love their masters not less than their studies, and should regard them as the parents not indeed of their bodies but of their minds. Such 2 attachments are of invaluable assistance to study. For under their influence they find it a pleasure to listen to their teachers, believe what they say and long to be like them, come cheerfully and gladly to school, are not angry when corrected, rejoice when praised, and seek to win their master's affection by the devotion with which they pursue their studies. For as it is the duty of the master to teach, so it is 3 the duty of the pupil to show himself teachable. The two obligations are mutually indispensable. And just as it takes two parents to produce a human being, and as the seed is scattered in vain, if the ground is hard and there is no furrow to receive it and bring it to growth, even so eloquence can never come to

271

nequit nisi sociata tradentis accipientisque con-
cordia.

X. In his primis operibus, quae non ipsa parva
sunt sed maiorum quasi membra atque partes, bene
instituto atque exercitato iam fere tempus appetet
aggrediendi suasorias iudicialesque materias; quarum
antequam viam ingredior, pauca mihi de ipsa ratione
declamandi dicenda sunt, quae quidem ut ex omni-
2 bus novissime inventa ita multo est utilissima.   Nam
et cuncta illa, de quibus diximus, in se fere continet,
et veritati proximam imaginem reddit, ideoque ita
est celebrata, ut plerisque videretur ad formandam
eloquentiam vel sola sufficere.   Neque enim virtus
ulla perpetuae duntaxat orationis reperiri potest,
quae non sit cum hac dicendi meditatione communis.
3 Eo quidem res ista culpa docentium reccidit, ut inter
praecipuas quae corrumperent eloquentiam causas
licentia atque inscitia declamantium fuerit.   Sed eo,
4 quod natura bonum est, bene uti licet.   Sint ergo
et ipsae materiae, quae fingentur, quam simillimae
veritatis, et declamatio, in quantum maxime potest,
imitetur eas actiones, in quarum exercitationem
5 reperta est.   Nam magos et pestilentiam et responsa
et saeviores tragicis novercas aliaque magis adhuc
fabulosa frustra inter sponsiones et interdicta quae-

---

¹ *sponsio* (= a wager) was a form of lawsuit in which the
litigant promised to pay a certain sum of money if he lost
his case.   The *interdict* was an order issued by the praetor

maturity, unless teacher and taught are in perfect sympathy.

X. These elementary stages are in themselves no small undertaking, but they are merely members and portions of the greater whole; when therefore the pupil has been thoroughly instructed and exercised in these departments, the time will as a rule have come for him to attempt deliberative and forensic themes. But before I begin to discuss these, I must say a few words on the theory of declamation, which is at once the most recent and most useful of rhetorical exercises. For it includes 2 practically all the exercises of which we have been speaking and is in close touch with reality. As a result it has acquired such a vogue that many think that it is the sole training necessary to the formation of an orator, since there is no excellence in a formal speech which is not also to be found in this type of rhetorical exercise. On the other hand the actual 3 practice of declamation has degenerated to such an extent owing to the fault of our teachers, that it has come to be one of the chief causes of the corruption of modern oratory; such is the extravagance and ignorance of our declaimers. But it is possible to make a sound use of anything that is naturally sound. The subjects chosen for themes should, therefore, be 4 as true to life as possible, and the actual declamation should, as far as may be, be modelled on the pleadings for which it was devised as a training. For we 5 shall hunt in vain among *sponsions*[1] and *interdicts* for magicians and plagues and oracles and stepmothers more cruel than any in tragedy, and other

commanding or prohibiting certain action. It occurred chiefly in disputes about property.

remus. Quid ergo? Nunquam haec supra fidem et
poetica, ut vere dixerim, themata iuvenibus tractare
permittamus, ut exspatientur et gaudeant materia et
6 quasi in corpus eant? Erit optimum; sed certe sint
grandia et tumida, non stulta etiam et acrioribus
oculis intuenti ridicula: ut, si iam cedendum est,
impleat se declamator aliquando, dum sciat, ut
quadrupedes, cum viridi pabulo distentae sunt, san-
guinis detractione curantur et sic ad cibos viribus
conservandis idoneos redeunt, ita sibi quoque tenu-
andas adipes, et quidquid humoris corrupti con-
traxerit, emittendum, si esse sanus ac robustus volet.
7 Alioqui tumor ille inanis primo cuiusque veri operis
conatu deprehendetur. Totum autem declamandi
opus qui diversum omni modo a forensibus causis
existimant, ii profecto ne rationem quidem, qua ista
8 exercitatio inventa sit, pervident. Nam si foro non
praeparat, aut scenicae ostentationi aut furiosae voci-
ferationi simillimum est. Quid enim attinet iudicem
praeparare, qui nullus est; narrare, quod omnes
sciant falsum; probationes adhibere causae, de qua
nemo sit pronuntiaturus? Et haec quidem otiosa
tantum; adfici vero et ira vel luctu permovere, cuius
est ludibrii, nisi quibusdam pugnae simulacris ad

---

[1] The themes of the *controversiae* often turned on the
supernatural and on crimes and incidents such as rarely or
never occur in actual life.

subjects still more unreal than these.[1]   What then?
are we never to permit young men to handle unreal
or, to be more accurate, poetic themes that they may
run riot and exult in their strength and display their
full stature? It were best to prohibit them absolutely. 6
But at any rate the themes, however swelling and
magnificent, should not be such as to seem foolish
and laughable to the eye of an intelligent observer.
Consequently, if we must make some concession, let
us allow the declaimer to gorge himself occasionally, as long as he realises that his case will be like
that of cattle that have blown themselves out with a
surfeit of green food : they are cured of their disorder
by blood-letting and then put back to food such as
will maintain their strength; similarly the declaimer
must be rid of his superfluous fat, and his corrupt
humours must be discharged, if he wants to be
strong and healthy. Otherwise, the first time he 7
makes any serious effort, his swollen emptiness will
stand revealed. Those, however, who hold that
declamation has absolutely nothing in common with
pleading in the courts, are clearly quite unaware of
the reasons which gave rise to this type of exercise.
For if declamation is not a preparation for the actual 8
work of the courts, it can only be compared to the
rant of an actor or the raving of a lunatic. For what
is the use of attempting to conciliate a non-existent
judge, or of stating a case which all know to be
false, or of trying to prove a point on which judgment will never be passed? Such waste of effort
is, however, a comparative trifle. But what can be
more ludicrous than to work oneself into a passion
and to attempt to excite the anger or grief of
our hearers, unless we are preparing ourselves by

verum discrimen aciemque iustam consuescimus?
9 Nihil ergo inter forense genus dicendi atque hoc
declamatorium intererit? Si profectus gratia dicimus, nihil. Utinamque adiici ad consuetudinem
posset, ut nominibus uteremur, et perplexae magis
et longioris aliquando actus controversiae fingerentur, et verba in usu cotidiano posita minus
timeremus, et iocos inserere moris esset; quae nos,
quamlibet per alia in scholis exercitati simus, tirones
10 in foro inveniunt. Si vero in ostentationem com-
paretur declamatio, sane paulum aliquid inclinare
11 ad voluptatem audientium debemus. Nam et in iis
actionibus, quae in aliqua sine dubio veritate versantur, sed sunt ad popularem aptatae delectationem,
quales legimus panegyricos, totumque hoc demonstrativum genus, permittitur adhibere plus cultus
omnemque artem, quae latere plerumque in iudiciis
debet, non confiteri modo sed ostentare etiam homi-
12 nibus in hoc advocatis. Quare declamatio, quoniam
est iudiciorum consiliorumque imago, similis esse
debet veritati; quoniam autem aliquid in se habet
13 ἐπιδεικτικόν, nonnihil sibi nitoris assumere. Quod
faciunt actores comici, qui neque ita prorsus, ut nos
vulgo loquimur, pronuntiant, quod esset sine arte,

such mimic combats for the actual strife and the
pitched battles of the law-courts? Is there then no 9
difference between our declamations and genuine
forensic oratory? I can only reply, that if we speak
with a desire for improvement, there will be no
difference. I wish indeed that certain additions
could be made to the existing practice; that we made
use of names, that our fictitious debates dealt with
more complicated cases and sometimes took longer
to deliver, that we were less afraid of words drawn
from everyday speech and that we were in the habit
of seasoning our words with jests. For as regards
all these points, we are mere novices when we come
to actual pleading, however elaborate the training
that the schools have given us on other points. And 10
even if display is the object of declamation, surely
we ought to unbend a little for the entertainment of
our audience. For even in those speeches which, 11
although undoubtedly to some extent concerned
with the truth, are designed to charm the multitude (such for instance as panegyrics and the oratory
of display in all its branches), it is permissible to
be more ornate and not merely to disclose all the
resources of our art, which in cases of law should as
a rule be concealed, but actually to flaunt them
before those who have been summoned to hear us.
Declamation therefore should resemble the truth, 12
since it is modelled on forensic and deliberative
oratory. On the other hand it also involves an
element of display, and should in consequence
assume a certain air of elegance. In this connexion 13
I may cite the practice of comic actors, whose delivery is not exactly that of common speech, since
that would be inartistic, but is on the other hand not

neque procul tamen a natura recedunt, quo vitio
periret imitatio; sed morem communis huius ser-
14 monis decore quodam scenico exornant. Sic quoque
aliqua nos incommoda ex iis, quas finxerimus, materiis
consequentur, in eo praecipue, quod multa in iis
relinquuntur incerta, quae sumimus ut videtur, aetates,
facultates, liberi, parentes, urbium ipsarum vires,
15 iura, mores, alia his similia; quin aliquando etiam
argumentum ex ipsis positionum vitiis ducimus. Sed
haec suo quaeque loco. Quamvis enim omne propositum operis a nobis destinati eo spectet, ut orator
instituatur, tamen, ne quid studiosi requirant, etiam
si quid erit, quod ad scholas proprie pertineat, in
transitu non omittemus.

XI. Iam hinc ergo nobis inchoanda est ea pars
artis, ex qua capere initium solent, qui priora omiserunt; quanquam video quosdam in ipso statim limine
obstaturos mihi, qui nihil egere huiusmodi praeceptis
eloquentiam putent, sed natura sua et vulgari modo
et scholarum exercitatione contenti rideant etiam
diligentiam nostram exemplo magni quoque nominis
professorum, quorum aliquis, ut opinor, interrogatus,
quid esset σχῆμα et νόημα, nescire se quidem sed, si

far removed from the accents of nature, for, if it were,
their mimicry would be a failure: what they do therefore is to exalt the simplicity of ordinary speech
by a touch of stage decoration. So too we shall 14
have to put up with certain inconveniences arising
from the nature of our fictitious themes; such draw-
backs occur more especially in connexion with those
numerous details which are left uncertain and which
we presume to suit our purpose, such as the ages of
our characters, their wealth, their families, or the
strength, laws and manners of the cities where our
scenes are laid, and the like. Sometimes we even 15
draw arguments from the actual flaws of the assump-
tions involved by the theme. But each of these
points shall be dealt with in its proper place. For
although the whole purpose of this work is the
formation of an orator, I have no intention of passing
over anything that has a genuine connexion with the
practice of the schools, for fear that students may
complain of the omission.

XI. I have now arrived at the point when I must
begin to deal with that portion of the art at which
those who have omitted the preceding stages generally commence. I can see, however, that certain
critics will attempt to obstruct my path at the very
outset: for they will urge that eloquence can dispense with rules of this kind and, in smug satisfaction with themselves and the ordinary methods
and exercises of the schools, will laugh at me for
my pains; in which they will be only following the
example of certain professors of no small reputation.
One of these gentlemen, I believe, when asked to
define a *figure* and a *thought*, replied that he did not
know what they were, but that, if they had anything

ad rem pertineret, esse in sua declamatione respon-
2 dit.   Alius percontanti, Theodoreus an Apollodoreus
esset?   Ego, inquit, parmularius sum.   Nec sane
potuit urbanius ex confessione inscitiae suae elabi.
Porro hi, quia et beneficio ingenii praestantes sunt
habiti et multa etiam memoria digna exclamaverunt,
plurimos habent similes negligentiae suae, paucis-
3 simos naturae.   Igitur impetu dicere se et viribus
uti gloriantur; neque enim opus esse probatione aut
dispositione in rebus fictis, sed, cuius rei gratia
plenum sit auditorium, sententiis grandibus, quarum
4 optima quaeque a periculo petatur.   Quin etiam in
cogitando, nulla ratione adhibita aut tectum in-
tuentes magnum aliquid, quod ultro se offerat,
pluribus saepe diebus expectant, aut murmure incerto velut classico instincti concitatissimum corporis motum non enuntiandis sed quaerendis verbis
5 accommodant.   Nonnulli certa sibi initia, priusquam
sensum invenerint, destinant, quibus aliquid diserti
subiungendum sit, eaque diu secum ipsi clareque
meditati desperata conectendi facultate deserunt et

---

[1] *i.e.* I care naught for your rival schools of rhetoric. I
give all my favour to the men armed with the buckler (the
gladiators known as *Thraces*). Such contests of the amphi-
theatre interest me far more than the contests between rival
schools of rhetoric.

to do with the subject, they would be found in
his declamation.   Another when asked whether he 2
was a follower of Theodorus or Apollodorus, replied,
"Oh! as for me, I am all for the Thracians."[1]
To do him justice, he could hardly have found a
neater way to avoid confessing his ignorance. These
persons, just because, thanks to their natural gifts,
they are regarded as brilliant performers and have,
as a matter of fact, uttered much that deserves to
be remembered, think that, while most men share
their careless habits, few come near them for talent.
Consequently they make it their boast that they 3
speak on impulse and owe their success to their
native powers; they further assert that there is no
need of proof or careful marshalling of facts when
we are speaking on fictitious themes, but only of
some of those sounding epigrams, the expectation of
which has filled the lecture-room; and these they
say are best improvised on the spur of the moment.
Further, owing to their contempt for method, when 4
they are meditating on some future effusion, they
spend whole days looking at the ceiling in the hope
that some magnificent inspiration may occur to
them, or rock their bodies to and fro, booming
inarticulately as if they had a trumpet inside them
and adapting their agitated movements, not to the
delivery of the words, but to their pursuit.   Some 5
again settle on certain definite openings long before they have thought what they are going to say,
with a view to using them as pegs for subsequent
snatches of eloquence, and then after practising
their delivery first in silent thought and then
aloud for hours together, in utter desperation of
providing any connecting links, abandon them and

ad alia deinceps atque inde alia non minus communia
6 ac nota devertunt. Qui plurimum videntur habere
rationis, non in causas tamen laborem suum sed in
locos intendunt, atque in iis non corpori prospiciunt
sed abrupta quaedam, ut forte ad manum venere,
7 iaculantur. Unde fit, ut dissoluta et ex diversis
congesta oratio cohaerere non possit similisque sit
commentariis puerorum, in quos ea, quae aliis declamantibus laudata sunt, regerunt. Magnas tamen
sententias et res bonas, ita enim gloriari solent,
elidunt; nam et barbari et servi; et si hoc sat est,
nulla est ratio dicendi.

XII. Ne hoc quidem negaverim, sequi plerumque
hanc opinionem, ut fortius dicere videantur indocti;
primum vitio male iudicantium, qui maiorem habere
vim credunt ea, quae non habent artem, ut effringere
quam aperire, rumpere quam solvere, trahere quam
2 ducere putant robustius. Nam et gladiator, qui
armorum inscius in rixam ruit, et luctator, qui totius
corporis nisu in id, quod semel invasit, incumbit,
fortior ab his vocatur; cum interim et hic frequenter
suis viribus ipse prosternitur, et illum vehementis

take refuge in one formula after another, each no
less hackneyed and familiar than the last. The 6
least unreasonable of them devote their attention not to the actual cases, but to their purple
patches, in the composition of which they pay no
attention to the subject-matter, but fire off a series
of isolated thoughts just as they happen to come to
hand. The result is a speech which, being com- 7
posed of disconnected passages having nothing in
common with each other, must necessarily lack
cohesion and can only be compared to a schoolboy's
notebook, in which he jots down any passages from
the declamations of others that have come in for a
word of praise. None the less they do occasionally
strike out some good things and some fine epigrams,
such as they make their boast. Why not ? slaves
and barbarians sometimes achieve the same effects,
and if we are to be satisfied with this sort of thing,
then good-bye to any theory of oratory.

XII. I must, however, admit that the general
opinion is that the untrained speaker is usually
the more vigorous. This opinion is due primarily
to the erroneous judgment of faulty critics, who
think that true vigour is all the greater for its lack
of art, regarding it as a special proof of strength to
force what might be opened, to break what might
be untied and to drag what might be led. Even a 2
gladiator who plunges into the fight with no skill at
arms to help him, and a wrestler who puts forth the
whole strength of his body the moment he has got
a hold, is acclaimed by them for his outstanding
vigour, although it is of frequent occurrence in such
cases for the latter to be overthrown by his own
strength and for the former to find the fury of his

3 impetus excipit adversarii mollis articulus. Sed
sunt in hac parte, quae imperitos etiam naturaliter
fallant; nam et divisio, cum plurimum valeat in
causis, speciem virium minuit, et rudia politis maiora
4 et sparsa compositis numerosiora creduntur. Est
praeterea quaedam virtutum vitiorumque vicinia,
qua maledicus pro libero, temerarius pro forti, effusus
pro copioso accipitur. Maledicit autem ineruditus
apertius et saepius vel cum periculo suscepti litiga-
5 toris, frequenter etiam suo. Adfert et ista res
opinionem, quia libentissime homines audiunt ea,
quae dicere ipsi noluissent. Illud quoque alterum
quod est in elocutione ipsa periculum minus vitat
conaturque perdite, unde evenit nonnunquam, ut
aliquid grande inveniat qui semper quaerit quod
nimium est; verum id et raro provenit, et cetera
vitia non pensat.
6 Propter hoc quoque interdum videntur indocti
copiam habere maiorem, quod dicunt omnia; doctis
est et electio et modus. His accedit, quod a cura
docendi quod intenderunt recedunt. Itaque illud
quaestionum et argumentorum apud corrupta iudicia

onslaught parried by his adversary with a supple
turn of the wrist. But there are many details in this 3
department of our art which the unskilled critic will
never notice. For instance, careful division under
heads, although of the utmost importance in actual
cases, makes the outward show of strength seem
less than the reality; the unhewn block is larger
than the polished marble, and things when scattered
seem more numerous than when placed together.
There is moreover a sort of resemblance between 4
certain merits and certain defects: abuse passes for
freedom of speech, rashness for courage, prodigality
for abundance. But the untrained advocate will
abuse too openly and too often, even though by so
doing he imperils the success of the case which he
has undertaken and not seldom his own personal
safety as well. But even such violence will win 5
men's good opinion, since they are only too pleased
to hear another say things which nothing would
have induced them to utter themselves. Such
speakers are also less careful to avoid that other
peril, the pitfall of style, and are so reckless in their
efforts that sometimes in their passion for extravagance they light upon some really striking expression. But such success is rare and does not
compensate for their other defects.

For the same reason the uninstructed sometimes 6
appear to have a richer flow of language, because
they say everything that can be said, while the
learned exercise discrimination and self-restraint.
To this must be added the fact that such persons
take no trouble to prove their contentions, and
consequently steer clear of the chilly reception
given in our decadent law-courts to arguments and

frigus evitant nihilque aliud, quam quod vel pravis
voluptatibus aures assistentium permulceat, quaerunt.
7 Sententiae quoque ipsae, quas solas petunt, magis
eminent, cum omnia circa illas sordida et abiecta
sunt; ut lumina non inter umbras, quemadmodum
Cicero dicit,[1] sed plane in tenebris clariora sunt.
Itaque ingeniosi vocentur, ut libet, dum tamen con-
8 stet contumeliose sic laudari disertum.   Nihilominus
confitendum est etiam detrahere doctrinam aliquid,
ut limam rudibus et cotes hebetibus et vino vetus-
tatem, sed vitia detrahit, atque eo solo minus est,
quod litterae perpolierunt, quo melius.

9   Verum hi pronuntiatione quoque famam dicendi
fortius quaerunt.   Nam et clamant ubique et omnia
levata, ut ipsi vocant, manu emugiunt, multo dis-
cursu, anhelitu, iactatione gestus, motu capitis
10 furentes.   Iam collidere manus, terrae pedem in-
cutere, femur, pectus, frontem caedere, mire ad
pullatum[2] circulum facit; cum ille eruditus, ut in
oratione multa summittere, variare, disponere, ita
etiam in pronuntiando suum cuique eorum, quae

---

[1] de Or. III. xxvi. 101.
[2] *pullatus* = wearing dark clothes, *i.e.* the common people,
as opposed to the upper classes wearing the white or purple-
bordered *toga*.

questions and seek only for such themes as may
beguile the ears of the public even at the cost of
appealing to the most perverted tastes.   Again, 7
their epigrams, the sole objects of their quest, seem
all the more striking because of the dreariness and
squalor of their context, since flashes are more
clearly seen against a background, not of mere
" shade," as Cicero[1] says, but of pitchy darkness.
Well, let the world credit them with as much genius
as it pleases, so long as it is admitted that such
praise is an insult to any man of real eloquence.
None the less it must be confessed that learning 8
does take something from oratory, just as the file
takes something from rough surfaces or the whet-
stone from blunt edges or age from wine ; it takes
away defects, and if the results produced after sub-
jection to the polish of literary study are less, they
are less only because they are better.

But these creatures have another weapon in their 9
armoury : they seek to obtain the reputation of
speaking with greater vigour than the trained orator
by means of their delivery.   For they shout on all
and every occasion and bellow their every utterance
" with uplifted hand," to use their own phrase,
dashing this way and that, panting, gesticulating
wildly and wagging their heads with all the frenzy
of a lunatic.   Smite your hands together, stamp 10
the ground, slap your thigh, your breast, your fore-
head, and you will go straight to the heart of the
dingier members of your audience.[2]   But the educated speaker, just as he knows how to moderate
his style, and to impart variety and artistic form to
his speech, is an equal adept in the matter of delivery and will suit his action to the tone of each

dicet, colori accommodare actum sciat, et, si quid sit
perpetua observatione dignum, modestus et esse et
11 videri malit.   At illi hanc vim appellant, quae est
potius violentia; cum interim non actores modo
aliquos invenias sed, quod est turpius, praeceptores
etiam, qui brevem dicendi exercitationem consecuti
omissa ratione ut tulit impetus, passim tumultuentur
eosque, qui plus honoris litteris tribuerunt, ineptos
et ieiunos et trepidos et infirmos, ut quodque verbum
12 contumeliosissimum occurrit, appellent.   Verum illis
quidem gratulemur sine labore, sine ratione, sine
disciplina disertis; nos, quando et praecipiendi
munus iam pridem deprecati sumus et in foro quoque dicendi, quia honestissimum finem putabamus
desinere dum desideraremur, inquirendo scribendo-
que talia consolemur otium nostrum, quae futura
usui bonae mentis iuvenibus arbitramur, nobis certe
sunt voluptati.

XIII. Nemo autem a me exigat id praeceptorum
genus, quod est a plerisque scriptoribus artium traditum, ut quasi quasdam leges immutabili necessitate
constrictas studiosis dicendi feram: utique prooemium et id quale, proxima huic narratio, quae lex
deinde narrandi, propositio post hanc vel, ut quibusdam placuit, excursio, tum certus ordo quaestionum
ceteraque, quae, velut si aliter facere fas non sit,

portion of his utterances, while, if he has any one
canon for universal observance, it is that he should
both possess the reality and present the appearance
of self-control. But the ranters confer the title of 11
force on that which is really violence. You may
also occasionally find not merely pleaders, but, what
is far more shameful, teachers as well, who, after a
brief training in the art of speaking, throw method
to the winds and, yielding to the impulse of the
moment, run riot in every direction, abusing those
who hold literature in higher respect as fools without life, courage or vigour, and calling them the
first and worst name that occurs to them. Still let 12
me congratulate these gentlemen on attaining eloquence without industry, method or study. As for
myself I have long since retired from the task of
teaching. in the schools and of speaking in the
courts, thinking it the most honourable conclusion to
retire while my services were still in request, and all
I ask is to be allowed to console my leisure by
making such researches and composing such instructions as will, I hope, prove useful to young men of
ability, and are, at any rate, a pleasure to myself.

XIII. Let no one however demand from me a rigid
code of rules such as most authors of textbooks have
laid down, or ask me to impose on students of rhetoric a system of laws immutable as fate, a system in
which injunctions as to the *exordium* and its nature
lead the way; then come the *statement of facts* and
the laws to be observed in this connexion: next the
proposition or, as some prefer, the *digression*, followed
by prescriptions as to the order in which the various
questions should be discussed, with all the other rules,
which some speakers follow as though they had no

2 quidam tanquam iussi sequuntur. Erat enim rhetorice res prorsus facilis ac parva, si uno et brevi
praescripto contineretur; sed mutantur pleraque
causis, temporibus, occasione, necessitate. Atque
ideo res in oratore praecipua consilium est, quia
3 varie et ad rerum momenta convertitur. Quid si
enim praecipias imperatori, quotiens aciem instruat,
derigat frontem, cornua utrinque promoveat, equites
pro cornibus locet? erit haec quidem rectissima
fortasse ratio, quotiens licebit; sed mutabitur natura
loci, si mons occurret, si flumen obstabit, collibus,
4 silvis, asperitate alia prohibebitur; mutabit hostium
genus, mutabit praesentis condicio discriminis; nunc
acie directa nunc cuneis, nunc auxiliis nunc legione
pugnabitur, nonnunquam terga etiam dedisse simu-
5 lata fuga proderit. Ita prooemium necessarium an
supervacuum, breve an longius, ad iudicem omni
sermone derecto an aliquando averso per aliquam
figuram dicendum sit, constricta an latius fusa narratio, continua an divisa, recta an ordine permutato,
causae docebunt. Itemque de quaestionum ordine,

---

¹ *i.e.* by the figure known as *apostrophe*, in which the
orator diverts his speech from the judge to some other
person : see IX. ii. 38.

choice but to regard them as orders and as if it were
a crime to take any other line.   If the whole of rhe- 2
toric could be thus embodied in one compact code,
it would be an easy task of little compass : but
most rules are liable to be altered by the nature of
the case, circumstances of time and place, and by
hard necessity itself. Consequently the all-important
gift for an orator is a wise adaptability since he is
called upon to meet the most varied emergencies.
What if you should instruct a general, as often as he 3
marshals his troops for battle, to draw up his front in
line, advance his wings to left and right, and station
his cavalry to protect his flank ? This will perhaps be
the best plan, if circumstances allow.   But it may
have to be modified owing to the nature of the ground,
if, for instance, he is confronted by a mountain, if a
river bars his advance, or his movements are hampered
by hills, woods or broken country.   Or again it may 4
be modified by the character of the enemy or the
nature of the crisis by which he is faced.   On one
occasion he will fight in line, on another in column,
on one he will use his auxiliary troops, on another his
legionaries ; while occasionally a feint of flight may
win the day.   So, too, with the rules of oratory.   Is 5
the *exordium* necessary or superfluous ? should it be
long or short ? addressed entirely to the judge or
sometimes directed to some other quarter by the
employment of some figure of speech ? [1]   Should the
statement of facts be concise or developed at some
length ? continuous or divided into sections ? and
should it follow the actual or an artificial order of
events ? The orator will find the answers to all these
questions in the circumstances of the case.   So, too,
with the order in which questions should be discussed,

6 cum in eadem controversia aliud alii parti prius
   quaeri frequenter expediat. Neque enim rogationi-
   bus plebisve scitis sancta sunt ista praecepta, sed
7 hoc quidquid est utilitas excogitavit. Non negabo
   autem sic utile esse plerumque, alioqui nec scribe-
   rem; verum, si eadem illa nobis aliud suadebit
   utilitas, hanc relictis magistrorum auctoritatibus
   sequemur.

8   Equidem id maxime *praecipiam ac repetens iterumque iterumque monebo :* res duas in omni actu spectet
   orator, quid deceat et quid expediat. Expedit
   autem saepe mutare ex illo constituto traditoque
   ordine aliqua et interim decet, ut in statuis atque
   picturis videmus variari habitus, vultus, status. Nam
9 recti quidem corporis vel minima gratia est; nempe
   enim adversa sit facies et demissa brachia et iuncti
   pedes et a summis ad ima rigens opus. Flexus ille
   et, ut sic dixerim, motus dat actum quendam et
   adfectum. Ideo nec ad unum modum formatae
10 manus et in vultu mille species. Cursum habent
   quaedam et impetum, sedent alia vel incumbunt;
   nuda haec, illa velata sunt, quaedam mixta ex
   utroque. Quid tam distortum et elaboratum quam
   est ille discobolos Myronis ? Si quis tamen,

---

[1] Verg. *Aen.* iii. 436.

since in any given debate it may often suit one party 6
best that such and such a question come up first,
while their opponents would be best suited by another.
For these rules have not the formal authority of laws
or decrees of the plebs, but are, with all they contain,
the children of expediency. I will not deny that it 7
is generally expedient to conform to such rules, otherwise I should not be writing now ; but if our friend
expediency suggests some other course to us, why,
we shall disregard the authority of the professors
and follow her.

For my part above all things 8

"This I enjoin and urge and urge anew "[1]

that in all his pleadings the orator should keep two
things constantly in view, what is becoming and what
is expedient. But it is often expedient and occasionally becoming to make some modification in the
time-honoured order. We see the same thing in
pictures and statues. Dress, expression and attitude
are frequently varied. The body when held bolt 9
upright has but little grace, for the face looks straight
forward, the arms hang by the side, the feet are
joined and the whole figure is stiff from top to toe.
But that curve, I might almost call it motion, with
which we are so familiar, gives an impression of action
and animation. So, too, the hands will not always be
represented in the same position, and the variety
given to the expression will be infinite. Some figures 10
are represented as running or rushing forward, others
sit or recline, some are nude, others clothed, while
some again are half-dressed, half-naked. Where can
we find a more violent and elaborate attitude than
that of the Discobolus of Myron? Yet the critic who

ut parum rectum, improbet opus, nonne ab
intellectu artis abfuerit, in qua vel praecipue
laudabilis est ipsa illa novitas ac difficultas?
11 Quam quidem gratiam et delectationem adferunt
figurae, quaeque in sensibus quaeque in verbis sunt;
mutant enim aliquid a recto atque hanc prae se
virtutem ferunt, quod a consuetudine vulgari reces-
12 serunt. Habet in pictura speciem tota facies;
Apelles tamen imaginem Antigoni latere tantum
altero ostendit, ut amissi oculi deformitas lateret.
Quid? non in oratione operienda sunt quaedam, sive
ostendi non debent sive exprimi pro dignitate non
13 possunt? Ut fecit Timanthes, opinor, Cythnius in
ea tabula, qua Coloten Teium vicit. Nam cum in
Iphigeniae immolatione pinxisset tristem Calchan-
tem, tristiorem Ulixen, addidisset Menelao, quem
summum poterat ars efficere, maerorem, consumptis
adfectibus, non reperiens, quo digne modo patris
vultum posset exprimere, velavit eius caput et suo
14 cuique animo dedit aestimandum. Nonne huic
simile est illud Sallustianum, *Nam de Carthagine
tacere satius puto quam parum dicere?* Propter quae
mihi semper moris fuit, quam minime alligare me ad
praecepta, quae καθολικά vocitant, id est (ut dicamus
quomodo possumus) universalia vel perpetualia. Raro
enim reperitur hoc genus, ut non labefactari parte

---

[1] *Jug.* xix.

disapproved of the figure because it was not upright,
would merely show his utter failure to understand the
sculptor's art, in which the very novelty and difficulty
of execution is what most deserves our praise. A 11
similar impression of grace and charm is produced by
rhetorical figures, whether they be *figures of thought*
or *figures of speech*. For they involve a certain de-
parture from the straight line and have the merit of
variation from the ordinary usage. In a picture the 12
full face is most attractive. But Apelles painted
Antigonus in profile, to conceal the blemish caused
by the loss of one eye. So, too, in speaking, there
are certain things which have to be concealed, either
because they ought not to be disclosed or because
they cannot be expressed as they deserve. Timanthes, 13
who was, I think, a native of Cythnus, provides an
example of this in the picture with which he won the
victory over Colotes of Teos. It represented the
sacrifice of Iphigenia, and the artist had depicted an
expression of grief on the face of Calchas and of still
greater grief on that of Ulysses, while he had given
Menelaus an agony of sorrow beyond which his art
could not go. Having exhausted his powers of emotional expression he was at a loss to portray the
father's face as it deserved, and solved the problem
by veiling his head and leaving his sorrow to the
imagination of the spectator. Sallust[1] did some- 14
thing similar when he wrote "I think it better to say
nothing of Carthage rather than say too little." It
has always, therefore, been my custom not to tie myself down to *universal* or *general* rules (this being the
nearest equivalent I can find for the Greek *catholic
rules*). For rules are rarely of such a kind that their
validity cannot be shaken and overthrown in some

15 aliqua et subrui possit. Sed de his plenius suo
quidque loco tractabimus. Interim nolo se iuvenes
satis instructos, si quem ex his, qui breves plerumque
circumferuntur, artis libellum edidicerint, et velut
decretis technicorum tutos putent. Multo labore,
assiduo studio, varia exercitatione, plurimis experimentis, altissima prudentia, praesentissimo consilio
16 constat ars dicendi. Sed adiuvatur his quoque, si
tamen rectam viam, non unam orbitam monstrent;
a qua declinare qui crediderit nefas, patiatur necesse
est illam per funes ingredientium tarditatem. Itaque
et stratum militari labore iter saepe deserimus compendio ducti; et, si rectum limitem rupti torrentibus
pontes inciderint, circumire cogemur, et, si ianua
17 tenebitur incendio, per parietem exibimus. Late
fusum opus est et multiplex et prope cotidie novum,
et de quo nunquam dicta erunt omnia. Quae sint
tamen tradita, quid ex his optimum, et si qua mutari,
adiici, detrahi melius videbitur, dicere experiar.

XIV. Rhetoricen in Latinum transferentes tum
oratoriam, tum oratricem nominaverunt. Quos equidem non fraudaverim debita laude, quod copiam
Romani sermonis augere temptarint. Sed non omnia

particular or other. But I must reserve each of these 15
points for fuller treatment in its proper place. For
the present I will only say that I do not want young
men to think their education complete when they
have mastered one of the small text-books of which
so many are in circulation, or to ascribe a talismanic
value to the arbitrary decrees of theorists. The art
of speaking can only be attained by hard work and
assiduity of study, by a variety of exercises and repeated trial, the highest prudence and unfailing
quickness of judgement. But rules are helpful all the 16
same so long as they indicate the direct road and do
not restrict us absolutely to the ruts made by others.
For he who thinks it an unpardonable sin to leave the
old, old track, must be content to move at much the
same speed as a tight-rope walker. Thus, for example,
we often leave a paved military road to take a short
cut or, finding that the direct route is impossible
owing to floods having broken down the bridges, are
forced to make a circuit, while if our house is on fire
and flames bar the way to the front door, we make
our escape by breaking through a party wall. The 17
orator's task covers a large ground, is extremely
varied and develops some new aspect almost every
day, so that the last word on the subject will never
have been said. I shall however try to set forth the
traditional rules and to point out their best features,
mentioning the changes, additions and subtractions
which seem desirable.

XIV. Rhetoric is a Greek term which has been
translated into Latin by *oratoria* or *oratrix*. I would
not for the world deprive the translators of the
praise which is their due for attempting to increase
the vocabulary of our native tongue; but translations

nos ducentes ex Graeco sequuntur sicut ne illos
quidem, quotiens utique suis verbis signare nostra
2 voluerunt. Et haec interpretatio non minus dura
est quam illa Plauti essentia atque queentia, sed ne
propria quidem; nam oratoria sic effertur ut elocutoria, oratrix ut elocutrix; illa autem de qua loquimur rhetorice talis est qualis eloquentia, nec dubie
apud Graecos quoque duplicem intellectum habet.
3 Namque uno modo fit appositum ars rhetorica ut
navis piratica, altero nomen rei, qualis est philosophia, amicitia. Nos ipsam nunc volumus significare substantiam ut grammatice litteratura est, non
litteratrix quemadmodum oratrix, nec litteratoria
quemadmodum oratoria; verum id in rhetorice non
4 fit. Ne pugnemus igitur, cum praesertim plurimis
alioqui Graecis sit utendum. Nam certe et philosophos et musicos et geometras dicam, nec vim
adferam nominibus his indecora in Latinum sermonem
mutatione. Denique cum M. Tullius etiam in ipsis
librorum, quos hac de re primum scripserat, titulis
Graeco nomine utatur, profecto non est verendum,
ne temere videamur oratori maximo de nomine artis
suae credidisse.
5 Igitur rhetorice (iam enim sine metu cavillationis
utemur hac appellatione) sic, ut opinor, optime
dividetur, ut de arte, de artifice, de opere dicamus.
Ars erit, quae disciplina percipi debet; ea est bene

---

[1] *sc.* essence and possibility. [2] A Stoic. *cp.* x. i. 124.
[3] See § 6 of next chapter.

from Greek into Latin are not always satisfactory,
just as the attempt to represent Latin words
in a Greek dress is sometimes equally unsuccessful.
And the translations in question are fully as 2
harsh as the *essentia* and *queentia* [1] of Plautus, [2]
and have not even the merit of being exact.
For *oratoria* is formed like *elocutoria* and *oratrix*
like *elocutrix*, whereas the rhetoric with which
we are concerned is rather to be identified with
eloquentia, and the word is undoubtedly used in two
senses by the Greeks. In the one case it is an 3
adjective i.e. *ars rhetorica*, the rhetorical art, like
piratic in the phrase *nauis piratica*, in the other it is
a noun like philosophy or friendship. It is as a sub-
stantive that we require it here; now the correct
translation of the Greek *grammatice* is *litteratura* not
litteratrix or *litteratoria*, which would be the forms
analogous to *oratrix* and *oratoria*. But in the case of
"rhetoric" there is no similar Latin equivalent. It is 4
best therefore not to quarrel about it, more especially
as we have to use Greek terms in many other cases.
For I may at least use the words *philosophus, musicus*
and *geometres* without outraging them by changing
them into clumsy Latin equivalents. Finally,
since Cicero gave a Greek title [3] to the earlier works
which he wrote on this subject, I may without fear
of rashness accept the great orator as sufficient
authority for the name of the art which he professed.

To resume, then, rhetoric (for I shall now use the 5
name without fear of captious criticism) is in my
opinion best treated under the three following heads,
the art, the artist and the work. The art is that
which we should acquire by study, and is the art of

dicendi scientia. Artifex est, qui percepit hanc
artem, id est, orator, cuius est summa bene dicere;
opus, quod efficitur ab artifice, id est, bona oratio.
Haec omnia rursus diducuntur in species; sed illa
sequentia suo loco, nunc quae de prima parte tractanda sunt, ordiar.

XV. Ante omnia, quid sit rhetorice. Quae finitur
quidem varie, sed quaestionem habet duplicem, aut
enim de qualitate ipsius rei aut de comprehensione
verborum dissensio est. Prima atque praecipua
opinionum circa hoc differentia, quod alii malos
quoque viros posse oratores dici putant; alii, quorum
nos sententiae accedimus, nomen hoc artemque,
de qua loquimur, bonis demum tribui volunt.

2 Eorum autem, qui dicendi facultatem a maiore ac
magis expetenda vitae laude secernunt, quidam
rhetoricen vim tantum, quidam scientiam sed non
virtutem, quidam usum, quidam artem quidem sed a
scientia et virtute diiunctam, quidam etiam pravi-
tatem quandam artis, id est κακοτεχνίαν, nomina-

3 verunt. Hi fere aut in persuadendo aut in dicendo
apte ad persuadendum positum orandi munus sunt
arbitrati. Id enim fieri potest ab eo quoque, qui vir
bonus non sit. Est igitur frequentissimus finis,
rhetoricen esse vim persuadendi. Quod ego vim
appello, plerique potestatem, nonnulli facultatem
vocant; quae res ne quid adferat ambiguitatis, *vim*

4 dico δύναμιν. Haec opinio originem ab Isocrate (si

speaking well. The artist is he who has acquired the art, that is to say, he is the orator whose task it is to speak well. The work is the achievement of the artist, namely good speaking. Each of these three *general* divisions is in its turn divided into *species*. Of the two latter divisions I shall speak in their proper place. For the present I shall proceed to a discussion of the first.

XV. The first question which confronts us is "What is rhetoric?" Many definitions have been given; but the problem is really twofold. For the dispute turns either on the quality of the thing itself or on the meaning of the words in which it is defined. The first and chief disagreement on the subject is found in the fact that some think that even bad men may be called orators, while others, of whom I am one, restrict the name of orator and the art itself to those who are good. Of those who 2 divorce eloquence from that yet fairer and more desirable title to renown, a virtuous life, some call rhetoric merely a power, some a science, but not a virtue, some a practice, some an art, though they will not allow the art to have anything in common with science or virtue, while some again call it a perversion of art or κακοτεχνία. These persons have as a 3 rule held that the task of oratory lies in persuasion or speaking in a persuasive manner: for this is within the power of a bad man no less than a good. Hence we get the common definition of rhetoric as the power of persuading. What I call a power, many call a capacity, and some a faculty. In order therefore that there may be no misunderstanding I will say that by power I mean δύναμις. This view 4 is derived from Isocrates, if indeed the treatise on

tamen revera Ars, quae circumfertur, eius est) duxit.
Qui, cum longe sit a voluntate infamantium oratoris
officia, finem artis temere comprehendit, dicens esse
rhetoricen persuadendi opificem, id est πειθοῦς δημι-
ουργόν; neque enim mihi permiserim eadem uti
declinatione, qua Ennius M. Cethegum *Suadae*
5 *medullam* vocat. Apud Platonem quoque Gorgias in
libro, qui nomine eius inscriptus est, idem fere dicit;
sed hanc Plato illius opinionem vult accipi non suam.
Cicero pluribus locis scripsit, officium oratoris esse
6 *dicere apposite ad persuadendum.* In rhetoricis etiam,
quos sine dubio ipse non probat, finem facit persuadere. Verum et pecunia persuadet et gratia et
auctoritas dicentis et dignitas, postremo aspectus
etiam ipse sine voce, quo vel recordatio meritorum
cuiusque vel facies aliqua miserabilis vel formae
7 pulchritudo sententiam dictat. Nam et Manium
Aquilium defendens Antonius, cum scissa veste
cicatrices, quas is pro patria pectore adverso suscepisset, ostendit, non orationis habuit fiduciam sed
oculis populi Romani vim attulit, quem illo ipso
aspectu maxime motum in hoc, ut absolveret reum,
8 creditum est. Servium quidem Galbam miseratione
sola, qua non suos modo liberos parvulos in contione

---

[1] This treatise is lost. It may have been the work of the
younger Isocrates.
[2] *Ann.* ix. 309 (Vahlen). The derivative to which he
objects is the rare word *suada.*   [3] *Gorg.* 453 A.
[4] *de Inv.* I. v. 6, *de Or.* I. xxxi. 138.

rhetoric[1] which circulates under his name is really from his hand. He, although far from agreeing with those whose aim is to disparage the duties of an orator, somewhat rashly defined rhetoric as πειθοῦς δημιουργός, the "worker of persuasion": for I cannot bring myself to use the peculiar derivative which Ennius[2] applies to Marcus Cethegus in the phrase *suadae medulla*, the "marrow of persuasion." Again Gorgias,[3] in the dialogue of Plato that takes 5 its title from his name, says practically the same thing, but Plato intends it to be taken as the opinion of Gorgias, not as his own. Cicero[4] in more than one passage defined the duty of an orator as "speaking in a persuasive manner." In his *Rhetorica*[5] too, 6 a work which it is clear gave him no satisfaction, he makes the end to be persuasion. But many other things have the power of persuasion, such as money, influence, the authority and rank of the speaker, or even some sight unsupported by language, when for instance the place of words is supplied by the memory of some individual's great deeds, by his lamentable appearance or the beauty of his person. Thus when Antonius in the course of his defence of 7 Manius Aquilius tore open his client's robe and revealed the honourable scars which he had acquired while facing his country's foes, he relied no longer on the power of his eloquence, but appealed directly to the eyes of the Roman people. And it is believed that they were so profoundly moved by the sight as to acquit the accused. Again there is a speech of 8 Cato, to mention no other records, which informs us that Servius Galba escaped condemnation solely by

[5] *cp.* III. i. 20 and Cic. *de Or.* I. ii. 5. The work in question is better known as the *de Inventione*.

produxerat, sed Galli etiam Sulpicii filium suis ipse
manibus circumtulerat, elapsum esse, cum aliorum
9 monumentis tum Catonis oratione testatum est. Et
Phrynen non Hyperidis actione, quanquam admirabili, sed conspectu corporis, quod illa speciosissimum
alioqui diducta nudaverat tunica, putant periculo
liberatam. Quae si omnia persuadent, non est hic,
10 de quo locuti sumus, idoneus finis. Ideoque dili-
gentiores sibi sunt visi, qui, cum de rhetorice idem
sentirent, existimaverunt eam vim dicendo persuadendi. Quem finem Gorgias in eodem, de quo
supra diximus, libro, velut coactus a Socrate facit; a
quo non dissentit Theodectes, sive ipsius id opus est,
quod de rhetorice nomine eius inscribitur, sive, ut
creditum est, Aristotelis, in quo est, finem esse
rhetorices ducere homines dicendo in id, quod actor
11 velit. Sed ne hoc quidem satis est comprehensum;
persuadent enim dicendo vel ducunt in id quod
volunt alii quoque, ut meretrices, adulatores, corrup-
tores. At contra non persuadet semper orator; ut
interim non sit proprius hic finis eius, interim sit
communis cum iis, qui ab oratore procul absunt.
12 Atqui non multum ab hoc fine abest Apollodorus,
dicens iudicialis orationis primum et super omnia
esse persuadere iudici et sententiam eius ducere in

---

[1] *Gorg.* p. 452 E.

the pity which he aroused not only by producing his
own young children before the assembly, but by
carrying round in his arms the son of Sulpicius
Gallus.   So also according to general opinion Phryne 9
was saved not by the eloquence of Hyperides, admirable as it was, but by the sight of her exquisite
body, which she further revealed by drawing aside
her tunic.   And if all these have power to persuade, the end of oratory, which we are discussing,
cannot adequately be defined as persuasion.   Con- 10
sequently those who, although holding the same
general view of rhetoric, have regarded it as the
power of persuasion by speaking, pride themselves on
their greater exactness of language.   This definition
is given by Gorgias, in the dialogue[1] mentioned
above, under compulsion from the inexorable logic of
Socrates.   Theodectes agrees with him, whether the
treatise on rhetoric which has come down to us
under his name is really by him or, as is generally
believed, by Aristotle.   In that work the end of
rhetoric is defined as the *leading of men by the
power of speech to the conclusion desired by the orator.*
But even this definition is not sufficiently compre- 11
hensive, since others besides orators persuade by
speaking or lead others to the conclusion desired, as
for example harlots, flatterers and seducers.   On
the other hand the orator is not always engaged on
persuasion, so that sometimes persuasion is not his
special object, while sometimes it is shared by
others who are far removed from being orators.   And 12
yet Apollodorus is not very far off this definition
when he asserts that the first and all-important task
of forensic oratory is *to persuade the judge and lead
his mind to the conclusions desired by the speaker.*   For

305

id, quod velit; nam et ipse oratorem fortunae subiicit, ut, si non persuaserit, nomen suum retinere
13 non possit. Quidam recesserunt ab eventu, sicut
Aristoteles dicit: *rhetorice est vis inveniendi omnia in
oratione persuasibilia.* Qui finis et illud vitium, de
quo supra diximus, habet et insuper quod nihil nisi
inventionem complectitur, quae sine elocutione non
14 est oratio. Hermagorae, qui finem eius esse ait persuasibiliter dicere, et aliis, qui eandem sententiam
non iisdem tantum verbis explicant ac finem esse
demonstrant dicere quae oporteat omnia ad persuadendum, satis responsum est, cum persuadere non
15 tantum oratoris esse convicimus. Addita sunt his
alia varie. Quidam enim *circa res omnes,* quidam
circa civiles modo versari rhetoricen putaverunt;
quorum verius utrum sit, in eo loco, qui huius quae-
16 stionis proprius est, dicam. Omnia subiecisse oratori
videtur Aristoteles, cum dixit vim esse videndi, quid
in quaque re possit esse persuasibile. Et Patrocles,[1]
qui non quidem adiicit *in quaque re,* sed nihil excipi-
endo idem ostendit; vim enim vocat inveniendi, quod
sit in oratione persuasibile; qui fines et ipsi solam
complectuntur inventionem. Quod vitium fugiens
Theodorus vim putat inveniendi et eloquendi cum
17 ornatu credibilia in omni oratione. Sed cum eodem

---

[1] latrocles, *B.* Iatrocles, *Radermacher.*

---

[1] *Rhet.* i. 2.

even Apollodorus makes the orator the sport of fortune by refusing him leave to retain his title if he
fails to persuade. Some on the other hand pay no 13
attention to results, as for example Aristotle,[1] who
says " *rhetoric is the power of discovering all means of
persuading by speech.*" This definition has not merely
the fault already mentioned, but the additional defect of including merely the power of invention,
which without style cannot possibly constitute
oratory. Hermagoras, who asserts that its end is to 14
speak persuasively, and others who express the same
opinion, though in different words, and inform us
that the end is to *say everything which ought to be
said with a view to persuasion,* have been sufficiently
answered above, when I proved that persuasion was
not the privilege of the orator alone. Various additions 15
have been made to these definitions. For some hold
that rhetoric is concerned with everything, while
some restrict its activity to politics. The question
as to which of these views is the nearer to the truth
shall be discussed later in its appropriate place. Aris- 16
totle seems to have implied that the sphere of the
orator was all-inclusive when he defined rhetoric as
the *power to detect every element in any given subject
which might conduce to persuasion ;* so too does Patrocles who omits the words *in any given subject,* but
since he excludes nothing, shows that his view is
identical. For he defines rhetoric as the *power to
discover whatever is persuasive in speech.* These definitions like that quoted above include no more than
the power of *invention* alone. Theodorus avoids this
fault and holds that it is the *power to discover and to
utter forth in elegant language whatever is credible in
every subject of oratory.* But, while others besides 17

modo credibilia quo persuasibilia etiam non orator
inveniat, adiiciendo *in omni oratione* magis quam
superiores concedit scelera quoque suadentibus pul-
18 cherrimae rei nomen. Gorgias apud Platonem suadendi se artificem in iudiciis et aliis coetibus esse
ait, de iustis quoque et iniustis tractare; cui Socrates
19 persuadendi, non docendi concedit facultatem. Qui
vero non omnia subiiciebant oratori, sollicitius ac
verbosius, ut necesse erat, adhibuerunt discrimina;
quorum fuit Ariston, Critolai Peripatetici discipulus,
cuius hic finis est, *scientia videndi et agendi in quaestionibus civilibus per orationem popularis persuasionis.*
20 Hic scientiam, quia Peripateticus est, non, ut
Stoici, virtutis loco ponit; popularem autem com-
prehendendo persuasionem etiam contumeliosus est
adversus artem orandi, quam nihil putat doctis per-
suasuram. Illud de omnibus, qui circa civiles demum
quaestiones oratorem iudicant versari, dictum sit,
excludi ab his plurima oratoris officia, illam certe
laudativam totam, quae est rhetorices pars tertia.
21 Cautius Theodorus Gadareus, ut iam ad eos veniamus,
qui artem quidem esse eam sed non virtutem putaverunt. Ita enim dicit (ut ipsis eorum verbis utar,
qui haec ex Graeco transtulerunt), *Ars inventrix et
iudicatrix et nuntiatrix decenti ornatu secundum mensio-
nem eius, quod in quoque potest sumi persuasibile, in
22 materia civili.* Itemque Cornelius Celsus, qui finem

---

[1] *Gorg.* 454 B.

orators may discover what is credible as well as persuasive, by adding the words *in every subject* he, to a greater extent than the others, concedes the fairest name in all the world to those who use their gifts as an incitement to crime. Plato makes Gorgias[1] say 18 that he is a master of persuasion in the law-courts and other assemblies, and that his themes are justice and injustice, while in reply Socrates allows him the power of persuading, but not of teaching. Those 19 who refused to make the sphere of oratory all-inclusive, have been obliged to make somewhat forced and long-winded distinctions: among these I may mention Ariston, the pupil of the Peripatetic Critolaus, who produced the following definition, "*Rhetoric is the science of seeing and uttering what ought to be said on political questions in language that is likely to prove persuasive to the people.*" Being a Peripatetic he 20 regards it as a science, not, like the Stoics, as a virtue, while in adding the words "*likely to prove persuasive to the people*" he inflicts a positive insult on oratory, in implying that it is not likely to persuade the learned. The same criticism will apply to all those who restrict oratory to political questions, for they exclude thereby a large number of the duties of an orator, as for example panegyric, the third department of oratory, which is entirely ignored. Turning 21 to those who regard rhetoric as an art, but not as a virtue, we find that Theodorus of Gadara is more cautious. For he says (I quote the words of his translators), "*rhetoric is the art which discovers and judges and expresses, with an elegance duly proportioned to the importance of all such elements of persuasion as may exist in any subject in the field of politics.*" Similarly Cornelius Celsus defines the end of rhetoric as

rhetorices ait dicere persuasibiliter in dubia civili
materia. Quibus sunt non dissimiles, qui ab aliis
traduntur; qualis est ille, *Vis videndi et eloquendi de*
rebus civilibus subiectis sibi cum quadam persuasione et
quodam corporis habitu et eorum, quae dicet, pronuntia-
23 *tione.* Mille alia, sed aut eadem aut ex eisdem
composita; quibus item, cum de materia rhetorices
dicendum erit, respondebimus. Quidam eam neque
vim neque scientiam neque artem putaverunt, sed
Critolaus usum dicendi (nam hoc τριβή significat),
24 Athenaeus fallendi artem. Plerique autem, dum
pauca ex Gorgia Platonis a prioribus imperite ex-
cerpta legere contenti neque hoc totum neque alia
eius volumina evolvunt, in maximum errorem inciderunt, creduntque eum in hac esse opinione, ut
rhetoricen non artem sed peritiam quandam gratiae
25 ac voluptatis existimet; et alio loco civilitatis par-
ticulae simulacrum et quartam partem adulationis,
quod duas partes civilitatis corpori adsignet, medici-
nam et quam interpretantur exercitatricem, duas
animo, legalem atque iustitiam; adulationem autem
medicinae vocet cocorum artificium, exercitatricis
mangonum, qui colorem fuco et verum robur inani
sagina mentiantur, legalis cavillatricem, iustitiae
26 rhetoricen. Quae omnia sunt quidem scripta in hoc
libro dictaque a Socrate, cuius persona videtur Plato

---

[1] *Gorg.* 462 c.   [2] *ib.* 463 d.
[3] *ib.* 464 b.   [4] *ib.* 464 b-465 e.

to speak persuasively on any doubtful subject within the field of politics. Similar definitions are given by others, such for instance as the following :— "*rhetoric is the power of judging and holding forth on such political subjects as come before it with a certain persuasiveness, a certain action of the body and delivery of the words.*" There are countless other definitions, 23 either identical with this or composed of the same elements, which I shall deal with when I come to the questions concerned with the subject matter of rhetoric. Some regard it as neither a power, a science or an art ; Critolaus calls it the *practice of speaking* (for this is the meaning of τριβή), Athenaeus styles it the *art of deceiving,* while the 24 majority, content with reading a few passages from the Gorgias of Plato, unskilfully excerpted by earlier writers, refrain from studying that dialogue and the remainder of Plato's writings, and thereby fall into serious error. For they believe that in Plato's view rhetoric was not an art, but a certain *adroitness in the production of delight and gratification,*[1] or with reference to another passage the 25 *shadow of a small part of politics*[2] and the *fourth department of flattery.* For Plato assigns[3] two departments of politics to the body, namely medicine and gymnastic, and two to the soul, namely law and justice, while he styles the art of cookery[4] a form of flattery of medicine, the art of the slave-dealer a flattery of gymnastic, for they produce a false complexion by the use of paint and a false robustness by puffing them out with fat : sophistry he calls a dishonest counterfeit of legal science, and rhetoric of justice. All these statements occur in the *Gorgias* and 26 are uttered by Socrates who appears to be the mouth-

significare quid sentiat; sed alii sunt eius sermones
ad coarguendos, qui contra disputant, compositi, quos
ἐλεγκτικούς vocant, alii ad praecipiendum, qui δογμα-
27 τικοί appellantur. Socrates autem seu Plato eam
quidem, quae tum exercebatur, rhetoricen talem
putat, nam et dicit his verbis τοῦτον τὸν τρόπον, ὃν
ὑμεῖς πολιτεύεσθε, veram autem et honestam intelligit.
Itaque disputatio illa contra Gorgian ita clauditur,
οὔκουν ἀνάγκη τὸν ῥητορικὸν δίκαιον εἶναι, τὸν δὲ δίκαιον
28 βούλεσθαι δίκαια πράττειν; Ad quod ille quidem con-
ticescit, sed sermonem suscipit Polus iuvenili calore
inconsideratior, contra quem illa de simulacro et
adulatione dicuntur. Tum Callicles adhuc concita-
tior, qui tamen ad hanc perducitur clausulam, τὸν
μέλλοντα ὀρθῶς ῥητορικὸν ἔσεσθαι, δίκαιον ἄνδρα δεῖ εἶναι
καὶ ἐπιστήμονα τῶν δικαίων; ut appareat, Platoni non
rhetoricen videri malum, sed eam veram nisi iusto ac
29 bono non contingere. Adhuc autem in Phaedro
manifestius facit, hanc artem consummari citra
iustitiae quoque scientiam non posse; cui opinioni
nos quoque accedimus. An aliter defensionem So-
cratis et eorum, qui pro patria ceciderant, laudem
30 scripsisset? quae certe sunt oratoris opera. Sed in
illud hominum genus, quod facilitate dicendi male
utebatur, invectus est. Nam et Socrates inhonestam

---

[1] 500 c.   [2] 460 c.   [3] 508 c.
[4] 261 A—273 E.   [5] Menexenus.

piece of the views held by Plato. But some of his
dialogues were composed merely to refute his
opponents and are styled *refutative,* while others are
for the purpose of teaching and are called *doctrinal.*
Now it is only rhetoric as practised in their own day 27
that is condemned by Plato or Socrates, for he
speaks of it as " the manner in which you engage in
public affairs " [1] : rhetoric in itself he regards as a
genuine and honourable thing, and consequently the
controversy with Gorgias ends with the words, " The
rhetorician therefore must be just and the just man
desirous to do what is just." [2] To this Gorgias 28
makes no reply, but the argument is taken up by
Polus, a hot-headed and headstrong young fellow,
and it is to him that Socrates makes his remarks
about " shadows" and "forms of flattery." Then
Callicles,[3] who is even more hot-headed, intervenes,
but is reduced to the conclusion that " he who would
truly be a rhetorician ought to be just and possess a
knowledge of justice." It is clear therefore that
Plato does not regard rhetoric as an evil, but holds
that true rhetoric is impossible for any save a just
and good man. In the *Phaedrus* [4] he makes it even 29
clearer that the complete attainment of this art is
impossible without the knowledge of justice, an
opinion in which I heartily concur. Had this not
been his view, would he have ever written the
Apology of Socrates or the Funeral Oration [5] in
praise of those who had died in battle for their
country, both of them works falling within the
sphere of oratory. It was against the class of men 30
who employed their glibness of speech for evil purposes that he directed his denunciations. Similarly
Socrates thought it incompatible with his honour to

sibi credidit orationem, quam ei Lysias reo composuerat; et tum maxime scribere litigatoribus, quae illi pro se ipsi dicerent, erat moris, atque ita iuri, quo non licebat pro altero agere, fraus adhibebatur.

31 Doctores quoque eius artis parum idonei Platoni videbantur, qui rhetoricen a iustitia separarent et veris credibilia praeferrent; nam id quoque dicit in

32 Phaedro. Consensisse autem illis superioribus videri potest etiam Cornelius Celsus, cuius haec verba sunt: *Orator simile tantum veri petit.* Deinde paulo post: *Non enim bona conscientia sed victoria litigantis est praemium.* Quae si vera essent, pessimorum hominum foret, haec tam perniciosa nocentissimis moribus dare instrumenta et nequitiam praeceptis adiuvare. Sed illi rationem opinionis suae viderint.

33 Nos autem ingressi formare perfectum oratorem, quem in primis esse virum bonum volumus, ad eos, qui de hoc opere melius sentiunt, revertamur. Rhetoricen autem quidam eandem civilitatem esse iudicaverunt; Cicero scientiae civilis partem vocat (civilis autem scientia idem quod sapientia est); quidam

34 eandem philosophiam, quorum est Isocrates. Huic eius substantiae maxime conveniet finitio, rhetoricen esse bene dicendi scientiam. Nam et orationis omnes virtutes semel complectitur et protinus etiam mores oratoris, cum bene dicere non possit nisi bonus.

35 Idem valet Chrysippi finis ille ductus a Cleanthe

---

[1] 267 A, with special reference to Tisias and Gorgias.
[2] *de Inv.* I. v. 6.

make use of the speech which Lysias composed for
his defence, although it was the usual practice in
those days to write speeches for the parties concerned to speak in the courts on their own behalf,
a device designed to circumvent the law which for-
bade the employment of advocates. Further the 31
teachers of rhetoric were regarded by Plato as quite
unsuited to their professed task. For they divorced
rhetoric from justice and preferred plausibility to
truth, as he states in the *Phaedrus.*[1] Cornelius Celsus 32
seems to have agreed with these early rhetoricians,
for he writes "The orator only aims at the semblance
of truth," and again a little later " The reward of
the party to a suit is not a good conscience, but victory." If this were true, only the worst of men
would place such dangerous weapons at the disposal
of criminals or employ the precepts of their art for
the assistance of wickedness. However I will leave
those who maintain these views to consider what
ground they have for so doing.

For my part, I have undertaken the task of mould- 33
ing the ideal orator, and as my first desire is that he
should be a good man, I will return to those who
have sounder opinions on the subject. Some however identify rhetoric with politics, Cicero [2] calls it a
department of the science of politics (and science of
politics and philosophy are identical terms), while
others again call it a *branch of philosophy,* among
them Isocrates. The definition which best suits its 34
real character is that which makes rhetoric the *science
of speaking well.* For this definition includes all the
virtues of oratory and the character of the orator as
well, since no man can speak well who is not good
himself. The definition given by Chrysippus, who 35

scientia recte dicendi. Sunt plures eiusdem, sed ad
alias quaestiones magis pertinent. Idem sentit et
finis hoc modo comprehensus, persuadere quod
36 oporteat, nisi quod artem ad exitum alligat. At
bene Areus dicere secundum virtutem orationis.
Excludunt a rhetorice malos et illi, qui scientiam
civilium officiorum eam putaverunt, si scientiam virtutem iudicant; sed anguste intra civiles quaestiones
coercent. Albutius, non obscurus professor atque
auctor, scientiam bene dicendi esse consentit, sed
exceptionibus peccat adiiciendo circa civiles quaestiones et credibiliter; quarum utrique iam respon-
37 sum est. Probabilis et illi voluntatis, qui recte
sentire et dicere rhetorices putaverunt.

Hi sunt fere fines maxime illustres et de quibus
praecipue disputatur. Nam omnes quidem persequi
neque attinet neque possum, cum pravum quoddam,
ut arbitror, studium circa scriptores artium extiterit,
nihil eisdem verbis, quae prior aliquis occupasset,
38 finiendi, quae ambitio procul aberit a me. Dicam
enim non utique quae invenero sed quae placebunt,
sicut hoc, rhetoricen esse bene dicendi scientiam;

derived it from Cleanthes, to the effect that it is the *science of speaking rightly*, amounts to the same thing. The same philosopher also gives other definitions, but they concern problems of a different character from that on which we are now engaged. Another definition defines oratory as the power of *persuading men to do what ought to be done*, and yields practically the same sense save that it limits the art to the result which it produces. Areus again defines it well as 36 *speaking according to the excellence of speech*. Those who regard it as the science of political obligations, also exclude men of bad character from the title of orator, if by science they mean virtue, but restrict it over-much by confining it to political problems. Albutius, a distinguished author and professor of rhetoric, agrees that rhetoric is the science of speaking well, but makes a mistake in imposing restrictions by the addition of the words *on political questions* and *with credibility*; with both of these restrictions I have already dealt. Finally those critics who hold that 37 the aim of rhetoric is *to think and speak rightly*, were on the correct track.

These are practically all the most celebrated and most discussed definitions of rhetoric. It would be both irrelevant and beyond my power to deal with all. For I strongly disapprove of the custom which has come to prevail among writers of text-books of refusing to define anything in the same terms as have been employed by some previous writer. I will have nothing to do with such ostentation. What I say 38 will not necessarily be my own invention, but it will be what I believe to be the right view, as for instance that oratory is the science of speaking well. For when the most satisfactory definition has been

cum reperto quod est optimum, qui quaerit aliud,
peius velit.

His approbatis, simul manifestum est illud quoque,
quem finem vel quid summum et ultimum habeat
rhetorice, quod τέλος dicitur, ad quod omnis ars
tendit; nam si est ipsa bene dicendi scientia, finis
eius et summum est bene dicere.

XVI. Sequitur quaestio, an utilis rhetorice. Nam
quidam vehementer in eam invehi solent, et, quod
sit indignissimum, in accusationem orationis utuntur

2 orandi viribus: eloquentiam esse, quae poenis eripiat
scelestos, cuius fraude damnentur interim boni, consilia ducantur in peius, nec seditiones modo turbae-
que populares sed bella etiam inexpiabilia excitentur;
cuius denique tum maximus sit usus, cum pro falsis

3 contra veritatem valet. Nam et Socrati obiiciunt
comici docere eum, quomodo peiorem causam meliorem faciat, et contra Tisian et Gorgian similia dicit

4 polliceri Plato. Et his adiiciunt exempla Graecorum
Romanorumque et enumerant, qui perniciosa non
singulis tantum sed rebus etiam publicis usi eloquentia turbaverint civitatium status vel everterint,
eoque et Lacedaemoniorum civitate expulsam et
Athenis quoque, ubi actor movere adfectus vetabatur,

5 velut recisam orandi potestatem. Quo quidem modo
nec duces erunt utiles nec magistratus nec medicina

found, he who seeks another, is merely looking for a worse one.

Thus much being admitted we are now in a position to see clearly what is the end, the highest aim, the ultimate goal of rhetoric, that τέλος in fact which every art must possess. For if rhetoric is the science of speaking well, its end and highest aim is to speak well.

XVI. There follows the question as to whether rhetoric is useful. Some are in the habit of denouncing it most violently and of shamelessly employing the powers of oratory to accuse oratory itself. "It is eloquence" they say "that snatches 2 criminals from the penalties of the law, eloquence that from time to time secures the condemnation of the innocent and leads deliberation astray, eloquence that stirs up not merely sedition and popular tumult, but wars beyond all expiation, and that is most effective when it makes falsehood prevail over the truth." The comic poets even accuse 3 Socrates of teaching how to make the worse cause seem the better, while Plato says that Gorgias and Tisias made similar professions. And to these they 4 add further examples drawn from the history of Rome and Greece, enumerating all those who used their pernicious eloquence not merely against individuals but against whole states and threw an ordered commonwealth into a state of turmoil or even brought it to utter ruin; and they point out that for this very reason rhetoric was banished from Sparta, while its powers were cut down at Athens itself by the fact that an orator was forbidden to stir the passions of his audience. On the showing of these critics not only 5 orators but generals, magistrates, medicine and philo-

nec denique ipsa sapientia. Nam et dux Flaminius
et Gracchi, Saturnini, Glauciae magistratus, et
in medicis venena et in his, qui philosophorum
nomine male utuntur, gravissima nonnunquam flagitia
6 deprehensa sunt. Cibos aspernemur; attulerunt
saepe valetudinis causas. Nunquam tecta subeamus;
super habitantes aliquando procumbunt. Non fabri-
cetur militi gladius; potest uti eodem ferro latro.
Quis nescit, ignes, aquas, sine quibus nulla sit vita,
et (ne terrenis immorer) solem lunamque, praecipua
siderum, aliquando et nocere?

7   Num igitur negabitur deformem Pyrrhi pacem
caecus ille Appius dicendi viribus diremisse? aut
non divina M. Tulli eloquentia et contra leges
agrarias popularis fuit et Catilinae fregit audaciam
et supplicationes, qui maximus honor victoribus bello
8 ducibus datur, in toga meruit? Nonne perterritos
militum animos frequenter a metu revocat oratio et
tot pugnandi pericula ineuntibus laudem vita potiorem esse persuadet? Neque vero me Lacedaemonii
atque Athenienses magis moverint quam populus
Romanus, apud quem summa semper oratoribus
9 dignitas fuit. Equidem nec urbium conditores reor
aliter effecturos fuisse ut vaga illa multitudo coiret
in populos, nisi docta voce commota; nec legum
repertores sine summa vi orandi consecutos, ut se

---

[1] *i.e.* though denouncing laws which would naturally be
popular.

sophy itself will all be useless.   For Flaminius was a
general, while men such as the Gracchi, Saturninus
and Glaucia were magistrates.   Doctors have been
caught using poisons, and those who falsely assume the
name of philosopher have occasionally been detected
in the gravest crimes.   Let us give up eating, it 6
often makes us ill; let us never go inside houses,
for sometimes they collapse on their occupants;
let never a sword be forged for a soldier, since
it might be used by a robber.   And who does
not realise that fire and water, both necessities of
life, and, to leave mere earthly things, even the sun
and moon, the greatest of the heavenly bodies, are
occasionally capable of doing harm.

On the other hand will it be denied that it was 7
by his gift of speech that Appius the Blind broke
off the dishonourable peace which was on the point
of being concluded with Pyrrhus?   Did not the
divine eloquence of Cicero win popular applause
even when he denounced the Agrarian laws,[1] did it
not crush the audacious plots of Catiline and win,
while he still wore the garb of civil life, the highest
honour that can be conferred on a victorious general,
a public thanksgiving to heaven?   Has not oratory 8
often revived the courage of a panic-stricken army
and persuaded the soldier faced by all the perils of
war that glory is a fairer thing than life itself?   Nor
shall the history of Sparta and Athens move me
more than that of the Roman people, who have
always held the orator in highest honour.   Never in 9
my opinion would the founders of cities have induced their unsettled multitudes to form communi-
ties had they not moved them by the magic of their
eloquence: never without the highest gifts of oratory

10 ipsi homines ad servitutem iuris astringerent. Quin ipsa vitae praecepta, etiamsi natura sunt honesta, plus tamen ad formandas mentes valent, quotiens pulchritudinem rerum claritas orationis illuminat. Quare, etiamsi in utramque partem valent arma facundiae, non est tamen aequum id haberi malum, quo bene uti licet.

11 Verum haec apud eos forsitan quaerantur, qui summam rhetorices ad persuadendi vim rettulerunt. Si vero est bene dicendi scientia, quem nos finem sequimur, ut sit orator in primis vir bonus, utilem

12 certe esse eam confitendum est. Et hercule deus ille princeps, parens rerum fabricatorque mundi, nullo magis hominem separavit a ceteris, quae quidem mortalia essent, animalibus, quam dicendi

13 facultate. Nam corpora quidem magnitudine, viribus, firmitate, patientia, velocitate praestantiora in illis mutis videmus, eadem minus egere acquisitae extrinsecus opis. Nam et ingredi citius et pasci et tranare aquas citra docentem natura ipsa sciunt. Et

14 pleraque contra frigus ex suo corpore vestiuntur, et arma iis ingenita quaedam et ex obvio fere victus, circa quae omnia multus hominibus labor est. Rationem igitur nobis praecipuam dedit eiusque nos

15 socios esse cum dis immortalibus voluit. Sed ipsa ratio neque tam nos iuvaret neque tam esset in nobis manifesta, nisi, quae concepissemus mente, promere etiam loquendo possemus, quod magis deesse ceteris

would the great legislators have constrained mankind to submit themselves to the yoke of law. Nay, 10
even the principles which should guide our life,
however fair they may be by nature, yet have greater
power to mould the mind to virtue, when the beauty
of things is illumined by the splendour of eloquence.
Wherefore, although the weapons of oratory may
be used either for good or ill, it is unfair to regard
that as an evil which can be employed for good.

These problems, however, may be left to those 11
who hold that rhetoric is the power to persuade. If
our definition of rhetoric as the science of speaking
well implies that an orator must be a good man,
there can be no doubt about its usefulness. And 12
in truth that god, who was in the beginning, the
father of all things and the architect of the universe,
distinguished man from all other living creatures
that are subject to death, by nothing more than
this, that he gave him the gift of speech. For as 13
regards physical bulk, strength, robustness, endurance or speed, man is surpassed in certain cases by
dumb beasts, who also are far more independent of
external assistance. They know by instinct without
need of any teacher how to move rapidly, to feed
themselves and swim. Many too have their bodies 14
clothed against cold, possess natural weapons and
have not to search for their food, whereas in all
these respects man's life is full of toil. Reason
then was the greatest gift of the Almighty, who
willed that we should share its possession with the
immortal gods. But reason by itself would help us 15
but little and would be far less evident in us, had
we not the power to express our thoughts in speech;
for it is the lack of this power rather than thought

animalibus quam intellectum et cogitationem quan-
16 dam videmus. Nam et mollire cubilia et nidos
texere et educare fetus et excludere, quin etiam
reponere in hiemem alimenta, opera quaedam nobis
inimitabilia (qualia sunt cerarum ac mellis) efficere,
nonnullius fortasse rationis est; sed quia carent
sermone, quae id faciunt, muta atque irrationalia
17 vocantur. Denique homines, quibus negata vox est,
quantulum adiuvat animus ille caelestis? Quare si
nihil a dis oratione melius accepimus, quid tam
dignum cultu ac labore ducamus, aut in quo malimus
praestare hominibus, quam quo ipsi homines ceteris
18 animalibus praestant, eo quidem magis, quod nulla
in arte plenius labor gratiam refert? Id adeo manifestum erit, si cogitaverimus, unde et quo usque iam
provecta sit orandi facultas; et adhuc augeri potest.
19 Nam ut omittam, defendere amicos, regere consiliis
senatum, populum, exercitum in quae velit ducere,
quam sit utile conveniatque bono viro, nonne pulchrum vel hoc ipsum est, ex communi intellectu
verbisque, quibus utuntur omnes, tantum adsequi
laudis et gloriae, ut non loqui et orare sed, quod
Pericli contigit, fulgurare ac tonare videaris?

XVII. Finis non erit, si exspatiari in parte hac et

---

[1] *cp*. Aristoph. *Ach.* 530: "Then in his wrath Pericles
the Olympian lightened and thundered and threw all Greece
into confusion."

and understanding, which they do to a certain extent possess, that is the great defect in other living
things. The construction of a soft lair, the weaving 16
of nests, the hatching and rearing of their young, and
even the storing up of food for the coming winter,
together with certain other achievements which we
cannot imitate, such as the making of honey and
wax, all these perhaps indicate the possession of a
certain degree of reason; but since the creatures that
do these things lack the gift of speech they are called
dumb and unreasoning beasts. Finally, how little 17
the heavenly boon of reason avails those who are
born dumb. If therefore we have received no fairer
gift from heaven than speech, what shall we regard
as so worthy of laborious cultivation, or in what
should we sooner desire to excel our fellow-men,
than that in which mankind excels all other living
things? And we should be all the more eager to do 18
so, since there is no art which yields a more grateful
recompense for the labour bestowed upon it. This
will be abundantly clear if we consider the origins
of oratory and the progress it has made; and it is
capable of advancing still further. I will not stop 19
to point out how useful and how becoming a task it is
for a good man to defend his friends, to guide the
senate by his counsels, and to lead peoples or armies
to follow his bidding; I merely ask, is it not a
noble thing, by employing the understanding which
is common to mankind and the words that are used
by all, to win such honour and glory that you seem
not to speak or plead, but rather, as was said of
Pericles, to thunder and lighten?[1]

XVII. However, if I were to indulge my own in-
clinations in expatiating on this subject, I should go

indulgere voluptati velim. Transeamus igitur ad
eam quaestionem, quae sequitur, an rhetorice ars
2 sit. Quod quidem adeo ex iis, qui praecepta dicendi
tradiderunt, nemo dubitavit, ut etiam ipsis librorum
titulis testatum sit, scriptos eos de arte rhetorica ;
Cicero vero eam, quae rhetorice vocetur, esse
artificiosam eloquentiam dicat. Quod non oratores
tantum vindicarunt, ut studiis aliquid suis praesti-
tisse videantur, sed cum iis philosophi et Stoici et
3 Peripatetici plerique consentiunt. Ac me dubitasse
confiteor, an hanc partem quaestionis tractandam
putarem ; nam quis est adeo non ab eruditione modo
sed a sensu remotus hominis, ut fabricandi quidem
et texendi et e luto vasa ducendi artem putet, rhetoricen autem, maximum ac pulcherrimum, ut supra
diximus, opus, in tam sublime fastigium existimet
4 sine arte venisse? Equidem illos, qui contra dis-
putaverunt, non tam id sensisse quod dicerent, quam
exercere ingenia materiae difficultate credo voluisse,
sicut Polycraten, cum Busirim laudaret et Clytaem-
nestram ; quanquam is, quod his dissimile non est,
composuisse orationem, quae est habita contra
Socraten, dicitur.
5 Quidam naturalem esse rhetoricen volunt et tamen
adiuvari exercitatione non diffitentur, ut in libris
Ciceronis de Oratore dicit Antonius, observationem
6 quandam esse non artem. Quod non ideo, ut pro
vero accipiamus, est positum, sed ut Antoni persona

---

[1] de Inv. I. v. 6. The titles in question are such as *Ars
rhetorica*, *Ars Hermagorae*, etc.

on for ever. Let us therefore pass to the next
question and consider whether rhetoric is an art.
No one of those who have laid down rules for 2
oratory has ever doubted that it is an art. It is clear
even from the titles of their books that their theme
is the art of rhetoric, while Cicero [1] defines rhetoric
as *artistic eloquence*. And it is not merely the orators
who have claimed this distinction for their studies
with a view to giving them an additional title to
respect, but the Stoic and Peripatetic philosophers for
the most part agree with them. Indeed I will confess 3
that I had doubts as to whether I should discuss this
portion of my inquiry, for there is no one, I will not
say so unlearned, but so devoid of ordinary sense, as
to hold that building, weaving or moulding vessels
from clay are arts, and at the same time to consider
that rhetoric, which, as I have already said, is the
noblest and most sublime of tasks, has reached such
a lofty eminence without the assistance of art. For 4
my own part I think that those who have argued
against this view did not realise what they were
saying, but merely desired to exercise their wits by
the selection of a difficult theme, like Polycrates,
when he praised Busiris and Clytemnestra; I may
add that he is credited with a not dissimilar performance, namely the composition of a speech which
was delivered against Socrates.

Some would have it that rhetoric is a natural gift 5
though they admit that it can be developed by practice.
So Antonius in the *de Oratore* [2] of Cicero styles it a *knack
derived from experience*, but denies that it is an art:
this statement is however not intended to be accepted 6
by us as the actual truth, but is inserted to make

[2] II. lvii. 232.

servetur, qui dissimulator artis fuit. Hanc autem
opinionem habuisse Lysias videtur. Cuius sententiae
talis defensio est, quod indocti et barbari et servi,
pro se cum loquuntur, aliquid dicant simile principio,
narrent, probent, refutent, et (quod vim habeat
7 epilogi) deprecentur. Deinde adiiciunt illas verborum cavillationes, nihil, quod ex arte fiat, ante
artem fuisse; atqui dixisse homines pro se et in alios
semper, doctores artis sero et circa Tisian et Coraca
primum repertos, orationem igitur ante artem fuisse
8 eoque artem non esse. Nos porro, quando coeperit
huius rei doctrina, non laboramus exquirere, quanquam apud Homerum et praeceptorem Phoenicem
cum agendi tum etiam loquendi et oratores plures et
omne in tribus ducibus orationis genus et certamina
quoque proposita eloquentiae inter iuvenes invenimus,
quin in caelatura clipei Achillis et lites sunt et
9 actores. Illud enim admonere satis est, omnia, quae
ars consummaverit, a natura initia duxisse. Aut
tollatur medicina, quae ex observatione salubrium
atque iis contrariorum reperta est, et, ut quibusdam
placet, tota constat experimentis; nam et vulnus
deligavit aliquis, antequam haec ars esset, et febrem
quiete et abstinentia, non quia rationem videbat, sed

---

[1] *Il*. ix. 432.
[2] *i.e.* the copious style by Nestor, the plain by Menelaus,
the intermediate by Ulysses.
[3] *Il*. xv. 284.   [4] *Il*. xviii. 497 *sqq*.

Antonius speak in character, since he was in the
habit of concealing his art. Still Lysias is said to
have maintained this same view, which is defended
on the ground that uneducated persons, barbarians
and slaves, when speaking on their own behalf, say
something that resembles an *exordium*, state the facts
of the case, prove, refute and plead for mercy just as
an orator does in his peroration. To this is added 7
the quibble that nothing that is based on art can
have existed before the art in question, whereas men
have always from time immemorial spoken in their
own defence or in denunciation of others: the
teaching of rhetoric as an art was, they say, a later
invention dating from about the time of Tisias and
Corax: oratory therefore existed before art and
consequently cannot be an art. For my part I am not 8
concerned with the date when oratory began to be
taught. Even in Homer we find Phoenix [1] as an
instructor not only of conduct but of speaking, while
a number of orators are mentioned, the various styles
are represented by the speeches of three of the
chiefs [2] and the young men are set to contend among
themselves in contests of eloquence: [3] moreover lawsuits and pleaders are represented in the engravings
on the shield of Achilles. [4] It is sufficient to call 9
attention to the fact that everything which art has
brought to perfection originated in nature. Otherwise we might deny the title of art to medicine,
which was discovered from the observation of
sickness and health, and according to some is
entirely based upon experiment: wounds were bound
up long before medicine developed into an art, and
fevers were reduced by rest and abstention from food,
long before the reason for such treatment was

10 quia id valetudo ipsa cogebat, mitigavit. Nec fabrica
sit ars; casas enim primi illi sine arte fecerunt; nec
musica; cantatur ac saltatur per omnes gentes aliquo
modo. Ita si rhetorice vocari debet sermo quicun-
11 que, fuisse eam, antequam esset ars, confitebor; si
vero non quisquis loquitur, orator est, et tum non
tanquam oratores loquebantur, necesse est, oratorem
factum arte nec ante artem fuisse fateantur. Quo
illud quoque excluditur, quod dicunt, non esse artis
id, quod faciat qui non didicerit, dicere autem
12 homines et qui non didicerint. Ad cuius rei confirmationem adferunt, Demaden remigem, et Aeschi-
nen hypocriten oratores fuisse. Falso; nam neque
orator esse, qui non didicit, potest, et hos sero potius
quam nunquam didicisse quis dixerit, quanquam
Aeschines ab initio sit versatus in litteris, quas pater
eius etiam docebat, Demaden neque non didicisse
certum sit, et continua dicendi exercitatio potuerit
tantum, quantuscunque postea fuit, fecisse; nam id
13 potentissimum discendi genus est. Sed et praestan-
tiorem, si didicisset, futurum fuisse dicere licet;
neque enim orationes scribere est ausus, ut eum
14 multum valuisse in dicendo sciamus. Aristoteles,
ut solet, quaerendi gratia quaedam subtilitatis suae

---

[1] A lost treatise, named after Gryllus, the son of
Xenophon.

known, simply because the state of the patient's health left no choice. So too building should not be 10 styled an art; for primitive man built himself a hut without the assistance of art. Music by the same reasoning is not an art; for every race indulges in some kind of singing and dancing. If therefore any kind of speech is to be called eloquence, I will admit that it existed before it was an art. If on the other 11 hand not every man that speaks is an orator and primitive man did not speak like an orator, my opponents must needs acknowledge that oratory is the product of art and did not exist before it. This conclusion also rules out their argument that men speak who have never learnt how to speak, and that which a man does untaught can have no connexion with art. In support of this contention they adduce 12 the fact that Demades was a waterman and Aeschines an actor, but both were orators. Their reasoning is false. For no man can be an orator untaught and it would be truer to say that these orators learned oratory late in life than that they never learned at all; although as a matter of fact Aeschines had an acquaintance with literature from childhood since his father was a teacher of literature, while as regards Demades, it is quite uncertain that he never studied rhetoric and in any case continuous practice in speaking was sufficient to bring him to such proficiency as he attained : for experience is the best of all schools. On the other hand it may fairly be asserted 13 that he would have achieved greater distinction, if he had received instruction : for although he delivered his speeches with great effect, he never ventured to write them for others. Aristotle, it is true, in his 14 *Gryllus*[1] produces some tentative arguments to

argumenta excogitavit in Gryllo; sed idem et de
arte rhetorica tris libros scripsit, et in eorum primo
non artem solum eam fatetur, sed ei particulam
15 civilitatis sicut dialectices adsignat.   Multa Critolaus
contra, multa Rhodius Athenodorus.   Agnon quidem
detraxit sibi inscriptione ipsa fidem, qua rhetorices
accusationem professus est.   Nam de Epicuro, qui
disciplinas omnes fugit, nihil miror.

16   Hi complura dicunt sed ex paucis locis ducta;
itaque potentissimis eorum breviter occurram, ne in
17 infinitum quaestio evadat.   Prima iis argumentatio
ex materia est.   Omnes enim artes aiunt habere
materiam, quod est verum; rhetorices nullam esse
propriam, quod esse falsum in sequentibus probabo.
18 Altera est calumnia nullam artem falsis assentiri
opinionibus, quia constitui sine perceptione non
possit, quae semper vera sit; rhetoricen assentiri falsis,
19 non esse igitur artem.   Ego rhetoricen nonnunquam
dicere falsa pro veris confitebor, sed non ideo in falsa
quoque esse opinione concedam, quia longe diversum
est, ipsi quid videri et, ut alii videatur, efficere.
Nam et imperator falsis utitur saepe, ut Hannibal,
cum inclusus a Fabio, sarmentis circum cornua boum

the contrary, which are marked by characteristic
ingenuity. On the other hand he also wrote three
books on the art of rhetoric, in the first of which
he not merely admits that rhetoric is an art, but
treats it as a department of politics and also of
logic. Critolaus and Athenodorus of Rhodes have 15
produced many arguments against this view, while
Agnon renders himself suspect by the very title of
his book in which he proclaims that he is going to
indict rhetoric. As to the statements of Epicurus
on this subject, they cause me no surprise, for he is
the foe of all systematic training.

These gentlemen talk a great deal, but the 16
arguments on which they base their statements are
few. I will therefore select the most important of
them and will deal with them briefly, to prevent the
discussion lasting to all eternity. Their first con- 17
tention is based on the subject-matter; for they
assert that all arts have their own subject-matter
(which is true) and go on to say that rhetoric has
none, which I shall show in what follows to be false.
Another slander is to the effect that no art will 18
acquiesce in false opinions: since an art must be
based on direct perception, which is always true:
now, say they, rhetoric does give its assent to false
conclusions and is therefore not an art. I will admit 19
that rhetoric sometimes substitutes falsehood for
truth, but I will not allow that it does so because its
opinions are false, since there is all the difference
between holding a certain opinion oneself and
persuading someone else to adopt an opinion. For
instance a general frequently makes use of falsehood: Hannibal when hemmed in by Fabius
persuaded his enemy that he was in retreat by

deligatis incensisque, per noctem in adversos montes
agens armenta speciem hosti abeuntis exercitus dedit,
sed illum fefellit, ipse, quid verum esset, non igno-
20 ravit.   Nec vero Theopompus Lacedaemonius, cum
permutato cum uxore habitu e custodia ut mulier
evasit, falsam de se opinionem habuit, sed custodibus
praebuit.   Item orator, cum falso utitur pro vero,
scit esse falsum eoque se pro vero uti; non ergo
21 falsam habet ipse opinionem, sed fallit alium.   Nec
Cicero, cum se tenebras offudisse iudicibus in causa
Cluenti gloriatus est, nihil ipse vidit.   Et pictor,
cum vi artis suae efficit, ut quaedam eminere in
opere, quaedam recessisse credamus, ipse ea plana
22 esse non nescit.   Aiunt etiam omnes artes habere
finem aliquem propositum, ad quem tendant; hunc
modo nullum esse in rhetorice, modo non praestari
eum, qui promittatur.   Mentiuntur; nos enim esse
23 finem iam ostendimus, et quis esset diximus.   Et
praestabit hunc semper orator, semper enim bene
dicet.   Firmum autem hoc, quod opponitur, adversus
eos fortasse sit, qui persuadere finem putaverunt.
Noster orator arsque a nobis finita non sunt posita in
eventu.   Tendit quidem ad victoriam qui dicit; sed
cum bene dixit, etiamsi non vincat, id quod arte con-
24 tinetur effecit.   Nam et gubernator vult salva nave

---

[1] See Livy, XXII. xvi.
[2] Probably a king of Sparta, 770-720 B.C.

tying brushwood to the horns of oxen, setting fire to them by night and driving the herds across the mountains opposite.[1] But though he deceived Fabius, he himself was fully aware of the truth. Again when the Spartan Theopompus changed 20 clothes with his wife and escaped from custody disguised as a woman, he deceived his guards, but was not for a moment deceived as to his own identity.[2] Similarly an orator, when he substitutes falsehood for the truth, is aware of the falsehood and of the fact that he is substituting it for the truth. He therefore deceives others, but not himself. When Cicero boasted that he had thrown 21 dust in the eyes of the jury in the case of Cluentius, he was far from being blinded himself. And when a painter by his artistic skill makes us believe that certain objects project from the picture, while others are withdrawn into the background, he knows perfectly well that they are really all in the same plane. My opponents further assert that every 22 art has some definite goal towards which it directs its efforts, but that rhetoric as a rule has no such goal, while at other times it professes to have an aim, but fails to perform its promise. They lie: I have already shown that rhetoric has a definite purpose and have explained what it is. And, what is more, the orator 23 will always make good his professions in this respect, for he will always speak well. On the other hand this criticism may perhaps hold good as against those who think persuasion the end of oratory. But our orator and his art, as we define it, are independent of results. The speaker aims at victory, it is true, but if he speaks well, he has lived up to the ideals of his art, even if he is defeated. Similarly a pilot will desire 24

in portum pervenire; si tamen tempestate fuerit
abreptus, non ideo minus erit gubernator dicetque

25 notum illud, *Dum clavum rectum teneam.* Et medicus
sanitatem aegri petit; si tamen aut valetudinis vi aut
intemperantia aegri aliove quo casu summa non contingit, dum ipse omnia secundum rationem fecerit,
medicinae fine non excidet. Ita oratori bene dixisse
finis est. Nam est ars ea, ut post paulum clarius

26 ostendemus, in actu posita non in effectu. Ita falsum
erit illud quoque, quod dicitur, artes scire quando
sint finem consecutae, rhetoricen nescire. Nam se
quisque bene dicere intelligit. Uti etiam vitiis rhetoricen, quod ars nulla faciat, criminantur, quia et

27 falsum dicat et adfectus moveat. Quorum neutrum
est turpe, cum ex bona ratione proficiscitur, ideoque
nec vitium. Nam et mendacium dicere etiam
sapienti aliquando concessum est, et adfectus, si aliter
ad aequitatem perduci iudex non poterit, necessario

28 movebit orator. Imperiti enim iudicant et qui frequenter in hoc ipsum fallendi sint, ne errent. Nam,
si mihi sapientes iudices dentur, sapientium contiones
atque omne consilium, nihil invidia valeat, nihil
gratia, nihil opinio praesumpta falsique testes: per-
quam sit exiguus eloquentiae locus et prope in sola

29 delectatione ponatur. Sin et audientium mobiles

---

[1] Ennius, *Ann.* 483 (Vahlen).

to bring his ship safe to harbour; but if he is swept out of his course by a storm, he will not for that reason cease to be a pilot, but will say in the well-known words of the old poet [1] "Still let me steer straight on!" So too the doctor seeks to heal the 25 sick; but if the violence of the disease or the refusal of the patient to obey his regimen or any other circumstance prevent his achieving his purpose, he will not have fallen short of the ideals of his art, provided he has done everything according to reason. So too the orator's purpose is fulfilled if he has spoken well. For the art of rhetoric, as I shall show later, is realised in action, not in the result obtained. From 26 this it follows that there is no truth in yet another argument which contends that arts know when they have attained their end, whereas rhetoric does not. For every speaker is aware when he is speaking well. These critics also charge rhetoric with doing what no art does, namely making use of vices to serve its ends, since it speaks the thing that is not and excites the passions. But there is no disgrace in doing 27 either of these things, as long as the motive be good: consequently there is nothing vicious in such action. Even a philosopher is at times permitted to tell a lie, while the orator must needs excite the passions, if that be the only way by which he can lead the judge to do justice. For judges are not always 28 enlightened and often have to be tricked to prevent them falling into error. Give me philosophers as judges, pack senates and assemblies with philosophers, and you will destroy the power of hatred, influence, prejudice and false witness; consequently there will be very little scope for eloquence whose value will lie almost entirely in its power to charm. But if, as is 29

animi et tot malis obnoxia veritas, arte pugnandum
est et adhibenda quae prosunt. Neque enim, qui
recta via depulsus est, reduci ad eam nisi alio flexu
potest.

30   Plurima vero ex eo contra rhetoricen cavillatio est,
quod ex utraque causae parte dicatur. Inde haec:
nullam esse artem contrariam sibi, rhetoricen esse
contrariam sibi; nullam artem destruere quod effecerit, accidere hoc rhetorices operi; item aut dicenda
eam docere aut non dicenda; ita vel per hoc non
esse artem, quod non dicenda praecipiat, vel per hoc,
quod, cum dicenda praeceperit, etiam contraria his
31 doceat. Quae omnia apparet de ea rhetorice dici,
quae sit a bono viro atque ab ipsa virtute seiuncta;
alioqui ubi iniusta causa est, ibi rhetorice non est,
adeo ut vix admirabili quodam casu possit accidere,
ut ex utraque parte orator, id est vir bonus, dicat.
32 Tamen quoniam hoc quoque in rerum naturam cadit,
ut duos sapientes aliquando iustae causae in diversum
trahant, (quando etiam pugnaturos eos inter se, si
ratio ita duxerit, credunt) respondebo propositis,
atque ita quidem, ut appareat, haec adversus eos
quoque frustra excogitata, qui malis moribus nomen
33 oratoris indulgent.   Nam rhetorice non est contraria

the case, our hearers are fickle of mind, and truth is
exposed to a host of perils, we must call in art to aid
us in the fight and employ such means as will help
our case. He who has been driven from the right road
cannot be brought back to it save by a fresh détour.

The point, however, that gives rise to the greatest 30
number of these captious accusations against rhetoric,
is found in the allegation that orators speak indifferently on either side of a case. From which they
draw the following arguments : no art is self-contradictory, but rhetoric does contradict itself; no art
tries to demolish what itself has built, but this does
happen in the operations of rhetoric; or again :—
rhetoric teaches either what ought to be said or what
ought not to be said ; consequently it is not an art
because it teaches what ought not to be said, or
because, while it teaches what ought to be said, it
also teaches precisely the opposite. Now it is obvious 31
that all such charges are brought against that type
of rhetoric with which neither good men nor virtue
herself will have anything to do ; since if a case be
based on injustice, rhetoric has no place therein and
consequently it can scarcely happen even under the
most exceptional circumstances that an orator, that
is to say, a good man, will speak indifferently on either
side. Still it is in the nature of things conceivable 32
that just causes may lead two wise men to take
different sides, since it is held that wise men may fight
among themselves, provided that they do so at the
bidding of reason. I will therefore reply to their
criticisms in such a way that it will be clear that these
arguments have no force even against those who concede the name of orator to persons of bad character.
For rhetoric is not self-contradictory. The conflict is 33

sibi. Causa enim cum causa, non illa secum ipsa
componitur. Nec, si pugnent inter se, qui idem
didicerunt, idcirco ars, quae utrique tradita est, non
erit ; alioqui nec armorum, quia saepe gladiatores sub
34 eodem magistro eruditi inter se componuntur ; nec
gubernandi, quia navalibus proeliis gubernator est
gubernatori adversus ; nec imperatoria, quia imperator cum imperatore contendit. Item non evertit
opus rhetorice, quod efficit. Neque enim positum
a se argumentum solvit orator sed ne rhetorice
quidem, quia apud eos, qui in persuadendo finem
putant, aut si quis (ut dixi) casus duos inter se bonos
viros composuerit, verisimilia quaerentur ; non autem,
si quid est altero credibilius, id ei contrarium est,
35 quod fuit credibile. Nam ut candido candidius et
dulci dulcius non est adversum, ita nec probabili
probabilius. Neque praecipit unquam non dicenda
nec dicendis contraria, sed quae in quaque causa
36 dicenda sunt. Non semper autem ei, etiamsi frequentissime, tuenda veritas erit ; sed aliquando exigit
communis utilitas, ut etiam falsa defendat.

Ponuntur hae quoque in secundo Ciceronis de
Oratore libro contradictiones : artem earum rerum
esse, quae sciantur ; oratoris omnem actionem opinione,
non scientia contineri, quia et apud eos dicat, qui

---

[1] II. vii. 30.

between case and case, not between rhetoric and
itself. And even if persons who have learned the
same thing fight one another, that does not prove
that what they have learned is not an art. Were
that so, there could be no art of arms, since gladiators
trained under the same master are often matched
against each other; nor would the pilot's art exist, 34
because in sea-fights pilots may be found on different
sides; nor yet could there be an art of generalship,
since general is pitted against general. In the same
way rhetoric does not undo its own work. For the
orator does not refute his own arguments, nor does
rhetoric even do so, because those who regard persuasion as its end, or the two good men whom chance has
matched against one another seek merely for proba-
bilities: and the fact that one thing is more credible
than another, does not involve contradiction between
the two. There is no absolute antagonism between 35
the probable and the more probable, just as there is
none between that which is white and that which is
whiter, or between that which is sweet and that
which is sweeter. Nor does rhetoric ever teach that
which ought not to be said, or that which is contrary
to what ought to be said, but solely what ought to be
said in each individual case. But though the orator 36
will as a rule maintain what is true, this will not
always be the case: there are occasions when the
public interest demands that he should defend what
is untrue.

The following objections are also put forward in
the second book of Cicero's *de Oratore* [1] :—" Art deals
with things that are known. But the pleading of an
orator is based entirely on opinion, not on knowledge,
because he speaks to an audience who do not know,

37 nesciant, et ipse dicat aliquando, quod nesciat. Ex
his alterum, id est, an sciat iudex, de quo dicatur,
nihil ad oratoris artem; alteri respondendum, *Ars
earum rerum est, quae sciuntur.* Rhetorice ars est bene
38 dicendi, bene autem dicere scit orator. Sed nescit,
an verum sit quod dicit. Ne hi quidem, qui ignem
aut aquam aut quattuor elementa aut corpora insecabilia esse, **ex** quibus res omnes initium duxerint,
tradunt, nec qui intervalla siderum et mensuras solis
ac terrae colligunt; disciplinam tamen suam artem
vocant. Quodsi ratio efficit, ut haec non opinari sed
propter vim probationum scire videantur, eadem
39 ratio idem praestare oratori potest. Sed an causa
vera sit, nescit. Ne medicus quidem, an dolorem
capitis habeat, qui hoc se pati dicet; curabit tamen,
tanquam id verum sit, et erit ars medicina. Quid
quod rhetorice non utique propositum habet semper
vera dicendi, sed semper verisimilia? scit autem esse
40 verisimilia quae dicit. Adiiciunt his, qui contra sentiunt, quod saepe, quae in aliis litibus impugnarunt
actores causarum, eadem in aliis defendant. Quod
non artis sed hominis est vitium. Haec sunt praecipua, quae contra rhetoricen dicantur; alia et minora
et tamen **ex** his fontibus derivata.

and sometimes himself states things of which he has
no actual knowledge." Now one of these points, 37
namely whether the judges have knowledge of what
is being said to them, has nothing to do with the art
of oratory. The other statement, that art is concerned
with things that are known, does however require an
answer. Rhetoric is the art of speaking well and the
orator knows how to speak well. "But," it is urged, 38
" he does not know whether what he says is true."
Neither do they, who assert that all things derive
their origin from fire or water or the four elements
or indivisible atoms; nor they who calculate the
distances of the stars or the size of the earth and sun.
And yet all these call the subject which they teach
an art. But if reason makes them seem not merely
to hold opinions but, thanks to the cogency of the
proofs adduced, to have actual knowledge, reason will
do the same service to the orator. " But," they say, 39
" he does not know whether the cause which he has
undertaken is true." But not even a doctor can tell
whether a patient who claims to be suffering from a
headache, really is so suffering : but he will treat him
on the assumption that his statement is true, and
medicine will still be an art. Again what of the fact
that rhetoric does not always aim at telling the truth,
but always at stating what is probable ? The answer
is that the orator knows that what he states is no
more than probable. My opponents further object 40
that advocates often defend in one case what they
have attacked in another. This is not the fault of the
art, but of the man. Such are the main points that
are urged against rhetoric ; there are others as well,
but they are of minor importance and drawn from the
same sources.

41 Confirmatur autem esse artem eam breviter. Nam
sive, ut Cleanthes voluit, ars est potestas via, id est
ordine, efficiens, esse certe viam atque ordinem in
bene dicendo nemo dubitaverit; sive ille ab omnibus
fere probatus finis observatur, artem constare ex per-
ceptionibus consentientibus et coexercitatis ad finem
utilem vitae, iam ostendemus nihil non horum in
42 rhetorice inesse.   Quid quod et inspectione et exercitatione ut artes ceterae constat?   Nec potest ars
non esse, si est ars dialectice, quod fere constat, cum
ab ea specie magis quam genere differat.   Sed nec
illa omittenda sunt, qua in re alius se inartificialiter
alius artificialiter gerat, in ea esse artem, et in eo
quod, qui didicerit, melius faciat quam qui non didi-
43 cerit, esse artem.   Atqui non solum doctus indoctum,
sed etiam doctior doctum in rhetorices opere supera-
bit, neque essent aliter eius tam multa praecepta
tamque magni, qui docerent; idque cum omnibus
confitendum est, tum nobis praecipue, qui rationem
dicendi a bono viro non separamus.

XVIII. Cum sint autem artium aliae positae in
inspectione, id est cognitione et aestimatione rerum,

---

[1] Fr. 790.   [2] *i.e.* since our ideals are so high.

That rhetoric is an art may, however, be proved in 41 a very few words. For if Cleanthes'[1] definition be accepted that "Art is a power reaching its ends by a definite path, that is, by ordered methods," no one can doubt that there is such method and order in good speaking: while if, on the other hand, we accept the definition which meets with almost universal approval that art consists in perceptions agreeing and cooperating to the achievement of some useful end, we shall be able to show that rhetoric lacks none of these characteristics. Again it is scarcely necessary 42 for me to point out that like other arts it is based on examination and practice. And if logic is an art, as is generally agreed, rhetoric must also be an art, since it differs from logic in *species* rather than in *genus*. Nor must I omit to point out that where it is possible in any given subject for one man to act without art and another with art, there must necessarily be an art in connexion with that subject, as there must also be in any subject in which the man who has received instruction is the superior of him who has not. But 43 as regards the practice of rhetoric, it is not merely the case that the trained speaker will get the better of the untrained. For even the trained man will prove inferior to one who has received a better training. If this were not so, there would not be so many rhetorical rules, nor would so many great men have come forward to teach them. The truth of this must be acknowledged by everyone, but more especially by us, since we concede the possession of oratory to none save the good man.[2]

XVIII. Some arts, however, are based on examination, that is to say on the knowledge and proper appreciation of things, as for instance astronomy,

qualis est astrologia, nullum exigens actum sed ipso
rei, cuius studium habet, intellectu contenta, quae
θεωρητικὴ vocatur; aliae in agendo, quarum in hoc
finis est et ipso actu perficitur nihilque post actum
operis relinquit, quae πρακτικὴ dicitur, qualis saltatio

2 est; aliae in effectu, quae operis, quod oculis subiicitur,
consummatione finem accipiunt, quam ποιητικὴν appel-
lamus, qualis est pictura : fere iudicandum est, rhetoricen in actu consistere ; hoc enim, quod est officii sui,

3 perficit. Atque ita ab omnibus dictum est. Mihi
autem videtur etiam ex illis ceteris artibus multum
assumere. Nam et potest aliquando ipsa res per se
inspectione esse contenta. Erit enim rhetorice in
oratore etiam tacente, et si desierit agere vel proposito vel aliquo casu impeditus, non magis desinet
esse orator quam medicus, qui curandi fecerit finem.

4 Nam est aliquis, ac nescio an maximus, etiam ex
secretis studiis fructus ac tum pura voluptas litterarum,
cum ab actu, id est opera, recesserunt et contempla-

5 tione sui fruuntur. Sed effectivae quoque aliquid
simile scriptis orationibus vel historiis, quod ipsum
opus in parte oratoria merito ponimus, consequetur.
Si tamen una ex tribus artibus habenda sit, quia
maxime eius usus actu continetur atque est in eo

which demands no action, but is content to understand
the subject of its study : such arts are called *theoretical*.
Others again are concerned with action : this is their
end, which is realised in action, so that, the action
once performed, nothing more remains to do : these
arts we style *practical*, and dancing will provide us
with an example. Thirdly there are others which 2
consist in producing a certain result and achieve their
purpose in the completion of a visible task : such we
style *productive*, and *painting* may be quoted as an
illustration. In view of these facts we must come to
the conclusion that, in the main, rhetoric is concerned
with action ; for in action it accomplishes that which
it is its duty to do. This view is universally accepted, 3
although in my opinion rhetoric draws largely on the
two other kinds of art. For it may on occasion be
content with the mere examination of a thing.
Rhetoric is still in the orator's possession even though
he be silent, while if he gives up pleading either
designedly or owing to circumstances over which he
has no control, he does not therefore cease to be an
orator, any more than a doctor ceases to be a doctor
when he withdraws from practice. Perhaps the 4
highest of all pleasures is that which we derive from
private study, and the only circumstances under
which the delights of literature are unalloyed are
when it withdraws from action, that is to say from
toil, and can enjoy the pleasure of self-contemplation.
But in the results that the orator obtains by writing 5
speeches or historical narratives, which we may reasonably count as part of the task of oratory, we shall
recognise features resembling those of a productive
art. Still, if rhetoric is to be regarded as one of these
three classes of art, since it is with action that its

frequentissima, dicatur activa vel administrativa, nam
et hoc eiusdem rei nomen est.

XIX. Scio, quaeri etiam, naturane plus ad eloquentiam conferat an doctrina. Quod ad propositum
quidem operis nostri nihil pertinet (neque enim consummatus orator nisi ex utroque fieri potest), plurimum tamen referre arbitror, quam esse in hoc loco
2 quaestionem velimus. Nam si parti utrilibet omnino
alteram detrahas, natura etiam sine doctrina multum
valebit, doctrina nulla esse sine natura poterit. Sin
ex pari coeant, in mediocribus quidem utrisque
maius adhuc credam naturae esse momentum, con-
summatos autem plus doctrinae debere quam naturae
putabo; sicut terrae nullam fertilitatem habenti
nihil optimus agricola profuerit, e terra uberi utile
aliquid etiam nullo colente nascetur, at in solo
fecundo plus cultor quam ipsa per se bonitas soli
3 efficiet. Et, si Praxiteles signum aliquod ex moları
lapide conatus esset exsculpere, Parium marmor
mallem rude; at si illud idem artifex expolisset,
plus in manibus fuisset quam in marmore. Denique
natura materia doctrinae est; haec fingit, illa fingi-
tur. Nihil ars sine materia, materiae etiam sine arte
pretium est, ars summa materia optima melior.

practice is chiefly and most frequently concerned, let us call it an active or administrative art, the two terms being identical.

XIX. I quite realise that there is a further question as to whether eloquence derives most from nature or from education. This question really lies outside the scope of our inquiry, since the ideal orator must necessarily be the result of a blend of both. But I do regard it as of great importance that we should decide how far there is any real question on this point. For if we make an absolute 2 divorce between the two, nature will still be able to accomplish much without the aid of education, while the latter is valueless without the aid of nature. If, on the other hand, they are blended in equal proportions, I think we shall find that the average orator owes most to nature, while the perfect orator owes more to education. We may take a parallel from agriculture. A thoroughly barren soil will not be improved even by the best cultivation, while good land will yield some useful produce without any cultivation; but in the case of really rich land cultivation will do more for it than its own natural fertility. Had Praxiteles attempted to carve 3 a statue out of a millstone, I should have preferred a rough block of Parian marble to any such statue. On the other hand, if the same artist had produced a finished statue from such a block of Parian marble, its artistic value would owe more to his skill than to the material. To conclude, nature is the raw material for education: the one forms, the other is formed. Without material art can do nothing, material without art does possess a certain value, while the perfection of art is better than the best material.

349

XX. Illa quaestio est maior, ex mediis artibus,
quae neque laudari per se nec vituperari possunt, sed
utiles aut secus secundum mores utentium fiunt,
habenda sit rhetorice, an sit, ut compluribus etiam
2 philosophorum placet, virtus. Equidem illud, quod
in studiis dicendi plerique exercuerunt et exercent,
aut nullam artem, quae ἀτεχνία nominatur, puto,
(multos enim video sine ratione, sine litteris, qua vel
impudentia vel fames duxit, ruentes) aut malam
quasi artem, quam κακοτεχνίαν dicimus. Nam et
fuisse multos et esse nonnullos existimo, qui facultatem dicendi ad hominum perniciem converterint.
3 Ματαιοτεχνία quoque est quaedam, id est supervacua
artis imitatio, quae nihil sane neque boni neque mali
habeat, sed vanum laborem, qualis illius fuit, qui
grana ciceris ex spatio distanti missa in acum continuo et sine frustratione inserebat, quem cum spec-
tasset Alexander, donasse dicitur eiusdem leguminis
modio, quod quidem praemium fuit illo opere dig-
4 nissimum. His ego comparandos existimo, qui in
declamationibus, quas esse veritati dissimillimas
volunt, aetatem multo studio ac labore consumunt.
Verum haec, quam instituere conamur et cuius
imaginem animo concepimus, quae bono viro con-
5 venit quaeque est vere rhetorice, virtus erit. Quod

XX. More important is the question whether rhetoric is to be regarded as one of the indifferent arts,
which in themselves deserve neither praise nor blame,
but are useful or the reverse according to the character of the artist; or whether it should, as not a few
even among philosophers hold, be considered as a
virtue. For my own part I regard the practice of rhe- 2
toric which so many have adopted in the past and still
follow to-day, as either no art at all, or, as the Greeks
call it, ἀτεχνία (for I see numbers of speakers without the least pretension to method or literary training rushing headlong in the direction in which
hunger or their natural shamelessness calls them);
or else it is a bad art such as is styled κακοτεχνία.
For there have, I think, been many persons and
there are still some who have devoted their powers
of speaking to the destruction of their fellow-men.
There is also an unprofitable imitation of art, a kind 3
of ματαιοτεχνία, which is neither good nor bad, but
merely involves a useless expenditure of labour, reminding one of the man who shot a continuous
stream of vetch-seeds from a distance through the
eye of a needle, without ever missing his aim, and
was rewarded by Alexander, who was a witness of
the display, with the present of a bushel of vetch-
seeds, a most appropriate reward. It is to such men 4
that I would compare those who spend their whole
time at the expense of much study and energy in
composing declamations, which they aim at making
as unreal as possible. The rhetoric on the other
hand, which I am endeavouring to establish and the
ideal of which I have in my mind's eye, that rhetoric
which befits a good man and is in a word the only
true rhetoric, will be a virtue. Philosophers arrive 5

philosophi quidem multis et acutis conclusionibus
colligunt, mihi vero etiam planiore hac proprieque
nostra probatione videtur esse perspicuum.

Ab illis haec dicuntur. Si consonare sibi in faciendis ac non faciendis virtus est, quae pars eius
prudentia vocatur, eadem in dicendis ac non dicendis
6 erit. Et si virtutes sunt, ad quas nobis etiam ante
quam doceremur initia quaedam ac semina sunt
concessa natura, ut ad iustitiam, cuius rusticis quoque ac barbaris apparet aliqua imago, nos certe sic
esse ab initio formatos, ut possemus orare pro nobis,
etiamsi non perfecte, tamen ut inessent quaedam (ut
7 dixi) semina eius facultatis, manifestum est. Non
eadem autem natura est iis artibus, quae a virtute
sunt remotae. Itaque cum duo sint genera orationis,
altera perpetua, quae rhetorice dicitur, altera concisa, quae dialectice (quas quidem Zeno adeo con-
iunxit, ut hanc compressae in pugnum manus, illam
explicatae diceret similem), etiam disputatrix virtus
erit. Adeo de hac, quae speciosior atque apertior
tanto est, nihil dubitabitur.   •
8 Sed plenius hoc idem atque apertius intueri ex
ipsis operibus volo. Nam quid orator in laudando
faciet nisi honestorum et turpium peritus? aut in

at this conclusion by a long chain of ingenious arguments; but it appears to me to be perfectly clear from the simpler proof of my own invention which I will now proceed to set forth.

The philosophers state the case as follows. If self-consistency as to what should and should not be done is an element of virtue (and it is to this quality that we give the name of prudence), the same quality will be revealed as regards what should be said and what should not be said, and if there are **6** virtues, of which nature has given us some rudimentary sparks, even before we were taught anything about them, as for instance justice, of which there are some traces even among peasants and barbarians, it is clear that man has been so formed from the beginning as to be able to plead on his own behalf, not, it is true, with perfection, but yet sufficiently to show that there are certain sparks of eloquence implanted in us by nature. The same nature, how- **7** ever, is not to be found in those arts which have no connexion with virtue. Consequently, since there are two kinds of speech, the continuous which is called rhetoric, and the concise which is called dialectic (the relation between which was regarded by Zeno as being so intimate that he compared the latter to the closed fist, the former to the open hand), even the art of disputation will be a virtue. Consequently there can be no doubt about oratory whose nature is so much fairer and franker.

I should like, however, to consider the point **8** more fully and explicitly by appealing to the actual work of oratory. For how will the orator succeed in panegyric unless he can distinguish between what is honourable and the reverse? How

suadendo nisi utilitate perspecta? aut in iudiciis, si iustitiae sit ignarus? Quid? non fortitudinem postulat res eadem, cum saepe contra turbulentas populi minas, saepe cum periculosa potentium offensa, nonnunquam, ut iudicio Miloniano, inter circumfusa militum arma dicendum sit; ut, si virtus non est, ne 9 perfecta quidem esse possit oratio. Quodsi ea in quoque animalium est virtus, qua praestat cetera vel pleraque, ut in leone impetus, in equo velocitas, hominem porro ratione atque oratione excellere ceteris certum est: cur non tam in eloquentia quam in ratione virtutem eius esse credamus, recteque hoc apud Ciceronem dixerit Crassus: *Est enim eloquentia una quaedam de summis virtutibus,* et ipse Cicero sua persona cum ad Brutum in epistulis, tum aliis etiam 10 locis virtutem eam appellet? At prooemium aliquando ac narrationem dicet malus homo et argumenta, sic ut nihil sit in iis requirendum. Nam et latro pugnabit acriter, virtus tamen erit fortitudo; et tormenta sine gemitu feret malus servus, tolerantia tamen doloris laude sua non carebit. Multa fiunt eadem sed aliter. Sufficiant igitur haec, quia de utilitate supra tractavimus.

---

[1] *de Or.* III. xiv. 55.   [2] Lost.

can he urge a policy, unless he has a clear perception of what is expedient? How can he plead in the law-courts, if he is ignorant of the nature of justice? Again, does not oratory call for courage, since it is often directed against the threats of popular turbulence and frequently runs into peril through incurring the hatred of the great, while sometimes, as for instance in the trial of Milo, the orator may have to speak in the midst of a crowd of armed soldiers? Consequently, if oratory be not a virtue, perfection is beyond its grasp. If, on the 9 other hand, each living thing has its own peculiar virtue, in which it excels the rest or, at any rate, the majority (I may instance the courage of the lion and the swiftness of the horse), it may be regarded as certain that the qualities in which man excels the rest are, above all, reason and powers of speech. Why, therefore, should we not consider that the special virtue of man lies just as much in eloquence as in reason? It will be with justice then that Cicero[1] makes Crassus say that "eloquence is one of the highest virtues," and that Cicero himself calls it a virtue in his letters to Brutus[2] and in other passages. "But," it may be urged, "a bad 10 man will at times produce an *exordium* or a *statement of facts,* and will argue a case in a manner that leaves nothing to be desired." No doubt; even a robber may fight bravely without courage ceasing to be a virtue; even a wicked slave may bear torture without a groan, and we may still continue to regard endurance of pain as worthy of praise. We can point to many acts which are identical with those of virtue, but spring from other sources. However, what I have said here must suffice, as I have already dealt with the question of the usefulness of oratory.

XXI. Materiam rhetorices quidam dixerunt esse orationem, qua in sententia ponitur apud Platonem Gorgias.[1] Quae si ita accipitur, ut sermo quacunque de re compositus dicatur oratio, non materia sed opus est, ut statuarii statua; nam et oratio efficitur arte sicut statua. Sin hac appellatione verba ipsa significari putamus, nihil haec sine rerum substantia 2 faciunt. Quidam argumenta persuasibilia; quae et ipsa in parte sunt operis et arte fiunt et materia egent. Quidam civiles quaestiones; quorum opinio non qualitate sed modo erravit, est enim haec materia 3 rhetorices sed non sola. Quidam, quia virtus sit rhetorice, materiam eius totam vitam vocant. Alii, quia non omnium virtutum materia sit tota vita, sed pleraeque earum versentur in partibus, sicut iustitia, fortitudo, continentia propriis officiis et suo fine intelliguntur, rhetoricen quoque dicunt in una aliqua parte ponendam, eique locum in ethice negotialem adsignant id est πραγματικόν.

4 Ego (neque id sine auctoribus) materiam esse rhetorices iudico omnes res quaecunque ei ad dicendum subiectae erunt. Nam Socrates apud Platonem dicere Gorgiae videtur, non in verbis esse materiam

---

[1] *Gorg.* 449 E.   [2] *Gorg.* 449 E.

XXI. As to the material of oratory, some have
asserted that it is speech, as for instance Gorgias[1] in
the dialogue of Plato. If this view be accepted in
the sense that the word "speech" is used of a discourse composed on any subject, then it is not the
material, but the work, just as a statue is the work
of the sculptor. For speeches like statues require
art for their production. If on the other hand
we interpret "speech" as indicating the words
themselves, they can do nothing unless they are
related to facts. Some again hold that the material
consists of persuasive arguments. But they form
part of the work, are produced by art and require
material themselves. Some say that political 2
questions provide the material. The mistake made
by these lies not in the quality of their opinion
but in its limitation. For political questions are
material for eloquence but not the only material.
Some, on the ground that rhetoric is a virtue, make the 3
material with which it deals to be the whole of life.
Others, on the ground that life regarded as a whole
does not provide material for every virtue, since
most of them are concerned only with departments
of life (justice, courage and self-control each having
their own duties and their own end), would consequently restrict oratory to one particular department
of life and place it in the practical or pragmatic
department of ethics, that is to say the department
of morals which deals with the business of life.

For my own part, and I have authority to support 4
me, I hold that the material of rhetoric is composed of
everything that may be placed before it as a subject
for speech. Plato, if I read him aright, makes
Socrates[2] say to Gorgias that its material is to be

sed in rebus.   Et in Phaedro palam, non in iudiciis
modo et contionibus, sed in rebus etiam privatis ac
domesticis rhetoricen esse demonstrat.   Quo mani-
5 festum est hanc opinionem ipsius Platonis fuisse.   Et
Cicero quodam loco materiam rhetorices vocat res,
quae subiectae sint ei, sed certas demum putat esse
subiectas.   Alio vero de omnibus rebus oratori
dicendum arbitratur his quidem verbis : *Quanquam
vis oratoris professioque ipsa bene dicendi hoc suscipere
ac polliceri videtur, ut omni de re, quaecunque sit pro-*
6 *posita, ornate ab eo copioseque dicatur.*   Atque adhuc
alibi : *Vero enim oratori, quae sunt in hominum vita,
quandoquidem in ea versatur orator atque ea est ei subiecta materies, omnia quaesita, audita, lecta, disputata,
tractata, agitata esse debent.*

7   Hanc autem, quam nos materiam vocamus, id est
res subiectas, quidam modo infinitam modo non
propriam rhetorices esse dixerunt, eamque artem
circumcurrentem vocaverunt, quod in omni materia
8 diceret, cum quibus mihi minima pugna est.   Nam
de omni materia dicere eam fatentur ; propriam
habere materiam, quia multiplicem habeat, negant.
Sed neque infinita est, etiamsi est multiplex ; et

---

[1] *Phaedr.* 261 A.   [2] *de Inv.* i. 5.
[3] *de Or.* I. vi. 21.   "I will not demand omniscience from
an orator, although " etc.   [4] *ib.* III. xiv. 54.

found in things not words; while in the *Phaedrus*[1]
he clearly proves that rhetoric is concerned not
merely with law-courts and public assemblies, but with
private and domestic affairs as well: from which it is
obvious that this was the view of Plato himself. Cicero 5
also in a passage[2] of one of his works, states that
the material of rhetoric is composed of the things
which are brought before it, but makes certain restrictions as to the nature of these things. In
another passage,[3] however, he expresses his opinion
that the orator has to speak about all kinds of things;
I will quote his actual words: "although the very
meaning of the name of orator and the fact that
he professes to speak well seem to imply a promise
and undertaking that the orator will speak with
elegance and fullness on any subject that may be
put before him." And in another passage[4] he says, 6
"It is the duty of the true orator to seek out, hear,
read, discuss, handle and ponder everything that be-
falls in the life of man, since it is with this that the
orator is concerned and this that forms the material
with which he has to deal."

But this material, as we call it, that is to say 7
the things brought before it, has been criticised by
some, at times on the ground that it is limitless, and
sometimes on the ground that it is not peculiar to
oratory, which they have therefore dubbed a *dis-
cursive* art, because all is grist that comes to its mill.
I have no serious quarrel with these critics, for they 8
acknowledge that rhetoric is concerned with every
kind of material, though they deny that it has any
peculiar material just because of that material's multiplicity. But in spite of this multiplicity, rhetoric
is not unlimited in scope, and there are other minor

aliae quoque artes minores habent multiplicem
materiam, velut architectonice, namque ea in omnibus, quae sunt aedificio utilia, versatur, et caelatura,

9 quae auro, argento, aere, ferro opera efficit. Nam
sculptura etiam lignum, ebur, marmor, vitrum,
gemmas praeter ea quae supra dixi complectitur.

10 Neque protinus non est materia rhetorices, si in
eadem versatur et alius. Nam si quaeram, quae sit
materia statuarii, dicetur aes; si quaeram quae sit
excusoris, id est fabricae eius quam Graeci χαλκευ-
τικὴν vocant, similiter aes esse respondeant. Atqui

11 plurimum statuis differunt vasa. Nec medicina ideo
non erit ars, quia unctio et exercitatio cum palae-
strica, ciborum vero qualitas etiam cum cocorum ei

12 sit arte communis. Quod vero de bono, utili, iusto
disserere philosophiae officium esse dicunt, non
obstat. Nam cum philosophum dicunt, hoc accipi
volunt virum bonum. Quare igitur oratorem, quem
a bono viro non separo, in eadem materia versari

13 mirer? cum praesertim primo libro iam ostenderim,[1]
philosophos omissam hanc ab oratoribus partem
occupasse, quae rhetorices propria semper fuisset,
ut illi potius in nostra materia versentur. Denique
cum sit dialectices materia de rebus subiectis dis-
putare, sit autem dialectice oratio concisa, cur non
eadem perpetuae quoque materia videatur?

---

[1] Pref. § 10 *sqq.*

arts whose material is characterised by the same multiplicity: such for instance is architecture, which deals with everything that is useful for the purpose of building: such too is the engraver's art which works on gold, silver, bronze, iron. As for sculpture, 9 its activity extends to wood, ivory, marble, glass and precious stones in addition to the materials already mentioned. And things which form the material for 10 other artists, do not for that reason cease forthwith to be material for rhetoric. For if I ask what is the material of the sculptor, I shall be told bronze; and if I ask what is the material of the maker of vessels (I refer to the craft styled χαλκευτική by the Greeks), the answer will again be bronze: and yet there is all the difference in the world between vessels and statues. Similarly medicine will not cease to be an 11 art, because, like the art of the gymnast, it prescribes rubbing with oil and exercise, or because it deals with diet like the art of cookery. Again, the 12 objection that to discourse of what is good, expedient or just is the duty of philosophy presents no difficulty. For when such critics speak of a philosopher, they mean a good man. Why then should I feel surprised to find that the orator whom I identify with the good man deals with the same material? There 13 is all the less reason, since I have already shown in the first book [1] that philosophers only usurped this department of knowledge after it had been abandoned by the orators: it was always the peculiar property of rhetoric and the philosophers are really trespassers. Finally, since the discussion of whatever is brought before it is the task of dialectic, which is really a concise form of oratory, why should not this task be regarded as also being the appropriate material for continuous oratory?

14 Solet a quibusdam et illud opponi: *Omnium igitur artium peritus erit orator, si de omnibus ei dicendum est.* Possem hic Ciceronis respondere verbis, apud quem hoc invenio: *Mea quidem sententia nemo esse poterit omni laude cumulatus orator, nisi erit omnium rerum magnarum atque artium scientiam consecutus;* sed mihi satis est eius esse oratorem rei de qua dicet non

15 inscium. Neque enim omnes causas novit, et debet posse de omnibus dicere. De quibus ergo dicet? De quibus didicit. Similiter de artibus quoque, de quibus dicendum erit, interim discet; et de quibus didicerit dicet.

16 Quid ergo? non faber de fabrica melius aut de musice musicus? Si nesciat orator, quid sit, de quo quaeratur, plane melius. Nam et litigator rusticus illitteratusque de causa sua melius, quam orator, qui nesciet quid in lite sit; sed accepta a musico, a fabro, sicut a litigatore melius orator

17 quam ipse qui docuerit. Verum et faber, cum de fabrica, et musicus, cum de musica, si quid confirmationem desideraverit, dicet. Non quidem erit orator, sed faciet illud quasi orator, sicut cum vulnus impe-

---

[1] *de Or.* I. vi. 20.

There is a further objection made by certain 14
critics, who say "Well then, if an orator has to speak on
every subject, he must be the master of all the arts."
I might answer this criticism in the words of Cicero,[1]
in whom I find the following passage :—"In my
opinion no one can be an absolutely perfect orator
unless he has acquired a knowledge of all important
subjects and arts." I however regard it as sufficient that an orator should not be actually ignorant
of the subject on which he has to speak. For he 15
cannot have a knowledge of all causes, and yet he
should be able to speak on all. On what then
will he speak? On those which he has studied.
Similarly as regards the arts, he will study those
concerning which he has to speak, as occasion may
demand, and will speak on those which he has
studied.

What then?—I am asked—will not a builder 16
speak better on the subject of building and a musician on music? Certainly, if the orator does not
know what is the question at issue. Even an illiterate peasant who is a party to a suit will speak
better on behalf of his case than an orator who does
not know what the subject in dispute may be. But
on the other hand if the orator receive instruction
from the builder or the musician, he will put forward what he has thus learned better than either,
just as he will plead a case better than his client,
once he has been instructed in it. The builder and 17
the musician will, however, speak on the subject of
their respective arts, if there should be any technical
point which requires to be established. Neither will
be an orator, but he will perform his task like an
orator, just as when an untrained person binds up a

ritus deligabit, non erit medicus, sed faciet ut
18 medicus. An huiusmodi res neque in laudem neque
in deliberationem neque in iudicium veniunt? Ergo
cum de faciendo portu Ostiensi deliberatum est, non
debuit sententiam dicere orator? atqui opus erat
19 ratione architectorum. Livores et tumores in corpore cruditatis an veneni signa sint, non tractat
orator? at est id ex ratione medicinae. Circa mensuras et numeros non versabitur? dicamus has
geometriae esse partes. Equidem omnia fere credo
posse casu aliquo venire in officium oratoris; quod si
non accidet, non erunt ei subiecta.

20   Ita sic quoque recte diximus, materiam rhetorices
esse omnes res ad dicendum ei subiectas; quod
quidem probat etiam sermo communis. Nam cum
aliquid, de quo dicamus, accepimus, positam nobis
esse materiam frequenter etiam praefatione testa-
21 mur. Gorgias quidem adeo rhetori de omnibus rebus
putavit esse dicendum, ut se in auditoriis interrogari
pateretur, qua quisque de re vellet. Hermagoras
quoque, dicendo materiam esse in causa et in quae-
22 stionibus, omnes res subiectas erat complexus. Sed
quaestiones si negat ad rhetoricen pertinere, dissentit
a nobis; si autem ad rhetoricen pertinent, ab hoc

---

[1] See III. v. 12-16.

wound, he will not be a physician, but he will be
acting as one. Is it suggested that such topics 18
never crop up in panegyric, deliberative or forensic
oratory? When the question of the construction of
a port at Ostia came up for discussion, had not the
orator to state his views? And yet it was a subject
requiring the technical knowledge of the architect.
Does not the orator discuss the question whether 19
livid spots and swellings on the body are sympto-
matic of ill-health or poison? And yet that is a
question for the qualified physician. Will he not
deal with measurements and figures? And yet we
must admit that they form part of mathematics. For
my part I hold that practically all subjects are
under certain circumstances liable to come up for
treatment by the orator. If the circumstances do
not occur, the subjects will not concern him.

We were therefore right in asserting that the 20
material of rhetoric is composed of everything that
comes before the orator for treatment, an assertion
which is confirmed by the practice of everyday
speech. For when we have been given a subject
on which to speak, we often preface our remarks by
calling attention to the fact that the matter has
been laid before us. Gorgias indeed felt so strongly 21
that it was the orator's duty to speak on every subject, that he used to allow those who attended his
lectures to ask him questions on any subject they
pleased. Hermagoras also asserted that the material
of oratory lay in the cause and the questions it
involved, thereby including every subject that can
be brought before it. If he denies that general 22
questions[1] are the concern of oratory, he disagrees
with me: but if they do concern rhetoric, that

quoque adiuvamur. Nihil est enim, quod non in
23 causam aut quaestionem cadat. Aristoteles tres
faciendo partes orationis, iudicialem, deliberativam,
demonstrativam, paene et ipse oratori subiecit omnia;
nihil enim non in haec cadit.

24 Quaesitum a paucissimis et de instrumento est.
Instrumentum voco, sine quo formari materia in id
quod velimus effici opus non possit. Verum hoc ego
non artem credo egere sed artificem. Neque enim
scientia desiderat instrumentum, quae potest esse
consummata, etiamsi nihil faciat, sed ille artifex,
ut caelator caelum et pictor penicilla. Itaque
haec in eum locum, quo de oratore dicturi sumus,
differamus.

supports my contention. For there is nothing which may not crop up in a cause or appear as a question for discussion. Aristotle [1] himself also by his tripartite 23 division of oratory, into forensic, deliberative and demonstrative, practically brought everything into the orator's domain, since there is nothing that may not come up for treatment by one of these three kinds of rhetoric.

A very few critics have raised the question as to 24 what may be the *instrument* of oratory. My definition of an instrument is *that without which the material cannot be brought into the shape necessary for the effecting of our object.* But it is not the art which requires an instrument, but the artist. Knowledge needs no instruments, for it may be complete although it produces nothing, but the artist must have them. The engraver cannot work without his chisel nor the painter without his brush. I shall therefore defer this question until I come to treat of the orator as distinct from his art.

[1] *Rhet.* I. iii. 3.

BOOK III

LIBER III

I. Quoniam in libro secundo quaesitum est, quid esset rhetorice et quis finis eius, artem quoque esse eam et utilem et virtutem, ut vires nostrae tulerunt, ostendimus, materiamque ei res omnes, de quibus dicere oporteret, subiecimus: iam hinc, unde coeperit, quibus constet, quo quaeque in ea modo invenienda atque tractanda sint, exsequar; intra quem modum plerique scriptores artium constiterunt, adeo ut Apollodorus contentus solis iudicialibus 2 fuerit. Nec sum ignarus, hoc a me praecipue, quod hic liber inchoat, opus studiosos eius desiderasse, ut inquisitione opinionum, quae diversissimae fuerunt, longe difficillimum, ita nescio an minimae legentibus futurum voluptati, quippe quod prope nudam prae-3 ceptorum traditionem desideret. In ceteris enim admiscere temptavimus aliquid nitoris, non iactandi ingenii gratia (namque in id eligi materia poterat uberior), sed ut hoc ipso adliceremus magis iuventutem ad cognitionem eorum, quae necessaria studiis arbitrabamur, si ducti iucunditate aliqua lectionis

BOOK III

1. In the second book the subject of inquiry was the nature and the end of rhetoric, and I proved to the best of my ability that it was an art, that it was useful, that it was a virtue and that its material was all and every subject that might come up for treatment. I shall now discuss its origin, its component parts, and the method to be adopted in handling and forming our conception of each. For most authors of text-books have stopped short of this, indeed Apollodorus confines himself solely to forensic oratory. I know that those who asked me to write 2 this work were specially interested in that portion on which I am now entering, and which, owing to the necessity of examining a great diversity of opinions, at once forms by far the most difficult section of this work, and also, I fear, may be the least attractive to my readers, since it necessitates a dry exposition of rules. In other portions of this work I have attempted to 3 introduce a certain amount of ornateness, not, I may say, to advertise my style (if I had wished to do that, I could have chosen a more fertile theme), but in order that I might thus do something to lure our young men to make themselves acquainted with those principles which I regarded as necessary to the study of rhetoric : for I hoped that by giving them something which was not unpleasant to read I might induce a greater readiness to learn those rules which I feared

libentius discerent ea, quorum ne ieiuna atque arida
traditio averteret animos et aures praesertim tam
4 delicatas raderet verebamur. Qua ratione se Lucretius dicit praecepta philosophiae carmine esse complexum; namque hac, ut est notum, similitudine
utitur:

> *Ac veluti pueris absinthia taetra medentes*
> *Cum dare conantur, prius oras pocula circum*
> *Aspirant* [1] *mellis dulci flavoque liquore,*

5 et quae sequuntur. Sed nos veremur, ne parum hic
liber mellis et absinthii multum habere videatur,
sitque salubrior studiis quam dulcior. Quin etiam
hoc timeo, ne ex eo minorem gratiam ineat, quod
pleraque non inventa per me sed ab aliis tradita
continebit, habeat etiam quosdam, qui contra sentiant
et adversentur, propterea quod plurimi auctores,
quamvis eodem tenderent, diversas tamen vias
muniverunt atque in suam quisque induxit sequentes.
6 Illi autem probant qualecunque ingressi sunt iter,
nec facile inculcatas pueris persuasiones mutaveris,
7 quia nemo non didicisse mavult quam discere. Est
autem, ut procedente libro patebit, infinita dissensio
auctorum, primo ad ea, quae rudia atque imperfecta
adhuc erant, adiicientibus quod invenissent scripto-

---

[1] inspirant, *A*: adspirant, *B*: contingunt, *MSS. of
Lucretius.*

---

[1] iv. 11. See also i. 936.

might, by the dryness and aridity which must necessarily characterise their exposition, revolt their minds
and offend their ears which are nowadays grown
somewhat over-sensitive. Lucretius has the same 4
object in mind when he states that he has set forth
his philosophical system in verse; for you will remember the well-known simile which he uses [1] :—

> " And as physicians when they seek to give
> A draught of bitter wormwood to a child,
> First smear along the edge that rims the cup
> The liquid sweets of honey, golden-hued,"

and the rest. But I fear that this book will have 5
too little honey and too much wormwood, and that
though the student may find it a healthy draught,
it will be far from agreeable. I am also haunted by
the further fear that it will be all the less attractive
from the fact that most of the precepts which it contains are not original, but derived from others, and
because it is likely to rouse the opposition of certain
persons who do not share my views. For there are
a large number of writers, who though they are all
moving toward the same goal, have constructed
different roads to it and each drawn their followers
into their own. The latter, however, approve of 6
the path on which they have been launched whatever its nature, and it is difficult to change the con-
victions implanted in boyhood, for the excellent reason
that everybody prefers to have learned rather than
to be in process of learning. But, as will appear in 7
the course of this book, there is an infinite diversity
of opinions among writers on this subject, since some
have added their own discoveries to those portions
of the art which were still shapeless and unformed,

ribus, mox, ut aliquid sui viderentur adferre, etiam
recta mutantibus.

8 Nam primus post eos, quos poetae tradiderunt,
movisse aliqua circa rhetoricen Empedocles dicitur.
Artium autem scriptores antiquissimi Corax et Tisias
Siculi, quos insecutus est vir eiusdem insulae Gorgias
9 Leontinus, Empedoclis, ut traditur, discipulus. Is
beneficio longissimae aetatis (nam centum et novem
vixit annos) cum multis simul floruit, ideoque et
illorum, de quibus supra dixi, fuit aemulus et ultra
10 Socraten usque duravit. Thrasymachus Chalce-
donius cum hoc et Prodicus Cius et Abderites Protagoras, a quo decem milibus denariorum didicisse
artem, quam edidit, Euathlus dicitur, et Hippias
Eleus et, quem Palameden Plato appellat, Alcidamas
11 Elaïtes. Antiphon quoque et orationem primus
omnium scripsit et nihilo minus et artem ipse composuit et pro se dixisse optime est creditus, etiam
Polycrates, a quo scriptam in Socraten diximus orationem, et Theodorus Byzantius ex iis et ipse, quos
12 Plato appellat λογοδαιδάλους. Horum primi communes locos tractasse dicuntur Protagoras, Gorgias,
adfectus Prodicus et Hippias et idem Protagoras et
Thrasymachus. Cicero in Bruto negat ante Periclea
scriptum quidquam, quod ornatum oratorium habeat;
eius aliqua ferri. Equidem non reperio quidquam

---

¹ About £312. ² *Phaedr.* 261 D.
³ *Phaedr.* 266 E. ⁴ vii. 27.

and subsequently have altered even what was perfectly sound in order to establish a claim to
originality.

The first writer after those recorded by the poets 8
who is said to have taken any steps in the direction
of rhetoric is Empedocles. But the earliest writers
of text-books are the Sicilians, Corax and Tisias,
who were followed by another from the same island,
namely Gorgias of Leontini, whom tradition asserts
to have been the pupil of Empedocles. He, thanks to 9
his length of days, for he lived to a hundred and nine,
flourished as the contemporary of many rhetoricians,
was consequently the rival of those whom I have
just mentioned, and lived on to survive Socrates.
In the same period flourished Thrasymachus of 10
Chalcedon, Prodicus of Ceos, Protagoras of Abdera,
for whose instructions, which he afterwards published
in a text-book, Euathlus is said to have paid 10,000 [1]
denarii, Hippias of Elis and Alcidamas of Elaea whom
Plato [2] calls Palamedes. There was Antiphon also, 11
who was the first to write speeches and who also wrote
a text-book and is said to have spoken most elo-
quently in his own defence ; Polycrates, who, as I
have already said, wrote a speech against Socrates,
and Theodorus of Byzantium, who was one of those
called "word-artificers" by Plato. [3] Of these Pro- 12
tagoras and Gorgias are said to have been the
first to treat commonplaces, Prodicus, Hippias,
Protagoras and Thrasymachus the first to handle
emotional themes. Cicero in the *Brutus* [4] states
that nothing in the ornate rhetorical style was
ever committed to writing before Pericles, and that
certain of his speeches are still extant. For my
part I have been unable to discover anything in

tanta eloquentiae fama dignum; ideoque minus
miror esse, qui nihil ab eo scriptum putent, haec
13 autem, quae feruntur, ab aliis esse composita.   His
successere multi, sed clarissimus Gorgiae auditorum
Isocrates, quanquam de praeceptore eius inter auctores non convenit; nos autem Aristoteli credimus.
14 Hinc velut diversae secari coeperunt viae.   Nam et
Isocratis praestantissimi discipuli fuerunt in omni
studiorum genere, eoque iam seniore (octavum enim
et nonagesimum implevit annum) postmeridianis
scholis Aristoteles praecipere artem oratoriam coepit,
noto quidem illo (ut traditur) versu ex Philocteta frequenter usus: *Turpe esse tacere et Isocraten pati dicere.*
Ars est utriusque, sed pluribus eam libris Aristoteles
complexus est.   Eodem tempore Theodectes fuit, de
15 cuius opere supra dictum est.   Theophrastus quoque
Aristotelis discipulus de rhetorice diligenter scripsit,
atque hinc vel studiosius philosophi quam rhetores
praecipueque Stoicorum ac Peripateticorum principes.
16 Fecit deinde velut propriam Hermagoras viam, quam
plurimi sunt secuti; cui maxime par atque aemulus

---

[1] *cp.* XII, ii. 22: x. 49, where Quintilian asserts that all
the writings of Pericles have been lost.

[2] Aristotle gave his esoteric lectures in the morning,
reserving the afternoon for those of more general interest:
see Aul. Gell. XX. v.

the least worthy of his great reputation for eloquence,[1] and am consequently the less surprised that there should be some who hold that he never committed anything to writing, and that the writings circulating under his name are the works of others. These 13 rhetoricians had many successors, but the most famous of Gorgias' pupils was Isocrates, although our authorities are not agreed as to who was his teacher: I however accept the statement of Aristotle on the subject. From this point the roads begin to 14 part. The pupils of Isocrates were eminent in every branch of study, and when he was already advanced in years (and he lived to the age of ninety-eight), Aristotle began to teach the art of rhetoric in his afternoon lectures,[2] in which he frequently quoted the well-known line from the *Philoctetes*[3] in the form

> " Isocrates still speaks. 'Twere shame should I
> Sit silent."

Both Aristotle and Isocrates left text-books on rhetoric, but that by Aristotle is the larger and contains more books. Theodectes, whose work I mentioned above, also lived about the same period ; while 15 Theophrastus, the pupil of Aristotle, produced some careful work on rhetoric. After him we may note that the philosophers, more especially the leaders of the Stoic and Peripatetic schools, surpassed even the rhetoricians in the zeal which they devoted to the subject. Hermagoras next carved out a path of 16 his own, which numbers have followed: of his rivals Athenaeus seems to have approached him most

---

[3] Probably the *Philoctetes* of Euripides. The original line was αἰσχρὸν σιωπᾶν, βαρβάρους δ' ἐᾶν λέγειν, which Aristotle travestied by substituting Ἰσοκράτην for βαρβάρους.

377

videtur Athenaeus fuisse. Multa post Apollonius
Molon, multa Areus, multa Caecilius et Halicarnas-
17 seus Dionysius. Praecipue tamen in se converterunt
studia Apollodorus Pergamenus, qui praeceptor Apol-
loniae Caesaris Augusti fuit, et Theodorus Gadareus,
qui se dici maluit Rhodium, quem studiose audisse,
cum in eam insulam secessisset, dicitur Tiberius
18 Caesar. Hi diversas opiniones tradiderunt, appella-
tique inde Apollodorei ac Theodorei ad morem certas
in philosophia sectas sequendi. Sed Apollodori
praecepta magis ex discipulis cognoscas, quorum
diligentissimus in tradendo fuit Latine Gaius Valgius,
Graece Atticus. Nam ipsius sola videtur Ars edita
ad Matium, quia ceteras missa ad Domitium epis-
tula non agnoscit. Plura scripsit Theodorus, cuius
auditorem Hermagoran sunt qui viderint.

19 Romanorum primus (quantum ego quidem sciam)
condidit aliqua in hanc materiam M. Cato ille censorius, post M. Antonius inchoavit; nam hoc solum
opus eius atque id ipsum imperfectum manet.
Secuti minus celebres; quorum memoriam, si quo
20 loco res poscet, non omittam. Praecipuum vero
lumen sicut eloquentiae ita praeceptis quoque eius
dedit, unicum apud nos specimen orandi docendique
oratorias artes, M. Tullius; post quem tacere mode-

---

[1] The younger Hermagoras, a rhetorician of the Augustan
age.

nearly. Later still much work was done by Apollonius Molon, Areus, Caecilius and Dionysius of Halicarnassus. But the rhetoricians who attracted 17 the most enthusiastic following were Apollodorus of Pergamus, who was the instructor of Augustus Caesar at Apollonia, and Theodorus of Gadara, who preferred to be called Theodorus of Rhodes: it is said that Tiberius Caesar during his retirement in that island was a constant attendant at his lectures. These 18 rhetoricians taught different systems, and two schools have arisen known as the Apollodoreans and the Theodoreans, these names being modelled on the fashion of nomenclature in vogue with certain schools of philosophy. The doctrines of Apollodorus are best learned from his pupils, among whom Caius Valgius was the best interpreter of his master's views in Latin, Atticus in Greek. The only text-book by Apollodorus himself seems to be that addressed to Matius, as his letter to Domitius does not acknowledge the other works attributed to him. The writings of Theodorus were more numerous, and there are some still living who have seen his pupil Hermagoras.

The first Roman to handle the subject was, to the 19 best of my belief, Marcus Cato, the famous censor, while after him Marcus Antonius began a treatise on rhetoric: I say " began," because only this one work of his survives, and that is incomplete. He was followed by others of less note, whose names I will not omit to mention, should occasion demand. But it was Cicero 20 who shed the greatest light not only on the practice but on the theory of oratory; for he stands alone among Romans as combining the gift of actual eloquence with that of teaching the art. With him for

stissimum foret, nisi et rhetoricos suos ipse adole-
scenti sibi elapsos diceret, et in oratoriis haec
minora, quae plerumque desiderantur, sciens omi-
21 sisset. Scripsit de eadem materia non pauca Cornificius, aliqua Stertinius, nonnihil pater Gallio;
accuratius vero priores Gallione Celsus et Laenas et
aetatis nostrae Verginius, Plinius, Tutilius. Sunt et
hodie clari eiusdem operis auctores, qui si omnia
complexi forent, consuluissent labori meo; sed parco
nominibus viventium; veniet eorum laudi suum
tempus, ad posteros enim virtus durabit, non per-
veniet invidia.

22 Non tamen post tot ac tantos auctores pigebit
meam quibusdam locis posuisse sententiam. Neque
enim me cuiusquam sectae velut quadam supersti-
tione imbutus addixi, et electuris quae volent facienda copia fuit, sicut ipse plurium in unum confero
inventa, ubicunque ingenio non erit locus, curae
testimonium meruisse contentus.

II. Nec diu nos moretur quaestio, quae rhetorices
origo sit. Nam cui dubium est, quin sermonem ab
ipsa rerum natura geniti protinus homines acceperint
(quod certe principium est eius rei), huic studium et
incrementum dederit utilitas, summam ratio et exer-
2 citatio? Nec video, quare curam dicendi putent

---

¹ *sc.* the *de Inventione.*

predecessor it would be more modest to be silent, but for the fact that he himself describes his Rhetorica[1] as a youthful indiscretion, while in his later works on oratory he deliberately omitted the discussion of certain minor points, on which instruction is generally desired. Cornificius wrote a good deal, Stertinius 21 something, and the elder Gallio a little on the same subject. But Gallio's predecessors, Celsus and Laenas, and in our own day Verginius, Pliny and Tutilius, have treated rhetoric with greater accuracy. Even to-day we have some distinguished writers on oratory who, if they had dealt with the subject more comprehensively, would have saved me the trouble of writing this book. But I will spare the names of the living. The time will come when they will reap their meed of praise; for their merits will endure to after generations, while the calumnies of envy will perish utterly.

Still, although so many writers have preceded me, 22 I shall not shrink from expressing my own opinion on certain points. I am not a superstitious adherent of any school, and as this book will contain a collection of the opinions of many different authors, it was desirable to leave it to my readers to select what they will. I shall be content if they praise me for my industry, wherever there is no scope for originality.

II. The question as to the origin of rhetoric need not keep us long. For who can doubt that mankind received the gift of speech from nature at its birth (for we can hardly go further back than that), while the usefulness of speech brought improvement and study, and finally method and exercise gave perfection? I cannot understand why some hold that 2 the elaboration of speech originated in the fact that

quidam inde coepisse, quod ii, qui in discrimen
aliquod vocabantur, accuratius loqui defendendi sui
gratia instituerint.   Haec enim ut honestior causa,
ita non utique prior est, cum praesertim accusatio
praecedat defensionem; nisi quis dicet, etiam gladium
fabricatum ab eo prius, qui ferrum in tutelam sui
3 quam qui in perniciem alterius compararit.   Initium
ergo dicendi dedit natura, initium artis observatio.
Homines enim, sicuti in medicina, cum viderent alia
salubria, alia insalubria, ex observatione eorum effe-
cerunt artem, ita, cum in dicendo alia utilia, alia
inutilia deprehenderent, notarunt ea ad imitandum
vitandumque, et quaedam secundum rationem eorum
adiecerunt ipsi quoque; haec confirmata sunt usu,
4 tum quae sciebat quisque docuit.   Cicero quidem
initium orandi conditoribus urbium ac legum latoribus dedit, in quibus fuisse vim dicendi necesse est;
cur tamen hanc primam originem putet, non video,
cum sint adhuc quaedam vagae et sine urbibus ac
sine legibus gentes, et tamen qui sunt in iis nati et
legationibus fungantur et accusent aliqua atque
defendant et denique alium alio melius loqui
credant.

III. Omnis autem orandi ratio, ut plurimi maxi-
mique auctores tradiderunt, quinque partibus constat,
inventione, dispositione, elocutione, memoria, pronuntiatione sive actione, utroque enim modo dicitur.
Omnis vero sermo, quo quidem voluntas aliqua enun-
2 tiatur, habeat necesse est rem et verba.   Ac si est

those who were in peril owing to some accusation being made against them, set themselves to speak with studied care for the purpose of their own defence. This, however, though a more honourable origin, cannot possibly be the earlier, for accusation necessarily precedes defence. You might as well assert that the sword was invented for the purpose of self-defence and not for aggression. It was, then, nature that created speech, and observation that originated the art of speaking. Just as men discovered the art of medicine by observing that some things were healthy and some the reverse, so they observed that some things were useful and some useless in speaking, and noted them for imitation or avoidance, while they added certain other precepts according as their nature suggested. These observations were confirmed by experience and each man proceeded to teach what he knew. Cicero,[1] it is true, attributes the origin of oratory to the founders of cities and the makers of laws, who must needs have possessed the gift of eloquence. But why he thinks this the actual origin, I cannot understand, since there still exist certain nomad peoples without cities or laws, and yet members of these peoples perform the duties of ambassadors, accuse and defend, and regard one man as a better speaker than another.

III. The art of oratory, as taught by most authorities, and those the best, consists of five parts :— *invention, arrangement, expression, memory,* and *delivery* or *action* (the two latter terms being used synonymously). But all speech expressive of purpose involves also a *subject* and *words.* If such expression is brief

[1] *de Inv.* i. 2.

brevis et una conclusione finitus, nihil fortasse ultra
desideret; at oratio longior plura exigit. Non tantum enim refert, quid et quo modo dicamus, sed
etiam quo loco; opus ergo est et dispositione. Sed
neque omnia, quae res postulat, dicere neque suo
quaeque loco poterimus nisi adiuvante memoria;
3 quapropter ea quoque pars quarta erit. Verum haec
cuncta corrumpit ac propemodum perdit indecora
vel voce vel gestu pronuntiatio. Huic quoque igitur
tribuendus est necessario quintus locus.

4   Nec audiendi quidam, quorum est Albutius, qui
tris modo primas esse partes volunt, quoniam memoria atque actio natura non arte contingant (quarum
nos praecepta suo loco dabimus), licet Thrasymachus
5 quoque idem de actione crediderit. His adiecerunt
quidam sextam partem, ita ut inventioni iudicium
subnecterent, quia primum esset invenire, deinde
iudicare. Ego porro ne invenisse quidem credo eum,
qui non iudicavit; neque enim contraria, communia,
stulta invenisse dicitur quisquam, sed non vitasse.
6 Et Cicero quidem in Rhetoricis iudicium subiecit
inventioni; mihi autem adeo tribus primis partibus
videtur esse permixtum (nam neque dispositio sine
eo neque elocutio fuerit), ut pronuntiationem quoque
7 vel plurimum ex eo mutuari putem. Quod hoc
audacius dixerim, quod in Partitionibus oratoriis ad

---

¹ Book II. chaps. ii. and iii.
² No such statement is found in the *de Inventione*.

and contained within the limits of one sentence, it
may demand nothing more, but longer speeches
require much more. For not only what we say
and how we say it is of importance, but also
the circumstances under which we say it. It is here
that the need of arrangement comes in. But it will
be impossible to say everything demanded by the
subject, putting each thing in its proper place, without
the aid of memory. It is for this reason that memory 3
forms the fourth department. But a delivery, which
is rendered unbecoming either by voice or gesture,
spoils everything and almost entirely destroys the
effect of what is said. Delivery therefore must be
assigned the fifth place.

Those (and Albutius is among them), who maintain 4
that there are only three departments on the ground
that memory and delivery (for which I shall give
instructions in their proper place[1]) are given us by
nature not by art, may be disregarded, although
Thrasymachus held the same views as regards delivery. Some have added a sixth department, sub- 5
joining *judgment* to *invention*, on the ground that it is
necessary first to *invent* and then to *exercise our judgment*. For my own part I do not believe that *invention*
can exist apart from *judgment*, since we do not say that a
speaker has *invented* inconsistent, two-edged or foolish
arguments, but merely that he has failed to avoid
them. It is true that Cicero in his Rhetorica[2] in- 6
cludes *judgment* under *invention ;* but in my opinion
judgment is so inextricably mingled with the first
three departments of rhetoric (for without *judgment*
neither *expression* nor *arrangement* are possible), that
I think that even delivery owes much to it. I say 7
this with all the greater confidence because Cicero in

easdem, de quibus supra dictum est, quinque pervenit partes. Nam cum dupliciter primum divisisset
in inventionem atque elocutionem, res ac dispositionem inventioni, verba et pronuntiationem elocutioni dedit quintamque constituit, communem ac
velut custodem omnium, memoriam. Idem in[1]
Oratore quinque rebus constare eloquentiam dicit,
in quibus postea scriptis certior eius sententia est.

8 Non minus mihi cupidi novitatis alicuius videntur
fuisse, qui adiecerunt ordinem, cum dispositionem
dixissent, quasi aliud sit dispositio quam rerum
ordine quam optimo collocatio. Dion inventionem
modo et dispositionem tradidit sed utramque duplicem, rerum et verborum, ut sit elocutio inventionis,
pronuntiatio dispositionis, his quinta pars memoriae,
accedat. Theodorei fere inventionem duplicem,
rerum atque elocutionis, deinde tris ceteras partes.

9 Hermagoras iudicium, partitionem, ordinem, quaeque sunt elocutionis, subiicit oeconomiae, quae
Graece appellata ex cura rerum domesticarum et hic
per abusionem posita nomine Latino caret.

10 Est et circa hoc quaestio, quod memoriam in
ordine partium quidam inventioni, quidam disposi-
tioni subiunxerunt; nobis quartus eius locus maxime
placet. Non enim tantum inventa tenere, ut dis-

---

[1] in libris de Oratore, *Spalding* (*sc.* I. xxxi. 142).

---

[1] i. 3.   [2] 14-17.

his *Partitiones oratoriae*[1] arrives at the same five-fold
division of which I have just spoken. For after an
initial division of oratory into *invention* and *expression*,
he assigns *matter* and *arrangement* to *invention*, *words*
and *delivery* to *expression*, and makes *memory* a fifth
department common to them all and acting as their
guardian. Again in the *Orator*[2] he states that eloquence consists of five things, and in view of the fact
that this is a later work we may accept this as his
more settled opinion. Others, who seem to me to 8
have been no less desirous than those mentioned
above to introduce some novelty, have added *order*,
although they had already mentioned arrangement,
as though *arrangement* was anything else than the
marshalling of arguments in the best possible order.
Dion taught that oratory consisted only of *invention*
and *arrangement*, but added that each of these departments was twofold in nature, being concerned with
words and things, so that *expression* comes under
invention, and *delivery* under *arrangement*, while *memory*
must be added as a fifth department. The followers
of Theodorus divide *invention* into two parts, the one
concerned with *matter* and the other with *expression*,
and then add the three remaining departments.
Hermagoras places *judgment*, *division*, *order* and 9
everything relating to *expression* under the heading
of *economy*, a Greek word meaning the management
of domestic affairs which is applied metaphorically to
oratory and has no Latin equivalent.

A further question arises at this point, since 10
some make *memory* follow *invention* in the list of
departments, while others make it follow *arrangement*.
Personally I prefer to place it fourth. For we ought
not merely to retain in our minds the fruits of our

ponamus, nec disposita, ut eloquamur, sed etiam
verbis formata memoriae mandare debemus. Hac
enim omnia, quaecunque in orationem collata sunt,
continentur.

11 Fuerunt etiam in hac opinione non pauci, ut has
non rhetorices partes esse existimarent sed opera
oratoris; eius enim esse invenire, disponere, eloqui
12 et cetera. Quod si accipimus, nihil arti relinquimus.
Nam bene dicere est oratoris, rhetorice tamen erit
bene dicendi scientia; vel, ut alii putant, artificis est
persuadere, vis autem persuadendi artis. Ita invenire quidem et disponere oratoris, inventio autem et
13 dispositio rhetorices propria videri potest. In eo
plures dissenserunt, utrumne hae partes essent rhetorices an eiusdem opera an, ut Athenaeus credit,
elementa, quae vocant στοιχεῖα. Sed neque elementa
recte quis dixerit, alioqui tantum initia erunt, ut
mundi vel umor vel ignis vel materia vel corpora
insecabilia; nec operum recte nomen accipient, quae
non ab aliis perficiuntur, sed aliud ipsa perficiunt:
14 partes igitur. Nam cum sit ex his rhetorice, fieri
non potest ut, cum totum ex partibus constet, non
sint partes totius ex quibus constat. Videntur
autem mihi, qui haec opera dixerunt, eo quoque
moti, quod in alia rursus divisione nollent in idem

invention, in order that we may be able to arrange
them, or to remember our *arrangement* in order that
we may express it, but we must also commit to
memory the words which we propose to use, since
memory embraces everything that goes to the composition of a speech.

There are also not a few who have held that these 11
are not *parts* of rhetoric, but rather *duties* to be
observed by the orator. For it is his business to
invent, arrange, express, etcetera. If, however, we
accept this view, we leave nothing to art. For 12
although the orator's task is to speak well, rhetoric
is the science of speaking well. Or if we adopt
another view, the task of the artist is to persuade,
while the power of persuasion resides in the art.
Consequently, while it is the duty of the orator to
invent and arrange, *invention* and *arrangement* may be
regarded as belonging to rhetoric. At this point 13
there has been much disagreement, as to whether
these are *parts* or *duties* of rhetoric, or, as Athenaeus
believes, *elements* of rhetoric, which the Greeks call
στοιχεῖα. But they cannot correctly be called *elements*. For in that case we should have to regard
them merely as first-principles, like the moisture, fire,
matter or atoms of which the universe is said to be
composed. Nor is it correct to call them duties, since
they are not performed by others, but perform something themselves. We must therefore conclude that
they are *parts*. For since rhetoric is composed of 14
them, it follows that, since a whole consists of parts,
these must be parts of the whole which they compose. Those who have called them *duties* seem to
me to have been further influenced by the fact that
they wished to reserve the name of *parts* for another

nomen incidere, partes enim rhetorices esse dicebant
laudativam, deliberativam, iudicialem. Quae si partes
15 sunt, materiae sunt potius quam artis. Namque in
his singulis rhetorice tota est, quia et inventionem
et dispositionem et elocutionem et memoriam et
pronuntiationem quaecunque earum desiderat. Itaque quidam genera tria rhetorices dicere maluerunt,
optime autem ii, quos secutus est Cicero, genera
causarum.

IV. Sed tria an plura sint, ambigitur. Nec dubie
prope omnes utique summae apud antiquos auctoritatis scriptores Aristotelem secuti, qui nomine tantum alio contionalem pro deliberativa appellat, hac
2 partitione contenti fuerunt. Verum et tum leviter
est temptatum, cum apud Graecos quosdam tum
apud Ciceronem in libris de Oratore, et nunc maximo
temporum nostrorum auctore prope impulsum, ut
non modo plura haec genera, sed paene innumera-
3 bilia videantur. Nam si laudandi ac vituperandi
officium in parte tertia ponimus, in quo genere
versari videbimur, cum querimur, consolamur, miti-
gamus, concitamus, terremus, confirmamus, praecipi-
mus, obscure dicta interpretamur, narramus, depre-
camur, gratias agimus, gratulamur, obiurgamus,
maledicimus, describimus, mandamus, renuntiamus,
4 optamus, opinamur, plurima alia? ut mihi in illa
vetere persuasione permanenti velut petenda sit
venia, quaerendumque, quo moti priores rem tam

---

[1] *de Or.* i. xxxi. 141 ; *Top.* xxiv. 91.   [2] *de Or.* ii. 10 *sq.*

division of rhetoric : for they asserted that the *parts* of rhetoric were, *panegyric, deliberative* and *forensic* oratory. But if these are parts, they are parts rather of the material than of the art. For each of them 15 contains the whole of rhetoric, since each of them requires *invention, arrangement, expression, memory* and *delivery.* Consequently some writers have thought it better to say that there are three *kinds* of oratory ; those whom Cicero[1] has followed seem to me to have taken the wisest course in terming them *kinds of causes.*

IV. There is, however, a dispute as to whether there are three kinds or more. But it is quite certain that all the most eminent authorities among ancient writers, following Aristotle who merely substituted the term *public* for *deliberative,* have been content with the threefold division. Still a feeble 2 attempt has been made by certain Greeks and by Cicero in his *de Oratore,*[2] to prove that there are not merely more than three, but that the number of kinds is almost past calculation : and this view has almost been thrust down our throats by the greatest authority[3] of our own times. Indeed if we place the 3 task of praise and denunciation in the third division, on what kind of oratory are we to consider ourselves to be employed, when we complain, console, pacify, excite, terrify, encourage, instruct, explain obscurities, narrate, plead for mercy, thank, congratulate, reproach, abuse, describe, command, retract, express our desires and opinions, to mention no other of the many possibilities ? As an adherent of the older view 4 I must ask for indulgence and must enquire what was the reason that led earlier writers to restrict a subject

[3] Unknown. Perhaps the elder Pliny.

late fusam tam breviter astrinxerint. Quos qui
errasse putant, hoc secutos arbitrantur, quod in his
5 fere versari tum oratores videbant; nam et laudes
ac vituperationes scribebantur, et ἐπιταφίους dicere
erat moris, et plurimum in consiliis ac iudiciis in-
sumebatur operae, ut scriptores artium pro solis
6 comprehenderint frequentissima. Qui vero defen-
dunt, tria faciunt genera auditorum, unum, quod ad
delectationem conveniat, alterum, quod consilium
accipiat, tertium, quod de causis iudicet. Mihi
cuncta rimanti et talis quaedam ratio succurrit, quod
omne orationis officium aut in iudiciis est aut extra
7 iudicia. Eorum, de quibus iudicio quaeritur, manifestum est genus; ea, quae ad iudicem non veniunt,
aut praeteritum habent tempus aut futurum; praeterita laudamus aut vituperamus, de futuris delibe-
8 ramus. Item omnia, de quibus dicendum est, aut
certa sint necesse est aut dubia. Certa, ut cuique
est animus, laudat aut culpat; ex dubiis partim nobis
ipsis ad electionem sunt libera, de his deliberatur;
partim aliorum sententiae commissa, de his lite
contenditur.
9　Anaximenes iudicialem et contionalem generales
partes esse voluit, septem autem species: hortandi,

of such variety to such narrow' bounds. Those who
think such authorities in error hold that they were
influenced by the fact that these three subjects
practically exhausted the range of ancient oratory.
For it was customary to write panegyrics and denun- 5
ciations and to deliver funeral orations, while the
greater part of their activities was devoted to the
law-courts and deliberative assemblies; as a result,
they say, the old writers of text-books only included
those kinds of oratory which were most in vogue. The 6
defenders of antiquity point out that there are three
kinds of audience: one which comes simply for the
sake of getting pleasure, a second which meets to receive advice, a third to give judgement on causes.
In the course of a thorough enquiry into the question
it has occurred to me that the tasks of oratory must
either be concerned with the law-courts or with themes
lying outside the law-courts. The nature of the 7
questions into which enquiry is made in the courts is
obvious. As regards those matters which do not
come before a judge, they must necessarily be concerned either with the past or the future. We praise
or denounce past actions, we deliberate about the
future. Again everything on which we have to 8
speak must be either certain or doubtful. We praise
or blame what is certain, as our inclination leads us:
on the other hand where doubt exists, in some cases
we are free to form our own views, and it is here that
deliberation comes in, while in others, we leave the
problem to the decision of others, and it is on these
that litigation takes place.

Anaximenes regarded forensic and public oratory 9
as *genera* but held that there were seven *species*:—
exhortation, dissuasion, praise, denunciation, accusa-

dehortandi, laudandi, vituperandi, accusandi, defendendi, exquirendi, quod ἐξεταστικόν dicit; quarum
duae primae deliberativi, duae sequentes demon-
strativi, tres ultimae iudicialis generis sunt partes.
10 Protagoran transeo, qui interrogandi, respondendi,
mandandi, precandi, quod εὐχωλήν dixit, partes solas
putat. Plato in Sophiste iudiciali et contionali tertiam adiecit προσομιλητικήν, quam sane permittamus
nobis dicere sermocinatricem; quae a forensi ratione
diiungitur et est accommodata privatis disputationi-
bus, cuius vis eadem profecto est quae dialecticae.
11 Isocrates in omni genere inesse laudem ac vituperationem existimavit.

  Nobis et tutissimum est auctores plurimos sequi,
12 et ita videtur ratio dictare. Est igitur, ut dixi,
unum genus, quo laus ac vituperatio continetur, sed
est appellatum a parte meliore laudativum; idem
alii demonstrativum vocant. Utrumque nomen ex
Graeco creditur fluxisse, nam ἐγκωμιαστικόν aut ἐπι-
13 δεικτικόν dicunt. Sed mihi ἐπιδεικτικόν non tam
demonstrationis vim habere quam ostentationis
videtur et multum ab illo ἐγκωμιαστικῷ differre; nam
ut continet laudativum in se genus, ita non intra hoc
14 solum consistit. An quisquam negaverit Panegyricos ἐπιδεικτικούς esse? Atqui formam suadendi
habent et plerumque de utilitatibus Graeciae loquuntur; ut causarum quidem genera tria sint, sed ea
tum in negotiis tum in ostentatione posita. Nisi

---

tion, defence, inquiry, or as he called it ἐξεταστικόν. The first two, however, clearly belong to deliberative, the next to demonstrative, the three last to forensic oratory. I say nothing of Protagoras, who 10 held that oratory was to be divided only into the following heads : question and answer, command and entreaty, or as he calls it εὐχωλή. Plato in his *Sophist* [1] in addition to public and forensic oratory introduces a third kind which he styles προσομιλητική, which I will permit myself to translate by "conversational." This is distinct from forensic oratory and is adapted for private discussions, and we may regard it as identical with dialectic. Isocrates [2] held that 11 praise and blame find a place in every kind of oratory.

The safest and most rational course seems to be to 12 follow the authority of the majority. There is, then, as I have said, one kind concerned with praise and blame, which, however, derives its name from the better of its two functions and is called *laudatory;* others however call it *demonstrative.* Both names are believed to be derived from the Greek in which the corresponding terms are *encomiastic,* and *epideictic.* The term *epideictic* seems to me however 13 to imply display rather than demonstration, and to have a very different meaning from *encomiastic.* For although it includes laudatory oratory, it does not confine itself thereto. Will any one deny the title 14 of *epideictic* to *panegyric* ? But yet *panegyrics* are advisory in form and frequently discuss the interests of Greece. We may therefore conclude that, while there are three kinds of oratory, all three devote themselves in part to the matter in hand, and in part to display. But it may be that Romans are not

QUINTILIAN

forte non ex Graeco mutuantes demonstrativum
vocant, verum id sequuntur, quod laus ac vituperatio
15 quale sit quidque demonstrat. Alterum est deli-
berativum, tertium iudiciale. Ceterae species in
haec tria incident genera, nec invenietur ex his ulla,
in qua non laudare ac vituperare, suadere ac dissua-
dere, intendere quid vel depellere debeamus. Illa
quoque sunt communia, conciliare, narrare, docere,
augere, minuere, concitandis componendisve adfecti-
16 bus animos audientium fingere. Ne iis quidem acces-
serim, qui laudativam materiam honestorum, deliberativam utilium, iudicialem iustorum quaestione
contineri putant, celeri magis ac rotunda usi distri-
butione quam vera. Stant enim quodammodo mutuis
auxiliis omnia. Nam et in laude iustitia utilitasque
tractatur et in consiliis honestas, et raro iudicialem
inveneris causam, in cuius non parte aliquid eorum,
quae supra diximus, reperiatur.

V. Omnis autem oratio constat aut ex iis, quae
significantur, aut et iis, quae significant, id est rebus
et verbis. Facultas orandi consummatur natura,
arte, exercitatione, cui partem quartam adiiciunt
2 quidam imitationis, quam nos arti subiicimus. Tria
sunt item, quae praestare debeat orator, ut doceat,
moveat, delectet. Haec enim clarior divisio quam
eorum, qui totum opus in res et in adfectus par-

borrowing from Greek when they apply the title
demonstrative, but are merely led to do so because
praise and blame demonstrate the nature of the
object with which they are concerned. The second 15
kind is *deliberative,* the third *forensic* oratory. All
other *species* fall under these three *genera :* you will
not find one in which we have not to praise or
blame, to advise or dissuade, to drive home or refute
a charge, while conciliation, narration, proof, exag-
geration, extenuation, and the moulding of the minds
of the audience by exciting or allaying their passions, are common to all three kinds of oratory. I 16
cannot even agree with those who hold that *laudatory* subjects are concerned with the question of
what is honourable, *deliberative* with the question of
what is expedient, and *forensic* with the question of
what is just : the division thus made is easy and
neat rather than true : for all three kinds rely on
the mutual assistance of the other. For we deal
with justice and expediency in *panegyric* and with
honour in *deliberations,* while you will rarely find a
forensic case, in part of which at any rate something
of those questions just mentioned is not to be found.

V. Every speech however consists at once of that
which is expressed and that which expresses, that is
to say of matter and words. Skill in speaking is
perfected by nature, art and practice, to which some
add a fourth department, namely imitation, which I
however prefer to include under art. There are also 2
three aims which the orator must always have in
view ; he must instruct, move and charm his hearers.
This is a clearer division than that made by those
who divide the task of oratory into that which relates
to things and that which concerns the emotions,

tiuntur. Non semper autem omnia in eam quae
tractabitur materiam cadent. Erunt enim quaedam
remotae ab adfectibus, qui ut non ubique habent
locum, ita quocunque irruperunt, plurimum valent.

3 Praestantissimis auctoribus placet alia in rhetorice
esse, quae probationem desiderent, alia quae non
desiderent, cum quibus ipse consentio. Quidam
vero, ut Celsus, de nulla re dicturum oratorem, nisi
de qua quaeratur, existimant, cui cum maxima pars
scriptorum repugnat tum etiam ipsa partitio ; nisi
forte laudare, quae constet esse honesta, et vituperare, quae ex confesso sint turpia, non est oratoris
officium.

4 Illud iam omnes fatentur, esse quaestiones aut in
scripto aut in non scripto ; in scripto de iure, in non
scripto de re. Illud rationale hoc legale genus
Hermagoras atque eum secuti vocant, id est νομικόν
5 et λογικόν. Idem sentiunt, qui omnem quaestionem
ponunt in rebus et in verbis.

Item convenit, quaestiones esse aut infinitas aut
finitas. Infinitae sunt, quae remotis personis et
temporibus et locis ceterisque similibus in utramque
partem tractantur, quod Graeci θέσιν dicunt, Cicero
propositum, alii quaestiones universales civiles, alii
quaestiones philosopho convenientes, Athenaeus
6 partem causae appellat. Hoc genus Cicero scientia
et actione distinguit, ut sit scientiae, *An providentia*

---

¹ *Top.* xxi. 79.
² *Top.* 81 ; *Part. Or.* xviii. 62.

since both of these will not always be present in the subjects which we shall have to treat. For some themes are far from calling for any appeal to the emotions, which, although room cannot always be found for them, produce a most powerful effect wherever they do succeed in forcing their way. The 3 best authorities hold that there are some things in oratory which require proof and others which do not, a view with which I agree. Some on the other hand, as for instance Celsus, think that the orator will not speak on any subject unless there is some question involved in it ; but the majority of writers on rhetoric are against him, as is also the threefold division of oratory, unless indeed to praise what is allowed to be honourable and to denounce what is admittedly disgraceful are no part of an orator's duty.

It is, however, universally agreed that all questions 4 must be concerned either with something that is written or something that is not. Those concerned with what is written are questions of law, those which concern what is not written are questions of fact. Hermagoras calls the latter *rational* questions, the former *legal* questions, for so we may translate λογικόν and νομικόν. Those who hold that every question con- 5 cerns either things or words, mean much the same.

It is also agreed that questions are either *definite* or *indefinite*. *Indefinite* questions are those which may be maintained or impugned without reference to persons, time or place and the like. The Greeks call them *theses*, Cicero[1] *propositions*, others *general questions relating to civil life*, others again *questions suited for philosophical discussion*, while Athenaeus calls them *parts of a cause.* Cicero[2] distinguishes two kinds, 6 the one concerned with *knowledge*, the other with *action.* Thus "Is the world governed by pro-

mundus regatur; actionis, *An accedendum ad rempublicam administrandam.* Prius trium generum, an sit? quid sit? quale sit? omnia enim haec ignorari possunt; sequens duorum, quo modo adipiscamur?

7 quo modo utamur? Finitae autem sunt ex complexu rerum, personarum, temporum, ceterorumque; hae ὑποθέσεις a Graecis dicuntur, causae a nostris. In his omnis quaestio videtur circa res personasque

8 consistere. Amplior est semper infinita, inde enim finita descendit. Quod ut exemplo pateat, infinita est, *An uxor ducenda?* finita, *An Catoni ducenda?* ideoque esse suasoria potest. Sed etiam remotae a personis propriis ad aliquid referri solent. Est enim simplex, *An respublica administranda?* refertur ad

9 aliquid, *An in tyrannide administranda?* Sed hic quoque subest velut latens persona; tyrannus enim geminat quaestionem, subestque et temporis et qualitatis tacita vis; nondum tamen hoc proprie dixeris causam. Hae autem, quas infinitas voco, et generales appellantur; quod si est verum, finitae speciales erunt. In omni autem speciali utique

10 inest generalis, ut quae sit prior. Ac nescio an in causis quoque, quidquid in quaestionem venit quali-

vidence ? " is a question of knowledge, while "Should
we enter politics?" is a question of action. The
first involves three questions, whether a thing
is, what it is, and of what nature : for all these
things may be unknown : the second involves two,
how to obtain power and how to use it. *Definite* 7
questions involve facts, persons, time and the like.
The Greeks call them *hypotheses,* while we call them
causes. In these the whole question turns on persons and facts. An *indefinite* question is always the 8
more comprehensive, since it is from the *indefinite*
question that the *definite* is derived. I will illustrate
what I mean by an example. The question "Should
a man marry?" is *indefinite ;* the question "Should
Cato marry ? " is *definite,* and consequently may be
regarded as a subject for a *deliberative* theme. But
even those which have no connexion with particular
persons are generally given a specific reference.
For instance the question " Ought we to take a share
in the government of our country? " is abstract,
whereas " Ought we to take part in the government
of our country under the sway of a tyrant ? " has a
specific reference. But in this latter case we may 9
say that a person is tacitly implied. For the
mention of a tyrant doubles the question, and
there is an implicit admission of time and quality ;
but all the same you would scarcely be justified in
calling it a cause or definite question. Those questions which I have styled indefinite are also called
general : if this is correct, we shall have to call definite
questions *special* questions. But in every special
question the general question is implicit, since the
genus is logically prior to the *species*. And perhaps 10
even in actual causes wherever the notion of quality
comes into question, there is a certain intrusion of

tatis, generale sit. *Milo Clodium occidit, iure occidit insidiatorem;* nonne hoc quaeritur, *An sit ius insidiatorem occidendi?* Quid in coniecturis? non illa generalia, *An causa sceleris odium? cupiditas? An tormentis credendum? Testibus an argumentis maior fides habenda?* Nam finitione quidem comprehendi

11 nihil non in universum certum erit. Quidam putant etiam eas thesis posse aliquando nominari, quae personis causisque contineantur, aliter tantummodo positas : ut causa sit, cum *Orestes accusatur :* thesis, *An Orestes recte sit absolutus;* cuius generis est, *An Cato recte Marciam Hortensio tradiderit.* Hi thesin a causa sic distinguunt, ut illa sit spectativae partis, haec activae; illic enim veritatis tantum gratia disputari, hic negotium agi.

12 Quanquam inutiles quidam oratori putant universales quaestiones, quia nihil prosit, quod constet ducendam esse uxorem vel administrandam rempublicam, si quis vel aetate vel valetudine impediatur. Sed non omnibus eiusmodi quaestionibus sic occurri potest, ut illis, sitne virtus finis? regaturne provi-

13 dentia mundus? Quin etiam in iis, quae ad per-

the abstract. "Milo killed Clodius: he was justified in killing one who lay in wait for him." Does not this raise the general question as to whether we have the right to kill a man who lies in wait for us? What again of conjectures? May not they be of a general character, as for instance, "What was the motive for the crime? hatred? covetousness?" or "Are we justified in believing confessions made under torture?" or "Which should carry greater weight, evidence or argument?" As for definitions, everything that they contain is undoubtedly of a general nature. There are some who hold that even those 11 questions which have reference to persons and particular cases may at times be called *theses,* provided only they are put slightly differently: for instance, if Orestes be accused, we shall have a *cause :* whereas if it is put as question, namely "Was Orestes rightly acquitted?" it will be a *thesis.* To the same class as this last belongs the question "Was Cato right in transferring Marcia to Hortensius?" These persons distinguish a *thesis* from a *cause* as follows: a *thesis* is theoretical in character, while a *cause* has relation to actual facts, since in the former case we argue merely with a view to abstract truth, while in the latter we have to deal with some particular act.

Some, however, think that general questions are 12 useless to an orator, since no profit is to be derived from proving that we ought to marry or to take part in politics, if we are prevented from so doing by age or ill health. But not all general questions are liable to this kind of objection. For instance questions such as "Is virtue an end in itself?" or "Is the world governed by providence?" cannot be countered in this way. Further in questions 13

sonam referuntur, ut non est satis generalem tractasse
quaestionem, ita perveniri ad speciem nisi illa prius
excussa non potest. Nam quomodo, an sibi uxor
ducenda sit, deliberabit Cato, nisi constiterit, uxores
esse ducendas? Et quomodo, an ducere debeat
Marciam, quaeretur, nisi Catoni ducenda uxor est?
14 Sunt tamen inscripti nomine Hermagorae libri, qui
confirmant illam opinionem, sive falsus est titulus
sive alius hic Hermagoras fuit. Nam eiusdem esse
quomodo possunt, qui de hac arte mirabiliter multa
composuit, cum, sicut ex Ciceronis quoque rhetorico
primo manifestum est, materiam rhetorices in thesis
et causas diviserit? Quod reprehendit Cicero ac
thesin nihil ad oratorem pertinere contendit totumque hoc genus quaestionis ad philosophos refert.
15 Sed me liberavit respondendi verecundia, et quod
ipse hos libros improbat, et quod in Oratore atque
his, quos de Oratore scripsit, et Topicis praecipit, ut
a propriis personis atque temporibus avocemus controversiam: quia latius dicere liceat de genere quam
de specie, et, quod in universo probatum sit, in parte
16 probatum esse necesse sit. Status autem in hoc
omne genus materiae iidem, qui in causas, cadunt.
Adhuc adiicitur, alias esse quaestiones in rebus ipsis,

---

[1] *de Inv.* i. 6.   [2] *Orator* xiv. 45.
[3] *de Or.* iii. 30; *Top.* 21.

which have reference to a particular person, although
it is not sufficient merely to handle the general
question, we cannot arrive at any conclusion on
the special point until we have first discussed the
general question. For how is Cato to deliberate
"whether he personally is to marry," unless the
general question "whether marriage is desirable"
is first settled? And how is he to deliberate
"whether he should marry Marcia," unless it is
proved that it is the duty of Cato to marry? There 14
are, however, certain books attributed to Hermagoras which support this erroneous opinion, though
whether the attribution is spurious or whether they
were written by another Hermagoras is an open
question. For they cannot possibly be by the
famous Hermagoras, who wrote so much that was
admirable on the art of rhetoric, since, as is clear
from the first book of the Rhetorica of Cicero,[1] he
divided the material of rhetoric into *theses* and *causes*.
Cicero objects to this division, contends that *theses*
have nothing to do with an orator, and refers all
this class of questions to the philosophers. But 15
Cicero has relieved me of any feeling of shame
that I might have in controverting his opinion, since
he has not only expressed his disapproval of his Rhetorica, but in the *Orator*,[2] the *de Oratore* and the
Topica[3] instructs us to abstract such discussions
from particular persons and occasions, "because
we can speak more fully on general than on special
themes, and because what is proved of the whole
must also be proved of the part." In all general 16
questions, however, the essential *basis* is the same as
in a cause or definite question. It is further
pointed out that there are some questions which

alias quae ad aliquid referantur: illud, *An uxor ducenda?* hoc, *An seni ducenda?* illud, *An fortis?* hoc, *An fortior?* et similia.

17 Causam finit Apollodorus, ut interpretatione Valgi discipuli eius utar, ita: *Causa est negotium omnibus suis partibus spectans ad quaestionem;* aut: *Causa est negotium, cuius finis est controversia.* Ipsum deinde negotium sic finit: *Negotium est congregatio personarum, locorum, temporum, causarum, modorum, casuum, factorum, instrumentorum, sermonum, scriptorum et non* 18 *scriptorum.* Causam nunc intelligamus ὑπόθεσιν, negotium περίστασιν. Sed et ipsam causam quidam similiter finierunt, ut Apollodorus negotium. Isocrates autem causam esse ait quaestionem finitam civilem aut rem controversam in personarum finitarum complexu; Cicero his verbis: *Causa certis personis, locis, temporibus, actionibus, negotiis cernitur, aut in omnibus aut in plerisque eorum.*

VI. Ergo cum omnis causa contineatur aliquo statu, priusquam dicere aggredior, quo modo genus

---

¹ Fr. 13 Sheehan.   ² *Top.* xxi. 80.
³ This chapter is highly technical and of little interest for the most part to any save professed students of the technique of the ancient schools of rhetoric. Its apparent obscurity will, however, be found to disappear on careful analysis. The one passage of general interest it contains is to be found in the extremely ingenious fictitious theme discussed in sections 96 *sqq.*

concern "things in themselves," while others have a particular reference; an example of the former will be the question "Should a man marry?" of the latter "Should an old man marry?"; or again the question whether a man is brave will illustrate the first, while the question whether he is braver than another will exemplify the second.

Apollodorus defines a *cause* in the following terms 17 (I quote the translation of his pupil Valgius):—"A cause is a matter which in all its parts bears on the question at issue," or again "a cause is a matter of which the question in dispute is the object." He then defines a *matter* in the following terms:— "A matter is a combination of persons, circumstances of place and time, motives, means, incidents, acts, instruments, speeches, the letter and the spirit of the law. Let us then understand a *cause* in the sense of 18 the Greek *hypothesis* or subject, and a *matter* in the sense of the Greek *peristasis* or collection of circumstances. But some, however, have defined a *cause* in the same way that Apollodorus defines a *matter*. Isocrates[1] on the other hand defines a *cause* as *some definite question concerned with some point of civil affairs, or a dispute in which definite persons are involved*; while Cicero[2] uses the following words:—"A *cause* may be known by its being concerned with certain definite persons, circumstances of time and place, actions, and business, and will relate either to all or at any rate to most of these."

VI.[3] Since every cause, then, has a certain essential *basis*[4] on which it rests, before I proceed to set forth how each kind of cause should be handled, I think I

---

[4] There is no exact English equivalent for *status*. *Basis* or *ground* are perhaps the nearest equivalents.

quodque causae sit tractandum, id quod est commune omnibus, quid sit status et unde ducatur et
quot et qui sint, intuendum puto. Quanquam id
nonnulli ad iudiciales tantum pertinere materias
putaverunt, quorum inscitiam, cum omnia tria genera
2 fuero exsecutus, res ipsa deprehendet. Quod nos
statum, id quidam constitutionem vocant, alii quaestionem, alii quod ex quaestione appareat, Theodorus
caput id est κεφάλαιον γενικώτατον, ad quod referantur
omnia. Quorum diversa appellatio, vis eadem est;
nec interest discentium, quibus quidque nominibus
3 appelletur, dum res ipsa manifesta sit. Statum
Graeci στάσιν vocant, quod nomen non primum ab
Hermagora traditum putant, sed alii ab Naucrate,
Isocratis discipulo, alii a Zopyro Clazomenio; quanquam videtur Aeschines quoque in oratione contra
Ctesiphontem uti hoc verbo, cum a iudicibus petit,
ne Demostheni permittant evagari, sed eum dicere
4 de ipso causae statu cogant. Quae appellatio dicitur
ducta vel ex eo, quod ibi sit primus causae congressus,
vel quod in hoc causa consistat. Et nominis quidem
haec origo; nunc quid sit. Statum quidam dixerunt
primam causarum conflictionem; quos recte sensisse,
5 parum elocutos puto. Non enim est status prima
conflictio, *fecisti, non feci;* sed quod ex prima con-

---

[1] § 206.

should first examine a question that is common to all
of them, namely, what is meant by *basis*, whence it
is derived and how many and of what nature such
bases may be. Some, it is true, have thought that
they were peculiar merely to forensic themes, but
their ignorance will stand revealed when I have
treated of all three kinds of oratory. That which I 2
call the *basis* some style the *constitution*, others the
question, and others again *that which may be inferred
from the question*, while Theodorus calls it the most *general
head*, κεφάλαιον γενικώτατον, to which everything
must be referred. These different names, however, all
mean the same thing, nor is it of the least importance
to students by what special name things are called,
as long as the thing itself is perfectly clear. The 3
Greeks call this essential *basis* στάσις, a name which
they hold was not invented by Hermagoras, but
according to some was introduced by Naucrates, the
pupil of Isocrates, according to others by Zopyrus of
Clazomenae, although Aeschines in his speech against
Ctesiphon[1] seems to employ the word, when he asks
the jury not to allow Demosthenes to be irrelevant
but to keep him to the *stasis* or *basis* of the case.
The term seems to be derived from the fact that it 4
is on it that the first collision between the parties to
the dispute takes place, or that it forms the *basis* or
standing of the whole case. So much for the origin of
the name. Now for its nature. Some have defined
the *basis* as being the *first conflict of the causes*. The
idea is correct, but the expression is faulty. For the 5
essential *basis* is not the first conflict, which we may
represent by the clauses "You did such and such
a thing" and "I did not do it." It is rather the
kind of question which arises from the first conflict,

flictione nascitur, id est genus quaestionis, *fecisti, non feci, an fecerit? Hoc fecisti, non hoc feci, quid fecerit?* Quia ex his apparet, illud coniectura, hoc finitione quaerendum, atque in eo pars utraque insistit, erit

6 quaestio coniecturalis vel finitivi status. Quid si enim dicat quis, *sonus est duorum inter se corporum conflictio:* erret, ut opinor, non enim sonus est conflictio sed ex conflictione. Sed hoc levius; intelligitur enim utcunque dictum. Inde vero ingens male interpretantibus innatus est error, qui, quia primam conflictionem legerant, crediderunt statum semper ex prima quaestione ducendum; quod est

7 vitiosissimum. Nam quaestio nulla non habet utique statum, constat enim ex intentione et depulsione; sed aliae sunt propriae causarum, de quibus ferenda sententia est, aliae adductae extrinsecus, aliquid tamen ad summam causae conferentes, velut auxilia quaedam, quo fit ut in controversia una plures quae-

8 stiones esse dicantur. Harum porro plerumque levissima quaeque primo loco fungitur. Namque et illud frequens est, ut ea, quibus minus confidimus, cum tractata sunt, omittamus, interim sponte nostra

which we may represent as follows. "You did it," "I did not," "Did he do it?," or "You did this," "I did not do this," "What did he do?" It is clear from these examples, that the first sort of question depends on *conjecture*, the second on *definition*, and that the contending parties rest their respective cases on these points: the *bases* of these questions will therefore be of a *conjectural* or *definitive* character respectively. Suppose it should be asserted that 6 sound is the conflict between two bodies, the statement would in my opinion be erroneous. For sound is not the actual conflict, but a result of the conflict. The error is, however, of small importance: for the sense is clear, whatever the expression. But this trivial mistake has given rise to a very serious error in the minds of those who have not understood what was meant: for on reading that the essential *basis* was the first conflict, they immediately concluded that the *basis* was always to be taken from the first question, which is a grave mistake. For every question has 7 its *basis*, since every question is based on assertion by one party and denial by another. But there are some questions which form an essential part of causes, and it is on these that we have to express an opinion; while others are introduced from without and are, strictly speaking, irrelevant, although they may contribute something of a subsidiary nature to the general contention. It is for this reason that there are said to be several questions in one matter of dispute. Of these questions it is often the most 8 trivial which occupies the first place. For it is a frequent artifice to drop those points in which we place least confidence, as soon as we have dealt with them; sometimes we make a free gift of them to our

velut donantes, interim ad ea quae sunt potentiora
9 gradum ex iis fecisse contenti.   Simplex autem
causa etiamsi varie defenditur, non potest habere
plus uno, de quo pronuntietur, atque inde erit status
causae, quod et orator praecipue sibi obtinendum et
iudex spectandum maxime intelligit; in hoc enim
causa consistet.   Ceterum quaestionum possunt esse
10 diversi.   Quod ut brevissimo pateat exemplo: cum
dicit reus, *Etiamsi feci, recte feci,* qualitatis utitur
statu; cum adiicit, *sed non feci,* coniecturam movet.
Semper autem firmius est non fecisse, ideoque in
eo statum esse iudicabo, quod dicerem, si mihi plus
11 quam unum dicere non liceret.   Recte igitur est
appellata causarum prima conflictio non quaestionum.
Nam et pro Rabirio Postumo Cicero prima parte
orationis in hoc intendit, ut actionem competere in
equitem Romanum neget; secunda, nullam ad eum
pecuniam pervenisse confirmat.   Statum tamen in
12 eo dicam fuisse, quod est potentius.   Nec in causa
Milonis circa primas quaestiones[1] iudicabo conflixisse
causam, sed ubi totis viribus insidiator Clodius ideoque
iure interfectus ostenditur.   Et hoc est, quod ante
omnia constituere in animo suo debeat orator, etiamsi

---

[1] After *quaestiones* the MSS. continue *quae sunt ante
prooemium positae.*   The words as they stand are absurd.
Halm therefore brackets the whole sentence as interpolated.
The alternative is to read *post* (Regius) or *ante pro prooemio*
(Baden), for which *cp.* IV. ii. 25 *sq.*, where Quintilian states
that these *primae quaestiones* have the "force of an
exordium" (*vim prooemii*).

opponents, while sometimes we are content to use them as a step to arguments which are of greater importance. A simple cause, however, although it 9 may be defended in various ways, cannot have more than one point on which a decision has to be given, and consequently the *basis* of the cause will be that point which the orator sees to be the most important for him to make and on which the judge sees that he must fix all his attention. For it is on this that the cause will stand or fall. On the other hand questions may have more *bases* than one.[1] A brief example 10 will show what I mean. When the accused says "Admitting that I did it, I was right to do it," he makes the *basis* one of *quality*; but when he adds "but I did not do it," he introduces an element of *conjecture*.[2] But denial of the facts is always the stronger line of defence, and therefore I conceive the *basis* to reside in that which I should say, if I were confined to one single line of argument. We are 11 right therefore in speaking of the first conflict of *causes* in contradistinction to the conflict of *questions*. For instance in the first portion of his speech on behalf of Rabirius Postumus Cicero contends that the action cannot lie against a Roman knight, while in the second he asserts that no money ever came into his client's hands. Still I should say that the *basis* was to be found in the latter as being the stronger of the two. Again in the case of Milo I do not consider 12 that the conflict is raised by the opening questions, but only when the orator devotes all his powers to prove that Clodius lay in wait for Milo and was therefore rightly killed. The point on which above all the orator must make up his mind, even although he may be going to

---

[1] See § 21.   [2] See § 30 *sqq.*

pro causa plura dicturus est, quid maxime liquere
iudici velit. Quod tamen ut primum cogitandum, ita
non utique primum dicendum erit.

13   Alii statum crediderunt primam eius, cum quo
ageretur, deprecationem. Quam sententiam his
verbis Cicero complectitur: *in quo primum insistit
quasi ad repugnandum congressa defensio.* Unde rursus
alia quaestio, an eum semper is faciat qui respondet.
Cui rei praecipue repugnat Cornelius Celsus dicens
non a depulsione sumi, sed ab eo qui propositionem
suam confirmet; ut, si hominem occisum reus negat,
status ab accusatore nascatur, quia is velit probare;
si iure occisum reus dicit, translata probationis ne-
14 cessitate idem a reo fiat, et sit eius intentio. Cui
non accedo equidem; nam est vero propius quod
contra dicitur, nullam esse litem, si is, cum quo
agatur, nihil respondeat, ideoque fieri statum a re-
15 spondente. Mea tamen sententia varium id est, et
accidit pro condicione causarum, quia et videri potest
propositio aliquando statum facere, ut in coniecturalibus causis; utitur enim coniectura magis qui agit,
(quo moti quidam eundem a reo infitialem esse
dixerunt) et in syllogismo tota ratiocinatio ab eo est

---

[1] *Top.* xxv. 93.
[2] *i.e.* where the law forms the major premiss, while the
minor premiss is the act which is brought under the law.

take up various lines of argument in support of his
case, is this: what is it that he wishes most to impress
upon the mind of the judge? But although this
should be the first point for his consideration, it does
not follow that it should be the first that he will make
in his actual speech.

Others have thought that the *basis* lay in the first 13
point raised by the other side in its defence. Cicero [1]
expresses this view in the following words:—"the
argument on which the defence first takes its stand
with a view to rebutting the charge." This involves
a further question as to whether the *basis* can only be
determined by the defence. Cornelius Celsus is
strongly against this view, and asserts that the *basis*
is derived not from the denial of the charge, but from
him who affirms his proposition. Thus if the accused
denies that anyone has been killed, the *basis* will
originate with the accuser, because it is the latter
who desires to prove: if on the other hand the
accused asserts that the homicide was justifiable, the
burden of proof has been transferred and the *basis*
will proceed from the accused and be affirmed by him.
I do not, however, agree. For the contrary is nearer 14
to the truth, that there is no point of dispute if the
defendant makes no reply, and that consequently the
basis originates with the defendant. But in my 15
opinion the origin of the *basis* varies and depends on
the circumstances of the individual case. For instance
in conjectural causes the affirmation may be regarded
as determining the *basis*, since *conjecture* is employed
by the plaintiff rather than the defendant, and consequently some have styled the *basis* originated
by the latter *negative*. Again in any *syllogism* [2]
the whole of the reasoning proceeds from him who

16 qui intendit. Sed quia videtur illic quoque necessitatem hos status exsequendi facere qui negat, (is enim si dicat, *non feci,* coget adversarium coniectura uti; et si dicat, *non habes legem,* syllogismo) concedamus ex depulsione nasci statum. Nihilominus enim res eo revertetur, ut modo is qui agit, modo is

17 cum quo agitur, statum faciat. Sit enim accusatoris intentio, *Hominem occidisti.* Si negat reus, faciat statum qui negat. Quid si confitetur, sed iure a se adulterum dicit occisum? nempe legem esse certum est quae permittat. Nisi aliquid accusator respondet, nulla lis est. *Non fuit,* inquit, *adulter;* ergo depulsio incipit esse actoris, ille statum faciet. Ita erit quidem status ex prima depulsione, sed ea fiet ab

18 accusatore non a reo. Quid? quod eadem quaestio potest eundem vel accusatorem facere vel reum: *Qui artem ludicram exercuerit, in quattuordecim primis ordinibus ne sedeat;* qui se praetori in hortis ostenderat neque erat productus, sedit in quattuordecim

19 ordinibus. Nempe intentio est: *Artem ludicram exercuisti;* depulsio: *Non exercui artem ludicram;*

---

affirms. But on the other hand he who in such cases [1] 16
denies appears to impose the burden of dealing with
such *bases* upon his opponent. For if he says " I did not
do it," he will force his opponent to make use of *conjecture*, and again, if he says "The law is against you,"
he will force him to employ the *syllogism*. Therefore
we must admit that a *basis* can originate in denial.
All the same we are left with our previous conclusion
that the *basis* is determined in some cases by the
plaintiff, in some by the defendant. Suppose the 17
accuser to affirm that the accused is guilty of homicide : if the accused denies the charge, it is he who
will determine the *basis*. Or again, if he admits that
he has killed a man, but states that the victim was
an adulterer and justifiably killed (and we know that
the law permits homicide under these circumstances),
there is no matter in dispute, unless the accuser has
some answer to make. Suppose the accuser does
answer however and deny that the victim was guilty
of adultery, it will be the accuser that denies, and it
is by him that the *basis* is determined. The *basis*,
then, will originate in the first denial of facts, but
that denial is made by the accuser and not the
accused. Again the same question may make the 18
same person either accuser or accused. " He who has
exercised the profession of an actor, is under no circumstances to be allowed a seat in the first fourteen
rows of the theatre." [2] An individual who had performed before the praetor in his private gardens, but
had never been presented on the public stage, has
taken his seat in one of the fourteen rows. The 19
accuser of course affirms that he has exercised the
profession of an actor : the accused denies that he has
exercised the profession. The question then arises

quaestio : *Quid sit artem ludicram exercere?* Si accu-
sabitur theatrali lege, depulsio erit rei ; si excitatus
fuerit de spectaculis et aget iniuriarum, depulsio erit
20 accusatoris. Frequentius tamen illud accidet, quod
est a plurimis traditum. Effugerunt has quaestiones
qui dixerunt, statum esse id, quod appareat ex intentione et depulsione, ut *Fecisti, Non feci* aut *Recte*
21 *feci.* Viderimus tamen, utrum id sit status an in eo
status. Hermagoras statum vocat, per quem subiecta
res intelligatur et ad quem probationes etiam partium
referantur. Nostra opinio semper haec fuit: cum
essent frequenter in causa diversi quaestionum status,
in eo credere statum causae, quod esset in ea potentissimum et in quo maxime res verteretur. Id si
quis generalem quaestionem vel caput generale dicere
malet cum hoc mihi non erit pugna, non magis, quam
si aliud adhuc, quo idem intelligatur, eius rei nomen
invenerit, quanquam tota volumina in hanc disputa-
tionem impendisse multos sciam ; nobis statum dici
22 placet. Sed cum in aliis omnibus inter scriptores
summa dissensio est, tum in hoc praecipue videtur
mihi studium quoque diversa tradendi fuisse ; adeo,
nec qui sit numerus nec quae nomina nec qui
generales quive speciales sint status, convenit.

---

[1] *i.e.* that the defendant makes the *basis* or *status.* See
§ 13.

as to the meaning of the " exercise of the profession
of actor." If he is accused under the law regarding
the seats in the theatre, the denial will proceed from
the accused ; if on the other hand he is turned out
of the theatre and demands compensation for assault,
the denial will be made by the accuser. The view 20
of the majority of writers[1] on this subject will,
however, hold good in most cases. Some have evaded
these problems by saying that a *basis* is that which
emerges from affirmations and denials, such as " You
did it," " I did not do it," or " I was justified in
doing it." But let us see whether this is the *basis* 21
itself or rather that in which the *basis* is to be found.
Hermagoras calls a *basis* that which enables the
matter in question to be understood and to which the
proofs of the parties concerned will also be directed.
My own opinion has always been that, whereas there
are frequently different *bases* of questions in connexion
with a cause, the *basis* of the cause itself is its most
important point on which the whole matter turns.
If anyone prefers to call that the *general question* or
general head of the cause, I shall not quarrel with him,
any more than I have done hitherto if he produced
a different technical term to express the same thing,
although I know that whole volumes have been
written on such disputes. I prefer however to call
it the *basis*. There is the greatest possible disagree- 22
ment among writers about this as about everything
else, but in this case as elsewhere they seem to me to
have been misled by a passion for saying something
different from their fellow-teachers. As a result
there is still no agreement as to the number and
names of *bases*, nor as to which are general and which
special.

23   Ac primum Aristoteles elementa decem constituit,
circa quae versari videatur omnis quaestio. Οὐσίαν,
quam Plautus essentiam vocat, neque sane aliud est
eius nomen Latinum; sed ea quaeritur, an sit.
Qualitatem, cuius apertus intellectus est. Quantitatem, quae dupliciter a posterioribus divisa est,
quam magnum et quam multum sit? Ad aliquid,
24 unde ducta est translatio et comparatio. Post haec
Ubi et Quando; deinde Facere, Pati, Habere, quod
est quasi armatum esse, vestitum esse. Novissime
κεῖσθαι, quod est compositum esse quodam modo, ut
calere, stare, irasci. Sed ex iis omnibus prima quattuor ad status pertinere, cetera ad quosdam locos
25 argumentorum videntur. Alii novem elementa
posuerunt, Personam, in qua de animo, corpore, extra
positis quaeratur, quod pertinere ad coniecturae et
qualitatis instrumenta video. Tempus, quod χρόνον
vocant, ex quo quaestio, an is quem, dum addicta
est, mater peperit, servus sit natus. Locum, unde
controversia videtur, an fas fuerit tyrannum in
templo occidere. An exulaverit, qui domi latuit
26 Tempus iterum, quod καιρόν appellant; hanc autem
videri volunt speciem illius temporis, ut aestatem

---

[1] *Categ.* ii. 7.
[2] See §§ 52, 68 *sqq.*, 84–86, which make the meaning of
translatio fairly clear. No exact rendering is satisfactory.
Literally it means "transference of the charge": the sense
is virtually the same as that of *exceptio* (a plea made by
defendant in bar of plaintiff's action). "Exception" is

To begin with Aristotle [1] lays down that there are 23
ten categories on which every question seems to turn.
First there is οὐσία, which Plautus calls *essence*, the
only available translation: under this category we inquire *whether a thing is*. Secondly there is *quality*,
the meaning of which is self-evident. Third comes
quantity, which was subdivided by later philosophers
as dealing with two questions as to *magnitude* and
number. Next *relation*, involving questions of *competence* [2] and *comparison*. This is followed by *when*
and *where*. Then come *doing, suffering* and *possessing*, 24
which for example are concerned with a person's being
armed or clothed. Lastly comes κεῖσθαι or *position*,
which means to be in a certain position, such for instance as being warm, standing or angry. Of these
categories the first four concern *bases*, the remainder
concern only certain *topics for argument*. Others 25
make the number of categories to be nine. *Person*,
involving questions concerning the mind, body or
external circumstances, which clearly has reference
to the means by which we establish *conjecture* or
quality. *Time*, or χρόνος, from which we get questions
such as whether a child is born a slave, if his mother
is delivered of him while assigned [3] to her creditors.
Place, from which we get such disputes as to whether
it is permissible to kill a tyrant in a temple, or
whether one who has hidden himself at home can be
regarded as an exile. Then comes *time* in another 26
sense, called καιρός by the Greeks, by which they
refer to a period of time, such as summer or winter;

too unfamiliar and technical a term. "Competence," despite
its vagueness, is perhaps the least unsatisfactory rendering.

[3] *addicti* were not technically *servi*, though in a virtual
condition of servitude, being the bondsmen of their creditors
till their debt was paid.

vel hiemem; huic subiicitur ille in pestilentia comis-
sator. Actum, id est πρᾶξιν, quod eo referunt, *sciens
commiserit an insciens? necessitate an casu?* et talia.
Numerum, qui cadit in speciem quantitatis, an Thra-
sybulo triginta praemia debeantur, quia tot tyrannos
27 sustulerit? Causam, cui plurimae subiacent lites,
quotiens factum non negatur, sed quia iusta ratione
sit factum, defenditur. Τρόπον, cum id, quod alio
modo fieri licet, alio dicitur factum; hinc est adulter
loris caesus vel fame necatus. Occasionem factorum,
quod est apertius, quam ut vel interpretandum vel
exemplo sit demonstrandum, tamen ἀφορμὰς ἔργων
28 vocant. Hi quoque nullam quaestionem extra haec
putant. Quidam detrahunt duas partes, numerum
et occasionem, et pro illo quod dixi actum subiiciunt
res, id est πράγματα. Quae ne praeterisse viderer,
satis habui attingere. Ceterum his nec status satis
ostendi nec omnes contineri locos credo, quod apparebit diligentius legentibus, quae de utraque re
dicam. Erunt enim plura multo, quam quae his
elementis comprehenduntur.

29 Apud plures auctores legi, placuisse quibusdam,
unum omnino statum esse coniecturalem. Sed

---

[1] There is no other reference to this theme.
[2] An adulterer caught *flagrante delicto* might be killed by
the husband or beaten. But to starve him to death in cold
blood would be illegal.

under this heading come problems such as that about
the man who held high revel in a time of pestilence.[1]
Action or πρᾶξις, to which they refer questions as to
whether an act was committed wittingly or unwittingly, by accident or under compulsion and the like.
Number, which falls under the category of quantity,
under which come questions such as whether the
state owes Thrasybulus thirty talents for ridding it of
the same number of tyrants. *Cause*, under which 27
heading come a large number of disputes, whenever
a fact is not denied, but the defence pleads that the
act was just and reasonable. Τρόπος or *manner*, which
is involved when a thing is said to have been done in
one way when it might have been done in another:
under this category come cases of such as that of the
adulterer who is scourged with thongs or starved to
death.[2] *Opportunity* for action, the meaning of which
is too obvious to need explanation or illustration:
the Greeks however call it ἔργων ἀφορμαί. These 28
authorities like Aristotle hold that no question can
arise which does not come under one of these heads.
Some subtract two of them, namely *number* and *opportunity*, and substitute for what I have called *action*,
things, or in Greek πράγματα. I have thought it sufficient to notice these doctrines, for fear someone might
complain of their omission. Still I do not consider
that *bases* are sufficiently determined by these categories, nor that the latter cover every possible kind
of topic, as will be clear to any that read carefully
what I have to say on both points. For there will be
found to be many topics that are not covered by
these categories.

I find it stated in many authors that some rhe- 29
toricians only recognise one kind of *basis*, the *con-*

quibus placuerit, neque illi tradiderunt neque ego usquam reperire potui. Rationem tamen hanc secuti dicuntur, quod res omnis signis colligeretur. Quo modo licet qualitatis quoque solum statum faciant, quia ubique, qualis sit cuiusque rei natura, quaeri potest. Sed utrocunque modo sequetur summa con-
30 fusio. Neque interest, unum quis statum faciat an nullum, si omnes causae sunt condicionis eiusdem. Coniectura dicta est a coniectu, id est directione quadam rationis ad veritatem, unde etiam somniorum atque ominum interpretes coniectores vocantur. Appellatum tamen est hoc genus varie, sicut sequentibus apparebit.

31   Fuerunt, qui duos status facerent: Archedemus coniecturalem et finitivum, exclusa qualitate, quia sic de ea quaeri existimabat, quid esset iniquum, quid iniustum, quid dicto audientem non esse;
32 quod vocat *de eodem et alio.* Huic diversa sententia eorum fuit, qui duos quidem status esse voluerunt, sed unum infitialem, alterum iuridicialem. Infitialis est, quem dicimus coniecturalem, cui ab infitiando nomen alii in totum dederunt, alii in partem, quia accusatorem coniectura, reum infitiatione uti puta-
33 verunt. Iuridicialis est qui Graece dicitur δικαιολο-γικός. Sed quemadmodum ab Archedemo qualitas exclusa est, sic ab his repudiata finitio. Nam subii-

---

[1] Fr. 11, Arnim.
[2] *i.e.* the question may be stated "Does it conform to our conception of injustice or is it something different?" Questions of quality are regarded as questions of definition.

jectural. But they have not mentioned who these rhetoricians are nor have I been able to discover. They are however stated to have taken this view on the ground that all our knowledge is a matter of inference from indications. On this line of reasoning they might regard all *bases* as *qualitative*, because we inquire into the nature of the subject in every case. But the adoption of either view leads to inextricable confusion. Nor does it matter whether one 30 recognises only one kind of *basis* or none at all, if all causes are of the same nature. *Coniectura* is derived from *conicere* " to throw together," because it implies the concentration of the reason on the truth. For this reason interpreters of dreams and all other phenomena are called *coniectores* "conjecturers." But the *conjectural basis* has received more names than one, as will appear in the sequel.

Some have recognised only two *bases*. Arche- 31 demus [1] for instance admits only the *conjectural* and *definitive* and refuses to admit the *qualitative*, since he held that questions of *quality* take the form of " What is unfair? what is unjust? what is disobedience?" which he terms questions about *identity* and *difference*.[2] A different view was held by those who 32 likewise only admitted two *bases*, but made them the *negative* and *juridical*. The *negative basis* is identical with that which we call the *conjectural*, to which some give the name of *negative* absolutely, others only in part, these latter holding that *conjecture* is employed by the accuser, *denial* only by the accused. The *juridical* is that known in Greek as 33 δικαιολογικός. But just as Archedemus would not recognise the *qualitative basis*, so these reject the *definitive* which they include in the *juridical*, holding

ciunt eam iuridiciali, quaerendumque arbitrantur
iustumne sit, sacrilegium appellari quod obiiciatur
34 vel furtum vel amentiam. Qua in opinione Pamphilus fuit, sed qualitatem in plura partitus est;
plurimi deinceps, mutatis tantum nominibus, in rem
de qua constet, et in rem de qua non constet. Nam
est verum nec aliter fieri potest, quam ut aut
certum sit factum esse quid aut non sit; si non est
certum, coniectura sit, si certum est, reliqui status.
35 Nam idem dicit Apollodorus, cum quaestionem aut
in rebus extra positis, quibus coniectura explicatur,
aut in nostris opinionibus existimat positam, quorum
illud πραγματικόν, 'ιος περὶ ἐννοίας vocat; idem, qui
ἀπρόληπτον et προληπτικόν dicunt, id est dubium et
36 praesumptum, quo significatur de quo liquet. Idem
Theodorus, qui de eo, An sit, et de accidentibus ei
quod esse constat, id est περὶ οὐσίας καὶ συμβεβηκότων,
existimat quaeri. Nam in his omnibus prius genus
coniecturam habet, sequens reliqua. Sed haec reliqua Apollodorus duo vult esse, qualitatem et de
nomine, id est finitivam; Theodorus, quid, quale,
37 quantum, ad aliquid. Sunt et qui de eodem et de
alio modo qualitatem esse modo finitionem velint.

---

[1] e.g. circumstantial evidence.
[2] ἀπρόληπτός lit. = unpresumed.

that in these questions we have to enquire whether
it is just that the act with which the accused is
charged should be called sacrilege or theft or mad-
ness. Pamphilus held this opinion but subdivided 34
quality into several different species. The majority
of later writers have classified *bases* as follows, involving however no more than a change of names :—
those dealing with ascertained facts and those
dealing with matters where there is a doubt. For
a thing must either be certain or uncertain : if
it is uncertain, the *basis* will be *conjectural;* if
certain, it will be some one of the other *bases*.
Apollodorus says the same thing when he states that 35
a question must either lie in *things external,*[1] which give
play to *conjecture,* or in our own *opinions :* the former
he calls πραγματικός, the latter περὶ ἐννοίας. The same
is said by those who employ the terms ἀπρόληπτὸς[2]
and προληπτικός, that is to say *doubtful* and *presump-
tive,* by this latter term meaning those facts which
are beyond a doubt. Theodorus agrees with them, 36
for he holds that the question is either as to whether
such and such a thing is really so, or is concerned
with the *accidents* of someting which is an admitted
fact: that is to say it is either περὶ οὐσίας or
περὶ συμβεβηκότων. For in all these cases the first
basis is *conjectural,* while the second belongs to one
of the other classes. As for these other classes of
basis, Apollodorus holds that there are two, one concerned with *quality* and the other with the *names* of
things, that is to say a *definitive basis*. Theodorus
makes them four, concerned with *existence, quality,
quantity* and *relation*. There are some too who make 37
questions of *identity* and *difference* come under the
head of *quality,* others who place it under the head

In duo et Posidonius dividit, vocem et res. In voce
quaeri putat an significet, quid, quam multa, quo
modo? in rebus coniecturam, quod κατ' αἴσθησιν vocat,
et qualitatem, et finitionem, cui nomen dat κατ' ἔννοιαν,
et ad aliquid. Unde et illa divisio est, alia esse
38 scripta, alia inscripta. Celsus Cornelius duos et ipse
fecit status generales, an sit? quale sit? Priori
subiecit finitionem, quia aeque quaeratur an sit
sacrilegus, qui nihil se sustulisse de templo dicit et
qui privatam pecuniam confitetur sustulisse. Qualitatem in rem et scriptum dividit. Scripto quattuor
partes legales, exclusa translatione; quantitatem et
39 mentis quaestionem coniecturae subiecit. Est etiam
alia in duos dividendi status ratio, quae docet, aut
de substantia controversiam esse, aut de qualitate;
ipsam porro qualitatem aut in summo genere con-
40 sistere aut in succedentibus. De substantia est
coniectura. Quaestio enim tractatur rei, an facta
sit? an fiat? an futura sit? interdum etiam mentis;
idque melius, quam quod iis placuit, qui statum
eundem facti nominaverunt, tanquam de praeterito

---

[1] Fr. p. 232, Bake.
[2] cp. § 23; *translatio* and *exceptio* are virtually identical.
The four classes are Intention, Ambiguity, Contradictory
Laws, Syllogism.
[3] *i.e.* the *conjectural basis* concerned with questions of fact.

of *definition*. Posidonius[1] divides them into two classes, those concerned with *words* and those concerned with *things*. In the first case he thinks that the question is whether a word has any meaning; if so, what is its meaning, how many meanings has it, and how does it come to mean what it means? In the latter case, we employ *conjecture*, which he calls κατ' αἴσθησιν, or inference from perception, *quality*, *definition* which he calls κατ' ἔννοιαν or rational inference, and *relation*. Hence also comes the division into things written and unwritten. Even Cornelius 38 Celsus stated that there were two general *bases*, one concerned with the question *whether a thing is*, the other with the question *of what kind it is*. He included *definition* under the first of these, because enquiry may equally be made as to whether sacrilege has been committed, when a man denies that he has stolen anything from a temple, and when he admits that he has stolen private money from a temple. He divides *quality* into *fact* and the *letter of the law*. Under the head of the *letter of the law* he places four classes, excluding questions of *competence*[2]: *quantity* and *intention* he places under the head of *conjecture*.[3] There is also another method of 39 dividing *bases* into two classes: according to this disputes are either about *substance* or *quality*, while *quality* is treated either in its most general sense or in its special senses. *Substance* is dealt with by *conjecture*: for in enquiring into anything, we ask 40 whether it has been done, is being done, or is likely to be done, and sometimes also consider its *intention*: this method is preferable to that adopted by those who style the conjectural *basis* a *basis of fact*, as though we only enquired into the past and what has

41 tantum et tantum de facto quaereretur. Pars
qualitatis, quae est de summo genere, raro in iudicium venit, quale est, idne sit honestum, quod vulgo
laudatur; succedentium autem aliae de communi
appellatione, ut sitne sacrilegus, qui pecuniam privatam ex templo furatus est; aut de re denominata,
ubi et factum esse certum est nec dubitatur, quid sit
quod factum est. Cui subiacent omnes de honestis,
42 iustis, utilibus quaestiones. His etiam ceteri status
contineri dicuntur, quia et quantitas modo ad coniecturam referatur, ut maiorne sol quam terra? modo
ad qualitatem, quanta poena quempiam quantove
praemio sit affici iustum? et translatio versetur circa
43 qualitatem, et definitio pars sit translationis; quin et
contrariae leges et ratiocinativus status, id est syllogismos, et plerumque scripti et voluntatis aequo
nitantur (nisi quod hic tertius aliquando coniecturam accipit, quid senserit legis constitutor); ambiguitatem vero semper coniectura explicari necesse
sit, quia, cum sit manifestum, verborum intellectum
esse duplicem, de sola quaeritur voluntate.

44 A plurimis tres sunt facti generales status, quibus
et Cicero in Oratore utitur, et omnia, quae aut in
controversiam aut in contentionem veniant, contineri

---

[1] See § 11 and the case cited in 38, where the accused
would argue that he was guilty not of sacrilege, but of
simple theft.
[2] When we argue that a certain case comes under a certain law. *cp.* § 15.   [3] *Or.* xiv. 45.

actually been done. The consideration of *quality* 41
under its most general aspect rarely comes up in
the courts; I refer to questions such as "whether
that is honourable which is generally praised." With
regard to the special aspects of *quality*, questions
sometimes occur about some common term, such as
whether sacrilege has been committed when a man
has stolen private money from a temple, or about
some act with a definite name, when there is no
doubt either as to the commission or the nature of
the act. Under this heading come all questions
about what is honourable, just or expedient. These 42
bases are said to contain others as well, because
quantity is sometimes concerned with *conjectural bases,*
as in the question whether the sun is bigger than
the earth, and sometimes with *qualitative bases,* as in
the question what reward or punishment it would
be just to assign to some particular person, while
questions of *competence* undoubtedly are concerned
with *quality,* and *definition* with questions of *competence.*[1] Further *contradictory laws* and the *ratiocinative* 43
basis or *syllogism*[2] and the majority of questions dealing with the *letter of the law* and *intention* are based
on equity, with the exception that this last question
sometimes admits of *conjecture* as, for instance, concerning the *intentions* of the legislator : *ambiguity,*
however, must always be explained by *conjecture,*
because as it is clear that the words admit of two
interpretations the only question is as to the
intention.

A large number of writers recognise *general bases ;* 44
Cicero adopts them in his *Orator,*[3] and holds that
everything that can form the subject of dispute or
discussion is covered by the three questions, *whether*

putat, Sitne? Quid sit? Quale sit? quorum nomina
45 apertiora sunt, quam ut dicenda sint. Idem[1] Patrocles sentit. Tres fecit et M. Antonius his quidem
verbis: *Paucae res sunt, quibus ex rebus omnes orationes
nascuntur, factum non factum, ius iniuria, bonum malum.*
Sed quoniam, quod iure dicimur fecisse, non hunc
solum intellectum habet, ut lege, sed illum quoque,
ut iuste fecisse videamur, secuti Antonium apertius
voluerunt eosdem status distinguere. Itaque dixerunt coniecturalem, legalem, iuridicialem; qui et
46 Verginio placent. Horum deinde fecerunt species,
ita ut legali subiicerent finitionem et alios, qui ex
scripto ducuntur, legum contrariarum, quae ἀντινομία
dicitur, et scripti et sententiae vel voluntatis, id est
κατὰ ῥητὸν καὶ διάνοιαν, et μετάληψιν, quam nos varie
translativam, transumptivam, transpositivam vocamus, συλλογισμόν, quem accipimus ratiocinativum
vel collectivum, ambiguitatis, quae ἀμφιβολία nominatur; quos posui, quia et ipsi a plerisque status
appellantur, cum quibusdam legales potius quaestiones eas dici placuerit.
47 Quattuor fecit Athenaeus, προτρεπτικὴν στάσιν vel
παρορμητικήν, id est exhortativum, qui suasoriae est
proprius; συντελικήν, qua coniecturam significari
magis ex his, quae sequuntur, quam ex ipso nomine

---

[1] Iatrocles, *B.*

---

[1] Conjectural, definitive, and qualitative.
[2] Concerned with questions of competence.

it is, what it is, and *of what kind it is.* The names of these three *bases* are too obvious for mention.[1] The same view is asserted by Patrocles. Marcus 45 Antonius stated that there were three *bases* in the following words:—"The things which form the ground of every speech are few and are as follows:—' Was a thing done or not done?' 'Was it just or unjust?' 'Was it good or bad?'" But since, when we are said to have been justified in doing anything, this does not merely mean that our action was legal, but further implies that it was just, those who follow Antonius attempt to differentiate these *bases* with greater exactness. They therefore called them *conjectural, legal* and *juridical,* a division which meets with the approval of Verginius as well. These 46 they then subdivided into species, placing *definition* under the head of the *legal basis,* together with all others which are concerned with the letter of the law : such as that of *contradictory laws,* or ἀντινομία, that which rests on the *letter of the law* and on *meaning* or *intention* (which the Greeks call κατὰ ῥητὸν καὶ διάνοιαν) and μετάληψις to which latter we give various names, styling it the *translative, transumptive* or *transpositive basis*[2]; the *syllogism,* which we call the *ratiocinative* or *deductive basis ;* and those which turn on *ambiguity* or ἀμφιβολία. I mention these because they are called *bases* by most writers, though some prefer to call them *legal questions.*

Athenaeus laid down that there were four *bases :* 47 the προτρεπτικὴ στάσις or παρορμητική, that is, the *hortative,* which is peculiar to deliberative themes ; the συντελική,[3] which is shown to be the *conjectural,* not so much from the name itself, but from what

[3] συντελική lit. = contributory.

apparet; ὑπαλλακτικήν, ea finitio est, mutatione enim
nominis constat; iuridicialem, eadem appellatione
Graeca qua ceteri usus. Nam est, ut dixi, multa in
48 nominibus differentia. Sunt qui ὑπαλλακτικήν translationem esse existiment, secuti hanc mutationis
significationem. Fecerunt alii totidem status, sed
alios, An sit? Quid sit? Quale sit? Quantum
49 sit? ut Caecilius et Theon. Aristoteles in rhetoricis, An sit, Quale, Quantum, et Quam multum sit?
quaerendum putat. Quodam tamen loco finitionis
quoque vim intelligit, quo dicit quaedam sic defendi,
Sustuli, sed non furtum feci; Percussi, sed non iniuriam
50 *feci.* Posuerat et Cicero in libris rhetoricis, facti,
nominis, generis, actionis; ut in facto coniectura, in
nomine finitio, in genere qualitas, in actione ius in-
telligeretur. Iuri subiecerat translationem. Verum
hic legales quoque quaestiones alio loco tractat ut
species actionis.

51 Fuerunt qui facerent quinque, coniecturam, finitionem, qualitatem, quantitatem, ad aliquid. Theodorus quoque, ut dixi, iisdem generalibus capitibus
utitur, An sit? Quid sit? Quale sit? Quantum
sit? Ad aliquid. Hoc ultimum maxime in com-
parativo genere versari putat, quoniam melius ac

---

[1] The defendant admits the act, but gives it a different
name, *e.g.* theft, not sacrilege. ὑπαλλακτική = changing.
[2] δικαιολογικός.   [3] Caec. fr. 49, Burkh.
[4] Ar. *Rhet.* 1416 b : 1374 a.   [5] *de Inv.* I. viii. 10.
[6] *Part. Or.* 31 and 38.   [7] § 36.

follows; the ὑπαλλακτική or *definitive*, for it consists
in a change of terms [1]; and the *juridical* to which
he gives the name employed by other Greek writers.[2]
For, as I have said, there is a great variety in the
names employed. There are some who, arguing from 48
its meaning of change, hold that ὑπαλλακτική is the
translative basis, which is concerned with *competence*.
Others, Caecilius [3] and Theon for instance, hold
that there are the same number of *bases*, but make
them of a different kind, namely, those covered by
the questions whether a thing is, what it is, of what
kind it is and how great it is.   Aristotle [4] in his 49
Rhetoric states that all enquiry turns on the questions *whether a thing is, of what kind it is, how great
it is,* and *of how many parts it consists.*   In one
place however he recognises the force of *definition*
as well, saying that certain points are defended
on the following lines:—" I took it, but did not
steal it." "I struck him, but did not commit an
assault." Cicero [5] again in his Rhetorica makes the 50
number of *bases* to be four, namely those concerned
with *fact, names, kinds,* and *legal action,* that is to say
conjecture is concerned with *fact, definition* with
names, quality with *kinds,* and *law* with *action*:
under this latter head of *law* he included questions of *competence.*   But in another passage he
treats [6] legal questions as a species of *action.*

Some writers have held that there are *five bases:* 51
the *conjectural, definitive, qualitative, quantitative* and
relative.   Theodorus, also, as I have said,[7] adopts the
same number of general heads, *whether a thing is, what
it is, of what kind it is, how great it is,* and *to what it refers.*
The last he considers to be chiefly concerned with
comparison, since better and worse, greater and less

peius, maius et minus nisi alio relata non intelligun-
52 tur. Sed in illas quoque translativas, ut supra sig-
nificavi, quaestiones incidit, An huic ius agendi sit?
vel, facere aliquid conveniat? An contra hunc?
An hoc tempore? An sic? omnia enim ista referri
53 ad aliquid necesse est. Alii sex status putant, coniecturam, quam γένεσιν vocant, et qualitatem, et
proprietatem, id est ἰδιότητα, quo verbo finitio ostenditur, et quantitatem, quam ἀξίαν dicunt, et com-
parationem, et translationem, cuius adhuc novum
nomen inventum est μετάστασις; novum, inquam, in
statu, alioqui ab Hermagora inter species iuridiciales
54 usitatum. Aliis septem esse placuit; a quibus nec
translatio nec quantitas nec comparatio recepta est,
sed in horum trium locum subditae quattuor legales
55 adiectaeque tribus illis rationalibus. Alii pervenerunt usque ad octo, translatione ad septem superiores
adiecta. A quibusdam deinde divisa ratio est, ut
status rationales appellarent, quaestiones (quemadmodum supra dixi) legales, ut in illis de re, in his de
scripto quaereretur. Quidam in diversum hos status
56 esse, illas quaestiones maluerunt. Sed alii rationales
tres putaverunt, An sit? Quid sit? Quale sit?
Hermagoras solus quattuor, coniecturam, proprietatem, translationem, qualitatem, quam per accidentia,

---

[1] See § 46.
[2] Conjectural, definitive, qualitative.
[3] § 46.

are meaningless terms unless referred to some
standard. But questions of *relation*, as I have already 52
pointed out, enter also into *translative* questions, that
is, questions of *competence*, since in cases such as
" Has this man a right to bring an action?" or " Is
it fitting that he should do such and such a thing,
or against this man, or at this time, or in this
manner?" For all these questions must be referred
to a certain standard. Others hold that there are 53
six *bases : conjecture* or γένεσις, *quality, particularity* or
ἰδιότης, by which word they mean *definition, quantity*
or ἀξία, *comparison* and *competence*, for which a new
term has been found in μετάστασις; I call it new
when applied to a *basis*, for Hermagoras employs it
to describe a species of *juridical question.* Others 54
think there are seven, while refusing to recognise
competence, quantity or *comparison*, in place of which
they substitute four *legal bases*,[1] completing the
seven by the addition of those three which they call
rational.[2] Others again make eight by the addition 55
of *competence* to the above-mentioned seven. Some
on the other hand have introduced a fresh method
of division, reserving the name of *bases* for the
rational, and giving the name of *questions* to the *legal*,
as I mentioned above,[3] since in the former the
problem is concerned with *facts*, in the latter with
the *letter of the law.* Some on the contrary reverse
this nomenclature calling the legal questions *bases*
and the rational grounds *questions.* But others have 56
thought that there are only three *rational bases*,
covered by the questions *whether a thing is, what it is,*
and *of what kind it is?* Hermagoras is alone in
thinking that there are four, namely *conjecture, particularity, competence*, and *quality :* to the latter he

id est κατὰ συμβεβηκός, vocat, hac interpretatione,
an illi accidat viro bono esse, vel malo. Hanc ita
dividit, de appetendis et fugiendis, quae est pars
57 deliberativa; de persona, ea ostenditur laudativa;
negotialem, quam πραγματικήν vocat, in qua de rebus
ipsis quaeritur, remoto personarum complexu, ut,
Sitne liber qui est in assertione, an divitiae super-
biam pariant, an iustum quid, an bonum sit.
Iuridicialem, in qua fere eadem sed certis destina-
tisque personis quaerantur: an ille iuste hoc fecerit,
58 vel bene.   Nec me fallit, in primo Ciceronis rhetorico aliam esse loci negotialis interpretationem, cum
ita scriptum sit: *Negotialis est, in qua, quid iuris ex
civili more et aequitate sit, consideratur ; cui diligentiae
59 praeesse apud nos iurisconsulti existimantur.*   Sed quod
ipsius de his libris iudicium fuerit, supra dixi.   Sunt
enim velut regestae in hos commentarios, quos ado-
lescens deduxerat, scholae, et si qua est in his culpa,
tradentis est, sive eum movit id, quod Hermagoras
prima in hoc loco posuit exempla ex quaestionibus
iuris, sive quod Graeci πραγματικοὺς vocant iuris in-
60 terpretes.   Sed Cicero quidem his pulcherrimos illos

---

[1] *assertio* = a trial in which the question of a person's
liberty is involved.   When waiting trial, this person is
described as *in assertione.*
[2] *de Inv.* I. xi. 14.   [3] See III. v. 15.

appends the phrase κατὰ συμβεβηκός, "according to
its accidents," illustrating his meaning by putting a
case where it is enquired whether a man *happen* to
be good or bad. He then subdivides *quality* into
four species : first that which is concerned with
things to be sought or avoided, which belongs to *deliberative* oratory : secondly those concerned with 57
persons, by which he indicates *panegyric :* thirdly the
practical or *pragmatic,* which is concerned *with things
in general* without reference to persons, and may be
illustrated by questions such as whether he is free
who is claimed as a slave and waiting the trial of his
case,[1] whether riches beget insolence, and whether a
thing is just or good ; lastly there is the *juridical*
species, under which practically the same questions
arise, but in relation to certain definite persons, as for
instance when it is asked whether that particular man
has done well or ill. I am aware that another explana- 58
tion is given by Cicero in the first book of his
Rhetorica[2] of the species known as *practical,*
where he says that it is "the department under
which we consider what is right according to civil
usage and equity : this department is regarded by
us as the special sphere of the lawyer." But I have 59
already mentioned[3] what his opinion was about this
particular work. The Rhetorica are simply a collection of school-notes on rhetoric which he worked
up into this treatise while quite a young man. Such
faults as they possess are due to his instructor. In the
present instance he may have been influenced by the
fact that the first examples given by Hermagoras of
this species are drawn from legal questions, or by the
fact that the Greeks call interpreters of the law
πραγματικοί. But for these early efforts Cicero substi- 60

439

de Oratore substituit, ideoque culpari, tanquam falsa praecipiat, non potest. Nos ad Hermagoran. Translationem hic primus omnium tradidit, quanquam semina eius quaedam citra nomen ipsum apud Aris-

61 totelen reperiuntur. Legales autem quaestiones has fecit, scripti et voluntatis (quam ipse vocat κατὰ ῥητὸν καὶ ὑπεξαίρεσιν, id est dictum et exceptionem, quorum prius ei cum omnibus commune est, exceptionis nomen minus usitatum), ratiocinativum, ambiguitatis,

62 legum contrariarum. Albutius eadem divisione usus detrahit translationem, subiiciens eam iuridiciali. In legalibus quoque quaestionibus nullum putat esse, qui dicatur ratiocinativus. Scio plura inventuros adhuc, qui legere antiquos studiosius volent, sed ne haec quoque excesserint modum vereor.

63 Ipse me paulum in alia, quam prius habuerim, opinione nunc esse confiteor. Et fortasse tutissimum erat famae modo studenti nihil ex eo mutare, quod multis annis non sensissem modo, verum etiam

64 approbassem. Sed non sustineo esse conscius mihi dissimulati (in eo praesertim opere, quod ad bonorum iuvenum aliquam utilitatem componimus) in ulla parte iudicii mei. Nam et Hippocrates, clarus arte medicinae, videtur honestissime fecisse, quod quosdam

---

[1] *Rhet.* II. xv. 8.   [2] *Epidem.* v. 14.

tuted his splendid *de Oratore* and therefore cannot be
blamed for giving false instruction. I will now
return to Hermagoras. He was the first rhetorician
to teach that there was a *basis* concerned with *competence,* although the elements of this doctrine are
found in Aristotle,[1] without however any mention of
the name. The legal questions were according to 61
Hermagoras of five kinds. First the letter of the
law and its intention; the names which he gives to
these are κατὰ ῥητόν and ὑπεξαίρεσις, that is to say
the letter of the law and the *exceptions* thereto: the
first of these classes is found in all writers, but the
term *exception* is less in use. The number is
completed by the *ratiocinative basis* and those
dealing with *ambiguity* and *contradictory laws.* Albutius 62
adopts this classification, but eliminates *competence,*
including it under the juridical *basis.* Further he
holds that in legal questions there is no *ratiocinative
basis.* I know that those who are prepared to
read ancient writers on rhetoric more carefully than
I have, will be able to discover yet more on this
subject, but I fear that I may have been too lengthy
even in saying what I have said.

I must admit that I am now inclined to take a 63
different view from that which I once held. It would
perhaps be safer for my reputation if I were to make
no modification in views which I not only held for so
many years, but of which I expressed my open appro-
bation. But I cannot bear to be thought guilty of 64
concealment of the truth as regards any portion of
my views, more especially in a work designed for the
profit of young men of sound disposition. For Hippocrates,[2] the great physician, in my opinion took the
most honourable course in acknowledging some of

errores suos, ne posteri errarent, confessus est; et
M. Tullius non dubitavit aliquos iam editos libros
aliis postea scriptis ipse damnare, sicut Catulum
atque Lucullum et hos ipsos, de quibus modo sum
65 locutus, artis rhetoricae. Etenim supervacuus foret
in studiis longior labor, si nihil liceret melius invenire
praeteritis. Neque tamen quidquam ex iis, quae
tum praecepi, supervacuum fuit; ad easdem enim
particulas haec quoque, quae nunc praecipiam, re-
vertentur; ita neminem didicisse poeniteat, colligere
tantum eadem ac disponere paulo significantius conor.
Omnibus autem satisfactum volo, non me hoc serius
66 demonstrare aliis, quam mihi ipse persuaserim. Secundum plurimos auctores servabam tris rationales
status, coniecturam, qualitatem, finitionem, unum
legalem. Hi mihi status generales erant. Legalem
in quinque species partiebar, scripti et voluntatis,
legum contrariarum, collectivum, ambiguitatis, trans-
67 lationis. Nunc quartum ex generalibus intelligo
posse removeri; sufficit enim prima divisio, qua
diximus alios rationales, alios legales esse; ita non
erit status, sed quaestionum genus; alioqui et ratio-
68 nalis status esset. Ex iis etiam, quos speciales
vocabam, removi translationem, frequenter quidem
(sicut omnes qui me secuti sunt meminisse possunt)
testatus et in ipsis etiam illis sermonibus me nolente

---

[1] The two books of the first edition of the *Academica*.
[2] *i.e.* the Rhetorica, better known as *de Inventione*.
[3] See III. v. 4.   [4] See I. Proem. 7.

his errors to prevent those who came after from being led astray, while Cicero had no hesitation about condemning some of his earlier works in books which he published later : I refer to his condemnation of his *Lucullus* and *Catulus* [1] and the books [2] on rhetoric which I have already mentioned. Indeed we should have no justification for protracting our studies if we were forbidden to improve upon our original views. Still none of my past teaching was superfluous : for the views which I am now going to produce will be found to be based on the same principles, and consequently no one need be sorry to have attended my lectures, since all that I am now attempting to do is to collect and rearrange my original views so that they may be somewhat more instructive. But I wish to satisfy everybody and not to lay myself open to the accusation that I have allowed a long time to elapse between the formation and publication of my views. I used to follow the majority of authorities in adhering to three *rational bases,* the *conjectural, qualitative* and *definitive,* and to one *legal basis.* [3] These were my *general bases.* The *legal basis* I divided into five *species,* dealing with the *letter of the law and intention, contradictory laws,* the *syllogism, ambiguity* and *competence.* It is now clear to me that the fourth of the *general bases* may be removed, since the original division which I made into *rational* and *legal bases* is sufficient. The fourth therefore will not be a *basis,* but a kind of *question ;* if it were not, it would form one of the *rational bases.* Further I have removed *competence* from those which I called *species.* For I often asserted, as all who have attended my lectures will remember, and even those discourses which were published against my will [4] included the state-

vulgatis hoc tamen complexus, vix in ulla controversia translationis statum posse reperiri, ut non et
alius in eadem recte dici videretur, ideoque a qui-
69 busdam eum exclusum. Neque ignoro multa trans-
ferri, cum in omnibus fere causis, in quibus cecidisse
quis formula dicitur, hae sint quaestiones, an huic,
an cum hoc, an hac lege, an apud hunc, an hoc tem-
70 pore liceat agere? et si qua sunt talia. Sed personae, tempora, actiones ceteraque propter aliquam
causam transferuntur; ita non est in translatione
quaestio sed in eo, propter quod transferuntur: *Non
debes apud praetorem petere fidei commissum, sed apud
consules, maior enim praetoria cognitione summa est.*
Quaeritur, an maior summa sit, facti controversia
71 est. *Non licet tibi agere mecum, cognitor enim fieri non
potuisti:* iudicatio, an potuerit. *Non debuisti interdi-
cere sed petere:* an recte interdictum sit, ambigitur.
72 Quae omnia succedunt legitimis quaestionibus. An
non praescriptiones (etiam in quibus maxime videtur
manifesta translatio) easdem omnes species habent,

---

sc. by getting an order for restitution.

ment, that the *basis* concerned with competence hardly ever occurs in any dispute under such circumstances that it cannot more correctly be given some other name, and that consequently some rhetoricians exclude it from their list of *bases*. I am, however, 69 well aware that the point of *competence* is raised in many cases, since in practically every case in which a party is said to have been ruled out of court through some error of form, questions such as the following arise : whether it was lawful for this person to bring an action, or to bring it against some particular person, or under a given law, or in such a court, or at such a time, and so on. But the question of *com-* 70 *petence* as regards persons, times, legal actions and the rest originates in some pre-existent cause : the question turns therefore not on *competence* itself, but on the cause with which the point of *competence* originates. " You ought to demand the return of a deposit not before the praetor but before the consuls, as the sum is too large to come under the praetor's jurisdiction." The question then arises whether the sum is too large, and the dispute is one of fact. " You have no right to bring an action against 71 me, as it is impossible for you to have been appointed to represent the actual plaintiff." It then has to be decided whether he could have been so appointed. " You ought not to have proceeded by interdict,[1] but to have put in a plea for possession." The point in doubt is whether the interdict is legal. All these points fall under the head of *legal questions*. For do 72 not even those special pleas, in which questions of *competence* make themselves most evident, give rise to the same species of question as those laws under which the action is brought, so that the enquiry is

quas eae leges, quibus agitur, ut aut de nomine aut
scripto et sententia vel ratiocinatione quaeratur?
Deinde status ex quaestione oritur; translatio non
habet quaestionem, de qua contendit orator, sed
73 propter quam contendit.   Hoc apertius, *Occidisti
hominem, Non occidi;* quaestio, an occiderit, status
coniectura.   Non est tale, *Habeo ius actionis, Non
habes,* ut sit quaestio, an habeat, et inde status.
Accipiat enim actionem necne, ad eventum pertinet,
non ad causam, et ad id, quod pronuntiat iudex, non
74 id, propter quod pronuntiat.   Hoc illi simile est,
Puniendus es, Non sum; videbit iudex, an puniendus
sit.   Sed non hic erit quaestio nec hic status.   Ubi
ergo?   *Puniendus es, hominem occidisti; Non occidi:*
An occiderit.   *Honorandus sum, Non es;* num statum
habet? non, ut puto.   *Honorandus sum, quia tyrannum
75 occidi; Non occidisti;* quaestio et status.   Similiter,
Non recte agis, Recte ago non habet statum.   Ubi est
ergo?   *Non recte agis ignominiosus.*   Quaeritur, an

---

¹ *e.g.* murder or manslaughter : sacrilege or theft.
² See § 70.
³ *sc.* the conjectural.

really concerned with the name of a given act,[1] with the letter of the law and its meaning, or with something that requires to be settled by argument? The *basis* originates from the question, and in cases of *competence* it is not the question concerning which the advocate argues that is involved, but the question on account of which he argues.[2] An example will make 73 this clearer. " You have killed a man." " I did not kill him." The *question* is whether he has killed him; the *basis* is the *conjectural*. But the following case is very different. " I have the right to bring this action." "You have not the right." The question is whether he has the right, and it is from this that we derive the *basis*. For whether he is allowed the right or not depends on the event, not on the cause itself, and on the decision of the judge, not on that on account of which he gives such a decision. The following is a similar 74 example. " You ought to be punished." " I ought not." The judge will decide whether he should be punished, but it is not with this that the *question* or the *basis* is concerned. Where then does the *question* lie? " You ought to be punished, for you have killed a man." " I did not kill him." The *question* is whether he killed him. " I ought to receive some honour." " You ought not." Does this involve a *basis*? I think not. " I ought to receive some honour for killing a tyrant." " You did not kill him." Here there is a *question* and a *basis*[3] as well. So, too, " You 75 are not entitled to bring this action," " I have," involves no *basis*. Where then is it to be found? " You have no right to bring this action, because you have been deprived of civil rights." In this case the question is whether he has been so deprived, or whether loss of civil rights debars a person from

ignominiosus sit; aut, an agere ignominioso liceat;
quaestiones et status. Ergo translativum genus
76 causae ut comparativum et mutuae accusationis. At
enim simile est illi *"Habeo ius, Non habes," "Occidisti,
Recte occidi."* Non nego, sed nec haec res statum
facit. Non enim sunt hae propositiones (alioqui
causa non explicabitur), sed, cum suis rationibus.
*Scelus commisit Horatius, sororem enim occidit. Non
commisit, debuit enim occidere eam, quae hostis mortem
maerebat.* Quaestio, an haec iusta causa; ita qua-
77 litas. Et similiter in translatione, *Non habes ius
abdicandi, quia ignominioso non est actio. Habeo ius,
quia abdicatio actio non est.* Quaeritur, quid sit actio:
finiemus *Non licet abdicare filium* syllogismo. Item
cetera per omnes et rationales et legales status.
78 Nec ignoro fuisse quosdam, qui translationem in
rationali quoque genere ponerent hoc modo, *Hominem occidi, iussus ab imperatore. Dona templi cogenti
tyranno dedi. Deserui tempestatibus, fluminibus, valetudine impeditus.* Id est, non per me stetit, sed per illud.
79 A quibus etiam liberius dissentio. Non enim actio
transfertur sed causa facti, quod accidit paene in omni

---

[1] *sc.* the conjectural or definitive basis and the qualitative.
[2] See III. x. 3 and 4.
[3] Disinheritance could only be effected by legal action.
[4] See § 15.

bringing an action. Here on the other hand we find
both *questions* and *bases*.[1] It is therefore to *kinds of
causes*, not to *bases* that the term *competence* applies:
other *kinds of cause* are the *comparative* and the *recri-
minatory*.[2] "But," it is urged, "the case 'I have a 76
right,' 'You have not,' is similar to 'You have killed
a man,' 'I was justified in so doing.'" I do not deny
it, but this does not make it a *basis*. For these statements are not propositions until the reasons for them
are added. If they were propositions as they stand,
the case could not proceed. " Horatius has committed
a crime, for he has killed his sister." " He has not
committed a crime, since it was his duty to kill her
for mourning the death of an enemy." The question
is whether this was a justifiable reason, and the *basis*
is one of *quality*. So too as regards *competence*. "You 77
have no right to disinherit, since a person who has
been deprived of civil rights is not allowed to take
legal action."[3] " I have the right, since disinheriting
is not legal action." The question here is what is legal
action. And we shall arrive at the conclusion that the
son's disinheritance is unlawful, by use of the *syllogism*.[4]
The case will be similar with all the *rational* and *legal
bases*. I am aware that there have been some who 78
placed *competence* among *rational bases*, using as
illustrations cases such as, " I killed a man under
orders from my general," " I gave the votive offerings
in a temple to a tyrant under compulsion," " I de-
serted owing to the fact that storms or floods or ill-
health prevented me from rejoining." That is to say
it was not due to me, but some external cause. From 79
these writers I differ even more widely: for it is not
the nature of the *legal action* itself which is involved
in the question of *competence*, but the cause of the act;

defensione. Deinde is, qui tali utitur patrocinio,
non recedit a forma qualitatis, dicit enim, se culpa
vacare; ut magis qualitatis duplex ratio facienda sit,
altera qua et factum defenditur, altera qua tantum
reus.

80   Credendum est igitur his, quorum auctoritatem
secutus est Cicero, tria esse, quae in omni disputa-
tione quaerantur, an sit, quid sit, quale sit? quod
ipsa nobis etiam natura praescribit. Nam primum
oportet subesse aliquid, de quo ambigitur; quod,
quid sit et quale sit, certe non potest aestimari, nisi
prius esse constiterit, ideoque ea prima quaestio.

81 Sed non statim, quod esse manifestum est, etiam
quid sit, apparet. Hoc quoque constituto novissima
qualitas superest, neque his exploratis aliud est ultra.
His infinitae quaestiones, his finitae continentur;
horum aliqua in demonstrativa, deliberativa, iudiciali

82 materia utique tractatur. Haec rursus iudiciales
causas et rationali parte et legali continent; neque
enim ulla iuris disceptatio nisi finitione, qualitate,

83 coniectura potest explicari. Sed instituentibus rudes
non erit inutilis latius primo fusa ratio et, si non
statim rectissima linea tensa, facilior tamen et apertior via. Discant igitur ante omnia quadripertitam

---

[1] (*A*) Absolute, when the deed is shown to be right. (*B*)
Relative, when the act is not defended, but the agent is
cleared of the guilt of the act.

[2] See § 44.

and this is the case in almost every defence. Finally he who adopts this line of defence, does not thereby abandon the *qualitative basis ;* for he states that he himself is free from blame, so that we really should differentiate between two kinds of *quality*,[1] one of which comes into play when both the accused person and his act are defended, and the other when the accused person alone is defended.

We must therefore accept the view of the authorities followed by Cicero,[2] to the effect that there are three things on which enquiry is made in every case : we ask *whether a thing is, what it is,* and *of what kind it is.* Nature herself imposes this upon us. For first of all there must be some subject for the question, since we cannot possibly determine *what a thing is,* or *of what kind it is,* until we have first ascertained *whether it is,* and therefore the first question raised is *whether it is.* But even when it is clear that a thing *is,* it is not immediately obvious *what it is.* And when we have decided what it is, there remains the question of its *quality.* These three points once ascertained, there is no further question to ask. These heads cover both *definite* and *indefinite questions.* One or more of them is discussed in every demonstrative, deliberative or forensic theme. These heads again cover all cases in the courts, whether we regard them from the point of view of *rational* or *legal questions.* For no legal problem can be settled save by the aid of *definition, quality* and *conjecture.* Those, however, who are engaged in instructing the ignorant will find it useful at first to adopt a slightly less rigid method : the road will not be absolutely straight to begin with, but it will be more open and will provide easier going. I would have them therefore learn above all things

in omnibus causis esse rationem, quam primam intueri debeat qui acturus est. Nam, ut a defensore
potissimum incipiam, longe fortissima tuendi se ratio
est, si quod obiicitur negari potest; proxima, si non
id, quod obiicitur, factum esse dicitur; tertia hones-
tissima, qua recte factum defenditur. Quibus si
deficiamur, ultima quidem sed iam sola superest
salus aliquo iuris adiutorio elabendi ex crimine, quod
neque negari neque defendi potest, ut non videatur
84 iure actio intendi. Hinc illae quaestiones sive
actiones sive translationes. Sunt enim quaedam
non laudabilia non natura sed iure concessa, ut in
XII tabulis debitoris corpus inter creditores dividi
licuit, quam legem mos publicus repudiavit; et
aliquid aequum sed prohibitum iure, ut libertas tes-
85 tamentorum. Accusatori nihilo plura intuenda sunt,
ut probet factum esse, hoc esse factum, non recte
factum, iure se intendere. Ita circa species easdem
lis omnis versabitur translatis tantum aliquando partibus, ut in causis, quibus de praemio agitur, recte
factum petitor probat.

86   Haec quattuor velut proposita formaeque actionis,
quae tum generales status vocabam, in duo (ut

---

[1] *e.g.* that the legal heir must receive at least a quarter of
the property.

that there are four different methods which may be employed in every case, and he who is going to plead should study them as first essentials. For, to begin with the defendant, far the strongest method of self-defence is, if possible, to deny the charge. The second best is when it is possible to reply that the particular act with which you are charged was never committed. The third and most honourable is to maintain that the act was justifiable. If none of these lines of defence are feasible, there remains the last and only hope of safety : if it is impossible either to deny the charge or justify the act, we must evade the charge with the aid of some point of law, making it appear that the action has been brought against us illegally. Hence arise those questions of *legal action* 84 or *competence.* For there are some things, which, although not laudable in themselves, are yet permitted by law ; witness the passage in the Twelve Tables authorising creditors to divide up a debtor's body amongst themselves, a law which is repudiated by public custom. There are also certain things which although equitable are prohibited by law ; witness the restrictions placed on testamentary disposition.[1] The 85 accuser likewise has four things which he must keep in mind : he must prove that something was done, that a particular act was done, that it was wrongly done, and that he brings his charge according to law. Thus every cause will turn on the same sorts of questions, though the parts of plaintiff and defendant will sometimes be interchanged : for instance in the case of a claim for a reward, it will be the plaintiff's task to show that what was done was right.

These four schemes or forms of action which I then 86 called *general bases* fall into two classes as I have

ostendi) genera discedunt rationale et legale. Rationale simplicius est, quia ipsius tantum naturae
contemplatione constat. Itaque in eo satis est os-
87 tendisse coniecturam, finitionem, qualitatem. Lega-
lium plures sint species necesse est, propterea quod
multae sunt leges et varias habent formas. Alia est
cuius verbis nitimur, alia cuius voluntate, alias nobis,
cum ipsi nullam habeamus, adiungimus, alias inter se
88 comparamus, alias in diversum interpretamur. Sic
nascuntur haec velut simulacra ex illis tribus, interim
simplicia, interim et mixta, propriam tamen faciem
ostendentia, ut scripti et voluntatis, quae sine dubio
aut qualitate aut coniectura continetur, et syllogismos, qui est maxime qualitatis, et leges contrariae,
quae iisdem, quibus scriptum et voluntas, constant,
et ἀμφιβολία, quae semper coniectura explicatur.
89 Finitio quoque utrique generi, quodque rerum quodque scripti contemplatione constat, communis est.
Haec omnia, etiamsi in illos tres status veniunt,
tamen, quia (ut dixi) habent aliquid velut proprium,
videntur demonstranda discentibus, et permittendum
ea dicere vel status legales vel quaestiones vel capita
quaedam minora, dum sciant, nihil ne in his quidem
90 praeter tria, quae praediximus, quaeri. At Quantum? et Quam multum? et Ad aliquid et, ut non-

---

[1] § 67, and III. v. 4.
[2] § 87.   [3] § 80.

shown,[1] namely, the *rational* and the *legal*. The *rational* is the simpler, as it involves nothing more than the consideration of the nature of things. In this connection, therefore, a mere mention of *conjecture, definition* and *quality* will suffice. *Legal questions* 87 necessarily have a larger number of species, since there are many laws and a variety of forms. In the case of one law we rely on the letter, in others on the spirit. Some laws we force to serve our turn, when we can find no law to support our case, others we compare with one another, and on others we put some novel interpretation. Thus from these three *bases* we 88 get three resemblances of *bases*: sometimes simple, sometimes complex, but all having a character of their own, as, for instance, when questions of the *letter of the law* and its *intention* are involved, for these clearly come under *conjecture* or *quality*; or again where the syllogism is involved, for this is specially connected with *quality*; or where contradictory laws are involved, for these are on the same footing as the *letter of the law and intention*; or yet again in cases of *ambiguity*, which is always resolved by *conjecture*. *Definition* also 89 belongs to both classes of question, namely those concerned with the consideration of *facts* and those concerned with the *letter of the law*. All these questions, although they come under the three *bases*, yet since, as I have mentioned,[2] they have certain characteristic features of their own, require to be pointed out to learners; and we must allow them to be called *legal bases* or *questions* or *minor heads*, as long as it is clearly understood that none of them involve any other *questions* than the three I have mentioned.[3] As regards questions of *quantity, number,* 90 *relation,* and, as some have thought, *comparison,* the

nulli putarunt, comparativus non eandem rationem
habent; sunt enim haec non ad varietatem iuris sed
ad solam rationem referenda, ideoque semper in
parte aut coniecturae aut qualitatis ponenda sunt, ut
Qua mente? et Quo tempore? et Quo loco?

91 Sed de singulis dicemus quaestionibus, cum tractare praecepta divisionis coeperimus. Hoc inter
omnes convenit, in causis simplicibus singulos status
esse causarum, quaestionum autem, quae velut subiacent his et ad illud, quo iudicium continetur, refe-
92 runtur, saepe in unam cadere plures posse; etiam
credo aliquando dubitari, quo statu sit utendum, cum
adversus unam intentionem plura opponuntur; et
sicut in colore dicitur narrationis, eum esse optimum,
quem actor optime tueatur, ita hic quoque posse dici,
eum statum esse faciendum, in quo tuendo plurimum
93 adhibere virium possit orator; ideoque pro Milone
aliud Ciceroni agenti placuit aliud Bruto, cum exercitationis gratia componeret orationem, cum ille iure
tanquam insidiatorem occisum et tamen non Milonis
consilio dixerit, ille etiam gloriatus sit occiso malo
94 cive: in coniunctis vero posse duos et tris inveniri
vel diversos, ut si quis aliud se non fecisse, aliud
recte fecisse defendat, vel generis eiusdem, ut si
95 quis duo crimina neget. Quod accidit etiam, si de
una re quaeratur aliqua sed eam plures petant, vel

---

[1] Book VII.

case is different. For these have no connexion with
the complexities of the law, but are concerned with
reason only. Consequently they must always be
regarded as coming under *conjecture* or *quality*, as, for
instance, when we ask with what purpose, or at what
time, or place something was done.

But I will speak of individual questions when I 91
come to handle the rules for *division*.[1] This much is
agreed to by all writers, that one *cause* possesses one
basis, but that as regards secondary questions related
to the main issue of the trial, there may frequently
be a number in one single cause. I also think there 92
is at times some doubt as to which *basis* should be
adopted, when many different lines of defence are
brought to meet a single charge; and, just as in regard to the complexion to be given to the statement
of the facts of the case, that complexion is said to be
the best which the speaker can best maintain, so in
the present connexion I may say that the best *basis*
to choose is that which will permit the orator to develop a maximum of force. It is for this reason that 93
we find Cicero and Brutus taking up different lines
in defence of Milo. Cicero says that Clodius was
justifiably killed because he sought to waylay Milo,
but that Milo had not designed to kill him; while
Brutus, who wrote his speech merely as a rhetorical
exercise, also exults that Milo has killed a bad citizen.
In complicated causes, however, two or three *bases* may 94
be found, or different *bases*: for instance a man may
plead that he did not do one thing, and that he was
justified in doing another, or to take another similar
class of case, a man may deny two of the charges.
The same thing occurs when there is a question 95
about some one thing which is claimed by a number

eodem iure ut proximitatis vel diverso, ut cum hic
testamento, ille proximitate nitetur.   Quotiens
autem aliud alii petitori opponitur, dissimiles esse
96 status necesse est, ut in illa controversia : *Testamenta
legibus facta rata sint.   Intestatorum parentium liberi
heredes sint.   Abdicatus ne quid de bonis patris capiat.
Nothus ante legitimum natus legitimus filius sit, post
legitimum natus tantum civis.   In adoptionem dare liceat.
In adoptionem dato redire in familiam liceat, si pater*
97 *naturalis sine liberis decesserit.   Qui ex duobus legitimis alterum in adoptionem dederat, alterum abdica-
verat, sustulit nothum; instituto herede abdicato
decessit.   Tres omnes de bonis contendunt.*   Nothum, qui non sit legitimus, Graeci vocant; Latinum
rei nomen, ut Cato quoque in oratione quadam testatus est, non habemus ideoque utimur peregrino.
98 Sed ad propositum.   Heredi scripto opponitur lex,
Abdicatus ne quid de bonis patris capiat; fit status
scripti et voluntatis, an ullo modo capere possit, an
ex voluntate patris, an heres scriptus.   Notho
duplex fit quaestio, quod post legitimos natus sit et

of persons, who may all of them rely on the same
kind of plea (for instance, on the right of the next of
kin), or may put in different claims, one urging that
the property was left him by will, another that he is
next of kin. Now whenever a different defence has
to be made against different claimants, there must be
different *bases*, as for example the well-known controversial theme : " Wills that are made in accordance 96
with law shall be valid. When parents die intestate,
their children shall be the heirs. A disinherited son
shall receive none of his father's property. A bastard,
if born before a legitimate son, shall be treated as
legitimate, but if born after a legitimate son shall be
treated merely as a citizen. It shall be lawful to give
a son in adoption. Every son given in adoption shall
have the right to re-enter his own family if his natural
father has died childless. A father of two legitimate 97
sons gave one in adoption, disinherited the other,
and acknowledged a bastard, who was born to him
later. Finally after making the disinherited son his
heir he died. All three sons lay claim to the
property." *Nothus* is the Greek word for a bastard ;
Latin, as Cato emphasized in one of his speeches, has
no word of its own and therefore borrows the foreign
term. But I am straying from the point. The son 98
who was made heir by the will finds his way barred
by the law " A disinherited son shall receive none of
his father's property." The *basis* is one resting on
the *letter of the law* and *intention*, and the problem is
whether he can inherit by any means at all ? can he
do so in accordance with the intention of his father ?
or in virtue of the fact that he was made heir by the
will ? The problem confronting the bastard is twofold, since he was born after the two legitimate sons

99 quod non sit ante legitimum natus. Prior syllogismon
habet, an pro non natis sint habendi, qui a familia
sunt alienati. Altera et scripti et voluntatis. Non
esse enim hunc natum ante legitimum convenit, sed
voluntate legis se tuebitur, quam dicet talem fuisse,
ut legitimus esset nothus tunc natus, cum alius legi-
100 timus in domo non esset. Scriptum quoque legis
excludet dicens, non utique, si postea legitimus
natus non sit, notho nocere; uteturque hoc argumento: *Finge solum natum nothum, cuius condicionis
erit? Tantum civis? atqui non erit post legitimum
natus. An filius? atqui non erit ante legitimos natus.
Quare si verbis legis stari non potest, voluntate standum*
101 *est.* Nec quemquam turbet, quod ex una lege duo
status fiant; duplex est, ita vim duarum habet.
Redire in familiam volenti dicitur ab altero primum,
Ut tibi redire liceat, heres sum. Idem status, qui in
petitione abdicati; quaeritur enim, an possit esse
102 heres abdicatus. Obiicitur communiter a duobus,
*Redire tibi in familiam non licet, non enim pater sine
liberis decessit.* Sed in hoc propria quisque eorum
quaestione nitetur. Alter enim dicet abdicatum

---

¹ The law is twofold as containing two separate, though
complementary, enactments on the position of bastards:
(a) *nothus . . . . filius sit*, (b) *post . . . . civis* (§ 96).

and was not born before a legitimate son. The first 99
problem involves a syllogism : are those sons who
have been cast out from their own family to be regarded as though they had never been born ? The
second is concerned with the letter of the law and
intention. For it is admitted that he was not born
before any legitimate son, but he will defend his
claim by appealing to the intention of the law, which
he will maintain to imply that the bastard, born when
there was no legitimate son in the family, should
rank as legitimate. He will dismiss the letter of the 100
law, pointing out that in any case the position of a
bastard is not prejudiced by the fact that no legitimate
son was born after him, and arguing as follows :—
"Suppose that the only son is a bastard, what will
his position be ? Merely that of a citizen ? and yet
he was not born after any legitimate son. Or
will he rank as a son in all respects ? But he
was not born before the legitimate sons. As it is
impossible to stand by the letter of the law we
must stand by its intentions." It need disturb no one 101
that one law should originate two *bases*. The law is
twofold, and therefore has the force of two laws.[1]
To the son who desires to re-enter the family, the
disinherited's first reply is, "Even though you are
allowed to re-enter the family, I am still the heir."
The *basis* will be the same as in the claim put forward
by the disinherited son, since the question at issue is
whether a disinherited son can inherit. Both the 102
disinherited and the bastard will object, "You cannot
re-enter the family, for our father did not die childless." But in this connexion each will rely on
his own particular question. For the disinherited son
will say that even a disinherited man does not cease

quoque inter liberos esse, et argumentum ducet ex
ipsa, qua repellitur, lege; supervacuum enim fuisse
prohiberi patris bonis abdicatum, si esset numero
alienorum; nunc quia filii iure futurus fuerit intes-
tati heres, oppositam esse legem, quae tamen non
id efficiat, ne filius sit, sed ne heres sit.   Status
103 finitivus, quid sit filius.   Rursus   nothus eisdem
colligit argumentis, non sine liberis patrem deces-
sisse, quibus in petitione usus est, ut probaret esse
se filium.   Nisi forte et hic finitionem movet, an
liberi sint etiam non legitimi.   Cadent ergo in
unam controversiam vel specialiter duo legitimi
status scripti et voluntatis et syllogismos et praeterea finitio, vel tres illi, qui natura soli sunt, coniectura in scripto et voluntate, qualitas in syllogismo,
et, quae per se est aperta, finitio.

104   Causa quoque et iudicatio et continens est in omni
genere causarum.   Nihil enim dicitur, cui non insit
ratio et quo iudicium referatur et quod rem maxime
contineat.   Sed quia magis haec variantur in litibus
et fere tradita sunt ab iis, qui de iudicialibus causis
aliqua composuerunt, in illam partem differantur.
Nunc, quia in tria genera causas divisi, ordinem
sequar.

---

¹ See § 82.   ² See § 88.
³ For discussion of these technical terms see chap. xi.
⁴ Chaps. iii. and iv.

to be a son, and will derive an argument from that
very law which denies his claim to the inheritance;
namely that it was unnecessary for a disinherited son
to be excluded from possession of his father's property
if he had ceased to be one of the family; but now,
since in virtue of his rights as son he would have
been his father's heir if he had died intestate, the
law is brought to bar his claim; and yet the law does
not deprive him of his position as son, but only of his
position as heir. Here the *basis* is *definitive*, as turning
on the definition of a son. Again the bastard in his 103
turn will urge that his father did not die childless,
employing the same arguments that he had used in
putting forward his claim that he ranked as a son;
unless indeed he too has recourse to definition, and
raises the question whether even bastards are not sons.
Thus in one case we shall have either two special
legal bases, namely the *letter of the law* and *intention,*
with the *syllogism* and also *definition,* or those three[1]
which are really the only *bases* strictly so called, *conjecture* as regards the *letter of the law and intention,*
quality in the *syllogism,*[2] and *definition,* which needs no
explanation.

Further every kind of case will contain a *cause,* a 104
point for the decision of the judge, and a *central argument.*[3]
For nothing can be said which does not contain a
reason, something to which the decision of the judge
is directed, and finally something which, more than
aught else, contains the substance of the matter at
issue. But as these vary in different cases and are as
a rule explained by writers on judicial causes, I will
postpone them to the appropriate portion of my work.
For the present I shall follow the order which I
prescribed by my division[4] of *causes* into three classes.

VII. Ac potissimum incipiam ab ea, quae constat laude ac vituperatione. Quod genus videtur Aristoteles atque eum secutus Theophrastus a parte negotiali, hoc est πραγματικῇ, removisse totamque ad solos auditores relegasse, et id eius nominis, quod
2 ab ostentatione ducitur, proprium est. Sed mos Romanus etiam negotiis hoc munus inseruit. Nam et funebres laudationes pendent frequenter ex aliquo publico officio atque ex senatus consulto magistratibus saepe mandantur, et laudare testem vel contra pertinet ad momentum iudiciorum, et ipsis etiam reis dare laudatores licet, et editi in Competitores, in L. Pisonem, in Clodium et Curionem libri vituperationem continent et tamen in Senatu loco sunt
3 habiti sententiae. Neque infitias eo, quasdam esse ex hoc genere materias ad solam compositas ostentationem, ut laudes deorum virorumque, quos priora tempora tulerunt. Quo solvitur quaestio supra tractata, manifestumque est errare eos, qui nunquam
4 oratorem dicturum nisi de re dubia putaverunt. An laudes Capitolini Iovis, perpetua sacri certaminis materia, vel dubiae sunt vel non oratorio genere tractantur?

---

1 *Rhet.* 1358 b. 2.   2 *sc.* ἐπιδεικτική.
3 The speech was known as *in Toga Candida.* Only fragments survive.
4 The *in Pisonem* survives, the *in Clodium et Curionem,* to which he refers again (v. x. 92), is lost.
5 III. v. 3.

464

VII. I will begin with the class of *causes* which are concerned with praise and blame. This class appears to have been entirely divorced by Aristotle,[1] and following him by Theophrastus, from the practical side of oratory (which they call πραγματική) and to have been reserved solely for the delectation of audiences, which indeed is shown to be its peculiar function by its name, which implies display.[2] Roman 2 usage on the other hand has given it a place in the practical tasks of life. For funeral orations are often imposed as a duty on persons holding public office, or entrusted to magistrates by decree of the senate. Again the award of praise or blame to a witness may carry weight in the courts, while it is also a recognised practice to produce persons to praise the character of the accused. Further the published speeches of Cicero directed against his rivals in the election to the consulship,[3] and against Lucius Piso, Clodius and Curio,[4] are full of denunciation, and were notwithstanding delivered in the senate as formal expressions of opinion in the course of debate. I do not deny that some compo- 3 sitions of this kind are composed solely with a view to display, as, for instance, panegyrics of gods and heroes of the past, a consideration which provides the solution of a question which I discussed a little while back,[5] and proves that those are wrong who hold that an orator will never speak on a subject unless it involves some problem. But what problem 4 is involved by the praise of Jupiter Capitolinus, a stock theme of the sacred Capitoline contest,[6] which is undoubtedly treated in regular rhetorical form?

[6] The quinquennial contest in honour of Jupiter Capitolinus, founded by Domitian in 86.

Ut desiderat autem laus, quae negotiis adhibetur,
probationem, sic etiam illa, quae ostentationi componitur, habet interim aliquam speciem probationis;
5 ut qui Romulum Martis filium educatumque a lupa
dicat, in argumentum caelestis ortus utatur his, quod
abiectus in profluentem non potuerit exstingui, quod
omnia sic egerit, ut genitum praeside bellorum deo
incredibile non esset, quod ipsum quoque caelo receptum temporis eius homines non dubitaverint.
6 Quaedam vero etiam in defensionis speciem cadent,
ut si in laude Herculis permutatum cum regina
Lydiae habitum et imperata, ut traditur, pensa orator
excuset. Sed proprium laudis est res amplificare et
ornare.

Quae materia praecipue quidem in deos et homines
cadit, est tamen et aliorum animalium, etiam caren-
7 tium anima. Verum in deis generaliter primum
maiestatem ipsius eorum naturae venerabimur, deinde proprie vim cuiusque et inventa, quae utile
8 aliquid hominibus attulerint. Vis ostenditur, ut in
Iove regendorum omnium, in Marte belli, in Nep-
tuno maris; inventa, ut artium in Minerva, Mercurio
litterarum, medicinae Apolline, Cerere frugum, Li-

However, just as panegyric applied to practical matters requires proof, so too a certain semblance of proof is at times required by speeches composed entirely for display. For instance, a speaker who tells 5 how Romulus was the son of Mars and reared by the she-wolf, will offer as proofs of his divine origin the facts that when thrown into a running stream he escaped drowning, that all his achievements were such as to make it credible that he was the offspring of the god of battles, and that his contemporaries unquestionably believed that he was translated to heaven. Some arguments will even wear a certain semblance 6 of defence: for example, if the orator is speaking in praise of Hercules, he will find excuses for his hero having changed raiment with the Queen of Lydia and submitted to the tasks which legend tells us she imposed upon him. The proper function however of panegyric is to amplify and embellish its themes.

This form of oratory is directed in the main to the praise of gods and men, but may occasionally be applied to the praise of animals or even of inanimate objects. In praising the gods our first step 7 will be to express our veneration of the majesty of their nature in general terms . next we shall proceed to praise the special power of the individual god and the discoveries whereby he has benefited the human race. For example, in the case of Jupiter, we shall 8 extol his power as manifested in the governance of all things, with Mars we shall praise his power in war, with Neptune his power over the sea; as regards inventions we shall celebrate Minerva's discovery of the arts, Mercury's discovery of letters, Apollo's of medicine, Ceres' of the fruits of the earth, Bacchus'

bero vini. Tum si qua ab iis acta vetustas tradidit,
commemoranda. Addunt etiam dis honorem parentes, ut si quis sit filius Iovis; addit antiquitas, ut
iis, qui sunt ex Chao; progenies quoque, ut Apollo
9 ac Diana Latonae. Laudandum in quibusdam quod
geniti immortales, quibusdam quod immortalitatem
virtute sint consecuti; quod pietas principis nostri
praesentium quoque temporum decus fecit.

10 Magis est varia laus hominum. Nam primum
dividitur in tempora, quodque ante eos fuit quoque
ipsi vixerunt; in iis autem, qui fato sunt functi,
etiam quod est insecutum. Ante hominem patria
ac parentes maioresque erunt, quorum duplex tractatus est : aut enim respondisse nobilitati pulchrum
11 erit aut humilius genus illustrasse factis. Illa quoque interim ex eo, quod ante ipsum fuit, tempore
trahentur, quae responsis vel auguriis futuram clari-
tatem promiserint, ut eum, qui ex Thetide natus
esset, maiorem patre suo futurum cecinisse dicuntur
12 oracula. Ipsius vero laus hominis ex animo et corpore et extra positis peti debet. Et corporis quidem
fortuitorumque cum levior, tum non uno modo tractanda est. Nam et pulchritudinem interim roburque

---

[1] *sc.* by Domitian's deification of his father Vespasian and
his brother Titus.

of wine. Next we must record their exploits as
handed down from antiquity. Even gods may derive honour from their descent, as for instance is
the case with the sons of Jupiter, or from their
antiquity, as in the case of the children of Chaos, or
from their offspring, as in the case of Latona, the
mother of Apollo and Diana. Some again may be 9
praised because they were born immortal, others
because they won immortality by their valour, a theme
which the piety of our sovereign has made the glory
even of these present times.[1]

There is greater variety required in the praise of 10
men. In the first place there is a distinction to be
made as regards time between the period in which
the objects of our praise lived and the time preceding their birth; and further, in the case of the
dead, we must also distinguish the period following
their death. With regard to things preceding a
man's birth, there are his country, his parents and his
ancestors, a theme which may be handled in two
ways. For either it will be creditable to the objects of
our praise not to have fallen short of the fair fame of
their country and of their sires or to have ennobled
a humble origin by the glory of their achievements.
Other topics to be drawn from the period preceding 11
their birth will have reference to omens or prophe-
cies foretelling their future greatness, such as the
oracle which is said to have foretold that the son of
Thetis would be greater than his father. The praise 12
of the individual himself will be based on his
character, his physical endowments and external
circumstances. Physical and accidental advantages
provide a comparatively unimportant theme, which
requires variety of treatment. At times for instance

prosequimur honore verborum, ut Homerus in Aga-
memnone atque Achille, et interim confert admira-
tioni multum etiam infirmitas, ut cum idem Tydea
13 parvum sed bellatorem dicit fuisse. Fortuna vero
tum dignitatem adfert, ut in regibus principibusque
(namque est haec materia ostendendae virtutis
uberior), tum quo minores opes fuerunt, maiorem
bene factis gloriam parit. Sed omnia, quae extra
nos bona sunt quaeque hominibus forte obtigerunt,
non ideo laudantur, quod habuerit quis ea, sed quod
14 iis honeste sit usus. Nam divitiae et potentia et
gratia, cum plurimum virium dent, in utramque
partem certissimum faciunt morum experimentum,
aut enim meliores sumus propter haec aut peiores.
15 Animi semper vera laus, sed non una per hoc opus
via ducitur. Namque alias aetatis gradus gestarum-
que rerum ordinem sequi speciosius fuit, ut in primis
annis laudaretur indoles, tum disciplinae, post hoc
operum id est factorum dictorumque contextus; alias
in species virtutum dividere laudem, fortitudinis,
iustitiae, continentiae ceterarumque, ac singulis ad-
signare, quae secundum quamque earum gesta erunt.
16 Utra sit autem harum via utilior, cum materia deli-
berabimus, dum sciamus gratiora esse audientibus,
quae solus quis aut primus aut certe cum paucis
fecisse dicetur, si quid praeterea supra spem aut

---

[1] *Iliad*, ii. 477.   [2] *Iliad*, ii. 180.
[3] *Iliad*, v. 801.

we extol beauty and strength in honorific terms, as
Homer does in the case of Agamemnon [1] and
Achilles [2]; at times again weakness may contribute
largely to our admiration, as when Homer says [3] that
Tydeus was small of stature but a good fighter.
Fortune too may confer dignity as in the case of 13
kings and princes (for they have a fairer field for
the display of their excellences) but on the other
hand the glory of good deeds may be enhanced by
the smallness of their resources.   Moreover the
praise awarded to external and accidental advantages
is given, not to their possession, but to their honourable employment.   For wealth and power and influ- 14
ence, since they are the sources of strength, are the
surest test of character for good or evil ; they make us
better or they make us worse.   Praise awarded to 15
character is always just, but may be given in various
ways.   It has sometimes proved the more effective
course to trace a man's life and deeds in due chrono-
logical order, praising his natural gifts as a child, then
his progress at school, and finally the whole course of
his life, including words as well as deeds.   At times
on the other hand it is well to divide our praises,
dealing separately with the various virtues, forti-
tude, justice, self-control and the rest of them and
to assign to each virtue the deeds performed under
its influence.   We shall have to decide which of 16
these two methods will be the more serviceable,
according to the nature of the subject ; but we
must bear in mind the fact that what most pleases
an audience is the celebration of deeds which our
hero was the first or only man or at any rate one of
the very few to perform : and to these we must add
any other achievements which surpassed hope or

exspectationem, praecipue quod aliena potius causa
17 quam sua. Tempus, quod finem hominis insequitur,
non semper tractare contingit; non solum quod
viventes aliquando laudamus, sed quod rara haec
occasio est, ut referri possint divini honores et
18 decreta et publice statuae constitutae. Inter quae
numeraverim ingeniorum monumenta, quae saeculis
probarentur. Nam quidam, sicut Menander, iustiora
posterorum quam suae aetatis iudicia sunt consecuti.
Adferunt laudem liberi parentibus, urbes conditoribus, leges latoribus, artes inventoribus nec non instituta quoque auctoribus, ut a Numa traditum deos
colere, a Publicola fasces populo summittere.

19 Qui omnis etiam in vituperatione ordo constabit,
tantum in diversum. Nam et turpitudo generis
opprobrio multis fuit, et quosdam claritas ipsa noti-
ores circa vitia et invisos magis fecit, et in quibusdam, ut in Paride traditum est, praedicta pernicies,
et corporis ac fortunae quibusdam mala contemptum,
sicut Thersitae atque Iro, quibusdam bona vitiis corrupta odium attulerunt, ut Nirea imbellem, Plis-
20 thenen impudicum a poetis accepimus. Et animo

---

[1] The handsomest warrior among the Greeks of Troy.
[2] Son of Atreus : the allusion is not known.

expectation, emphasising what was done for the sake
of others rather than what he performed on his
own behalf. It is not always possible to deal with 17
the time subsequent to our hero's death : this is
due not merely to the fact that we sometimes praise
him, while still alive, but also that there are but few
occasions when we have a chance to celebrate the
award of divine honours, posthumous votes of thanks,
or statues erected at the public expense. Among 18
such themes of panegyric I would mention monu-
ments of genius that have stood the test of time.
For some great men like Menander have received
ampler justice from the verdict of posterity than
from that of their own age. Children reflect glory
on their parents, cities on their founders, laws on
those who made them, arts on their inventors and
institutions on those that first introduced them ; for
instance Numa first laid down rules for the worship
of the gods, and Publicola first ordered that the
lictors' rods should be lowered in salutation to the
people.

The same method will be applied to denunciations 19
as well, but with a view to opposite effects. For humble
origin has been a reproach to many, while in some
cases distinction has merely served to increase the
notoriety and unpopularity of vices. In regard to
some persons, as in the story of Paris, it has been
predicted that they would be the cause of destruction
to many, some like Thersites and Irus have been
despised for their poverty and mean appearance,
others have been loathed because their natural advantages were nullified by their vices : the poets for
instance tell us that Nireus[1] was a coward and
Pleisthenes[2] a debauchee. The mind too has as 20

473

totidem vitia, quot virtutes sunt, nec minus quam in
laudibus duplici ratione tractantur.   Et post mortem
adiecta quibusdam ignominia est, ut Maelio, cuius
domus solo aequata, Marcoque Manlio, cuius prae-
21 nomen e familia in posterum exemptum est; et
parentes malorum odimus; et est conditoribus
urbium infame contraxisse aliquam perniciosam
ceteris gentem, qualis est primus Iudaicae supersti-
tionis auctor; et Gracchorum leges invisae; et si
quod est exemplum deforme posteris traditum, quale
libidinis vir Perses in muliere Samia instituere ausus
22 dicitur primus.   Sed in viventibus quoque iudicia
hominum velut argumenta sunt morum, et honos
aut ignominia veram esse laudem vel vituperationem
probat.

23   Interesse tamen Aristoteles putat, ubi quidque
laudetur aut vituperetur.   Nam plurimum refert,
qui sint audientium mores, quae publice recepta
persuasio, ut illa maxime quae probant esse in eo,
qui laudabitur, credant, aut in eo, contra quem
dicemus, ea quae oderunt.   Ita non dubium erit
24 iudicium, quod orationem praecesserit.   Ipsorum
etiam permiscenda laus semper, nam id benevolos
facit; quotiens autem fieri poterit, cum materiae
utilitate iungenda.   Minus Lacedaemone studia

---

[1] Moses.   [2] *Rhet.* i. 9.

many vices as virtues, and vice may be denounced, as virtue may be praised, in two different ways. Some have been branded with infamy after death like Maelius, whose house was levelled with the ground, or Marcus Manlius, whose first name was banished from his family for all generations to come. The vices of the children bring hatred on 21 their parents; founders of cities are detested for concentrating a race which is a curse to others, as for example the founder of the Jewish superstition;[1] the laws of Gracchus are hated, and we abhor any loathsome example of vice that has been handed down to posterity, such as the criminal form of lust which a Persian is said to have been the first to practise on a woman of Samos. And even in the 22 case of the living the judgment of mankind serves as a proof of their character, and the fairness or foulness of their fame proves the orator's praise or blame to be true.

Aristotle[2] however thinks that the place and sub- 23 ject of panegyrics or denunciations make a very considerable difference. For much depends on the character of the audience and the generally received opinion, if they are to believe that the virtues of which they approve are pre-eminently characteristic of the person praised and the vices which they hate of the person denounced. For there can be little doubt as to the attitude of the audience, if that attitude is already determined prior to the delivery of the speech. It will be wise 24 too for him to insert some words of praise for his audience, since this will secure their good will, and wherever it is possible this should be done in such a manner as to advance his case. Literature

litterarum quam Athenis honores merebuntur, plus patientia ac fortitudo. Rapto vivere quibusdam honestum, aliis cura legum. Frugalitas apud Sybaritas forsitan odio foret, veteribus Romanis summum luxuria crimen. Eadem in singulis differentia.

25 Maxime favet iudex, qui sibi dicentem assentiri putat. Idem praecipit illud quoque (quod mox Cornelius Celsus prope supra modum invasit), quia sit quaedam virtutibus ac vitiis vicinitas, utendum proxima derivatione verborum, ut pro temerario fortem, pro prodigo liberalem, pro avaro parcum vocemus; quae eadem etiam contra valent. Quod quidem orator, id est vir bonus, nunquam faciet, nisi forte communi utilitate ducetur.

26 Laudantur autem urbes similiter atque homines. Nam pro parente est conditor, et multum auctoritatis adfert vetustas, ut iis, qui terra dicuntur orti; et virtutes ac vitia circa res gestas eadem quae in singulis, illa propria quae ex loci positione ac munitione sunt. Cives illis ut hominibus liberi decori.

27 Est laus et operum, in quibus honor, utilitas, pulchritudo, auctor spectari solet. Honor ut in templis, utilitas ut in muris, pulchritudo vel auctor

476

will win less praise at Sparta than at Athens, endurance and courage more. Among some races the life of a freebooter is accounted honourable, while others regard it as a duty to respect the laws. Frugality might perhaps be unpopular with the Sybarites, whilst luxury was regarded as a crime by the ancient Romans. Similar differences of opinion are found in individuals. A judge is most favourable to 25 the orator whose views he thinks identical with his own. Aristotle also urges a point, which at a later date Cornelius Celsus emphasised almost to excess, to the effect that, since the boundary between vice and virtue is often ill-defined, it is desirable to use words that swerve a little from the actual truth, calling a rash man brave, a prodigal generous, a mean man thrifty; or the process may, if necessary, be reversed. But this the ideal orator, that is to say a good man, will never do, unless perhaps he is led to do so by consideration for the public interest.

Cities are praised after the same fashion as men. 26 The founder takes the place of the parent, and antiquity carries great authority, as for instance in the case of those whose inhabitants are said to be sprung from the soil. The virtues and vices revealed by their deeds are the same as in private individuals. The advantages arising from site or fortifications are however peculiar to cities. Their citizens enhance their fame just as children bring honour to their parents.

Praise too may be awarded to public works, 27 in connexion with which their magnificence, utility, beauty and the architect or artist must be given due consideration. Temples for instance will be praised for their magnificence, walls for

utrobique. Est et locorum, qualis Siciliae apud
Ciceronem, in quibus similiter speciem et utilitatem
intuemur; speciem in maritimis, planis, amoenis;
utilitatem in salubribus, fertilibus. Erit et dictorum
honestorum factorumque laus generalis, erit et rerum
28 omnis modi. Nam et somni et mortis scriptae
laudes et quorundam a medicis ciborum.

Itaque, ut non consensi hoc laudativum genus
circa solam versari honesti quaestionem, sic qualitate maxime contineri puto; quanquam tres status
omnes cadere in hoc opus possint, iisque usum
C. Caesarem in vituperando Catone notaverit Cicero.
Totum autem habet aliquid simile suasoriis, quia
plerumque eadem illic suaderi, hic laudari solent.

VIII. Deliberativas quoque miror a quibusdam
sola utilitate finitas. Ac si quid in his unum sequi
oporteret, potior fuisset apud me Ciceronis sententia,
qui hoc materiae genus dignitate maxime contineri
putat. Nec dubito, quin ii, qui sunt in illa priore
sententia, secundum opinionem pulcherrimam ne
utile quidem, nisi quod honestum esset, existimarint.
2 Et est haec ratio verissima, si consilium contingat
semper bonorum atque sapientium. Verum apud
imperitos, apud quos frequenter dicenda sententia
est, populumque praecipue, qui ex pluribus constat

---

[1] *in Verr.* ii. 1 *sqq.*, iv. 48.
[2] Quality, conjecture, definition. See chap. vi. for explanation of this term.   [3] *Top.* xxv. 94.
[4] *de Or.* ii. lxxxii. 334.

their utility, and both for their beauty or the skill of
the architect. Places may also be praised, witness
the praise of Sicily in Cicero.[1] In such cases
we consider their beauty and utility : beauty calls for
notice in places by the sea, in open plains and
pleasant situations, utility in healthy or fertile
localities. Again praise in general terms may be
awarded to noble sayings or deeds. Finally things
of every kind may be praised. Panegyrics have 28
been composed on sleep and death, and physicians
have written eulogies on certain kinds of food.

While therefore I do not agree that panegyric
concerns only questions regarding what is honourable, I do think that it comes as a rule under
the heading of *quality*, although all three *bases*[2] may
be involved in Panegyric and it was observed by
Cicero[3] that all were actually used by Gaius Caesar
in his denunciation of Cato. But *panegyric* is akin
to *deliberative* oratory inasmuch as the same things
are usually praised in the former as are advised
in the latter.

VIII. I am surprised that *deliberative* oratory also
has been restricted by some authorities to questions
of expediency. If it should be necessary to assign
one single aim to deliberative I should prefer
Cicero's[4] view that this kind of oratory is primarily
concerned with what is honourable. I do not doubt
that those who maintain the opinion first mentioned
adopt the lofty view that nothing can be expedient
which is not good. That opinion is perfectly sound 2
so long as we are fortunate enough to have wise and
good men for counsellors. But as we most often
express our views before an ignorant audience, and
more especially before popular assemblies, of which

indoctis, discernenda sunt haec et secundum com-
3 munes magis intellectus loquendum. Sunt enim
multi, qui etiam, quae credunt honesta, non tamen
satis eadem utilia quoque existiment, et quae turpia
esse dubitare non possunt, utilitatis specie ducti
probent, ut foedus Numantinum iugumque Cau-
4 dinum. Ne qualitatis quidem statu, in quo et
honestorum et utilium quaestio est, complecti eas
satis est. Nam frequenter in his etiam coniecturae
locus est, nonnunquam tractatur aliqua finitio, aliquando etiam legales possunt incidere tractatus, in
privata maxime consilia, si quando ambigetur an
5 liceat. De coniectura paulo post pluribus. Interim
est finitio apud Demosthenen, Det Halonnesum
Philippus, an reddat? apud Ciceronem in Philippicis,
Quid sit tumultus? Quid? non illa similis iudicialium quaestio de statua Servi Sulpici, an iis demum
ponenda sit, qui in legatione ferro sunt interempti?
6 Ergo pars deliberativa, quae eadem suasoria dicitur,

---

[1] Mancinus was surrounded on retreat from Numantia in
137 B.C., while the surrender at the Caudine Forks took
place in 321 B.C. In both cases the Senate refused to ratify
the humiliating treaties which had been made the price of
the release of the Roman armies.

[2] For *conjecture* see III. vi. 30 *sqq.*

[3] Halonnesus had belonged to Athens, but had been seized
by pirates. Philip ejected the pirates. The Athenians asked
him to restore it; he replied that it belonged to him and
that there could be no question of restoration, but if they
asked for it as a gift he promised to give it them.

the majority is usually uneducated, we must distinguish between what is honourable and what is expedient and conform our utterances to suit ordinary understandings. For there are many who do not 3 admit that what they really believe to be the honourable course is sufficiently advantageous, and are misled by the prospect of advantage into approving courses of the dishonourable nature of which there can be no question : witness the Numantine treaty and the surrender of the Caudine Forks.[1] Nor does 4 it suffice to restrict deliberative oratory to the *basis* of *quality* which is concerned with questions of honour and expediency. For there is often room for conjecture as well. Sometimes again *definition* is necessary or *legal* problems require handling ; this is especially the case when advice has to be given on private matters, where there is some doubt of the legality of the course under consideration. Of *conjecture*[2] I shall speak more fully a little later on. Returning to *definition* for the moment, we 5 find it in the question raised by Demosthenes, "whether Philip should give or restore Halonnesus,"[3] and to that discussed by Cicero in the *Philippics*[4] as to the nature of a *tumultus*. Again does not the question raised in connection with the statue of Servius Sulpicius[5] as to " whether statues should be erected only in honour of those ambassadors who perish by the sword" bear a strong resemblance to the questions that are raised in the law courts ? The 6 *deliberative* department of oratory (also called the

[4] VIII. i. 2, where the question is discussed as to whether the war with Antony is *bellum* or *tumultus*, the latter being the technical name for any grave national emergency such as civil war or a Gallic invasion within the bounds of Italy.   [5] *Phil.* ix. 1.

de tempore futuro consultans quaerit etiam de praeterito. Officiis constat duobus suadendi ac dissuadendi.

Prooemio, quale est in iudicialibus, non ubique eget, quia conciliatus est ei quisque, quem consulit. Initium tamen quodcunque debet habere aliquam prooemii speciem; neque enim abrupte nec unde libuit incipiendum, quia est aliquid in omni materia
7 naturaliter primum. In senatu et utique in contionibus eadem ratio quae apud iudices, adquirendae sibi plerumque eorum, apud quos dicendum sit, benevolentiae. Nec mirum, cum etiam in panegyricis petatur audientium favor, ubi emolumentum non in utilitate aliqua, sed in sola laude consistit.
8 Aristoteles quidem nec sine causa putat et a nostra et ab eius, qui dissentiet, persona duci frequenter in consiliis exordium, quasi mutuantibus hoc nobis a iudiciali genere, nonnunquam etiam, ut minor res maiorve videatur; in demonstrativis vero prooemia
9 esse maxime libera existimat. Nam et longe a materia duci, ut in Helenae laude Isocrates fecerit; et ex aliqua rei vicinia, ut idem in Panegyrico, cum queritur plus honoris corporum quam animorum virtutibus dari; et Gorgias in Olympico laudans eos, qui primi tales instituerint conventus. Quos secutus

---

[1] *Rhet.* iii. 14.
[2] The speech opens with a disquisition on the absurd and trivial nature of much that is contained in the speeches of sophists and rhetoricians.

advisory department), while it deliberates about the future, also enquires about the past, while its functions are twofold and consist in advising and dissuading.

Deliberative oratory does not always require an *exordium*, such as is necessary in forensic speeches, since he who asks an orator for his opinion is naturally well disposed to him. But the commencement, whatever be its nature, must have some resemblance to an *exordium.* For we must not begin abruptly or just at the point where the fancy takes us, since in every subject there is something which naturally comes first. In addressing the senate or the people the same 7 methods apply as in the law courts, and we must aim as a rule at acquiring the goodwill of our audience. This need cause no surprise, since even in *panegyric* we seek to win the favour of our hearers when our aim is praise pure and simple, and not the acquisition of any advantage. Aristotle,[1] it is true, holds, not 8 without reason, that in *deliberative* speeches we may often begin with a reference either to ourselves or to our opponent, borrowing this practice from *forensic* oratory, and sometimes producing the impression that the subject is of greater or less importance than it actually is. On the other hand he thinks that in *demonstrative* oratory the *exordium* may be treated with the utmost freedom, since it is sometimes drawn from 9 irrelevant material, as for example in Isocrates' Praise of Helen,[2] or from something akin to the subject, as for instance in the *Panegyricus* of the same author, when he complains that more honour is given to physical than to moral excellence, or as Gorgias in his speech delivered at the Olympic games praises the founders of the great national games. Sallust seems

videlicet C. Sallustius in bello Iugurthino et Catilinae nihil ad historiam pertinentibus principiis orsus est.

10 Sed nunc ad suasoriam, in qua, etiam cum prooemio utemur, breviore tamen et velut quodam capite tantum et initio debebimus esse contenti. Narrationem vero nunquam exigit privata deliberatio, eius duntaxat rei, de qua dicenda sententia est;

11 quia nemo ignorat id de quo consulit. Extrinsecus possunt pertinentia ad deliberationem multa narrari. In contionibus saepe est etiam illa, quae ordinem

12 rei docet, necessaria. Adfectus ut quae maxime postulat. Nam et concitanda et lenienda frequenter est ira, et ad metum, cupiditatem, odium, conciliationem impellendi animi. Nonnunquam etiam movenda miseratio, sive, ut auxilium obsessis feratur, suadere oportebit sive sociae civitatis eversionem deflebimus. Valet autem in consiliis auctoritas

13 plurimum. Nam et prudentissimus esse haberique et optimus debet, qui sententiae suae de utilibus atque honestis credere omnes velit. In iudiciis enim vulgo fas habetur indulgere aliquid studio suo; consilia nemo est qui neget secundum mores dari.

to have imitated these authors in his *Jugurthine War*
and in the introduction to his *Catiline,* which has no
connection with his narrative.

But it is time for me to return to *deliberative* oratory 10
in which, even when we introduce an *exordium,* we
must content ourselves with a brief prelude, which
may amount to no more than a mere heading.   As
regards the *statement of facts,* this is never required in
speeches on private subjects, at least as regards the
subject on which an opinion has to be given, because
everyone is acquainted with the question at issue.
Statements as to external matters which are relevant 11
to the discussion may however frequently be introduced.   In addressing public assemblies it will often
be necessary to set forth the order of the points
which have to be treated.   As regards appeals to the 12
emotions, these are especially necessary in *deliberative*
oratory.   Anger has frequently to be excited or
assuaged and the minds of the audience have to be
swayed to fear, ambition, hatred, reconciliation.   At
times again it is necessary to awaken pity, whether it
is required, for instance, to urge that relief should be
sent to a besieged city, or we are engaged in deplor-
ing the overthrow of an allied state.   But what really
carries greatest weight in *deliberative* speeches is the
authority of the speaker.   For he, who would have 13
all men trust his judgment as to what is expedient
and honourable, should both possess and be regarded as possessing genuine wisdom and excellence
of character.   In *forensic* speeches the orator may,
according to the generally received opinion, indulge
his passion to some extent.   But all will agree that
the advice given by a speaker should be in keeping
with his moral character.

14 Graecorum quidem plurimi omne hoc officium
contionale esse iudicaverunt et in sola reipublicae
administratione posuerunt. Quin et Cicero in hac
maxime parte versatur. Ideoque suasuris de pace,
bello, copiis, operibus, vectigalibus haec duo esse
praecipue nota voluit, vires civitatis et mores, ut ex
natura cum ipsarum rerum tum audientium ratio
15 suadendi duceretur. Nobis maior in re videtur
varietas, nam et consultantium et consiliorum plurima sunt genera.

Quare in suadendo et dissuadendo tria primum
spectanda erunt, quid sit de quo deliberetur, qui
16 sint qui deliberent, qui sit qui suadeat. Rem, de
qua deliberatur, aut certum est posse fieri aut
incertum. Si incertum, haec erit quaestio sola aut
potentissima; saepe enim accidet, ut prius dicamus,
ne si possit quidem fieri, esse faciendum, deinde
fieri non posse. Cum autem de hoc quaeritur,
coniectura est, an Isthmos intercidi, an siccari
palus Pomptina, an portus fieri Ostiae possit, an
Alexander terras ultra Oceanum sit inventurus.
17 Sed in iis quoque quae constabit posse fieri, coniectura aliquando erit, si quaeretur, an utique
futurum sit, ut Carthaginem superent Romani; ut

---

[1] *de Orat.* ii. 82.
[2] The theme of a *suasoria* of the elder Seneca (*Suas.* i.).
" Alexander deliberates whether to sail forth into the ocean."

The majority of Greek writers have held that this 14
kind of oratory is entirely concerned with addressing
public assemblies and have restricted it to politics.
Even Cicero [1] himself deals chiefly with this department. Consequently those who propose to offer advice
upon peace, war, troops, public works or revenue must
thoroughly acquaint themselves with two things, the
resources of the state and the character of its people,
so that the method employed in tendering their advice may be based at once on political realities and
the nature of their hearers. This type of oratory 15
seems to me to offer a more varied field for eloquence,
since both those who ask for advice and the answers
given to them may easily present the greatest diversity.

Consequently there are three points which must
be specially borne in mind in advice or dissuasion:
first the nature of the subject under discussion,
secondly the nature of those who are engaged in the
discussion, and thirdly the nature of the speaker who
offers them advice. As to the subject under discussion 16
its practicability is either certain or uncertain. In
the latter case this will be the chief, if not
the only point for consideration; for it will often
happen that we shall assert first that something
ought not to be done, even if it can be done, and
secondly, that it cannot be done. Now when
the question turns on such points as to whether the
Isthmus can be cut through, the Pontine Marshes
drained, or a harbour constructed at Ostia, or whether
Alexander is likely to find land beyond the Ocean,[2]
we make use of *conjecture.* But even in connection 17
with things that are undoubtedly feasible, there may
at times be room for *conjecture,* as for instance in
questions such as whether Rome is ever likely to

redeat Hannibal, si Scipio exercitum in Africam
transtulerit ; ut servent fidem Samnites, si Romani
arma deposuerint.   Quaedam et fieri posse et futura
esse credibile est, sed aut alio tempore aut alio loco
aut alio modo.

18 Ubi coniecturae non erit locus, alia sunt intuenda.
Et primum aut propter ipsam rem, de qua sententiae rogantur, consultabitur aut propter alias inter-
venientes extrinsecus causas.   Propter ipsam deliberant Patres conscripti, an stipendium militi
19 constituant ? Haec materia simplex erit. Accedunt
causae aut faciendi, ut deliberant patres conscripti,
an Fabios dedant Gallis bellum minitantibus ; aut
non faciendi, ut deliberat C. Caesar, an perseveret
in Germaniam ire, cum milites passim testamenta
20 facerent.   Hae suasoriae duplices sunt. Nam et
illic causa deliberandi est, quod bellum Galli mini-
tentur ; esse tamen potest quaestio, dedendine
fuerint etiam citra hanc denuntiationem, qui contra
fas, cum legati missi essent, proelium inierint,
regemque, ad quem mandata acceperant, truci-
21 darint.   Et hic nihil Caesar sine dubio deliberaret
nisi propter hanc militum perturbationem ; est
tamen locus quaerendi, an citra hunc quoque casum

---

[1] *sc.* at the Caudine Forks : see above, § 3.
[2] See Livy, v. 36.
[3] See Caesar, *Gallic War*, i. 39, where this detail is
recorded, also 40 where the speech made to his troops is
given.

conquer Carthage, whether Hannibal will return to
Africa if Scipio transports his army thither, or whether
the Samnites are likely to keep faith if the Romans
lay down their arms.[1] There are some things too
which we may believe to be both feasible and likely
to be carried into effect, but at another time or place
or in another way.

When there is no scope for conjecture, our atten- 18
tion will be fixed on other points.   In the first place
advice will be asked either on account of the actual
thing on which the orator is required to express his
views, or on account of other causes which affect it
from without.   It is on the actual thing that the
senate for instance debates, when it discusses such
questions as whether it is to vote pay for the troops.
In this case the material is simple.   To this however 19
may be added reasons for taking action or the reverse,
as for example if the senate should discuss whether
it should deliver the Fabii to the Gauls when the
latter threaten war,[2] or Gaius Caesar should deliberate
whether he should persist in the invasion of Germany,
when his soldiers on all sides are making their wills.[3]
These deliberative themes are of a twofold nature. 20
In the first case the reason for deliberation is the
Gallic threat of war, but there may still be a further
question as to whether even without such threat of
war they should surrender those who, contrary to the
law of nations, took part in a battle when they had
been sent out as ambassadors and killed the king
with whom they had received instructions to treat.
In the second case Caesar would doubtless never deli- 21
berate on the question at all, but for the perturbation
shown by his soldiers; but there is still room for
enquiry whether quite apart from this occurrence it

penetrandum in Germaniam fuerit. Semper autem
de eo prius loquemur, de quo deliberari etiam
detractis sequentibus possit.

22 Partes suadendi quidam putaverunt honestum,
utile, necessarium. Ego non invenio huic tertiae
locum. Quantalibet enim vis ingruat, aliquid fortasse pati necesse sit, nihil facere ; de faciendo
23 autem deliberatur. Quodsi hanc vocant necessitatem, in quam homines graviorum metu coguntur,
utilitatis erit quaestio ; ut si obsessi et impares et
aqua ciboque defecti de facienda ad hostem dedi-
tione deliberent et dicatur, *necesse est ;* nempe
sequitur, ut hoc subiiciatur, *alioqui pereundum est :*
ita propter id ipsum non est necesse, quia perire
potius licet. Denique non fecerunt Saguntini nec
24 in rate Opitergina circumventi. Igitur in his quoque causis aut de sola utilitate ambigetur aut quaestio inter utile atque honestum consistet. At enim
si quis liberos procreare volet, necesse habet ducere
uxorem. Quis dubitat? sed ei, qui pater vult fieri,
25 liqueat necesse est uxorem esse ducendam. Itaque
mihi ne consilium quidem videtur, ubi necessitas est,
non magis quam ubi constat, quid fieri non possit.

---

[1] In 218 B.C., when besieged by Hannibal. See Livy,
xxi. 14.

[2] C. Antonius was blockaded in an island off the Dalmatian
coast which he held for Caesar 49 B.C. Reinforcements on
rafts were sent to his rescue. Most were captured ; but in
one case, of a raft carrying 1,000 men from Opitergium in

would be wise to penetrate into Germany. But it must be remembered that we shall always speak first on that subject which is capable of discussion quite apart from the consequences.

Some have held that the three main considerations 22 in an advisory speech are honour, expediency and necessity. I can find no place for the last. For however great the violence which may threaten us, it may be necessary for us to suffer something, but we are not compelled to do anything; whereas the subject of deliberation is primarily whether we shall do anything. Or if by necessity they mean that into which we are 23 driven by fear of worse things, the question will be one of expediency. For example, if a garrison is besieged by overwhelmingly superior forces and, owing to the failure of food and water supplies, discusses surrender to the enemy, and it is urged that it is a matter of necessity, the words "otherwise we shall perish" must needs be added: consequently there is no necessity arising out of the circumstances themselves, for death is a possible alternative. And as a matter of fact the Saguntines[1] did not surrender, nor did those who were surrounded on the raft from Opitergium.[2] It follows 24 that in such cases also the question will be either one of expediency alone or of a choice between expediency and honour. "But," it will be urged, "if a man would beget children, he is under the necessity of taking a wife." Certainly. But he who wishes to become a father must needs be quite clear that he must take a wife. It appears to me, therefore, that 25 where necessity exists, there is no room for deliberation, any more than where it is clear that a thing is

Venetia, surrender was scorned and the men slew each other rather than yield. See Lucan, iv. 462; Florus, ii. 33.

Omnis enim deliberatio de dubiis est. Melius igitur, qui tertiam partem dixerunt δυνατόν, quod nostri possibile nominant, quae ut dura videatur appellatio, 26 tamen sola est. Quas partes non omnes in omnem cadere suasoriam manifestius est, quam ut docendum sit. Tamen apud plerosque earum numerus augetur, a quibus ponuntur ut partes, quae superiorum species sunt partium. Nam fas, iustum, pium, aequum, mansuetum quoque (sic enim sunt interpretati τὸ ἥμερον) et si qua adhuc adiicere quis eiusdem generis 27 velit, subiici possunt honestati. An sit autem facile, magnum, iucundum, sine periculo, ad quaestionem pertinet utilitatis. Qui loci oriuntur ex contradictione : *Est quidem utile sed difficile, parvum, iniucun-* 28 *dum, periculosum.* Tamen quibusdam videtur esse nonnunquam de iucunditate sola consultatio, ut si de aedificando theatro, instituendis ludis deliberetur. Sed neminem adeo solutum luxu puto, ut nihil in 29 causa suadendi sequatur praeter voluptatem. Praecedat enim semper aliquid necesse est, ut in ludis honor deorum, in theatro non inutilis laborum remissio, deformis et incommoda turbae, si id non sit,

not feasible. For deliberation is always concerned with questions where some doubt exists. Those therefore are wiser who make the third consideration for deliberative oratory to be τὸ δυνατόν or "possibility" as we translate it; the translation may seem clumsy, but it is the only word available. That all these 26 considerations need not necessarily obtrude themselves in every case is too obvious to need explanation. Most writers, however, say that there are more than three. But the further considerations which they would add are really but *species* of the three *general* considerations just mentioned. For right, justice, piety, equity and mercy (for thus they translate τὸ ἥμερον), with any other virtues that anyone may be pleased to add, all come under the heading of that which is honourable. On the other hand, if the question 27 be whether a thing is easy, great, pleasant or free from danger, it comes under questions of expediency. Such topics arise from some contradiction; for example a thing is expedient, but difficult, or trivial, or unpleasant, or dangerous. Some however hold that at 28 times deliberation is concerned solely with the question whether a thing is pleasant, as for instance when discussion arises as to whether a theatre should be built or games instituted. But in my opinion you will never find any man such a slave to luxury as not to consider anything but pleasure when he delivers an advisory speech. For there must needs be something on every 29 occasion that takes precedence of pleasure: in proposing the institution of public games there is the honour due to the gods; in proposing the erection of a theatre the orator will consider the advantages to be derived from relaxation from toil, and the unbecoming and undesirable struggle for places which will arise if

conflictatio, et nihilominus eadem illa religio, cum
theatrum veluti quoddam illius sacri templum voca-
30 bimus. Saepe vero et utilitatem despiciendam esse
dicimus, ut honesta faciamus, ut cum illis Opiter-
ginis damus consilium, ne se hostibus dedant, quanquam perituri sint, nisi fecerint; et utilia honestis
praeferimus, ut cum suademus, ut bello Punico servi
31 armentur. Sed neque hic plane concedendum est
esse id inhonestum, liberos enim natura omnes et
eisdem constare elementis et fortasse antiquis etiam
nobilibus ortos dici potest; et illic, ubi manifestum
periculum est, opponenda alia, ut crudelius etiam
perituros adfirmemus, si se dediderint, sive hostis non
servaverit fidem, sive Caesar vicerit, quod est vero
32 similius. Haec autem, quae tantum inter se pug-
nant, plerumque nominibus deflecti solent. Nam
et utilitas ipsa expugnatur ab iis, qui dicunt, non
solum potiora esse honesta quam utilia, sed ne utilia
quidem esse, quae non sint honesta; et contra, quod
nos honestum, illi vanum, ambitiosum, stolidum,
33 verbis quam re probabilius vocant. Nec tantum
inutilibus comparantur utilia, sed inter se quoque
ipsa, ut si ex duobus eligamus, in altero quid sit
magis, in altero quid sit minus. Crescit hoc adhuc.
Nam interim triplices etiam suasoriae incidunt: ut
cum Pompeius deliberabat, Parthos an Africam an
Aegyptum peteret. Ita non tantum, utrum melius

---

[1] After the battle of Cannae : Livy, xxii. 57.
[2] After his defeat at Pharsalus.

there is no proper accommodation; religion, too, has
its place in the discussion, for we shall describe the
theatre as a kind of temple for the solemnization of a
sacred feast. Often again we shall urge that honour 30
must come before expediency; as for instance when
we advise the men of Opitergium not to surrender to
the enemy, even though refusal to do so means
certain death. At times on the other hand we prefer
expediency to honour, as when we advise the arming
of slaves in the Punic War.[1] But even in this case we 31
must not openly admit that such a course is dishonourable: we can point out that all men are free by
nature and composed of the same elements, while
the slaves in question may perhaps be sprung
from some ancient and noble stock; and in the
former case when the danger is so evident,
we may add other arguments, such as that they
would perish even more cruelly if they surrendered,
should the enemy fail to keep faith, or Caesar (a
more probable supposition) prove victorious. But 32
in such a conflict of principles it is usual to modify
the names which we give them. For expediency is
often ruled out by those who assert not merely that
honour comes before expediency, but that nothing
can be expedient that is not honourable, while others
say that what we call honour is vanity, ambition and
folly, as contemptible in substance as it is fair in
sound. Nor is expediency compared merely with 33
inexpediency. At times we have to choose between
two advantageous courses after comparison of their
respective advantages. The problem may be still
more complicated, as for instance when Pompey
deliberated whether to go to Parthia, Africa or
Egypt.[2] In such a case the enquiry is not which of

sed quid sit optimum, quaeritur, itemque contra.
34 Nec unquam incidet in hoc genere materiae dubitatio rei, quae undique secundum nos sit. Nam ubi
contradictioni locus non est, quae potest esse causa
dubitandi? Ita fere omnis suasoria nihil est aliud
quam comparatio, videndumque, quid consecuturi
simus et per quid, ut aestimari possit, plus in eo
quod petimus sit commodi, an vero in eo per quod
35 petimus incommodi. Est utilitatis et in tempore
quaestio, *expedit sed non nunc ;* et in loco, *non hic ;*
et in persona, *non nobis, non contra hos ;* et in genere
agendi, *non sic ;* et in modo, *non in tantum.*

Sed personam saepius decoris gratia intuemur,
quae et in nobis et in iis, qui deliberant, spectanda
36 est. Itaque quamvis exempla plurimum in consiliis
possint, quia facillime ad consentiendum homines
ducuntur experimentis, refert tamen, quorum auctoritas et quibus adhibeatur. Diversi sunt enim
37 deliberantium animi, duplex condicio. Nam con-
sultant aut plures aut singuli ; sed in utrisque differentia, quia et in pluribus multum interest, senatus

two courses is better or worse, but which of three or more. On the other hand in *deliberative* oratory there 34 will never be any doubt about circumstances wholly in our favour. For there can clearly be no doubt about points against which there is nothing to be said. Consequently as a rule all *deliberative* speeches are based simply on comparison, and we must consider what we shall gain and by what means, that it may be possible to form an estimate whether there is more advantage in the aims we pursue or greater disadvantage in the means we employ to that end. A 35 question of expediency may also be concerned with time (for example, "it is expedient, but not now") or with place ("it is expedient, but not here") or with particular persons ("it is expedient, but not for us" or "not as against these") or with our method of action ("it is expedient, but not thus") or with degree ("it is expedient, but not to this extent").

But we have still more often to consider personality with reference to what is becoming, and we must consider our own as well as that of those before whom the question is laid. Consequently, 36 though examples are of the greatest value in deliberative speeches, because reference to historical parallels is the quickest method of securing assent, it matters a great deal whose authority is adduced and to whom it is commended. For the minds of those who deliberate on any subject differ from one another and our audience may be of two kinds. For those who ask us for ad- 37 vice are either single individuals or a number, and in both cases the factors may be different. For when advice is asked by a number of persons it makes a considerable difference whether they are

sīc an populus, Romani an Fidenates, Graeci an
barbari, et in singulis, Catoni petendos honores sua-
deamus an C. Mario, de ratione belli Scipio prior an
38 Fabius deliberet.   Proinde intuenda sexus, dignitas,
aetas.   Sed mores praecipue discrimen dabunt.   Et
honesta quidem honestis suadere facillimum est; si
vero apud turpes recta obtinere conabimur, ne videamur exprobrare diversam vitae sectam, cavendum.
39 Et animus deliberantis non ipsa honesti natura, quam
ille non respicit, permovendus, sed laude, vulgi
opinione, et si parum proficiet haec vanitas, secutura
ex his utilitate, aliquanto vero magis obiiciendo
40 aliquos, si diversa fecerint, metus.   Namque praeter
id quod his levissimi cuiusque animus facillime ter-
retur, nescio an etiam naturaliter apud plurimos plus
valeat malorum timor quam spes bonorum, sicut
facilior eisdem turpium quam honestorum intellectus
41 est.   Aliquando bonis quoque suadentur parum de-
cora, dantur parum bonis consilia, in quibus ipsorum
qui consulunt spectatur utilitas.   Nec me fallit, quae
statim cogitatio subire possit legentem : Hoc ergo
42 praecipis ? et hoc fas putas ?   Poterat me liberare
Cicero, qui ita scribit ad Brutum, praepositis plurimis,

---

[1] The letter is lost.   The argument of the quotation is as
follows.   The policy which I advise is honourable, but it
would be wrong for me to urge Caesar to follow it, since it is
contrary to his interests.

the senate or the people, the citizens of Rome or
Fidenae, Greeks or barbarians, and in the case of
single individuals, whether we are urging Cato or
Gaius Marius to stand for office, whether it is the
elder Scipio or Fabius who is deliberating on his plan
of campaign.   Further sex, rank, and age, must be 38
taken into account, though it is character that will
make the chief difference.   It is an easy task to
recommend an honourable course to honourable
men, but if we are attempting to keep men of bad
character to the paths of virtue, we must take care
not to seem to upbraid a way of life unlike our own.
The minds of such an audience are not to be moved 39
by discoursing on the nature of virtue, which they
ignore, but by praise, by appeals to popular opinion,
and if such vanities are of no avail, by demonstration
of the advantage that will accrue from such a policy,
or more effectively perhaps by pointing out the
appalling consequences that will follow the opposite
policy.   For quite apart from the fact that the minds 40
of unprincipled men are easily swayed by terror, I
am not sure that most men's minds are not more
easily influenced by fear of evil than by hope of
good, for they find it easier to understand what is
evil than what is good.   Sometimes again we urge 41
good men to adopt a somewhat unseemly course,
while we advise men of poor character to take a
course in which the object is the advantage of
those who seek our advice.   I realise the thought
that will immediately occur to my reader : " Do you
then teach that this should be done or think it
right ? "   Cicero [1] might clear me from blame in the
matter ; for he writes to Brutus in the following
terms, after setting forth a number of things that

quae honeste suaderi Caesari possint: *Simne bonus
vir, si haec suadeam? Minime. Suasoris enim finis est
utilitas eius, cui quisque suadet. At recta sunt. Quis
negat? sed non est semper rectis in suadendo locus.*
Sed quia est altior quaestio nec tantum ad suasorias
pertinet, destinatus est mihi hic locus duodecimo,
43 qui summus futurus est, libro. Nec ego quidquam
fieri turpiter velim. Verum interim haec vel ad
scholarum exercitationes pertinere credantur, nam
et iniquorum ratio noscenda est, ut melius aequa
44 tueamur. Interim si quis bono inhonesta suadebit,
meminerit non suadere tanquam inhonesta, ut quidam declamatores Sextum Pompeium ad piraticam
propter hoc ipsum quod turpis et crudelis sit, impel-
lunt; sed dandus illis deformibus color idque etiam
apud malos. Neque enim quisquam est tam malus,
45 ut videri velit. Sic Catilina apud Sallustium loquitur, ut rem sceleratissimam non malitia, sed indig-
natione videatur audere. Sic Atreus apud Varium:
—Iam fero (inquit) *infandissima, Iam facere cogor.*
Quanto magis eis, quibus cura famae fuit, conser-
46 vandus est hic velut ambitus? Quare et, cum
Ciceroni dabimus consilium, ut Antonium roget, vel
etiam ut Philippicas (ita vitam pollicente eo) exurat,
non cupiditatem lucis allegabimus (haec enim si

---

[1] Chap. xii.   [2] *Cat.* xx.
[3] For examples of this theme see the elder Seneca (*Suas.*
vi. and vii.).

might honourably be urged on Caesar : " Should I be
a good man to advise this ? No. For the end of him
who gives advice is the advantage of the man to
whom he gives it. But, you say, your advice is right.
Certainly, but there is not always room for what
is right in giving advice." However, this is a
somewhat abstruse question, and does not concern
deliberative oratory alone. I shall therefore reserve
it for my twelfth and concluding book.[1] For my part 43
I would not have anything done dishonourably. But
for the meantime let us regard these questions as at
least belonging to the rhetorical exercises of the
schools : for knowledge of evil is necessary to enable
us the better to defend what is right. For the 44
present I will only say that if anyone is going to urge
a dishonourable course on an honourable man, he
should remember not to urge it as being dishonourable, and should avoid the practice of certain declaimers who urge Sextus Pompeius to piracy just
because it is dishonourable and cruel. Even when we
address bad men, we should gloss over what is un-
sightly. For there is no man so evil as to wish to
seem so. Thus Sallust makes Catiline [2] speak as one 45
who is driven to crime not by wickedness but by indignation, and Varius makes Atreus say :

" My wrongs are past all speech,
    And such shall be the deeds they force me to."

How much more has this pretence of honour to be
kept up by those who have a real regard for their
own good name ! Therefore when we advise Cicero 46
to beg Antonius for mercy or even to burn the
Philippics if Antonius promises to spare him on that
condition,[3] we shall not emphasise the love of life in
our advice (for if that passion has any force with

valet in animo eius, tacentibus quoque nobis valet),
47 sed ut reipublicae se servet hortabimur. Hac illi
opus est occasione, ne eum talium precum pudeat.
Et C. Caesari suadentes regnum adfirmabimus stare
iam rempublicam nisi uno regente non posse. Nam
qui de re nefaria deliberat, id solum quaerit, quomodo quam minimum peccare videatur.

48 Multum refert etiam, quae sit persona suadentis;
quia anteacta vita si illustris fuit aut clarius genus
aut aetas aut fortuna adfert expectationem, providendum est, ne quae dicuntur ab eo qui dicit dissentiant. At his contraria summissiorem quendam
modum postulant. Nam quae in aliis libertas est, in
aliis licentia vocatur, et quibusdam sufficit auctoritas,
quosdam ratio ipsa aegre tuetur.

49 Ideoque longe mihi difficillimae videntur prosopopoeiae, in quibus ad reliquum suasoriae laborem
accedit etiam personae difficultas. Namque idem
illud aliter Caesar, aliter Cicero, aliter Cato suadere
debebit. Utilissima vero haec exercitatio, vel quod
duplicis est operis, vel quod poetis quoque aut
historiarum futuris scriptoribus plurimum confert
50 Verum et oratoribus necessaria. Nam sunt multae
a Graecis Latinisque compositae orationes, quibus
alii uterentur, ad quorum condicionem vitamque

---

[1] Julius Caesar.

him, it will have it none the less if we are silent),
but we shall exhort him to save himself in the interest of the state.   For he needs some such reason 47
as that to preserve him from feeling shame at en-
treating such a one as Antony.   Again if we urge
Gaius Caesar [1] to accept the crown we shall assert
that the state is doomed to destruction unless controlled by a monarchy.   For the sole aim of the man
who is deliberating about committing a criminal act
is to make his act appear as little wicked as possible.

It also makes a great deal of difference who it is 48
that is offering the advice : for if his past has been
illustrious, or if his distinguished birth or age or
fortune excite high expectations, care must be taken
that his words are not unworthy of him.   If on the
other hand he has none of these advantages he will
have to adopt a humbler tone.   For what is regarded
as liberty in some is called licence in others.   Some
receive sufficient support from their personal
authority, while others find that the force of reason
itself is scarce sufficient to enable them to maintain
their position.

Consequently I regard *impersonation* as the most 49
difficult of tasks, imposed as it is in addition to the
other work involved by a deliberative theme.   For
the same speaker has on one occasion to impersonate
Caesar, on another Cicero or Cato.   But it is a most
useful exercise because it demands a double effort
and is also of the greatest use to future poets and
historians, while for orators of course it is absolutely
necessary.   For there are many speeches composed 50
by Greek and Latin orators for others to deliver, the
words of which had to be adapted to suit the position and character of those for whom they were

aptanda quae dicebantur fuerunt. An eodem modo
cogitavit aut eandem personam induit Cicero, cum
scriberet Cn. Pompeio et cum T. Ampio ceterisve;
ac non uniuscuiusque eorum fortunam, dignitatem,
res gestas intuitus omnium, quibus vocem dabat,
etiam imaginem expressit? ut melius quidem sed
51 tamen ipsi dicere viderentur. Neque enim minus
vitiosa est oratio, si ab homine quam si ab re, cui
accommodari debuit, dissidet; ideoque Lysias optime
videtur in iis, quae scribebat indoctis, servasse veritatis fidem. Enimvero praecipue declamatoribus
considerandum est, quid cuique personae conveniat,
qui paucissimas controversias ita dicunt ut advocati,
plerumque filii, parentes, divites, senes, asperi, lenes,
avari, denique superstitiosi, timidi, derisores fiunt;
ut vix comoediarum actoribus plures habitus in pronuntiando concipiendi sint quam his in dicendo.
52 Quae omnia possunt videri prosopopoeiae, quam ego
suasoriis subieci, quia nullo alio ab iis quam persona distat. Quanquam haec aliquando etiam in
controversias ducitur, quae ex historiis compositae
53 certis agentium nominibus continentur. Neque
ignoro plerumque exercitationis gratia poni et
poeticas et historicas, ut Priami verba apud Achillem

---

[1] Nothing is known of these speeches.

written.   Do you suppose that Cicero thought in the
same way or assumed the same character when he
wrote for Gnaeus Pompeius and when he wrote for
Titus Ampius and the rest?[1]   Did he not rather bear
in mind the fortune, rank and achievements of each
single individual and represent the character of all
to whom he gave a voice so that though they spoke
better than they could by nature, they still might
seem to speak in their own persons?   For a speech 51
which is out of keeping with the man who delivers
it is just as faulty as the speech which fails to suit
the subject to which it should conform.   It is for
this reason that Lysias is regarded as having shown
the highest art in the speeches which he wrote for
uneducated persons, on account of their extraordin-
ary realism.   In the case of declaimers indeed it is
of the first importance that they should consider
what best suits each character: for they rarely play
the rôle of advocates in their declamations.   As a
rule they impersonate sons, parents, rich men, old
men, gentle or harsh of temper, misers, superstitious persons, cowards and mockers, so that hardly
even comic actors have to assume more numerous
rôles in their performances on the stage than
these in their declamations.   All these rôles may 52
be regarded as forming part of *impersonation,*
which I have included under *deliberative* themes,
from which it differs merely in that it involves the
assumption of a rôle.   It is sometimes introduced
even with controversial themes, which are drawn
from history and involve the appearance of definite
historical characters as pleaders.   I am aware also 53
that historical and poetical themes are often set for
the sake of practice, such as Priam's speech to

aut Sullae dictaturam deponentis in contione. Sed
haec in partem cedent trium generum, in quae
causas divisimus. Nam et rogare, indicare, rationem
reddere et alia, de quibus supra dictum est, varie
atque ut res tulit in materia iudiciali, deliberativa,
54 demonstrativa, solemus. Frequentissime vero in iis
utimur ficta personarum, quas ipsi substituimus,
oratione, ut apud Ciceronem pro Caelio Clodiam et
Caecus Appius et Clodius frater, ille in castiga-
tionem, hic in exhortationem vitiorum compositus,
alloquitur.

55 Solent in scholis fingi materiae ad deliberandum
similiores controversiis et ex utroque genere com-
mixtae, ut cum apud C. Caesarem consultatio de
poena Theodoti ponitur. Constat enim accusatione
et defensione causa eius, quod est iudicialium pro-
56 prium. Permixta tamen est et utilitatis ratio, an
pro Caesare fuerit occidi Pompeium, an timendum
a rege bellum, si Theodotus sit occisus, an id
minime opportunum hoc tempore et periculosum et
57 certe longum sit futurum. Quaeritur et de honesto,
deceatne Caesarem ultio Pompeii, an sit verendum, ne peiorem faciat suarum partium causam, si
58 Pompeium indignum morte fateatur. Quod genus
accidere etiam veritati potest.

---

[1] xiv. *sqq*

Achilles or Sulla's address to the people on his
resignation of the dictatorship. But these will fall
under one or other of the three classes into which
I have divided causes. For entreaty, statement,
and argument, with other themes already mentioned,
are all of frequent occurrence in *forensic, deliberative*
or *demonstrative* subjects, according as circumstances
demand, and we often introduce fictitious speeches 54
of historical persons, whom we select ourselves.
Cicero for instance in the *pro Caelio* [1] makes both
Appius Caecus and her brother Clodius address
Clodia, the former rebuking her for her immorality,
the latter exhorting her thereto.

In scholastic declamations the fictitious themes for 55
deliberative speeches are often not unlike those of
controversial speeches and are a compromise between
the two forms, as for instance when the theme set is
a discussion in the presence of Gaius Caesar of the
punishment to be meted out to Theodotus; for it consists of accusation and defence, both of them peculiar
to forensic oratory. But the topic of expediency also 56
enters into the case, in such questions as whether it
was to Caesar's advantage that Pompeius should be
slain; whether the execution of Theodotus would
involve the risk of a war with the king of Egypt;
whether such a war would be highly inopportune at
such a critical moment, would prove dangerous and
be certain to last a long time. There is also a question 57
of honour. Does it befit Caesar to avenge Pompeius'
death? or is it to be feared that an admission that
Pompeius did not deserve death will injure the cause
of the Caesarian party? It may be noted that dis- 58
cussions of such a kind may well occur in actual
cases.

Non simplex autem circa suasorias error in plerisque declamatoribus fuit, qui dicendi genus in iis diversum atque in totum illi iudiciali contrarium esse existimaverunt. Nam et principia abrupta et concitatam semper orationem et in verbis effusiorem, ut ipsi vocant, cultum adfectaverunt, et earum breviores utique commentarios quam legalis materiae facere

59 laborarunt. Ego porro ut prooemio video non utique opus esse suasoriis, propter quas dixi supra causas, ita cur initio furioso sit exclamandum, non intelligo; cum proposita consultatione rogatus sententiam, si modo est sanus, non quiritet, sed quam maxime potest civili et humano ingressu mereri adsensum

60 deliberantis velit. Cur autem torrens et utique aequaliter concitata sit in ea dicentis oratio, cum vel praecipue moderationem consilia desiderent? Neque ego negaverim, saepius subsidere in controversiis impetum dicendi prooemio, narratione, argumentis; quae si detrahas, id fere supererit, quo suasoriae constant, verum id quoque aequalius erit non tumul-

61 tuosius atque turbidius. Verborum autem magnificentia non validius est adfectanda suasorias declamantibus, sed contingit magis; nam et personae fere magnae fingentibus placent, regum, principum,

Declaimers have however often been guilty of an error as regards deliberative themes which has involved a series of consequences. They have considered deliberative themes to be different and absolutely opposed to forensic themes. For they have always affected abrupt openings, an impetuous style and a generous embellishment, as they call it, in their language, and have been especially careful to make shorter notes for *deliberative* than for *forensic* themes. For my part while I realise that *deliberative* themes 59 do not require an *exordium,* for reasons which I have already stated, I do not, however, understand why they should open in such a wild and exclamatory manner. When a man is asked to express his opinion on any subject, he does not, if he is sane, begin to shriek, but endeavours as far as possible to win the assent of the man who is considering the question by a courteous and natural opening. Why, I ask, in 60 view of the fact that deliberations require moderation above all else, should the speaker on such themes indulge in a torrential style of eloquence kept at one high level of violence? I acknowledge that in controversial speeches the tone is often lowered in the *exordium,* the *statement of facts* and the *argument,* and that if you subtract these three portions, the remainder is more or less of the *deliberative* type of speech, but what remains must likewise be of a more even flow, avoiding all violence and fury. With 61 regard to magnificence of language, *deliberative* declaimers should avoid straining after it more than others, but it comes to them more naturally. For there is a preference among those who invent such themes for selecting great personages, such as kings, princes, senators and peoples, while the theme itself

senatus, populi et res ampliores; ita cum verba rebus
62 aptentur, ipso materiae nitore clarescunt. Alia
veris consiliis ratio est, ideoque Theophrastus quam
maxime remotum ab omni adfectione in deliberativo
genere voluit esse sermonem, secutus in hoc auctoritatem praeceptoris sui, quanquam dissentire ab eo
63 non timide solet. Namque Aristoteles idoneam
maxime ad scribendum demonstrativam proximam-
que ab ea iudicialem putavit, videlicet quoniam prior
illa tota esset ostentationis, haec secunda egeret
artis, vel ad fallendum, si ita poposcisset utilitas,
64 consilia fide prudentiaque constarent. Quibus in
demonstrativa consentio, nam et omnes alii scriptores idem tradiderunt; in iudiciis autem consiliisque
secundum condicionem ipsius, quae tractabitur, rei
65 accommodandam dicendi credo rationem. Nam et
Philippicas Demosthenis iisdem quibus habitas in
iudiciis orationes video eminere virtutibus, et Ciceronis sententiae et contiones non minus clarum,
quam est in accusationibus ac defensionibus, eloquentiae lumen ostendunt. Dicit tamen idem de
suasoria hoc modo: *Tota autem oratio simplex et gravis*
66 *et sententiis debet ornatior esse quam verbis.* Usum
exemplorum nulli materiae magis convenire merito
fere omnes consentiunt, cum plerumque videantur

---

[1] *Rhet.* iii. 12.   [2] *Part. or.* xxvii. 97.

is generally on a grander scale. Consequently since the words are suited to the theme, they acquire additional splendour from the magnificence of the matter. In actual deliberations the case is different, 62 and consequently Theophrastus laid it down that in the *deliberative* class of oratory the language should as far as possible be free from all affectation: in stating this view he followed the authority of his instructor, although as a rule he is not afraid to differ from him. For Aristotle[1] held that the *demonstrative* 63 type of oratory was the best suited for writing and that the next best was *forensic* oratory: his reason for this view was that the first type is entirely concerned with display, while the second requires art, which will even be employed to deceive the audience, if expedience should so demand, whereas advice requires only truth and prudence. I agree with this view as 64 regards *demonstrative* oratory (in fact all writers are agreed on this point), but as regards *forensic* and *deliberative* themes I think that the style must be suited to the requirements of the subject which has to be treated. For I notice that the *Philippics* of Demosthenes 65 are pre-eminent for the same merits as his forensic speeches, and that the opinions expressed by Cicero before the senate or the people are as remarkable for the splendour of their eloquence as the speeches which he delivered in accusing or defending persons before the courts. And yet Cicero[2] says of *deliberative* oratory that the whole speech should be simple and dignified, and should derive its ornament rather from the sentiments expressed than the actual words. As regards the use of examples practically all authori- 66 ties are with good reason agreed that there is no subject to which they are better suited, since as a

respondere futura praeteritis, habeaturque experi-
67 mentum velut quoddam rationis testimonium. Bre-
vitas quoque aut copia non materiae genere sed modo
constat. Nam ut in consiliis plerumque simplicior
quaestio est, ita saepe in causis minor.

Quae omnia vera esse sciet, si quis non orationes
modo, sed historias etiam (namque in iis contiones
atque sententiae plerumque suadendi ac dissuadendi
funguntur officio), legere maluerit quam in commen-
68 tariis rhetorum consenescere. Inveniet enim nec
in consiliis abrupta initia et concitatius saepe in
iudiciis dictum et verba aptata rebus in utroque genere
et breviores aliquando causarum orationes quam sen-
69 tentiarum. Ne illa quidem in iis vitia deprehendet,
quibus quidam declamatores laborant, quod et contra
sentientibus inhumane conviciantur et ita plerumque
dicunt, tanquam ab iis qui deliberant utique dissentiant, ideoque obiurgantibus similiores sunt quam
70 suadentibus. Haec adolescentes sibi scripta sciant,
ne aliter quam dicturi sunt exerceri velint et in
desuescendis morentur. Ceterum, cum advocari
coeperint in consilia amicorum, dicere sententiam in

rule history seems to repeat itself and the experience
of the past is a valuable support to reason. Brevity 67
and copiousness are determined not so much by the
nature as by the compass of the subject. For, just as
in *deliberations* the question is generally less complicated, so in *forensic* cases it is often of less
importance.

Anyone who is content to read not merely speeches,
but history as well, in preference to growing grey over
the notebooks of the rhetoricians, will realise the
truth of what I say : for in the historians the speeches
delivered to the people and the opinions expressed
in the senate often provide examples of advice and
dissuasion. He will find an avoidance of abrupt 68
openings in *deliberative* speeches and will note that
the *forensic* style is often the more impetuous of the
two, while in both cases the words are suited to the
matter and *forensic* speeches are often shorter than
deliberative. Nor will he find in them those faults into 69
which some of our declaimers fall, namely a coarse
abuse of those who hold opposite opinions and a
general tendency to speak in such a way as to make
it seem that the speaker's views are in opposition to
those of the persons who ask his advice. Consequently
their aim seems to be invective rather than persuasion.
I would have my younger readers realise that these 70
words are penned for their special benefit that they
may not desire to adopt a different style in their
exercises from that in which they will be required to
speak, and may not be hampered by having to unlearn what they have acquired. For the rest if they
are ever summoned to take part in the counsels of
their friends, or to speak their opinions in the senate,
or advise the emperor on some point on which he

senatu, suadere si quid consulet princeps, quod
praeceptis fortasse non credunt, usu docebuntur.

IX. Nunc de iudiciali genere, quod est praecipue
multiplex, sed officiis constat duobus intentionis ac
depulsionis. Cuius partes, ut plurimis auctoribus
placuit, quinque sunt: prooemium, narratio, pro-
batio, refutatio, peroratio. His adiecerunt quidam
partitionem, propositionem, excessum; quarum pri-
2 ores duae probationi succedunt. Nam proponere
quidem, quae sis probaturus, necesse est, sed et
concludere; cur igitur si illa pars causae est, non et
haec sit? Partitio vero dispositionis est species,
ipsa dispositio pars rhetorices et per omnes materias
totumque earum corpus aequaliter fusa, sicut in-
3 ventio, elocutio. Ideoque eam non orationis totius
partem unam esse credendum est sed quaestionum
etiam singularum. Quae est enim quaestio, in qua
non promittere possit orator, quid primo, quid
secundo, quid tertio sit loco dicturus? quod est
proprium partitionis. Quam ergo ridiculum est,
quaestionem quidem speciem esse probationis, partitionem autem, quae sit species quaestionis, partem
4 totius orationis vocari? Egressio vero vel, quod usi-
tatius esse coepit, excessus, sive est extra causam,
non potest esse pars causae, sive est in causa, adiu-
torium vel ornamentum partium est earum, ex quibus
egreditur. Nam si, quidquid in causa est, pars
causae vocabitur, cur non argumentum, similitudo,

may consult them, they will learn from practice
what they cannot perhaps put to the credit of the
schools.

IX. I now come to the forensic kind of oratory,
which presents the utmost variety, but whose duties
are no more than two, the bringing and rebutting
of charges. Most authorities divide the forensic
speech into five parts : the *exordium*, the *statement of
facts*, the *proof*, the *refutation*, and the *peroration*.
To these some have added the *partition into heads*,
proposition and *digression*, the two first of which
form part of the *proof*. For it is obviously 2
necessary to *propound* what you are going to *prove*
as well as to conclude. Why then, if *proposition* is a
part of a speech, should not *conclusion* be also ? *Partition* on the other hand is merely one aspect of
arrangement, and *arrangement* is a part of rhetoric
itself, and is equally distributed through every theme
of oratory and their whole body, just as are *invention*
and *style*. Consequently we must regard *partition* 3
not as one part of a whole speech, but as a part of
each individual question that may be involved. For
what question is there in which an orator cannot
set forth the order in which he is going to make
his points? And this of course is the function of *partition*. But how ridiculous it is to make each question an aspect of *proof*, but *partition* which is an
aspect of a question a part of the whole speech. As 4
for *digression* (*egressio*, now more usually styled
excessus), if it lie outside the case, it cannot be part
of it, while, if it lie within it, it is merely an acces-
sory or ornament of that portion of the case from
which *digression* is made. For if anything that lies
within the case is to be called part of it, why not

locus communis, adfectus, exempla partes vocentur?

5 Tamen nec iis adsentior, qui detrahunt refutationem tanquam probationi subiectam, ut Aristoteles; haec enim est, quae constituat, illa, quae destruat. Hoc quoque idem aliquatenus novat, quod prooemio non narrationem subiungit sed propositionem. Verum id facit, quia propositio ei genus, narratio species videtur, et hac non semper, illa semper et ubique credit opus esse.

6 Verum ex his quas constitui partibus non, ut quidque primum dicendum, ita primum cogitandum est; sed ante omnia intueri oportet, quod sit genus causae, quid in ea quaeratur, quae prosint, quae noceant, deinde quid confirmandum sit ac refellen-
7 dum, tum quo modo narrandum. Expositio enim probationum est praeparatio, nec esse utilis potest, nisi prius constiterit, quid debeat de probatione promittere. Postremo intuendum, quemadmodum iudex sit conciliandus. Neque enim nisi totius causae partibus diligenter inspectis scire possumus, qualem nobis facere animum cognoscentis expediat, severum an mitem, concitatum an remissum, adversum gratiae an obnoxium.

8 Neque ideo tamen eos probaverim, qui scribendum

---

[1] *Rhet.* ii. 26.   [2] *Rhet.* iii. 13.

call *argument, comparison, commonplace, pathos, illustration* parts of the case? On the other hand I 5
disagree with those who, like Aristotle,[1] would remove *refutation* from the list on the ground that it
forms part of the *proof* : for the *proof* is construc-
tive, and the *refutation* destructive. Aristotle [2] also
introduces another slight novelty in making *proposition*, not *statement of facts*, follow the *exordium*. This
however he does because he regards *proposition* as
the *genus* and *statement of facts* as the *species*, with
the result that he holds that, whereas the former is
always and everywhere necessary, the latter may
sometimes be dispensed with.

It is however necessary to point out as regards 6
these five parts which I have established, that that
which has to be spoken first is not necessarily that
which requires our first consideration. But above
all we must consider the nature of the case,
the question at issue and the arguments for and
against. Next we must consider what points are
to be made, and what refuted, and then how the
facts are to be stated. For the *statement of facts* is 7
designed to prepare the way for the *proofs* and must
needs be unprofitable, unless we have first determined what *proofs* are to be promised in the *statement*. Finally we must consider how best to win the
judge to take our view. For we cannot be sure until
we have subjected all the parts of the case to careful
scrutiny, what sort of impression we wish to make
upon the judge : are we to mollify him or increase
his severity, to excite or relax his interest in the
case, to render him susceptible to influence or the
reverse?

I cannot however approve the view of those who 8

quoque prooemium novissime putant. Nam ut con
ferri materiam omnem et, quid quoque loco [1] sit opus,
constare decet, antequam dicere aut scribere ordi-
amur, ita incipiendum ab iis, quae prima sunt. Nam
nec pingere quisquam aut fingere coepit a pedibus,
nec denique ars ulla consummatur ibi, unde ordien-
dum est. Quid fiet alioqui, si spatium componendi
orationem stilo non fuerit? nonne nos haec inversa
consuetudo deceperit? Inspicienda igitur materia
est, quo praecepimus ordine, scribenda, quo dicemus.

X. Ceterum causa omnis, in qua pars altera agentis
est, altera recusantis, aut unius rei controversia constat aut plurium. Haec simplex dicitur, illa coniuncta. Una controversia est per se furti, per se
adulterii. Plures aut eiusdem generis, ut in pecuniis
repetundis, aut diversi, ut si quis sacrilegii et homi-
cidii simul accusetur. Quod nunc in publicis iudiciis
non accidit, quoniam praetor certa lege sortitur,
principum autem et senatus cognitionibus frequens
est et populi fuit; privata quoque iudicia saepe unum
iudicem habere multis et diversis formulis solent.
2 Nec aliae species erunt, etiamsi unus a duobus dumtaxat eandem rem atque ex eadem causa petet aut

---

[1] quoque loco, *Regius*: quoque, *MSS.*

---

[1] In the permanent courts (*quaestiones perpetuae*). There
were separate courts for different offences. In cases brought
before the Senate or the Emperor a number of different
charges might be dealt with at once.

think that the *exordium* should actually be written last. For though we must collect all our material and determine the proper place for each portion of it, before we begin to speak or write, we must commence with what naturally comes first. No one begins a portrait 9 by painting or modelling the feet, and no art finds its completion at the point where it should begin. Otherwise what will happen if we have not time to write our speech? Will not the result of such a reversal of the proper order of things be that we shall be caught napping? We must therefore review the subject-matter in the order laid down, but write our speech in the order in which we shall deliver it.

X. Every cause in which one side attacks and the other defends consists either of one or more controversial questions. In the first case it is called *simple,* in the second *complex.* An example of the first is when the subject of enquiry is a theft or an adultery taken by itself. In *complex* cases the several questions may all be of the same kind, as in cases of extortion, or of different kinds, as when a man is accused at one and the same time of homicide and sacrilege. Such cases no longer arise in the public courts, since the praetor allots the different charges to different courts in accordance with a definite rule; but they still are of frequent occurrence in the Imperial or Senatorial courts, and were frequent in the days when they came up for trial before the people.[1] Private suits again are often tried by one judge, who may have to determine many different points of law. There are no other *species* of *forensic* 2 causes, not even when one person brings the same suit on the same grounds against two different

duo ab uno aut plures a pluribus, quod accidere in
hereditariis litibus interim scimus, quia quamvis in
multis personis causa tamen una est, nisi si condicio
personarum quaestiones variaverit.

3 Diversum his tertium genus, quod dicitur comparativum; cuius rei tractatus in parte causae
frequens est, ut cum apud centumviros post alia
quaeritur et hoc, uter dignior hereditate sit. Rarum
est autem, ut in foro iudicia propter id solum con-
stituantur, sicut divinationes, quae fiunt de accusatore constituendo, et nonnunquam inter delatores,
4 uter praemium meruerit. Adiecerunt quidam
numero mutuam accusationem, quae ἀντικατηγορία
vocatur, aliis videlicet succedere hanc quoque com-
parativo generi existimantibus, cui similis erit
petitionum invicem diversarum, quod accidit vel
frequentissime. Id si et ipsum vocari debet ἀντικατηγορία (nam proprio caret nomine) duo genera erunt
eius, alterum quo litigatores idem crimen invicem
intentant, alterum quo aliud atque aliud. Cui et
petitionum condicio par est.

5 Cum apparuerit genus causae, tum intuebimur,
negeturne factum, quod intenditur, an defendatur,
an alio nomine appelletur, an a genere actionis
repellatur; unde sunt status.

---

[1] A civil court specially concerned with questions of
inheritance.

[2] *Divinatio* is a trial to decide between the claims of two
persons to appear as accuser, there being no public prosecutor
at Rome. *cp.* Cicero's *Divinatio in Caecilium.*

persons, or two persons bring the same suit against one, or several against several, as occasionally occurs in lawsuits about inheritances. Because although a number of parties may be involved, there is still only one suit, unless indeed the different circumstances of the various parties alter the questions at issue.

There is however said to be a third and different 3 class, the *comparative*. Questions of comparison frequently require to be handled in portions of a cause, as for instance in the centumviral court,[1] when after other questions have been raised the question is discussed as to which of two claimants is the more deserving of an inheritance. It is rare however for a case to be brought into court on such grounds alone, as in *divinations*[2] which take place to determine who the accuser shall be, and occasionally when two informers dispute as to which has earned the reward. Some again have added a fourth class, namely 4 *mutual accusation*, which they call ἀντικατηγορία. Others, however, regard it as belonging to the *comparative* group, to which indeed the common case of reciprocal suits on different grounds bears a strong resemblance. If this latter case should also be called ἀντικατηγορία (for it has no special name of its own), we must divide *mutual accusation* into two classes, in one of which the parties bring the same charge against each other, while in the other they bring different charges. The same division will also apply to claims.

As soon as we are clear as to the kind of cause on 5 which we are engaged, we must then consider whether the act that forms the basis of the charge is denied or defended, or given another name or excepted from that class of action. Thus we determine the *basis* of each case.

XI. His inventis, intuendum deinceps Hermagorae videtur, quid sit quaestio, ratio, iudicatio,
continens, vel, ut alii vocant, firmamentum. Quaestio latius intelligitur omnis, de qua in utramque
partem vel in plures partes dici credibiliter potest.
2 In iudiciali autem materia dupliciter accipienda est :
altero modo, quo dicimus multas quaestiones habere
controversiam, quo etiam minores omnes complecti-
mur, altero, quo significamus summam illam, in qua
causa vertitur ; de hac nunc loquor, ex qua nascitur
3 status, an factum sit, quid factum sit, an recte
factum sit. Has Hermagoras et Apollodorus et
alii plurimi scriptores proprie quaestiones vocant,
Theodorus, ut dixi, capita generalia, sicut illas
minores aut ex illis pendentes specialia. Nam et
quaestionem ex quaestione nasci et speciem in
4 species dividi convenit. Hanc igitur quaestionem
veluti principalem vocant ζήτημα. Ratio autem est,
qua id, quod factum esse constat, defenditur. Et
cur non utamur eodem, quo sunt usi omnes fere,
exemplo ? Orestes matrem occidit, hoc constat ;
dicit se iuste fecisse : status erit qualitatis ; quaestio,
an iuste fecerit, ratio, quod Clytaemnestra maritum
suum, patrem Orestis, occidit ; hoc αἴτιον dicitur.

---

[1] This highly technical chapter will be largely unintelligible
to those who have not read chapter vi. Those who have no
stomach for such points would do well to skip §§ 1–20 ; they
will however find consolation in § 21 *sqq.*, where Quintilian
says what he really thinks of such technicalities.

XI. As soon as these points are ascertained, the next step, according to Hermagoras, should be to consider what is the *question at issue*, the *line of defence*, the *point for the judge's decision* and the *central point*, or, as others call it, the *foundation* of the case.[1] The *question* in its more general sense is taken to mean everything on which two or more plausible opinions may be advanced. In *forensic* subjects however it 2 must be taken in two senses: first in the sense in which we say that a controversial matter involves many questions, thereby including all minor questions; secondly in the sense of the main question on which the case turns. It is of this, with which the *basis* originates, that I am now speaking. We ask whether a thing has been done, what it is that has been done, and whether it was rightly done. To 3 these Hermagoras and Apollodorus and many other writers have given the special name of *questions*; Theodorus on the other hand, as I have already said, calls them *general heads*, while he designates minor questions or questions dependent on these *general heads* as *special heads*. For it is agreed that question may spring from question, and species be subdivided into other species. This main question, then, they 4 call the ζήτημα. The *line of defence* is the method by which an admitted act is defended. I see no reason why I should not use the same example to illustrate this point that has been used by practically all my predecessors. Orestes has killed his mother: the fact is admitted. He pleads that he was justified in so doing: the *basis* will be one of quality, the *question*, whether he was justified in his action, the *line of defence* that Clytemnestra killed her husband, Orestes' father. This is called the αἴτιον or *motive*.

Κρινόμενον autem iudicatio, an oportuerit vel nocen-
5 tem matrem a filio occidi. Quidam diviserunt αἴτιον
et αἰτίαν, ut esset altera, propter quam iudicium
constitutum est, ut occisa Clytaemnestra, altera, qua
factum defenditur, ut occisus Agamemnon. Sed
tanta est circa verba dissensio, ut alii αἰτίαν causam
iudicii, αἴτιον autem facti vocent, alii eadem in contrarium vertant. Latinorum quidam haec initium
et rationem vocaverunt, quidam utrumque eodem
6 nomine appellant. Causa quoque ex causa, id est
αἴτιον ἐξ αἰτίου, nasci videtur, quale est: Occidit
Agamemnonem Clytaemnestra, quia ille filiam communem immolaverat et captivam pellicem adduce-
bat. Iidem putant et sub una quaestione plures esse
rationes, ut si Orestes et alteram adferat causam
matris necatae, quod responsis sit impulsus; quot
autem causas faciendi, totidem iudicationes; nam et
haec erit iudicatio, an responsis parere debuerit.
7 Sed et una causa plures habere quaestiones et iudicationes (ut ego arbitror) potest, ut in eo, qui, cum
adulteram deprehensam occidisset, adulterum, qui
tum effugerat, postea in foro occidit. Causa enim
est una, adulter fuit; quaestiones et iudicationes, an

The point for the decision of the judge is known as
the κρινόμενον, and in this case is whether it was
right that even a guilty mother should be killed by
her son. Some have drawn a distinction between 5
αἴτιον and αἰτία, making αἴτιον mean the cause of the
trial, namely the murder of Clytemnestra, αἰτία the
motive urged in defence, namely the murder of
Agamemnon. But there is such lack of agreement
over these two words, that some make αἰτία the cause
of the trial and αἴτιον the motive of the deed, while
others reverse the meanings. If we turn to Latin
writers we find that some have given these causes the
names of *initium*, the beginning, and *ratio*, the reason,
while others give the same name to both. Moreover 6
cause seems to spring from *cause*, or as the Greeks say
αἴτιον ἐξ αἰτίου, as will be seen from the following :—
Clytemnestra killed Agamemnon, because he had
sacrificed their daughter and brought home a captive
woman as his paramour. The same authors think
that there may be several *lines of defence* to one
question : for instance Orestes may urge that he
killed his mother because driven to do so by oracles.
But the number of *points for the decision of the judge*
will be the same as the number of alleged *motives* for
the deed : in this case it will be whether he ought to
have obeyed the oracles. But one alleged *motive* may 7
also in my opinion involve several questions and several
points for the decision of the judge, as for instance
in the case when the husband caught his wife in
adultery and slew her and later slew the adulterer,
who had escaped, in the market place. The *motive* is
but one : " he was an adulterer." But there arise
as *questions* and *points for decision by the judge*, whether

8 illo tempore, an illo loco licuerit occidere. Sed
sicut, cum sint plures quaestiones omnesque suos
status habeant, causae tamen status unus sit, ad
quem referuntur omnia, ita iudicatio maxime propria,
9 de qua pronuntiatur. Συνέχον autem (quod, ut dixi,
continens alii, firmamentum alii putant, Cicero *fir-
missimam argumentationem defensoris et adpositissimam
ad iudicationem*) quibusdam id videtur esse, post quod
nihil quaeritur, quibusdam id quod ad iudicationem
10 firmissimum adfertur. Causa facti non in omnes
controversias cadit. Nam quae fuerit causa faciendi,
ubi factum negatur? At ubi causa tractetur, negant
eodem loco esse iudicationem quo quaestionem,
idque et in Rhetoricis Cicero et in Partitionibus
11 dicit. Nam in coniectura est quaestio ex illo
Factum, non factum an factum sit. Ibi ergo iudicatio, ubi quaestio, quia in eadem re prima quaestio
et extrema disceptatio. At in qualitate, *Matrem
Orestes occidit: recte, non recte,* an recte occiderit, quaestio nec statim iudicatio. Quando ergo?
*Illa patrem meum occiderat; sed non ideo tu matrem
12 debuisti occidere;* an debuerit, hic iudicatio. Firma-

---

[1] *De Inv.* i. xiv. 19.
[2] *De Inv. l.c.: Part. Or.* xxx. 104.

it was lawful to kill him at that time and at that place. But just as, although there be several *questions*, 8 each with its special *basis*, the *basis* of the case is but one, namely that to which all else is referred, even so the real *point for the decision of the judge* is, strictly speaking, that on which judgment is given. As for 9 the σύνεχον, the *central argument*, as I have mentioned it is called by some, or the *foundation* as it is called by others, or as Cicero [1] styles it *the strongest argument of the defender and the most relevant to the decision of the judge,* some regard it as being the point after which all enquiry ceases, others as the main point for adjudication. The *motive* of the deed does not arise 10 in all controversial cases. For how can there be a *motive* for the deed, when the deed is denied? But when the *motive* for the deed does come up for discussion, they deny that the *point for the decision of the judge* rests on the same ground as *the main question at issue,* and this view is maintained by Cicero [2] in his Rhetorica and *Partitiones*. For when it has been 11 asserted and denied that a deed was done, the question whether it was done is resolved by *conjecture,* and the *decision of the judge* and the *main question* rest on the same ground, since the first question and the final decision are concerned with the same point. But when it is stated and denied that Orestes was justified in killing his mother, considerations of *quality* are introduced : the *question* is whether he was justified in killing her, but this is not yet the point for the *decision of the judge.* When, then, does it become so ? " She killed my father." " Yes, but that did not make it your duty to murder your mother." The *point for the decision of the judge* is whether it was his duty to kill her. As regards the *foundation,* I will put 12

527

mentum autem verbis ipsius ponam: *si velit Orestes
dicere eiusmodi animum matris suae fuisse in patrem
suum, in se ipsum ac sorores, in regnum, in famam
generis et familiae, ut ab ea poenas liberi potissimum sui*
13 *petere debuerint.* Utuntur alii et talibus exemplis:
*Qui bona paterna consumpserit, ne contionetur; in opera
publica consumpsit;* quaestio, an, quisquis consump-
14 serit, prohibendus sit: iudicatio, an, qui sic. Vel,
ut in causa militis Arrunti, qui Lusium tribunum
vim sibi inferentem interfecit, quaestio, an iure
fecerit, ratio, quod is vim afferebat; iudicatio, an
indemnatum, an tribunum a milite occidi opor-
15 tuerit. Alterius etiam status quaestionem, alterius
iudicationem putant. Quaestio qualitatis, an recte
Clodium Milo occiderit. Iudicatio coniecturalis, an
16 Clodius insidias fecerit. Ponunt et illud, saepe
causam in aliquam rem dimitti, quae non sit propria
quaestionis, et de ea iudicari. A quibus multum
dissentio. Nam et illa quaestio, an omnes, qui
paterna bona consumpserint, contione sint prohi-
bendi, habeat oportet suam iudicationem. Ergo non
alia quaestio alia iudicatio erit, sed plures quaesti-

---

[1] *de Inv. l.c.*

it in the words of Cicero [1] himself :—" The foundation
is the strongest argument for the defence, as for
instance, if Orestes were ready to say that the disposition of his mother towards his father, himself and
his sisters, the kingdom, the reputation of the race
and the family were such that it was the peculiar duty
of her children to punish her." Others again use 13
illustrations such as the following :—" He who has
spent his patrimony, is not allowed to address the
people." " But he spent it on public works." The
question is whether everyone that spends his patrimony
is to be prohibited, while the *point for decision* is
whether he who spent it in such a way is to be
prohibited. Or again take the case of the soldier 14
Arruntius, who killed the tribune Lusius for assaulting
his honour. The *question* is whether he was justified
in so doing, *the line of defence,* that the murdered man
made an assault upon his honour, *the point for the
decision of the judge,* whether it was right that a man
should be killed uncondemned or a tribune by a
soldier. Some even regard the *basis* of the *question* 15
as being different from the *basis* of the *decision.*
The *question* as to whether Milo was justified in
killing Clodius, is one of *quality.* The *point for the
decision of the judge,* namely whether Clodius lay in
wait for Milo, is a matter for *conjecture.* They also 16
urge that a case is often diverted to the consideration
of some matter irrelevant to the *question,* and that it is
on this matter that judgment is given. I strongly
disagree. Take the question whether all who have
spent their patrimony are to be prohibited from
addressing the people. This *question* must have its
point for decision, and therefore the *question* and the
point for decision are not different, but there are more

17 ones et plures iudicationes. Quid? non in causa
Milonis ipsa coniectura refertur ad qualitatem? nam
si est insidiatus Clodius, sequitur, ut recte sit occisus.

Cum vero in aliquam rem missa causa recessum est
a quaestione, quae erat, et hic constituta quaestio,
ubi iudicatio est.[1]

18 Paulum in his secum etiam Cicero dissentit. Nam
in Rhetoricis (quemadmodum supra dixi) Hermagoran est secutus; in Topicis ex statu effectam contentionem κρινόμενον existimat, idque Trebatio, qui
iuris erat consultus, adludens *qua de re agitur* appellat; quibus id contineatur, *continentia, quasi firma-
menta defensionis, quibus sublatis defensio nulla sit;*
19 at in Partitionibus oratoriis firmamentum, quod
opponitur defensioni, quia continens, quod primum
sit, ab accusatore dicatur, ratio a reo, ex rationis et
firmamenti quaestione disceptatio sit iudicationum.

Verius igitur et brevius ii, qui statum et continens
et iudicationem idem[2] esse voluerunt; continens
20 autem id esse, quo sublato lis esse non possit. Hoc
mihi videntur utramque causam complexi, et quod

---

[1] causa est recessum est a quaestione quae erat et hic constituta quaestio iudicatio est, *A* : causa est recessum et a
quaestione quae erat hic constituta quaestio ubi iudicatio
est, *B. The reading and meaning are very uncertain.*
[2] idem, *added by Regius.*

than one *question* and more than one *point for decision*
in the case.   Again, in the case of Milo, is not the 17
question of fact ultimately referred to the *question of
quality*?   For if Clodius lay in wait for Milo, it follows
that he was justifiably killed.   But when the case is
shifted to some other point far removed from the
original question, even in this case the *question* will
be found to reside in the *point for decision*.

As regards these questions Cicero is slightly in- 18
consistent with himself.   For in the Rhetorica, as I
have already mentioned, he followed Hermagoras,
while in the *Topica*[1] he holds that the κρινόμενον or
disputed point is originated by the *basis*, and in
addressing the lawyer Trebatius on this subject he
calls it the *point at issue*, and describes the elements
in which it resides as *central arguments* or *foundations
of the defence which hold it together and the removal of
which causes the whole defence to fall to the ground*.   But 19
in the *Partitiones Oratoriae*[2] he gives the name of
foundation to that which is advanced against the defence, on the ground that the *central argument*, as it
logically comes first, is put forward by the accuser,
while *the line of defence* is put forward by the accused,
and the *point for the decision of the judge* arises from
the question jointly raised by the *central argument*
and the *line of defence*.

The view therefore of those who make the *basis*,
the *central argument*, and the *point for the decision of
the judge* identical, is at once more concise and nearer
to the truth.   The *central argument*, they point out,
is that the removal of which makes the whole case fall
to the ground.   In this *central argument* they seem to 20
me to have included both the alleged causes, that

---

[1] *Top.* xxv. 95.   [2] xxix. 103.

Orestes matrem et quod Clytaemnestra Agamemnonem occiderit. Iidem iudicationem et statum consentire semper existimarunt, neque enim aliud eorum rationi conveniens fuisset.

21 Verum haec adfectata subtilitas circa nomina rerum ambitiose laborat, a nobis in hoc assumpta solum, ne parum diligenter inquisisse de opere, quod aggressi sumus, videremur; simplicius autem instituenti non est necesse per tam minutas rerum par-

22 ticulas rationem docendi concidere. Quo vitio multi quidem laborarunt, praecipue tamen Hermagoras, vir alioqui subtilis et in plurimis admirandus, tantum diligentiae nimium sollicitae, ut ipsa eius reprehensio

23 laude aliqua non indigna sit. Haec autem brevior et vel ideo lucidior multo via neque discentem per ambages fatigabit nec corpus orationis in parva momenta diducendo consumet. Nam qui viderit, quid sit, quod in controversiam veniat, quid in eo et per quae velit efficere pars diversa, quid nostra, quod in primis est intuendum, nihil eorum ignorare,

24 de quibus supra diximus, poterit. Neque est fere quisquam modo non stultus atque ab omni prorsus

Orestes killed his mother and that Clytemnestra killed Agamemnon. The same authorities have likewise always held that the *basis* and the *point for the decision* of the judge are in agreement; any other opinion would have been inconsistent with their general views.

But this affectation of subtlety in the invention of 21 technical terms is mere laborious ostentation: I have undertaken the task of discussing them solely that I might not be regarded as having failed to make sufficient inquiry into the subject which I have chosen as my theme. But it is quite unnecessary for an instructor proceeding on less technical lines to destroy the coherence of his teaching by attention to such minute detail. Many however suffer from this draw- 22 back, more especially Hermagoras who, although he labours these points with such anxious diligence, was a man of penetrating intellect and in most respects deserves our admiration, so that even where we must needs blame him, we cannot withhold a certain meed of praise. But the shorter method, which for that 23 very reason is also by far the most lucid, will not fatigue the learner by leading him through a maze of detail, nor destroy the coherence of his eloquence by breaking it up into a number of minute departments. For he who has a clear view of the main issue of a dispute, and divines the aims which his own side and his opponents intend to follow and the means they intend to employ (and it is to the intentions of his own side that he must pay special attention), will without a doubt be in possession of a knowledge of all the points which I have discussed above. And there is hardly 24 anyone, unless he be a born fool without the least acquaintance with the practice of speaking, who does

usu dicendi remotus, quin sciat, et quid litem faciat,
(quod ab illis causa vel continens dicitur) et quae sit
inter litigantes quaestio, et de quo iudicari oporteat;
quae omnia idem sunt.   Nam et de eo quaestio est,
quod in controversiam venit, et de eo iudicatur, de
25 quo quaestio est.   Sed non perpetuo intendimus in
haec animum et cupiditate laudis utcunque acqui-
rendae vel dicendi voluptate evagamur, quando
uberior semper extra causam materia est, quia in
controversia pauca sunt, extra omnia, et hic dicitur
de his, quae accepimus, illic, de quibus volumus.
26 Nec tam hoc praecipiendum est, ut quaestionem,
continens, iudicationem inveniamus (nam id quidem
facile est), quam ut intueamur semper, aut certe si
digressi fuerimus saltem respiciamus, ne plausum
adfectantibus arma excidant.   Theodori schola, ut
27 dixi, omnia refert ad *capita*.   His plura intelliguntur: uno modo summa quaestio item ut status, altero
ceterae quae ad summam referuntur, tertio propositio
cum adfirmatione; ut dicimus, *Caput rei est,* apud
Menandrum κεφάλαιόν ἐστιν.   In universum autem,
quidquid probandum est, erit caput; sed id maius
aut minus.

---

[1] Perhaps a gloss referring to the late rhetorician Menander. If genuine, the words must refer to the comic poet.

not know what is the main issue of a dispute (or as
they call it the *cause* or *central argument*) and what is
the *question* between the parties and the *point on which
the judge has to decide,* these three being identical.
For the *question* is concerned with the matter in dispute and the *decision of the judge* is given on the
point involved in the *question.* Still we do not keep 25
our attention rigidly fixed on such details, but the
desire to win praise by any available means and the
sheer delight in speaking make us wander away from
the subject, since there is always richer material for
eloquence outside the strict theme of the case, inasmuch as the points of any given dispute are always
few, and there is all the world outside, and in the one
case we speak according to our instructions, in the
other on the subjects of our own choice. We should 26
teach not so much that it is our duty to discover the
question, the *central argument,* and the *point for the decision of the judge* (an easy task), as that we should
continually keep our attention on our subject, or if
we digress, at least keep looking back to it, lest in
our desire to win applause we should let our weapons
drop from our grasp. The school of Theodorus, as I 27
have said, groups everything under *heads,* by which
they mean several things. First they mean the *main
question,* which is to be identified with the *basis*;
secondly they mean the other questions dependent
on the *main question,* thirdly the *proposition* and the
statement of the proofs. The word is used as we use it
when we say "It is the head of the whole business,"
or, as Menander says, κεφάλαιον ἐστιν.[1] But generally
speaking, anything which has to be proved will be a
head of varying degrees of importance.

28   Et quoniam, quae de his erant a scriptoribus
artium tradita, verbosius etiam quam necesse erat
exposuimus, praeterea, quae partes essent iudicialium
causarum, supra dictum est, proximus liber a prima,
id est exordio incipiet.

I have now set forth the principles laid down by 28
the writers of text-books, though I have done so
at a greater length than was necessary. I have
also explained what are the various parts of forensic
causes. My next book therefore shall deal with
the *exordium.*

INDEX

(Only those names are included which seem to require some explanation; a complete index will be contained in Vol. IV.)

Accius, I. vii. 14; I. viii. 11. Famous tragic poet, *fl.* 140 B.C.

Aelius Stilo, I. vi. 37. Famous as a philologist, *circa* 100 B.C.

Aeschines, II. xvii. 12; III. vi. 3. Attic orator, contemporary and opponent of Demosthenes.

Agnon, II. xvii. 15. Academic philosopher and rhetorician, teacher of Carneades, second century.

Albutius Silus, C., II. xv. 36; III. iii. 4; III. vi. 62. Rhetorician of the Augustan period.

Alcidamas, III. i. 10. Rhetorician from Elaea, pupil of Gorgias, *fl.* 425 B.C.

Ampius, T., III. viii. 50. T. Ampius Balbus, trib. pleb. 68 B.C., praetor 59. Friend and correspondent of Cicero.

Anaximenes of Lampsacus, III. iv. 9. A rhetorician, who accompanied Alexander on his campaigns.

Antigonus, II. xiii. 12. King of Asia, after Alexander's death.

Antipho, III. i. 11. Orator and instructor of Thucydides.

Antonius, M., II. xv. 7; II. xvii. 5 *sq.*; III. i. 19; III. vi. 45. With L. Crassus, the most famous Roman orator prior to Cicero, of whom he was an elder contemporary.

Antonius Gnipho, I. vi. 23. A famous grammarian and rhetorician, contemporary with Cicero.

Antonius Rufus I. v. 43. An early grammaria,n of uncertain date. Possibly also a dramatic poet.

Apelles, II. xiii. 12. A famous Greek painter, *fl.* 330 B.C.

Apollodorus of Pergamus, II. xv. 12; III. i. 1, 17; III. v. 17; III. vi. 35 *sq.*; III. xi. 3. Cp. II. xi. 2; II. xv. 12; III. i. 18. A distinguished rhetorician of the Augustan age.

Apollonius Molon of Rhodes, III. i. 16. A famous rhetorician. Cicero was among his pupils.

Appius Caecus, II. xvi. 7; III. viii. 54. Consul 307 B.C.; specially famous for the speech by which he persuaded the senate to reject Pyrrhus' terms of peace. The earliest great orator of Rome.

Aquilius Manius, II. xv. 8. Accused of maladministration in Sicily, 98 B.C.

Archedemus, III. vi. 31, 33. A rhetorician of the generation following Aristotle.

Archimedes, I. x. 48. The famous mathematician of Syracuse, who perished in the sack of that city by the Romans, 212 B.C., after prolonging the siege by his skill in the construction of siege engines.

Archytas, I. x. 17. Pythagorean philosopher, mathematician and statesman of Tarentum, *fl.* 400 B.C.

Areus, II. xv. 36; III. i. 16. Stoic

539

INDEX

INDEX

before Octavian, Antony and Lepidus for remission of part of the tax imposed on married women.

Hortensius, I. v. 12; II. i. 1, 11; III. v. 11. The leading orator at Rome when Cicero first made his appearance at the bar, and the latter's most serious rival.

Hyperbolus, I. x. 18. Athenian demagogue at end of fifth century B.C.

Hyperides, II. xv. 9. Attic orator contemporary with Demosthenes and ranked as second only to him.

Hypobolimaeus, I. x. 18. "The Supposititious Son," a lost play of Menander.

Irus, III. vii. 19. A beggar who fights Odysseus in the *Odyssey*.

Isocrates, II. viii. 11; II. xv. 4, 33; III. i. 13 *sqq.*; III. iv. 11; III. v. 18; III. vi. 3; III. viii. 9. Famous orator and founder of the science and technique of Greek rhetoric. 436–338 B.C.

Italia, I. vi. 31. From ἰταλοι = oxen, *i.e.*, Oxland.

Labienus, I. v. 8. Orator and historian under Augustus.

Laelia, I. i. 6. Daughter of Laelius the wise and wife of Scaevola. She was famous for the pure Latinity of her conversation.

Laenas, Popilius, III. i. 21. Rhetorician probably of the reign of Tiberius.

Latium, I. vi. 31. Probably from *latus* = the broad lands : popularly derived from *latere*, because Saturn lay hid there.

Leonidas, I. i. 9. Uncle and tutor of Alexander the Great.

Lucilius, I. v. 56; I. vi. 8; I. vii. 15, 19; I. viii. 11. The founder of Roman satire. D. 103 B.C.

Maelius, Spurius, III. vii. 20. Bought up corn in time of dearth and sold it cheap to the people in 440 B.C. Was suspected of wishing to seize the supreme power and killed in the following year.

M. Manlius Capitolinus, III. vii. 20. Saved Rome from the Gauls, but was subsequently suspected of aiming at supreme power and hurled from the Tarpeian rock in 384 B.C.

Marcellus Victorius, Ep. ad Tryph. 1; 1 Pr. 5. Nothing is known of him except for the fact that Statius dedicated the Fourth Book of the *Silvae* to him.

Matius, III. i. 18. A friend of Augustus.

Messala, I. v. 15, 61; I. vi. 42; I. vii. 23, 34. Distinguished orator and philologist of the Augustan age.

Milo of Croton, I. ix. 5. A famous athlete of the sixth century B.C.

Modestus, I. vi. 36. Probably Iulius Modestus, a grammarian who flourished in the principate of Tiberius.

Naucrates, III. vi. 3. Orator and rhetorician, famous for the funeral oration on Mausolus, king of Caria, in 352 B.C.

Nicias, I. x. 48. Athenian statesman and general, was captured with his army in Sicily owing to his refusal to march during eclipse of the moon, 413 B.C.

Nireus, III. vii. 19. The handsomest man in the Greek army at Troy.

Pacuvius, I. v. 67; I. viii. 11; I. xii. 18. Famous tragic poet, 220–130 B.C.

Palaemon, Remmius, I. iv. 20; I. vi. 35. Famous *grammaticus*, taught Quintilian, *fl. circa* 30 A.D.

Palamedes, III. i. 10. Greek chief in the Trojan war, put to death on false accusation of treachery. He was later regarded by the sophists as their prototype.

Pamphilus, III. vi. 34. A rhetorician mentioned by Aristotle.

Patrocles, II. xv. 16; III. vi. 44.

542

INDEX

Rhetorician otherwise unknown. Some read Iatrocles.

Paulus, L., I. x. 47. The famous general, surnamed Macedonicus, on account of his successful campaign in Macedonia (168 B.C.) during which the incident referred to occurred.

Pedianus, Asconius, I. vii. 24. Distinguished historian and critic, contemporary with Quintilian.

Pericles, I. x. 47. The eclipse in question occurred in 430 B.C. on the eve of an expedition to the Peloponnese.

Phoenix, II. iii. 12. The tutor of Achilles in the *Iliad*.

Plautus, II. xiv. 2 ; III. vi. 23. Probably the Stoic Rubellius Plautus, d. 62 A.D.

Plisthenes, III. vii. 19. A son of Atreus. The allusion is uncertain.

Plotius, II. iv. 42. A rhetorician and older contemporary of Cicero.

Pollio, Asinius, I. v. 8, 56 ; I. vi. 42 ; I. viii. 11. Famous orator, poet and historian of the Augustan age.

Polycrates, II. xvii. 4 ; III. i. 11. An Athenian rhetorician, contemporary with Socrates.

Posidonius, III. vi. 37. Famous philosopher of the Middle Stoa, who taught at Rome in the time of Cicero.

Prodicus of Cos, III. i. 10, 12. Sophist of the fifth century B.C.

Protagoras of Abdera, III. i. 10, 12. Sophist of the fifth century B.C.

Publicola, I. vi. 31 ; III. vii. 18. Name (= friend of the people) given to M. Valerius, consul in opening year of the republic.

Pythicus, I. vi. 31. Cognomen in the family of Sulpicius Camerinus (see Dio, 63, 18) ; origin unknown.

Quirinalis, collis, I. vi. 31. Variously derived from Quirinus, Quirites, and the Sabine town of Cures.

Saturninus, II. xvi. 5. Tribune and demagogue, killed 100 B.C.

Sisenna, I. v. 13. Historian and man of letters with a passion for rare words ; an elder contemporary of Cicero.

Sophron, I. x. 17. Famous Sicilian writer of mimes, *fl.* 450 B.C.

Sotades, I. viii. 6. Alexandrian writer of indecent lampoons, third century B.C.

Stertinius, III. i. 21. Stoic writer of the Augustan age.

Subura, I. vii. 29. A quarter of Rome near the Esquiline.

Sulpicius, Gallus, I. x. 47 ; II. xv. 8. Astronomer. Consul 166 B.C. A relative of Servius Sulpicius Galba, *q.v.*

Sulpicius, Servius, III. viii. 5. Distinguished orator contemporary with Cicero, died on an embassy to Mark Antony.

Theodectes, I. iv. 18 ; II. xv. 10 ; III. i. 14. Rhetorician of first half of fourth century B.C.

Theodorus (i), of Byzantium, III. i. 11. Rhetorician contemporary with Plato.

Theodorus (ii), of Gadara, II. xv. 16, 21 ; III. i. 17 ; III. vi. 2, 36, 51 ; III. xi. 3. Famous rhetorician of the Augustan age. *Theodorei* = his followers.

Theodotus, III. viii. 55. Rhetorician of Samos, by whose advice Pompey was murdered ; was put to death by Brutus, 43 B.C.

Theon, III. vi. 48. Stoic and rhetorician of the Augustan age.

Theopompus (i), II. viii. 11. Famous Greek historian of latter half of fourth century B.C.

Theopompus (ii), of Sparta, II. xvii. 20. (?) King of Sparta, eighth century B.C.

Thersites, III. vii. 19. The misshapen demagogue of the *Iliad*.

Thrasybulus, III. vii. 26. Overthrew the Thirty tyrants of Athens, 404 B.C.

INDEX